In His Own Right

COLUMBIA STUDIES IN CONTEMPORARY AMERICAN HISTORY
WILLIAM E. LEUCHTENBURG AND ALAN BRINKLEY, GENERAL EDITORS

COLUMBIA STUDIES IN CONTEMPORARY AMERICAN HISTORY
WILLIAM E. LEUCHTENBURG AND ALAN BRINKLEY, GENERAL EDITORS

Lawrence S. Wittner, *Rebels Against War: The American Peace Movement, 1941-1960*   1969

Davis R. B. Ross, *Preparing for Ulysses: Politics and Veterans During World War II*   1969

John Lewis Gaddis, *The United States and the Origins of the Cold War, 1941-1947*   1972

George C. Herring, Jr., *Aid to Russia, 1941-1946: Strategy, Diplomacy, the Origins of the Cold War*   1973

Alonzo L. Hamby, *Beyond the New Deal: Harry S. Truman and American Liberalism*   1973

Richard M. Fried, *Men Against McCarthy*   1976

Steven F. Lawson, *Black Ballots: Voting Rights in the South, 1944-1969*   1976

Carl M. Brauer, *John F. Kennedy and the Second Reconstruction*   1977

Maeva Marcus, *Truman and the Steel Seizure Case: The Limits of Presidential Power*   1977

Morton Sosna, *In Search of the Silent South: Southern Liberals and the Race Issue*   1977

Robert M. Collins, *The Business Response to Keynes, 1929-1964*   1981

Robert M. Hathaway, *Ambiguous Partnership: Britain and America, 1944-1947*   1981

Leonard Dinnerstein, *America and the Survivors of the Holocaust*   1982

Lawrence S. Wittner, *American Intervention in Greece, 1943-1949*   1982

Nancy Bernkopf Tucker, *Patterns in the Dust: Chinese-American Relations and the Recognition Controversy, 1949-1950*   1983

Catherine A. Barnes, *Journey from Jim Crow: The Desegregation of Southern Transit*   1983

Steven F. Lawson, *In Pursuit of Power: Southern Blacks and Electoral Politics, 1965-1982*   1985

David R. Colburn, *Racial Change and Community Crisis: St. Augustine, Florida, 1877-1980*   1985

Henry William Brands, *Cold Warriors: Eisenhower's Generation and the Making of American Foreign Policy*   1988

Marc S. Gallicchio, *The Cold War Begins in Asia: American East Asian Policy and the Fall of the Japanese Empire.*   1988

Melanie Billings-Yun, *Decision Against War: Eisenhower and Dien Bien Phu*   1988

Walter L. Hixson, *George F. Kennan: Cold War Iconoclast*   1989

Robert D. Schulzinger, *Henry Kissinger: Doctor of Diplomacy*   1989

Henry William Brands, *The Specter of Neutralism: The United States and the Emergence of the Third World, 1947-1960*   1989

Mitchell K. Hall, *Because of Their Faith: CALCAV and Religious Opposition to the Vietnam War*   1990

David L. Anderson, *Trapped By Success: The Eisenhower Administration and Vietnam, 1953-1961*   1991

Steven M. Gillon, *The Democrats' Dilemma: Walter F. Mondale and the Liberal Legacy*   1992

Wyatt C. Wells, *Economist in an Uncertain World: Arthur F. Burns and the Federal Reserve, 1970-1978*   1994

Stuart Svonkin, *Jews Against Prejudice: American Jews and the Fight for Civil Liberties*   1997

Doug Rossinow, *The Politics of Authenticity: Liberalism, Christianity, and the New Left in America*   1998

Campbell Craig, *Destroying the Village: Eisenhower and Thermonuclear War.*   1998

Brett Gary, *The Nervous Liberals: Propaganda Anxieties from World War I to the Cold War*   1999

Andrea Friedman, *Prurient Interests: Gender, Democracy, and Obscenity in New York City, 1909-1945*   2000

In His Own Right

The Political Odyssey of Senator
Robert F. Kennedy

Joseph A. Palermo

COLUMBIA UNIVERSITY PRESS   NEW YORK

COLUMBIA UNIVERSITY PRESS
Publishers Since 1893
New York, Chichester, West Sussex
Copyright © 2001 Columbia University Press
All rights reserved

Library of Congress Cataloging-in-Publication Data

Palermo, Joseph A.
    In his own right: the political odyssey of Senator Robert F. Kennedy /
    Joseph A. Palermo.
        p. cm. — (Columbia studies in contemporary American history)
    Includes bibliographical references (p.) and index.
    ISBN 0-231-12068-0 (cloth : alk. paper)
    1. Kennedy, Robert F., 1925–1968. 2. Kennedy, Robert F., 1925–1968—Political
    and social views. 3. Legislators—United States—Biography. 4. United States.
    Congress. Senate—Biography. 5. Presidential candidates—United States—
    Biography. 6. United States—Politics and government—1963–1969.
    7. United States—Social conditions—1960–1980. I. Title. II. Series.

E840.8.K4 P26 2001
973.922′092—dc21
[B]   00-069373

For my parents, Lorayne Mary Palermo and Joseph Nick Palermo, and my children, Dante Joseph Palermo, Palesa Bianca Palermo, and Marco Blake Palermo

Contents

Preface

Robert F. Kennedy's role in American politics during the 1960s defies definition. He was a junior senator from New York, but at the same time he was much more than that. The public perceived him as possessing the intangible qualities that arose from his close identification with his brother, the slain President John F. Kennedy. From 1965 to 1968, Kennedy struggled to find his voice in national affairs, and in that time he embarked on a political journey unique in American history.

In January 1965, Kennedy began serving in his first elective office as United States senator. By the spring, he started questioning the U.S. intervention in Vietnam, even before President Lyndon Johnson decided to send combat troops. He did not arrive at his views on the war in a vacuum, but was persuaded by the antiwar activists, non-governmental organizations, scholars, and ordinary citizens aligned with the emergent peace movement.

A barrage of letters, telegrams, and copies of paid media advertisements bombarded Kennedy's office from civic groups and individual activists. Soldiers serving in Vietnam, student peace organizers, refugee volunteers, black community activists, and Latino farm workers implored Kennedy to take ever tougher stands against the war, racism, and poverty. He forged his own political identity profoundly affected by this spirit of citizen mobilization. One of the goals of this book is to examine this often overlooked body of correspondence in order to illustrate the moral power of the appeals to higher conscience that Kennedy received.

Throughout his Senate years, Kennedy was in a crucial dialogue with the peace movement, which constantly prodded him to take bolder action against Johnson's Vietnam policy. In August 1965, following the turning point of the Watts riot in Los Angeles, Kennedy became deeply committed to the maturing civil rights and antipoverty struggles. In March 1966, he embraced wholeheartedly the cause of César Chávez's United Farm Workers Union. Kennedy often needed cajoling by progressive civic and religious groups to take political gambles, but he showed repeatedly that at pivotal moments he would stand up for their goals. One intriguing aspect of Kennedy's political odyssey in the 1960s is his transformation from Cold Warrior with a limited understanding of dissent to a national leader whose political strength was heavily indebted to a mobilized citizenry.

Books on Kennedy are generally either traditional biographies, where the subject's character and psychology are placed under a microscope, or memoirs and journalistic accounts from individuals who knew or worked with Kennedy. The three early works which I have found the most useful are Jack Newfield's *Robert Kennedy: A Memoir* (1969), which is a poignant account from a sympathetic left-leaning journalist; *On His Own*, written in 1970 by William Vanden Heuvel and Milton Gwirtzman, a first-hand chronicle from two of Kennedy's close colleagues; and Arthur M. Schlesinger, Jr.'s 1978 masterpiece of biography, *Robert Kennedy and His Times*, which is one of the most comprehensive works on Kennedy. Dozens of subsequent books have been written which deepen our understanding of Kennedy's Senate years. Yet none of these studies utilize archival sources to explore his relations with civic groups, citizen activists, and social movements of the period.

This book is not a complete account of Kennedy's personal life during his Senate years, which one historian calls his "time of self-actualization." What it offers is an analysis of his evolving critique of the Vietnam War, his views on racism and poverty, and his communication with his growing national constituency. My study is based on extensive archival research in Kennedy's Senate papers and those from his 1968 campaign held in the John Fitzgerald Kennedy Library in Boston. I also draw upon the Democratic National Committee papers, White House files, and other collections held in the Lyndon Baines Johnson Library in Austin. I have paid particular attention to Kennedy's critiques of Vietnam policy, because it was his stand on the war which ultimately led him to run for president in 1968. I also trace his three-year battle with the Democratic leadership at the highest level.

In June 1968, when Kennedy was cut down and his presidential campaign brutally ended, the effort of countless citizens' groups and individuals, once so purposeful, swirled out of control and quickly lost its focus. It is as if the candidate were at the hub of a great wheel of social forces that lost its bearings after his violent removal. His direct links to the activism of the period made him an indispensable leader. His disappearance from American politics tore a gaping hole in the organized progressive movement of the 1960s, and his message of hope seemed to go with him. American politics became more cynical and less inspiriting after Robert Kennedy's assassination.

In 1968, I was a boy growing up in San Jose, California, and I can vividly recall watching Kennedy's televised victory speech from the Ambassador Hotel after he won the California primary. My two draft-age uncles were Kennedy volunteers, and there was Kennedy campaign literature scattered around the house. My working-class Catholic family supported Kennedy with a rare enthusiasm, and I can remember the sadness, fear, and disappointment that descended upon us all when he was killed. Perhaps the initial impetus for me to explore this topic arose from this childhood experience.

Some of the questions I seek to answer include: What was the nature of Kennedy's dialogue with citizens active in the peace, civil rights, farm worker, and antipoverty movements? How did Kennedy make the transformation from being a political operator known for "ruthlessness" toward his opponents, to becoming, by 1968, a "tribune of the underclass"? What is the significance of the coalition Kennedy put together in his California primary bid? What effects did his personal and political rivalry with Lyndon Johnson have on the Democratic Party? And finally, what does Kennedy's challenge to the Democratic leadership tell us about the effects of the Vietnam War on mainstream American liberalism?

Robert Kennedy's leadership role was a product of the social movements of the 1960s. Well-known activists and political players such as Benjamin Spock, Allard Lowenstein, Eugene McCarthy, Martin Luther King, Jr., César Chávez, and others are an integral part of the story, as well as the hundreds of ordinary citizens who influenced Kennedy's views throughout his Senate years. Looming over the entire period was the often antagonistic presence of Lyndon Johnson. It is my hope that this book will contribute to our understanding of the interdependence of Kennedy's leadership as a public citizen and the social activism of the 1960s.

Acknowledgments

I would like to express my profound thanks to Richard Polenberg, who guided me through the early stages of this project. For his kindness, help, and encouragement when I needed it most, I shall always be grateful; he came through for me with support and guidance from the time I began my research to the day of publication. Singular thanks are due William E. Leuchtenburg, whose generosity, graciousness, and skills as a historian have been a constant source of inspiration to me; I was extremely fortunate to have had the opportunity to work with a scholar of his depth and experience. His interest in this project sustained me through the difficult times. I also owe a debt of gratitude to the other gifted historians who read parts of this work: George McTurnan Kahin commented on the chapters where I discuss the Vietnam War, and kindly gave me access to his personal papers; Thomas Borstelmann asked tough questions that helped improve my early drafts; and James N. Giglio provided invaluable criticism that strongly influenced the shape of the final product.

The editor-in-chief of Columbia University Press, Kate Wittenberg, is the most thoughtful and supportive editor with whom any new author could hope to work; my deepest thanks go out to her for her encouragement throughout the revision process. Her patience and expertise brought this book to completion. I would like to extend my appreciation to the other fine editors at Columbia University Press, especially to James Burger and Leslie Bialler. Special thanks to Robert Hemenway, whose copyediting showed a sharp eye and provided insightful queries which added greatly to the clarity of the book.

Thanks also to the archivists at the John Fitzgerald Kennedy Library in Boston, and the Lyndon Baines Johnson Library in Austin: Allan Goodrich, the chief audiovisual archivist, James Hill, June Payne, and Vinnie Calarese at the JFKL; and Allen Fisher at the LBJL.

I must also offer my special thanks to the colleagues who have helped me along the way: Walter LaFeber, R. Laurence Moore, Thomas Holloway, Daniel Usner, Stuart Davis, Bruce Roebel, and Katherine Gottschalk at Cornell University; Nigel Young, Joy Meeker, and the Peace Studies Department at Colgate University; Andrew Rotter at Colgate; Sandford Gutman at the State University of New York at Cortland; Beatrice Farnsworth at Wells College; David Anderson; Robert Dallek; Maxwell Kennedy; Scott Brown; Douglas F. Dowd; Saul Landau; James O'Connor; and Helene Berinsky. Thanks also to the John S. Knight Writing Program at Cornell, and to the Peace History Society.

For courtesies large and small, I must thank my close friends and family in Ithaca and beyond. A special thanks must go out to Andrew Farnsworth for his upbeat encouragement, and to Jeffrey Marinacci for his spirited dialogues and insights. Thanks also to my dear life-long friend Brian Burman.

I must also thank my Nana, Genevieve Bosworth; Christopher Palermo; Patricia Collier; Gerry and Donald Thompson; Geraldine and Carl Palermo Sr.; and Anthony, Mary, Irene, Carol, Lucy, Michael, and Carl Palermo. Thanks to Jackie Martin; Judy Burkhard; Jennifer Evangelista; Sharon Bahringer; and Leslie Horowitz. A warm and special thanks goes out to Eric Aceto, Michael Cerza, Peter Dougan, and Charles Shew for their brotherhood in music; I must also thank the other members of my musical family: Jordan Aceto, Kathy Aelias, Amy and Sharon Beltaine, Max Buckholtz, Clint Burke, Darin Brandi, Uniit Carruyo, Jeff Coleman, Peter DeBoer, Peter Dodge, Everett Fox, Tino Gonzales, Daniel Janis, Chad Lieberman, Dan Merwin, Anthony (Babatunde) Milliner, Dennis Montgomery, Sim and Asa Redmond, Hank Roberts, Doug Robinson, Kimara Sajn, Taz, Scott Vomvolakis, and Bill and Rick Walker.

Thank you, Wayne and Alice Lyon. And a special salute to the members of the TCI: Sam and Tali Fridman, Ibe Ibeike-Jonah, Kevin and Michelle Thompson, Miguel Pineros Soler, Holly Manslank, Tomas Vence, and Margaret Gordona. A healthy thanks also to Lisa Fernandez; Courtney Ballard; Lisa Patti; Claire Thurston; Debbie and Dr. George Dougan; Bill Burman; and Bea Goldman.

I would like to give my warm appreciation to Carl Maloney and the Iona

School; Shea and Osha Maloney; Kat Morgenstern; Joan Spielholz; Mauro Lelli (my friend in Firenze); Leonardo Venturi; Mamdoh Badran; Art Stern; Andre LeClair; Goxwa Borg; Jane Roberts; Barbara Cerza; Kelly, Casey, and Jade Shew; Jody Schwan; Woody McKenzie; Dan Kress; John Sullivan; Debra Ash; Dave Hinkle, Scott, Shawn Tubridy, Eric and Mary Ott, and everyone at the Rongovian Embassy in Trumansburg, New York; Scott Pardee; Alan Cohen; John Lenz; Monty; John Meyer; Wendy Kenigsberg; Reg, Chick, Dewi, Karen, and Carol at Maxie's Supper Club and Oyster Bar in Ithaca, New York.

My greatest appreciation and deepest affection go to my parents, Lorayne Mary and Joseph Nick Palermo, and to my kind and caring children: Dante Joseph Palermo, Palesa Bianca Palermo, and Marco Blake Palermo.

In His Own Right

Prologue: The Odyssey Begins

On November 22, 1963, Attorney General Robert Kennedy enjoyed a pleasant lunch with some aides from the Justice Department at his home, Hickory Hill, in McLean, Virginia. At about 1:45 P.M. he received a phone call from J. Edgar Hoover, the Director of the Federal Bureau of Investigation, no friend of the attorney general's, who informed him that President John F. Kennedy had been shot in Dallas. While Robert Kennedy dashed around Hickory Hill changing clothes and trying to contact officials more knowledgeable about events in Texas, a second call came in from Captain Tazewell Shepard, President Kennedy's naval aide. His brother, Shepard told him, was dead. Robert Kennedy's life would never be the same.

With the nation in a state of grief-ridden shock, Robert Kennedy showed remarkable stoicism while tending to arrangements for transporting his brother's body back to Washington, and consoling his sister-in-law, Jacqueline Kennedy. During the days just after the assassination, he was a source of strength for friends and for family. The presence of John Kennedy's young children in the White House intensified the nation's sense of tragedy, and Robert Kennedy assumed a new role in the lives of his six-year-old niece, Caroline, and his nephew, John Jr., whose third birthday sadly fell on the day of his father's funeral.

Kennedy, who had celebrated his thirty-eighth birthday just two days before his brother's murder, found himself cast into a personal and political wilderness. He entered a long period of grief and mourning which gave him a greater appreciation of the suffering of others. Democrats who had iden-

Kennedy carry Texas and six other southern states,[6] would win him a central role in the new administration. But the Vice President quickly discovered that any influence he had hoped for paled in comparison to that of the President's 35-year-old brother. In December 1960, despite Robert's youth and inexperience, and cries of nepotism, President-elect Kennedy appointed his younger brother attorney general.[7] He became the second youngest attorney general in United States history, the youngest in over 140 years, and the first brother of a president to hold the position. Moreover, he functioned as President Kennedy's trusted adviser on all policy questions, foreign and domestic. The antipathy between Johnson and Robert Kennedy grew steadily during the one thousand days of the Kennedy Administration.[8]

When he became attorney general, Kennedy had a limited knowledge of the racial injustices that African Americans had been organizing against for decades. In power, the Kennedy brothers wished blacks would move slowly in demanding an end to racial segregation in the South. They preferred to focus the Administration's attention on fighting the Cold War, facing down Soviet Premier Nikita Khrushchev, and rolling back Communism in Cuba. They initially saw the civil rights protests in the South as a nuisance, and a grand distraction from the more important field of foreign relations. Also, the civil rights movement exposed the segregationist wing of the Democratic Party, threatened to upset the political balance in the "Solid South," and divided the party at a time when President Kennedy desperately needed every Democratic vote in Congress.

The President and the Attorney General would have liked to avoid the issue of civil rights altogether, but the nonviolent movement had been gaining momentum for years. In 1961, following a series of bloody clashes between segregationists and the "freedom riders" who sought to integrate interstate transportation in Alabama, Attorney General Kennedy called for a cessation of the protests, and a cooling-off period. James Farmer, the executive director of the Congress of Racial Equality (C.O.R.E.), and an organizer of the freedom rides, responded that blacks had been "cooling off for 350 years," and if they cooled off any more, they would be in a deep freeze.[9] The protesters forced Kennedy's hand; he had to repeatedly improvise federal protection for the freedom riders in the form of U.S. marshals. Thus began Robert Kennedy's education about the effects of racial injustice in America.

As attorney general, Kennedy offered some modest civil rights reforms. He strengthened the Justice Department's moribund Civil Rights Division, increased the number of African Americans employed in the department, implemented a program to prevent juvenile delinquency, and enforced federal court orders which integrated universities in Mississippi and Alabama. But these moves were met with criticism from civil rights activists for not going far enough, while Southern Democrats attacked President Kennedy for enflaming the passions of the demonstrators with his idealistic rhetoric. By the summer of 1963, the Administration had reached an uneasy truce with mainstream civil rights leaders, including Martin Luther King, Jr., of the Southern Christian Leadership Conference (S.C.L.C.), and Roy Wilkins of the National Association for the Advancement of Colored People (N.A.A.C.P.).

In June 1963, Attorney General Kennedy prevailed in a nationally televised confrontation with Alabama Governor George Wallace after Wallace stood "in the schoolhouse door" to prevent the admission of James Hood and Vivian Malone, the first blacks ever to attend the University of Alabama. The drafting of what became the 1964 Civil Rights Act arose out of this dramatic conflict. Kennedy had been the only Cabinet member to urge his brother to send to Congress a comprehensive civil rights bill. In August 1963, the March on Washington further demonstrated to the nation the depth of African-American opposition to segregation, and the crying need for prompt Congressional action on civil rights.

As attorney general, Robert Kennedy had been thrust into the center of what became the nation's most pressing moral battle involving racial politics since Reconstruction. In the early 1960s, his previous lack of empathy with black suffering shifted along with the national mood. Despite the Administration's initial reluctance to embrace the cause, the civil rights protesters, employing the Gandhian principles of nonviolent civil disobedience, had succeeded in placing race relations on the front burner of American politics. The movement had initiated an evolution in Robert Kennedy's thinking on race and poverty.

On November 22, 1963, Lyndon Johnson assumed the presidency under uniquely grave conditions. He promised the nation continuity, and he retained nearly all of President Kennedy's key advisers. A number of Kennedy partisans called for drafting Robert as vice president as a tribute to his slain brother. National opinion polls showed that three out of four Democrats wanted Kennedy to be Johnson's running mate.[10] Democratic organizers promoted a vice-presidential write-in for Kennedy in the New Hampshire primary. In March 1964, more than 25,000 Democrats wrote in Kennedy's name for vice president, just 3,700 fewer than wrote in Johnson's name as their choice for president.[11]

But Johnson had no intention of remaining in the shadow of another Kennedy, and he thwarted efforts to place Robert Kennedy on the ticket.[12] Kennedy coyly refused to take his name out of the running. Johnson paid Robert back for his earlier arrogance by building up the Attorney General's hopes for the vice presidency, only to squelch them definitively in favor of Minnesota Senator Hubert Humphrey, whom Johnson knew he could control. With evident delight, Johnson privately mocked Kennedy's sullen reaction when he heard he was denied the post.[13] The press bombarded Kennedy with queries about his feelings at being refused a place on the ticket; thereafter, the news media consistently magnified the Kennedy-Johnson feud. Kennedy's days in the Johnson Cabinet were numbered.

After months of mourning for his brother, and seeking solace in Aeschylus and Camus, Kennedy slowly began to assess the new political reality. At the urging of Democratic officials who saw an opportunity, he decided to run for the Senate seat that was opening up in New York. A successful Senate bid would give him an independent voice in national politics free from the shackles of the Johnson Administration. His decision to run arose from a desire to protect his brother's presidential legacy, but also reflected his own growing ambitions.

In July 1964, as the Democratic National Convention in Atlantic City neared, Johnson feared that delegates, still swept with lingering emotion over the assassination of John Kennedy, might draft his brother as the vice-presidential nominee. Johnson ordered the FBI to monitor the Attorney General's contacts and actions at the convention, and made sure that Kennedy did not address the assembly until after Humphrey had been safely confirmed as his running mate.[14] Johnson's political instincts might have been accurate: on the final day, when Kennedy stood at the podium to introduce a film tribute to his brother, he received a standing ovation that lasted twenty-two minutes, by far the longest of the convention.

In November 1964, for the first time, Kennedy tested himself before the voters, and challenged the incumbent senator, Kenneth Keating. Keating was a liberal Republican from Rochester, who had served on the Judiciary Committee that voted to approve Kennedy's appointment as attorney general. Keating was popular among moderate and independent voters, and the race was a tough one. Kennedy's opponents labeled him a carpetbagger, and accused him of manipulating the voters of New York merely to advance his national political career. President Johnson campaigned for Kennedy in New York City, and his lengthy coattails in his landslide victory over Arizona Senator Barry Goldwater helped Kennedy win.[15] Thus began the most difficult and important phase of Robert Kennedy's personal and political journey.

1 On His Own: Kennedy's Evolving Critique of the War, May 1965–February 1966

> I do not believe we should be under the self-delusion that this military effort will bring Ho Chi Minh or the Viet Cong to their knees.
> —Robert F. Kennedy, May 6, 1965

On January 5, 1965, Kennedy began his term as the junior senator from New York, joining the ranks of Senate Democrats who commanded a 36-seat majority at the start of the 89th Congress. The adjustment to being one voice in a hundred frustrated Kennedy. His earlier posts had not prepared him for the club-like atmosphere and cloakroom dealings of the Senate. Back in 1957, as the chief counsel of the Senate Rackets Investigating Committee, Kennedy, at the age of 31, had directed a staff of seventy, and guided an elaborate investigation through months of highly publicized hearings. In 1960, he had managed the national campaign that won John Kennedy the presidency. From 1961 to 1964, as attorney general, he had presided over a department with 33,000 employees. In addition to his Justice Department duties, he had served President Kennedy as his confidant, adviser, and roving ambassador. He had therefore grown accustomed to wielding a degree of executive power unfamiliar to most senators. His forceful management style, which demanded hard work and excellence from his staff, pointed to his experience as a decision maker.

Early on, Kennedy's stature as the brother and former close aide of the late president set him apart from other senators. In June 1965, his speech in the Senate on nuclear proliferation, unlike that of other junior members, filled the press gallery and drew more than fifty senators as spectators. Whenever he prepared to give a major address, an atmosphere of anticipation prevailed; senators and the press recognized the potential importance of his remarks.[1] Moreover, from the time of President Kennedy's assassination, treat any future President."[2]

In 1965 and 1966, Robert Kennedy, like other United States senators, scrambled to keep up with the Johnson Administration's growing commitment to a military solution in Vietnam. His views, like those of millions of Americans, evolved over time. Although Kennedy cautiously edited his statements to temper his political and personal rivalry with President Lyndon Johnson,[3] his criticisms stiffened throughout his first eighteen months in the Senate. It became increasingly evident to Kennedy that Johnson's masterful crafting of public support for the war, beginning with the Gulf of Tonkin incident of August 1964, had been built upon hidden deceits and false premises.

As the junior senator from New York with no committee assignments expressly relating to foreign affairs, Kennedy did not possess a springboard from which to question the president's prerogative in foreign policy. Also, Kennedy's philosophical commitment to a strong executive, especially in foreign affairs, never wavered. Premature criticism or Monday-morning quarterbacking angered Johnson, and played into the hands of a Washington press corps eager to portray Kennedy's growing opposition to the war as little more than cynical political posturing.

Kennedy was in a delicate position when criticizing the Administration's actions in Southeast Asia, because of President John Kennedy's role in promoting a greater American military presence there. Johnson had retained most of President Kennedy's key foreign policy advisers, including Secretary of State Dean Rusk, Secretary of Defense Robert McNamara, and National Security Adviser McGeorge Bundy, all of whom became central figures in formulating Johnson's Vietnam policies.[4] Administration officials never tired of emphasizing that their Vietnam policy was consistent with President Kennedy's; attacking Johnson on the war would be like attacking the late President. Robert Kennedy and his advisers, who witnessed what they saw as "simplistic Texas nationalism" engulf the White House, never accepted this argument.[5]

However, political considerations did not prevent Kennedy from criticizing the substance of U.S. policy in Vietnam. He stopped short of repudiating

the United States commitment to South Vietnam, which had been maintained since the administration of President Harry Truman. Yet throughout
1965 and 1966, he denounced the bombing of North Vietnam, questioned
the wisdom of escalating the number of American combat troops, and
spoke out against Johnson's policy of blocking key Vietnamese political
organizations from gaining a share of power in the Saigon regime. Kennedy
argued that despite the Administration's claims that it was seeking peace,
its military actions and diplomatic stance precluded any hope for a negotiated settlement.[6]

In 1965, Kennedy's views shifted steadily away from a technocratic or
tactical critique of the war to a more fundamental questioning of the United
States' ultimate goals in Vietnam, especially as they related to Johnson's calls
for unconditional negotiations.

At each new stage of the U.S. intervention, Kennedy stressed political
development inside South Vietnam over military conquest. He criticized
the class injustices and vestiges of colonialism in Vietnamese society, saying
that the inequality of land ownership impeded the American objective of
winning popular support for the government. He pointed out that the National Liberation Front, by far the most powerful political body fighting the
United States in South Vietnam, drew its support largely from landless peas-
ants, while the U.S.-backed regime in Saigon represented the elite and the
landowning class.[7] He believed that only internal reforms which the Vietnamese themselves enacted offered any hope of ending the conflict. "It is
not our war," he said in January 1966.[8]

Whenever the Johnson Administration offered cease-fires, such as the two
in December 1965, Kennedy urged the United States and its South Vietnamese allies to extend them, refrain from fighting, and begin a peace dialogue. When these cease-fires invariably failed, he issued statements of regret
they did not lead to negotiations. As with the cease-fires, Kennedy advocated
extending the bombing halts of North Vietnam that Johnson periodically
offered, and publicly disagreed whenever the President ordered the resumption of bombing.[9]

Johnson had marshaled a formidable coalition of bipartisan supporters
behind his Vietnam policies. In addition to powerful members of Congress,
such as the Chairman of the Senate Arms Services Committee, Henry
"Scoop" Jackson of Washington, and Speaker of the House John McCormack of Massachusetts, Johnson had the backing of foreign policy and military experts, and World War II heroes such as General Omar Bradley and

former President Dwight Eisenhower. Prominent Republicans, including North Dakota Senator Karl Mundt, a member of the Foreign Relations Committee, and House Minority Leader Gerald Ford of Michigan, strongly believed in the purposes of the war, and their criticisms of Johnson centered on the notion that he had not sufficiently unleashed the United States military in Vietnam. Johnson also counted on the backing of syndicated columnists, among them Joseph Alsop, Drew Pearson, Robert Novak, and dozens of less influential commentators.

A Harris poll taken in May 1965 showed that 57 percent of Americans approved of Johnson's handling of the war, which at that time included what McGeorge Bundy called the sustained reprisal bombing of North Vietnam ("Rolling Thunder"), and a dramatic increase in American ground forces. Throughout 1965 and 1966, whenever Johnson bombed North Vietnam his popularity increased, which illustrated the general hawkishness of the American electorate.[10]

The antiwar movement at the time was "inchoate and without structure," according to the democratic socialist Michael Harrington, writing in October 1965.[11] Liberals and peace advocates of all ideological stripes struggled to keep up with Johnson's gradual escalation of the war. In 1965 and 1966, aside from a few dozen teach-ins on college campuses, and a smattering of small protests in New York, Washington, D.C., and San Francisco, the peace movement had a negligible effect on the public discourse.[12] The movement grew in size and scope in subsequent years, and opened up the debate on the war, but during the initial stages of the United States' direct military involvement in Vietnam its influence remained marginal. The press, too, inched its way slowly in criticizing the fundamental U.S. aims in Vietnam. Most reporters identified fully and unselfconsciously with the anti-Communist Cold War mission, and commonly closed their pieces by suggesting better ways for the American military to annihilate the "Viet Cong."[13] The relative lack of political clout in 1965 and 1966 of the antiwar forces, along with the compliance of the press, made Kennedy's early public criticisms of the war all the more important in influencing the national debate.

In May 1965, Adam Walinsky, a brilliant 30-year-old member of Kennedy's Senate staff and an early opponent of the Vietnam War, used an upcoming vote for a $700 million appropriations bill for South Vietnam to prod Kennedy to take a stand against what he saw as a radical shift in United States policy in Southeast Asia. Although Walinsky felt "somewhat silly" telling his boss what to do, he said other staff members, such as Kennedy's

29-year-old legislative aide, Peter Edelman, agreed that the senator should speak out against Congress surrendering any right of stopping the present course in Vietnam.[14]

In a speech on the Senate floor on May 6, Kennedy offered his earliest criticisms of American policy. Although agreeing with Johnson that a unilateral American withdrawal "would be an explicit and gross betrayal of those in Vietnam who have been encouraged by our support to oppose the spread of communism," he quickly added that "the course of purposely enlarging the war would be a deep and terrible decision." Kennedy sought what he called a third course for the United States in Vietnam. "I do not believe we should be under the self-delusion that this military effort will bring Ho Chi Minh or the Vietcong to their knees," he said.[15]

Kennedy called for a solution in Vietnam that was probably impossible to achieve: an ironclad United States guarantee of a fully non-Communist South Vietnam, without a greatly expanded American military effort.[16] Yet midway through the speech, he made a revealing connection between Johnson's handling of the conflict and the recent U.S. invasion of the Dominican Republic. On April 14, 1965, Johnson had sent 23,000 U.S. troops into the Dominican Republic to crush what he considered an anti-U.S. revolution on the island. Foreign capitals, especially in Latin America, generally viewed the intervention as a heavy-handed expression of old-style Yankee imperialism.[17]

Kennedy said that Johnson's Dominican invasion, along with his Vietnam policies, were part of a "seamless web" which relied too heavily upon brute military force. He referred to the invasion as "the tragic events of the last few days in our own hemisphere," and argued that Johnson's unilateral intervention made a mockery of the Organization of American States, trampled the sovereignty of a neighboring state, and imperiled the structure of international law in the hemisphere. Kennedy also saw the invasion as a severe blow to the goals of the Alliance for Progress, one of President Kennedy's legacies which Robert Kennedy championed. Johnson had claimed that the invasion prevented another Cuba in the hemisphere, and he was probably surprised when Kennedy, who had been a zealous opponent of Fidel Castro, criticized the intervention. A Gallup poll found that more than three-quarters of Americans favored the military action.[18]

Kennedy read into the Congressional Record a highly critical article from the Christian Science Monitor, which reported that most Dominicans, regardless of political affiliation, opposed the invasion. He criticized the Administration for failing to differentiate between Communists and non-Communist democrats. Our objective, he said, "must surely be not to drive the genuine democrats in the Dominican revolution into association with the Communists by blanket characterizations and condemnation of their revolution."[19] Kennedy later in the speech admonished the Administration for doing the same thing in Vietnam.

Kennedy's coupling of Johnson's Vietnam policy with the invasion of the Dominican Republic revealed, albeit indirectly, that he had rejected the Administration's growing reliance on military force in Southeast Asia. In July 1965, when Johnson decided to leap into the chilly waters of a massive American commitment of ground forces in Vietnam,[20] Kennedy repeatedly called for a negotiated settlement, and emphatically stated there could be no progress in South Vietnam without making political and social reform the centerpiece of American policy. Kennedy remained a consistent critic of the Administration's moves to "internationalize" the war (through bombing North Vietnam), and "Americanize" it, through escalating the number of U.S. combat troops. At this time, Kennedy privately shared his deep concern about Vietnam with his friend, the *New York Times* columnist Anthony Lewis. Although he believed Johnson was a very popular figure, he predicted that "the popularity of the Chief Executive will dissipate if the involvement and casualties grow to serious proportions." He feared that this could interfere with the enormously important legislation in the domestic field, which Kennedy supported.[21]

When it came to the subject of Vietnam, Kennedy relied upon diverse sources of information including academics, journalists, and military officials.[22] In August 1965, Lieutenant Colonel John Paul Vann wrote Kennedy from Bao Trai, South Vietnam, saying that he had been struck by some of the senator's recent speeches. In Vann's view, Kennedy "indicat[ed] comprehension of the problems we face here."[23] At that time, Vann served as an adviser to the Agency for International Development (A.I.D.) in its "pacification" effort, a pivotal component of U.S. policy in Vietnam. According to Vann, Kennedy understood "the extremely difficult task of wet-nursing a reluctant hierarchy to be responsive to its own people"; Kennedy had also displayed "cognizance of the need for discrimination when the enemy is mixed up with the population."[24]

Other people with knowledge of the conflict reached out to Kennedy from Vietnam. In the fall of 1965, after hearing a Radio Bangkok broadcast in which Kennedy called for China to be included in nuclear arms talks, his friend from the New York Times, R. W. (Johnny) Apple, offered his impressions of the United States position. Like Vann, Apple discerned serious flaws in Johnson's military policies. From his vantage point in Saigon, Apple concluded that bombers weren't the solution, because "they made as many new VC as they destroyed." Apple wanted the Johnson Administration to realize that this was a war "in which our technological superiority ultimately will count for very little."[25] In his view, the United States military accomplished nothing by seizing an area of the South Vietnamese countryside only to have it quickly reclaimed by the enemy.[26] Apple subsequently became one of the New York Times' most prominent political analysts.

Vann and Apple both privately expressed to Kennedy their criticisms of the Administration's military tactics in Vietnam, without touching on the United States' ultimate goals. In 1965, Kennedy also followed this course. By the end of the year, however, he had moved toward a more sophisticated understanding of the South Vietnamese political context. His opposition to the Dominican intervention, coupled with the remarks about the desirability of "revolution" he had made during a November 1965 tour of Latin America,[27] showed that Kennedy's former attraction to counterinsurgency had waned considerably since the heady days of his brother's administration. He began to reject technocratic critiques in favor of a fundamental questioning of United States goals in Southeast Asia.

Starting in early 1965, Kennedy corresponded with Cornell University's Southeast Asian specialist, George McTurnan Kahin, who had sent him articles spelling out the political reality inside South Vietnam. Kennedy read these materials carefully, and sometimes exchanged comments with Walinsky or another aide on one of Kahin's finer points.[28] He wrote Kahin that his information and opinions were of great interest,[29] and Kahin remained in contact with Walinsky throughout the mid-1960s. Kahin later met with Kennedy after returning from a trip to Vietnam, and he found the New York senator sympathetic to his views of the conflict; Kahin's analysis was informed by an intricate knowledge of Saigon politics, and repudiated the United States position.[30]

Kahin shared his opinion with Kennedy that Johnson's Vietnam "experts" were unrealistic in their belief that "the shifting coalition in Saigon can command enough popular loyalty to give the U.S. a sufficient fulcrum for effective and sustained political leverage."[31] In March 1965, Kahin argued that the U.S.-backed South Vietnamese military would continue to deteriorate, and render the American presence there unmanageable, despite an enormous escalation in combat troops.[32] Kennedy grappled with Kahin's informed analysis throughout 1965 and 1966.

In late 1965, Kennedy publicly linked the war in Vietnam with the drain of resources away from domestic antipoverty programs. In December 1965, he commented on the meaning of the Watts riot in Los Angeles, which had broken out four months earlier. He responded to the findings of the McCone Commission, which analyzed the riot's causes.[33] To give the Vietnam War priority over domestic programs designed to alleviate long-festering social injustices, Kennedy believed, "would be to invite the very internal conflagration of which we have been warned—to invite a society so irretrievably split that no war will be worth fighting, and no war will be possible to fight."[34] From that point on, the deterioration of race relations at home and the extravagant expenditures for the Vietnam War remained linked in Kennedy's thinking.

In addition to speaking out against the war's drain of resources from social programs, Kennedy publicly supported the right to dissent of those who opposed the war. He defended the academic freedom and free speech rights of the Rutgers historian Eugene Genovese after former Vice President Richard Nixon and other prominent prowar figures called for revoking Genovese's tenure because he had said at a teach-in that he welcomed the victory of America's enemies in Vietnam.[35] Kennedy also upheld the rights of student activists who resisted the draft. Although he said he would not choose that path if he were of draft age, he nonetheless saw draft resistance as a valid form of protest. At a time when prowar Democrats and Republicans alike were known to accuse antiwar protesters of treason, the defense by a former attorney general of their right to dissent had a legitimizing influence.

In November 1965, at a press conference at the University of Southern California, Kennedy reiterated his defense of the rights of students to resist conscription. A reporter then queried him about a related issue:

PRESS: What about giving blood to the North Vietnamese?
KENNEDY: I think that would be a good idea.
PRESS: Is that going too far?
KENNEDY: If we've given all the blood that is needed to the South Vietnamese. I'm in favor of giving anybody who needs blood, I'm in favor of them having blood.
PRESS: Even to the North Vietnamese?
KENNEDY: Yes.

PRESS: Senator, there's one view that a lot of this difficulty was touched
   off by a lack of . . .
KENNEDY: I'd rather concentrate on the South Vietnamese and those
   who need it, but I'm in favor of giving blood to anyone who needs it.[36]

Editorialists and political commentators seized upon this exchange, rid-
iculing Kennedy for his approval of giving blood to enemy soldiers who
killed American boys.[37] The conservative Arizona senator and 1964 Republican presidential nominee Barry Goldwater publicly questioned Kennedy's
loyalty to the nation. Soon, the far right John Birch society had set up telephone lines in Washington, D.C. and other cities, where a tape-recorded
message asked callers: "Isn't advocating the giving of blood to the enemy
treason?"[38] A few months later, Alabama Governor George Wallace, whom
Kennedy, as attorney general, had forced to accept the integration of the
University of Alabama, referred to Kennedy simply as that "fellow who advocated giving blood to the Vietcong."[39]

Two years later, Kennedy's press secretary, Frank Mankiewicz, was still
sending out disclaimers to angry constituents explaining that Kennedy had
not advocated sending blood to North Vietnamese troops or to the National
Liberation Front, which was fighting the Americans in South Vietnam. Kennedy's defense of blood plasma going to "anyone who needs it," Mankiewicz
said by way of clarification, applied only to the Vietnamese civilian population.[40] The unexpected and lingering public flap over Kennedy's brief col-
loquy with student reporters eventually became somewhat humorous to him.
In a private exchange with the conservative columnist William F. Buckley,
Jr., Kennedy complimented Buckley on an article he had recently written
on the author Gore Vidal, with whom Kennedy had a long-standing feud,
adding jokingly: "I have changed my platform for 1968 from 'Let's give blood
to the Viet Cong' to 'Let's give Gore Vidal to the Viet Cong.'"[41]

Throughout 1965, Kennedy stopped short of breaking cleanly with the
Johnson Administration on the war. Given President Kennedy's earlier Southeast Asia policies, he found it awkward to attack Johnson for standing by the
Saigon regime, despite its astounding levels of corruption and Machiavellian
factionalism. Johnson never tired of accurately pointing out that his commitment to the Republic of South Vietnam remained consistent with the policies
of three previous administrations. Kennedy conceded this point, but he never
accepted the notion that his late brother would have followed an identical
path in internationalizing and Americanizing the conflict. Senator Ernest

Gruening of Alaska agreed with Kennedy on this point. Gruening, who had been one of two senators who voted against the Tonkin Gulf Resolution in August 1964, wrote Kennedy in late 1965: "The nature and form of our present commitment can in no way be compared with the previous commitments of either President Eisenhower or President Kennedy."[42]

In December 1965, the fighting in South Vietnam entered a lull when Johnson instituted two separate cease-fires as part of a highly publicized "peace offensive." Kennedy favored prolonging the cease-fire period: "American and South Vietnamese troops should not be the first to attack if the Viet Cong substantially honors the additional hours of the truce period established by our side," he said. Such an extension might "provide an avenue by which the conflict can be brought from the battlefield to the conference table." To further the prospect of peace talks, Kennedy urged the Administration to restate "its willingness to enter into unconditional discussions by all diplomatic means."[43] Kennedy's stand on the cease-fire and a negotiated settlement prompted two small citizens' groups in Cambridge, Massachusetts, and New Haven, Connecticut, to gather about 1,100 signatures on two separate petitions endorsing his peace proposals.[44] These actions were an early indication that Kennedy's words on the war could generate direct grassroots citizen action.

On January 11, 1966, Kennedy expressed his "reservations" about Johnson's Vietnam policies, particularly the bombing of North Vietnam, to an audience of millions on NBC's *Today* show. He also said that neither the executive branch nor the legislative branch had "satisfactorily discussed" the fundamental issues involved in a negotiated settlement. The Administration, in Kennedy's view, had failed to explain to the American people what it was willing to give up to secure peace in Vietnam. President Johnson kept a full transcript of Kennedy's *Today* show interview.[45]

On January 31, 1966, Johnson ordered a resumption of the bombing of North Vietnam, and thereby canceled the 37-day bombing pause, which had been in effect since December 24. He also approved Operation Masher, which the *New York Times* described as "the largest amphibious operation by United States Marines since the 1950 Inchon landing in Korea."[46] These decisions marked an end to the Administration's "peace offensive," which was Johnson's attempt to show that he had gone the extra mile for peace before launching the next seemingly inevitable phase of the U.S. military buildup.[47] Kennedy found Johnson's decision regrettable: "Obviously the resumption of bombing in the North is not a policy and we should not delude ourselves that it offers a painless method of winning the war. For if we regard bombing as the answer in Vietnam we are headed straight for disaster."[48]

Kennedy had long advocated international agreements on the proliferation of nuclear weapons, and one of his concerns was that the large-scale U.S. bombing of a Soviet ally close to the Chinese border could lead to World War Three:[49] "The danger is that the decision to resume [bombing] may become the first step in a series of steps on a road from which there is no turning back—a road which leads to catastrophe for all mankind. That cannot be permitted to happen."[50]

As he did in his May 1965 address, Kennedy stressed in remarks to the Senate the class injustices that existed in South Vietnam, and he argued that the success of the U.S.-backed regime depended on comprehensive reform: "We are spending far more on military efforts than on all the education, land reform, and welfare programs which might convince a young South Vietnamese that his future is not best served by the Communists."[51]

In January 1966, George Kahin testified before the House Foreign Relations Committee, and sent Kennedy red-penciled excerpts of his testimony, commenting: "I strongly urge that you persist in enlightened criticism of our badly mistaken policy in Vietnam."[52] Kennedy replied that he hoped they could meet face-to-face to discuss the situation: "You have sent me articles and letters which were very useful as guides to [my] understanding of Southeast Asia problems," he wrote.[53] Kahin highlighted for Kennedy those parts of his testimony in which he argued that a peaceful settlement could be reached only if the U.S.-backed government in Saigon recognized the de facto political power of the National Liberation Front. Kahin believed the N.L.F. was a far more powerful force in South Vietnam than the Administration had acknowledged, and that it could be neither militarily destroyed nor excluded from the political life of the country. Kennedy, who apparently did not share this opinion in August 1965 when Kahin first broached the subject,[54] five months later had accepted this analysis of Vietnamese political reality.

In early 1966, Ambassador-at-Large W. Averell Harriman, Defense Secretary Robert McNamara, and General Maxwell Taylor—three officials who supported the war, and remained close to Kennedy—urged him to travel to South Vietnam to see for himself what the United States had accomplished. The Administration often invited important critics to travel to Vietnam as a means of coopting them to the cause.[55] Kennedy considered taking them up on their offer, but his key political aide, Frederick Dutton, who was one of Kennedy's shrewdest strategists, strongly advised against it. Referring to Vietnam as "the indigestible lump in this country's gut," Dutton believed a trip to South Vietnam would very probably have little tangible benefit for the country or for Kennedy. The invitation, he wrote Kennedy, appeared to be "an unconscious effort by McNamara, Taylor and Harriman to have you help pull their and President Johnson's badly charred chestnuts out of a fire that they are all letting get out of control."[56] Kennedy passed on their offer.

Dutton also rejected the portrayal of the war as the direct legacy of Presidents Kennedy and Eisenhower: "It is a whole new mess," he wrote, that most nations in the world opposed "despite the growing self-righteousness and simplistic Texas nationalism of the White House."[57] Like other friends and advisers, Dutton believed that Kennedy could do more good by allowing other senators, such as J. William Fulbright of Arkansas and Eugene McCarthy of Minnesota, both of the Foreign Relations Committee, to "illuminate the problem," with Kennedy then adding his support.[58] Kennedy adopted this tactic, which he hoped might temper the media's obsession with portraying his criticisms of the war as part of a personal vendetta against Johnson.

In February 1966, Massachusetts Senator Edward Kennedy, who had begun serving his older brother's career in ways similar to those in which Robert had served John, presided over hearings of his subcommittee of the Senate Judiciary Committee on Refugees and Escapees. He heard testimony from government officials, refugee workers, physicians, and others who worked with the displaced population of South Vietnam. The younger Kennedy's subcommittee became an important voice in the Vietnam debate in subsequent years. Senator Fulbright, the chairman of the Foreign Relations Committee, also held hearings from February 4th through the 18th which reached a wide television audience. The Fulbright Committee called civilian and military experts to testify, and debated the Johnson Administration's request for supplemental appropriations that would greatly expand the American military commitment.[59]

Robert Kennedy followed the televised hearings intensely in his Senate office, and occasionally strolled over to the hearing room when an important witness testified. Fulbright and other committee members posed vague questions that Kennedy did not like. They allowed representatives of the Administration to skirt the concrete problems of the political role of the N.L.F. in South Vietnam, and its implications for Johnson's call for unconditional negotiations.[60] Kennedy was ready to make a statement on Vietnam which reflected his frustration with the Fulbright hearings. The day after the hearings concluded, he decided to raise some of the issues he felt the committee had neglected.

On Saturday morning, February 19, 1966, Kennedy called a brief press conference to address the crucial matter of the political role of the National Liberation Front. This public statement on Vietnam, like his earlier criticisms of the Administration, would exhibit caution and restraint, and avoid singling out Johnson for blame. He held the press conference in his office in the New Senate Office Building, and despite the presence of sharp-witted journalists, such as I. F. Stone who sat in the front row, the atmosphere seemed non-momentous.

Kennedy opened by speaking of the American tradition of dissent, citing as an example Abraham Lincoln's opposition to the Mexican War; he quoted Supreme Court Justice Oliver Wendell Holmes on freedom of expression, and commented on the historical role of the Senate in debating issues of war and peace. He reiterated his concern that the war drained resources from antipoverty programs. Although he made it clear he did not advocate a unilateral withdrawal from Vietnam, calling such a move "a repudiation of commitments undertaken and confirmed by three administrations," he nonetheless challenged the Administration to live up to its oft-stated desire for a negotiated settlement.

As he had done in May 1965, Kennedy searched for a third course for the United States in Vietnam, between unilateral withdrawal and military victory. But unlike his earlier statements, which vaguely set out how to achieve this goal, a more sophisticated analysis of South Vietnamese politics now informed Kennedy's views. "Whatever the exact status of the National Liberation Front—puppet or partly independent," he said:

> any negotiated settlement must accept the fact that there are discontented elements in South Viet Nam, Communist and non-Communist, who desire to change the existing political and economic system of the country. There are three things you can do with such groups: kill or repress them, turn the country over to them, or admit them to a share of power and responsibility. The first two are now possible only through force of arms.[61]

The only course, therefore, was to recognize the de facto political power of the N.L.F. In Kennedy's view, the role of the N.L.F. was "at the heart of the hope for a negotiated settlement. *It may mean a compromise government fully acceptable to neither side,*" he added, but "we must be willing to face the uncertainties of election, and the possibility of an eventual vote on re-unification."[62] This idea was a bitter pill for the war's supporters to swallow.

Kennedy disagreed with the Administration's short-sighted refusal to ac-knowledge the N.L.F., the strongest force fighting the United States in South Vietnam. Although he had chosen to publicly avoid the issue, Kennedy knew the State Department had squelched repeated offers by the Vietnam-ese to exchange prisoners of war, because it required a degree of official recognition of the N.L.F., which held twenty-seven Americans at that time.[63]

The United States, Kennedy said, had to clarify its terms and reveal enough of its intentions to Hanoi to "eliminate any reasonable fear that we ask them to talk only to demand their surrender." In calling for N.L.F. participation in South Vietnamese politics, Kennedy went further than Sen-ator Fulbright or any other member of the Foreign Relations Committee.[64] He had illuminated the contradictory nature of Johnson's call for negotia-tions, and he touched a sensitive nerve.

Frustrated by the missed opportunities of both the Senate hearings and the bombing pause, Kennedy questioned the Administration's practice of assuaging its critics with rhetorical pleasantries about seeking peace while it plowed ahead in pursuing military victory. The crux of the issue was that Johnson had called for peace talks without offering any concessions. Ken-nedy warned that the United States had to give "some reason for the Viet Cong to come to the conference table" or "be prepared for a long and bloody fight which eventually may bring in China."[65] A negotiated settlement meant "*that each side must concede matters that are important in order to preserve positions that are essential,*" he said.[66] With that, Kennedy concluded the press conference, and rather naively looked forward to a relaxing weekend skiing with his family in Vermont.

Kennedy was ill-prepared for the Administration's counterattack and the highly publicized confrontation between himself and senior Johnson offi-cials which ensued during the following week. "RFK Wants Viet Reds in Coalition" read some headlines, and the *Chicago Tribune* ran the story of Kennedy's press conference under the simple headline: "Ho Chi Ken-nedy."[67] Since his proposals had been consistent with the Administration's stated goals of a negotiated settlement, the hostile press reaction revealed the media's prowar framing of the debate. Coming on the heels of the "blood for the Viet Cong" controversy, and his defense of the rights of Americans who called for an N.L.F. victory or resisted the draft, this latest blast from the news media had a chilling effect on Kennedy.

After receiving a transcript of Kennedy's press conference, Vice President Hubert Humphrey told reporters on a flight from Wellington, New Zealand, to Manila: "I do not believe we should write a prescription for Viet Nam which includes a dose of arsenic." Humphrey had recently visited a half-dozen Asian countries including South Vietnam. He likened Kennedy's call to include the N.L.F. in a political settlement to "having a fox in the chicken coop," or "an arsonist in the fire department." Humphrey called the N.L.F. a "stooge" of Hanoi, and said the United States would only deal with it in any future negotiations as part of a North Vietnamese delegation. The U.S. goal in Vietnam, Humphrey stressed, was to ensure that "the rule of reason prevails rather than the rule of the jungle."[68]

In Saigon, South Vietnam's nominal head of state, Air Vice Marshall Nguyen Cao Ky, was furious at Kennedy. "The so-called National Liberation Front does not liberate anybody," he snapped to reporters. "They killed 11,000 of our troops last year and 22,000 of the innocent people in the countryside. They murdered them. They are 1,000 percent Communist and they are illegal," Ky barked. "So let's not talk about the National Liberation Front anymore."[69]

The Administration's strategy for countering Kennedy was simple: Johnson remained above the fray while his underlings discredited the young senator's prescription for a settlement. The day after Kennedy's press conference, McGeorge Bundy, Johnson's special assistant for national security affairs, and Undersecretary of State George Ball appeared on two separate Sunday morning television programs to defend the Administration. Both officials had served as aides to President Kennedy, which added to their credibility as critics of the late President's younger brother.

Bundy, who had been a Harvard dean, a Kennedy family friend, and then one of Johnson's most hawkish civilian advisers, said on NBC's *Meet the Press* that admitting the N.L.F. "to a share of the power and responsibility" in South Vietnam would not be a "useful or helpful step."[70] Most disturbing to Kennedy was Bundy's suggestion that President Kennedy, if he were alive, would agree with Johnson on this issue. Bundy paraphrased John Kennedy's line that forming a coalition with Communists was like trying to ride a tiger.[71] He had originally planned to embarrass Kennedy by quoting hard-line remarks about Vietnam that Kennedy himself had made back in 1962, but Johnson prevailed upon him not to do so if he valued his friendship with the senator.[72]

Kennedy cut short his ski weekend and returned to Washington to deal with the controversy. His friend General Maxwell Taylor, who supported the war and had been President Kennedy's military adviser, as well as Johnson's Ambassador to South Vietnam, tried to smooth over the conflict. Taylor told reporters he believed Kennedy's position was "very close" to his own, which favored "unconditional negotiations followed by free elections."[73] White House Press Secretary Bill Moyers had written Taylor's statement, which had been cleared with President Johnson. "Kennedy has managed to create the image of division among us," Moyers subsequently wrote Johnson, "thus escaping the necessity of clarifying his own position."[74] Kennedy had tried with little success to meet the Johnson forces halfway, and blunt the edges of the dispute.

Bundy sent Kennedy a transcript of his *Meet the Press* appearance, and Kennedy focused on a paragraph where Bundy said there would be "trouble" if U.S. officials considered "the usefulness of putting Communists in a position of power and responsibility."[75] In his letter accompanying the transcript, Bundy informed Kennedy that he had tried to avoid criticizing him directly, but insisted he had to make his "own position clear simply because of the very bad impact it would have both in Saigon and in Hanoi if anyone thought that the Administration was in favor of forming a popular front."[76] Bundy offered to use a future speaking engagement as a forum to publicly "dissociate" Kennedy from "the notion of a popular front imposed with our support before free elections."[77] Kennedy had said nothing about creating a "popular front" in Vietnam, a tainted term from the era when such governments were associated with the spread of Communist influence in Europe.

Bundy told Kennedy to use Johnson's press secretary, Bill Moyers, as his chief White House liaison before his next Vietnam statement.[78] But Kennedy had contacted Moyers beforehand: "I did, in fact, call him the day before I made the speech," he wrote Bundy, "read excerpts of the major points to him on the telephone and we discussed it briefly." Kennedy told Bundy that he had asked Moyers if there was anything further that needed to be done to apprise the Administration of his proposals prior to his press conference, and it was Moyers's judgment that there was nothing. Moyers had even expressed his appreciation to Kennedy for contacting him ahead of time.[79]

Kennedy did not appreciate Bundy's overwhelmingly negative and highly public reaction to his views, which he thought he had cleared with the White House press secretary. He decided to expunge the last paragraph from his response to Bundy:

> Actually, I wanted really to make myself clear—I have no fault at all to find in your protecting the position of the administration—that is your responsibility. But my statement was not directed at you personally. I would have obviously appreciated a call before you dealt with it and me on Sunday afternoon. Perhaps a call would not have taken any more time than for someone to look up the quote of President Kennedy to use against my position.[80]

Undersecretary of State George Ball, a closet dove among Johnson's hawkish foreign policy set, exhibited the opposite tendencies when he publicly slapped down Kennedy's assessment of the N.L.F. Appearing on ABC's *Issues and Answers*, Ball called Kennedy's proposals "absurd" and "impossible," even though Kennedy's views were almost identical to Ball's own privately held opinions about U.S. Vietnam policy.[81] Adhering to the Administration's public line on Vietnam despite his own serious misgivings, Ball, the team player, said the N.L.F. was an instrument of North Vietnam, and any coalition with it would quickly result in a Communist government in Saigon. The United States, he concluded, was "not going to deliver the South Vietnamese people to the administrations of a Communist regime, because that is what this war is all about."[82] Ball's reputation as a cautious foreign policy liberal, and like Bundy, a former adviser to President Kennedy, gave his criticism added credibility.

Like Bundy, Ball also sought to clarify his position in a private letter to Kennedy; both officials wished to stay on the senator's good side. Ball denied that he thought Kennedy's views were absurd or impossible, and said he was speaking "only in reference to the current demands of the National Liberation Front." Ball toyed with the notion that he might have misinterpreted Kennedy's proposal as a call for a coalition government prior to elections, rather than "the participation of the Viet Cong in the electoral process."[83] Ball's point was moot, since N.L.F. participation in any election would require a degree of recognition. Whether Kennedy called for a coalition government before or after elections became the key point of departure for Ball, because the Administration had already formally endorsed "free elections" in South Vietnam.

In a handwritten note to Ball, Kennedy said he "was taken a little aback" given that he was familiar with Ball's views on the matter. Kennedy pointed to a "very good memorandum" on Vietnam that Ball had written in April 1965 which seemed to support Kennedy's position. He was therefore "surprised" when Ball publicly chastised him for making an argument that expressed ideas similar to Ball's own.[84] Kennedy knew well the schizophrenic nature of Ball's public and private stands on the war: publicly, he toed the Administration's line; privately he called for disengagement.[85]

The counterattack against Kennedy prompted a few members of Congress to jump into the fray. Senator George Aiken of Vermont, the ranking Republican on the Foreign Relations Committee, who was not known as a Johnson ally, said on the CBS program *Face the Nation* that Kennedy's suggestion was "considerably out of order," and that it was not "up to the United States to offer the Viet Cong a share in the Saigon government."[86] Kennedy's senior colleague in the Senate from New York, Republican Jacob Javits, with whom Kennedy had a good professional and personal relationship, called the proposal a "way out suggestion" unlikely to lead to negotiations.[87]

For the next three days, Kennedy's stand on the N.L.F. became the focus of surprisingly intense media coverage, mainly because of the Administration's strident reaction. On Monday, February 21, 1966, Kennedy appeared on NBC's *Today* show to clarify his position. Despite trying to cool the dispute, he remained firm in his conviction that the "dissident elements" in South Vietnam "must be brought into any peace talks." The Administration's reaction, he said, showed "confusion" on its part over U.S. military and political goals in Vietnam. The United States' "political objectives should be absolutely clear," Kennedy reiterated. "If we want to destroy the Viet Cong we should be prepared for a long and bloody fight which eventually may bring in China."[88]

The following evening, February 22, Kennedy seemed to back off from the statements he had made on February 19 and on the *Today* show. He contended that he was closer to the Administration's view than the press had understood. This backpedaling on Kennedy's part led Dutton to privately criticize him for "inject[ing] confusion and offhandedness about a critical issue."[89] "You will end up being attacked for foxes-and-chickens by

the hard-liners," Dutton wrote, "for compromising your Saturday principles by the peace groups, and for muddled handling of the subject by a lot
of others. If I were Humphrey," he added, "I would try to clobber you" for
"wobbling on an issue of war and peace."[90] Four days later, Humphrey had
his chance.

The following Sunday, February 28, 1966, Kennedy appeared on *Face
the Nation*, which aired about one hour prior to an appearance by Hubert
Humphrey on *Issues and Answers*. Given that political commentators widely
recognized Humphrey and Kennedy as potential rivals for the Democratic
presidential nomination in 1972, they played up the domestic political significance of what became a televised sparring match. One columnist wrote
that their performances were "vaguely reminiscent of the 1960 television
debates between presidential candidates John F. Kennedy and Richard
Nixon."[91]

On *Face The Nation*, Kennedy once again addressed the issue of the
political role of the N.L.F. in South Vietnam: "I think that statements that
are made that we will never deal with assassins and we will never deal with
murderers," referring to some of Humphrey's remarks during the week,
"makes it difficult for them (the Vietcong) to believe that they are being
asked to the negotiating table other than to surrender."[92]

Humphrey, who had the opportunity to view Kennedy's appearance before he spoke, retorted that the N.L.F. "engage[d] in assassination, murder,
pillage, conquest, and I can't for the life of me see why the United States of
America would want to propose that such an outfit be made part of any
government." Humphrey drew a domestic analogy by boasting that he
helped "to purge the liberal movement of any Communist influence. You
didn't have any coalition with Commies" in the Americans for Democratic
Action, he said. In an uncharacteristic swipe at Kennedy, Humphrey added:
"I have just never believed that a person of liberal persuasion—and I guess
there are many definitions of that these days—should spend his time trying
to find out how he can accommodate himself, or someone else, with the
Communist thrust for power."[93] The following day, the *Washington Post*
reported that overall, Kennedy gave the impression of being "reasonable,
moderate, and calm, while Humphrey took a harder line, using tough language at times."[94]

A week after the controversy subsided, Kennedy told the *Christian Science
Monitor* that the only goal of his February 19 statement was to further "public
enlightenment to the realities involved in bringing about negotiations." Feel-

ing burned by the experience, he retreated. When asked if he would speak out again on the subject, he replied: "I have made the point."[95] Kennedy had been clearly caught off guard by the intensity of the news media's and Administration officials' attacks on him for simply pointing out that no Saigon regime could survive that denied the N.L.F. a political voice.

However, Kennedy received support for his February 19 statement from diverse sources. Senator Fulbright stopped short of endorsing his position, but accepted the premise that the N.L.F. should be one of the principal parties at the bargaining table.[96] The leaders of the liberal California Democratic Council, which was winding up a convention in Bakersfield when Kennedy's statement made headlines, endorsed his stand, and hoped it would hasten a change in U.S. Vietnam policy.[97]

George Kahin sent a letter to Kennedy which he and nine of his Cornell colleagues signed stating: "We strongly endorse your wise and realistic statement of February 19 on Vietnam." Included among the signatories were the economics professor and outspoken steering committee member of the National Committee for the Mobilization to End the War in Vietnam, Douglas Dowd, and the China specialist, Knight Biggerstaff.[98] Senator Frank Church of Idaho forwarded Kennedy copies of several *Washington Post* articles, which described George Ball's earlier challenge to the premises of the Administration's policies in Southeast Asia, implying that Ball's criticisms of Kennedy had been disingenuous or at least contradictory.[99] Walter Lippmann defended Kennedy's position in his syndicated column, and Pennsylvania Senator Joseph Clark read the Lippmann article into the *Congressional Record*.[100] "Senator Kennedy has gone to the heart of the matter," Lippmann wrote, "in fixing public attention on the simple truth that if the administration wants to negotiate, it will have to negotiate with the enemy who is in fact arrayed against us."[101]

Lippmann's wife, Helen Byrne Lippmann, wrote a letter congratulating Kennedy on his statement: "I believe that what at present may appear as idealistic courage will turn in the not so distant future to be politically popular realism."[102] In a handwritten reply, Kennedy said he appreciated the support "particularly at this time when my thoughts seem to have stirred up so much controversy and, I gather, bad feelings."[103] In a similar vein, Theodore Sorensen, who had been President Kennedy's key speech writer and currently worked for Johnson, wrote Kennedy: "What you said may prove in the long run (like JFK's Algerian speech [of 1957]) to be even wiser than it appears now."[104]

A day before the controversy began, the octogenarian pacifist A. J. Muste wrote Kennedy that "it has been gratifying to note that in a number of instances you have expressed doubt about aspects of the war in Vietnam and the current foreign policy of our government."[105] The actor Robert Vaughn, famous for his television role as the Man from U.N.C.L.E., wrote the senator after reading his February 19 statement: "Your rational realism in this matter is applauded resoundingly by this citizen."[106] The *New York Times* columnist Anthony Lewis privately complimented Kennedy for "a great statement."[107]

The former head of the Justice Department's Civil Rights Division when Kennedy was attorney general, Burke Marshall, wrote that despite the "good deal of trouble" it caused, "it is far and away the most constructive statement that has been made."[108] The defense Kennedy received from citizens and public figures for his February 1966 stand illustrates the important role he played in broadening the debate about Vietnam, and publicly ventilating issues that the Johnson Administration would have preferred to keep foggy.

Still, in mid-March 1966, the findings of a poll conducted by researchers from Stanford University and the University of Chicago confirmed previously published commercial polls that 61 percent of the American public still favored Johnson's handling of the war, while 29 percent opposed it.[109] But the survey also revealed that the majority of Americans were beginning to have reservations about continuing the war when faced with its costs, both in money and manpower. Eighty-eight percent of the respondents favored negotiations with representatives of the National Liberation Front in South Vietnam if they agreed to bargain.[110]

* * *

Kennedy lost the media battle with the Administration over the political role of the N.L.F. But he succeeded in moving the public debate toward a more realistic understanding of the influence of the N.L.F., and the folly of trying to militarily destroy an umbrella political organization, which included non-Communist nationalists whose support the Saigon regime badly needed. Kennedy outlined the key challenges facing the United States in seriously pursuing a negotiated settlement. Despite the strongly negative responses of Humphrey, Bundy, and Ball, Kennedy succeeded at least in opening up the debate.[111]

When he served in his brother's Cabinet, Kennedy had been a true believer in the methods of counterinsurgency to stymie wars of national liberation in the Third World. He sat on a special National Security Council committee designed to promote these techniques. However, the doctrines of counterinsurgency never worked in practice as well as they promised to do on paper, and the political and military environment in Vietnam demonstrated their limitations. Kennedy questioned his earlier faith in counterinsurgency, and came to agree with a Special Forces sergeant who wrote him from Vietnam in November 1965 that winning political support in the countryside of South Vietnam was "a hell of a lot more important than killing VC."[112]

In the wake of the "fox in the chicken coop" controversy, Dutton presented a set of proposals to Kennedy about how best to avoid future scraps with the Administration. He singled out Kennedy's stand on the war in Vietnam as both an opportunity and a vulnerability. He advised Kennedy not to "go too liberal on other public matters for now," because this would only throw fuel on the fire. He also suggested that Kennedy state his position "in terms of its being the logical extension of, not opposition to, the administration's stand," which Kennedy had attempted to do with his backpedaling from his original February 19 statement. Finally, Dutton wrote: "Use a little more patriotic rhetoric to support your Viet Nam position. A little political bunting can be helpful even when, as at present, you are making a jarring if historically important contribution to the evolution of national thinking on an emotional problem."[113] Dutton tried his best to salvage Kennedy's image at a time when many editorialists had gone on the offensive against him.[114] Kennedy generally followed Dutton's advice for the remainder of 1966.

It took years for the growing peace movement in the United States, with not much help from the national news media, to establish itself as a viable political force, and Kennedy drifted down a similar path; his views on the war did not remain fixed in place in 1965, but evolved through time as they did for millions of other Americans. His correspondence with Kahin and others knowledgeable about Vietnam shows an openness to a wide range of opinion. Given his role as the most prominent dove in the Democratic Party, along with his media-fueled rivalry with Johnson and Humphrey, Kennedy refused to throw caution to the wind in voicing his opposition. He could seriously damage his own political future and that of the Democratic Party. However, these constraints did not prevent him from speaking out against the direction of Johnson's Vietnam policies.

Cold War liberals of the 89th and 90th Congresses who disputed Johnson's course in Vietnam had to couch their disagreement in cautious terms.

Coming down too hard on Johnson for his foreign policy could impede the historic progress in the domestic field, which included sweeping legislation affecting civil rights, health care, education, and antipoverty programs. Moreover, Johnson appeared to have a reasonable prescription for success in Vietnam. He weighed his military options carefully and chose the middle road, ostensibly displaying restraint.[115]

By the end of 1965, there were 185,000 American troops in South Vietnam, and more than a thousand had been killed in battle. At various times in 1965 and early 1966, Kennedy pressed for a negotiated settlement, and tried to hold the Administration to its word about its stated desire for peace. He opposed Johnson's bombing of North Vietnam, saying it blocked any prospect for peace talks, swelled the ranks of the enemy, and threatened to bring China into the conflict. (He also supported a G.I. Bill for Vietnam veterans at a time when both the Veterans Administration and the Defense Department opposed it.)[116]

In February 1966, it was still conceivable that Johnson might achieve his goals in Southeast Asia. Although Kennedy had predicted privately in the summer of 1965 that the war could become a serious liability for Johnson, possibly blocking his domestic agenda, the President remained a popular figure, and no one could predict when, or if, this would wear off. The ultimate effects of the war on United States domestic opinion were equally unpredictable given the seemingly hawkish nature of the electorate. It was uncertain whether or not the peace movement could widen the debate on the war.

Finally, the Johnson Administration practiced a high degree of deception concerning the true nature of the war that was not widely exposed until Johnson was out of office. Secretary of State Dean Rusk and Kennedy's close friend, Secretary of Defense Robert McNamara, argued adeptly that the U.S.-backed government of South Vietnam was stronger politically and militarily than it really was; that it possessed greater popular support than it really did; and that the American troops were there only for a temporary mission to honor established U.S. diplomatic commitments. They also consistently claimed the war was going better for the United States than was truthfully the case.

In February 1966, Kennedy had taken a bolder stand on the issue of the role of the N.L.F. in a negotiated peace in Vietnam than any other senator, including the members of the Foreign Relations Committee. However, at that time he was not yet ready to repudiate the U.S. commitment to South

Vietnam. He faced serious political constraints: if he came out too strongly against Johnson on the war, the Washington press corps would interpret it as part of a personal vendetta, calculated to further his own political ambitions; and if he remained too cautious following his periodic criticisms of the war he would certainly be charged with hypocrisy. These political limitations continued to plague him for the next two years.

2

A Slow Path to Peace: Kennedy Calls for a Negotiated Settlement, March 1966–March 1967

If we don't find a solution, if we can't negotiate, if we cannot keep our commitments with honor, we can always go back to fighting. We can always go back to the war. . . . Before we take the final plunge to even greater escalation, I think that we should try negotiations.

—Robert F. Kennedy, the *Today* show, March 7, 1967

Throughout 1966, Kennedy remained cautious in voicing his criticisms of President Johnson's Vietnam policies. He shifted his focus from foreign policy to domestic projects, such as the public-private partnership in developing a poverty zone in Brooklyn, his work with the subcommittee on migrant labor, and his highly publicized trip to South Africa that June. As the 1966 midterm elections approached, Kennedy campaigned for Democratic candidates all over the country, and strengthened his ties to some of the party's regional power brokers. He consciously toned down his criticisms of the war and Johnson's foreign policy to avoid damaging the Democrats' chances in state, local, and Congressional races.

Kennedy's reticence in expressing his opposition to the war did not mean he remained silent. He criticized the bombing, the escalation, and the Americanizing of the conflict. He publicly agreed with other senators who challenged Johnson's policies, many of whom, unlike Kennedy, held committee assignments directly relating to foreign policy. Sometimes he led the way in calls for a negotiated settlement on television news programs and political talk shows.

Throughout 1966, Kennedy worked in behalf of the families of the American prisoners of war in Vietnam, and impelled the State Department to explore new avenues to negotiate their release. Active duty servicemen, as well as the wives of P.O.W.'s, wrote Kennedy seeking his assistance in securing the release of friends and loved ones who were missing in action in Vietnam.[1] Kennedy instructed Adam Walinsky, his key aide on Vietnam issues, to keep P.O.W. families apprised of his efforts to help them;[2] he quietly labored at this task with no fanfare, and sought no overt political gain from it.

In April 1966, Kennedy contacted the State Department and asked to discuss privately diplomatic initiatives to win the release of American P.O.W.'s. The State Department sent Philip Heymann, an administrator from the Bureau of Security and Consular Affairs. The senator expressed to Heymann his disappointment in the Administration's lack of progress in pursuing the P.O.W. problem: "Not enough is being done for these servicemen and their families," Kennedy told Heymann at the start of the stormy, forty-five minute meeting in his Senate office. He alluded to the story that the N.L.F. had been willing to trade an American prisoner of war for a captured Viet Cong one-for-one, but the United States had refused. When the State Department official denied having knowledge of the case, Kennedy said he had read about it himself in the *Washington Post*.[3]

Heymann reported that there were more than eighty American prisoners inside North Vietnam, and that the N.L.F. held about twenty-seven. Kennedy suggested that with the help of the State Department the families of the downed fliers could organize a committee, and hire a lawyer to go to Vietnam to represent them. Heymann scoffed at the idea, saying they probably would be refused visas. Kennedy then pointed out that the New Left activist and scholar Staughton Lynd had received a visa, and perhaps Lynd might even assume the role of intermediary. Heymann was taken aback at Kennedy's suggestion of using a noted leftist as a possible United States diplomatic emissary. But Kennedy continued to search for an avenue the Administration might have overlooked in aiding the release of prisoners. He reiterated his central point that "everything possible should at least be fully explored for the benefit of the prisoners."[4]

Heymann remained committed to the Administration's hard-line position on negotiating the release of P.O.W.'s. Any direct talks with the N.L.F., he argued, could not be undertaken in South Vietnam because it "might result in some degree of recognition of the VC." The "consequences of sitting down with the Viet Cong," he said, were "more important" in the State Department's view than the twenty-seven prisoners who were in their hands. Kennedy disputed this logic, noting that "the situation would be unstable for some time," and "meanwhile our servicemen were still prisoners."[5]

When Heymann said he doubted the possibility of any prisoner exchange, Kennedy, drawing on his past experience as a presidential adviser, countered by pointing out that the State Department, including the sitting Secretary of State, Dean Rusk, had been convinced that Fidel Castro would never agree to prisoner exchanges, yet they were successfully negotiated. He urged Heymann to find out what terms North Vietnam and the N.L.F. demanded for the release of U.S. servicemen, and suggested using contacts through the Soviet Embassy. When Heymann also rejected this course, saying the Russians had refused to play the role of honest brokers, Kennedy proposed using a full-time third-party negotiator, as had been done during the Cuban prisoner exchange. Heymann brushed this suggestion aside as well, saying that the State Department already had such contacts.[6]

In a follow-up letter to the meeting, Kennedy wrote Secretary of State Rusk: "My talk with Mr. Heymann convinced me that not enough is being done for these men, or their families. Too often, it seems to me, we neglect a possible course of action because we think it will not work—instead of trying it to see whether it works or not." In Kennedy's view, Heymann had tried to obscure the fact that "no approaches had been made through the Soviet Union, [and] no efforts had been made to find a non-governmental third party to negotiate on behalf of the prisoners or their families." He asked to be kept informed about "whatever ideas you or the Department have," and "any steps that are taken or progress that is made."[7]

Rusk wrote back a few weeks later, and blamed America's enemies for the lack of progress in this area. The United States efforts, he wrote, had "unfortunately resulted in no useful response from the other side." The Secretary of State ignored the earlier case, to which Kennedy alluded, where the N.L.F. offered to exchange a prisoner. Rusk agreed to keep Kennedy informed about further actions.[8] Kennedy's private efforts on behalf of American P.O.W.'s in Vietnam were consistent with his earlier calls for recognizing the N.L.F. He opposed the Administration's intransigence on issues vitally affecting the lives of U.S. servicemen and their families.

Later that month, in a statement on the Senate floor, Kennedy commented on recent clashes between American and North Vietnamese fighter aircraft near the Chinese border. He strongly disagreed with a State Department spokesman who said there would be "no sanctuary" for newly supplied enemy aircraft, "even over the border of China." Kennedy noted that violating China's air space could provoke the intervention of Chinese troops in Vietnam. He decried the Administration's reckless behavior at a time when the volatility of China's domestic life was revealing itself in the early rumblings of Mao Tse-tung's Cultural Revolution. "Even accepting our basic policy," he said, "it appears to me neither prudent nor wise to undertake risks of a still wider war until some progress has been made toward achieving the stability that is essential for the successful prosecution of our efforts in Viet Nam."[9] This stand was consistent with his earlier calls to avoid internationalizing the conflict, which formed the basis of Kennedy's opposition to the bombing of North Vietnam.

No amount of bombing North Vietnam, Kennedy emphasized, would enhance the political stability of the South Vietnamese government, as the Johnson Administration had reasoned. The U.S.-backed government in Saigon refused to speak with either the Communists or the Buddhist leaders of the non-Communist opposition, who were then leading prodemocracy demonstrations in the five northernmost provinces of South Vietnam.[10] Since the true political struggle was in the South, Kennedy called the Administration's obsession with the North counterproductive:

> There is still great political instability in South Viet Nam. And South Viet Nam is where the war is being fought. . . . Without a viable political structure in South Viet Nam, the efforts and sacrifice of our fighting men will be wasted. But no military action in North Viet Nam or China can create or contribute to the creation of such a political structure in South Viet Nam.[11]

Once again, Kennedy was drawing attention to the political nature of the conflict and the centrality of the N.L.F. He had recognized, long before Johnson's Vietnam advisers (with the possible *private* exception of George Ball), that the N.L.F. represented a broad-based political movement inside South Vietnam. Kennedy understood the significance of the military cadres of the N.L.F.—what U.S. officials derisively labeled the "Viet Cong"—but he also understood their secondary role when compared to the political movement they represented, which included non-Communist nationalists, Buddhists, civil servants, and students.

On April 27, 1966, Kennedy appeared on Walter Cronkite's CBS evening news and on the *Huntley and Brinkley Report*, where he summarized the main points of his Senate statement. He outlined, once again, the risks involved in provoking China, as well as the perennial political instability of the Republic of South Vietnam. His renewed public criticism of the Administration's Vietnam policies sparked a reaction from the White House. Johnson's key media specialist, the former president of NBC Robert

Kintner, shared with the President his impressions of Kennedy's television performances. Kennedy's statement had been "so uncomplicated," Kintner wrote, it was sure to "appeal to a great many people, as well as to the New York Times, etc." He believed Kennedy had "painted" Johnson as recklessly using the armed forces in Vietnam, which hurt the President's public image.[12] Kintner mapped out for Johnson a media strategy to counter Kennedy's criticisms. The response, he wrote, should "come from someone who is obviously not a part of the Administration, who has a liberal stature, and is on the Eastern Seaboard."[13] He suggested Johnson order his press secretary, Bill Moyers, to appear on television to present the Administration's rebuttal.

A week following Kintner's warning to Johnson, Kennedy appeared again on TV, this time on the *Today* show, where he called for a bombing halt, a cease-fire, and a negotiated settlement.[14] Senate doves, including South Dakota Senator George McGovern, publicly praised Kennedy's remarks. Kennedy sent a handwritten note to McGovern: "I hope we shall make some progress in this area of the world as well as elsewhere. But sometimes when I read the statements of our representatives in the executive branch of the gov[ernment] I become quite discouraged. The problems are so immense [and] the needs too great to prevent some of the more unfortunate errors of judgment and action—at least that is the way it appears to me."[15]

On June 29, 1966, the day Johnson announced the bombing of the North Vietnamese port city of Haiphong, Kennedy released to the press a statement denouncing the President's latest action. "I am sure that all Americans are concerned at this expansion of the war in Vietnam," it quoted him as saying. "It seems to me that the major question to be answered with respect to the bombings is this: Will this step effectively prevent North Vietnam from supplying the Viet Cong in the South with sufficient men and materiel to enable them to continue the war at the levels they desire?"

"Unfortunately," he continued, "past escalations have often been accompanied by assurances and predictions that this would be the case."[16] And he went on: "These hopes have not been fulfilled. Had these predictions been correct, the bombings announced today would not have been necessary. Indeed, on each occasion, the effort from the North has either increased in spite of our efforts, or taken a different and more dangerous course.

I regret that it has seemed necessary to take this step. We must all hope that the predictions based on this latest heightening of the battle will prove to be realistic ones."[17]

As he had in many of his public statements in 1965, Kennedy questioned Johnson's Vietnam policies on what might be considered tactical grounds. Yet he also pointed the way toward formally recognizing the political power of the N.L.F., and exploring avenues for a negotiated settlement.

In July 1966, reports surfaced in the press that hard-liners in North Vietnam contemplated hostile actions against Americans under their control as retaliation for the stepped-up United States bombing. Kennedy implored Hanoi to refrain from reprisals against American prisoners. Such acts, he said, were "contrary to the laws of war, contrary to all past practices in this war, [and] a plunge into barbarism which could serve the interest of no man and no nation."[18] Kennedy opposed the bombing of North Vietnam, in part, because he feared it would lead to just such reprisals against American P.O.W.'s.

As the 1966 midterm elections neared, Kennedy campaigned for Democratic candidates at the state, local, and Congressional levels. The Democrats' uncommonly large majorities in the House of Representatives (295 to 140), the Senate (68 to 32), and the statehouses (33 to 17), seemed certain to lose ground. In his stump speeches, Kennedy trumpeted the domestic successes of Presidents Kennedy and Johnson, while toning down his criticisms of the Administration's Southeast Asia policy. For example, in September 1966 at the New Hampshire Democratic State Convention, where Kennedy helped the Johnson loyalists Senator Thomas McIntyre and Governor John King, he avoided the war issue altogether, and instead enumerated the domestic accomplishments of the Democratic Congress and Administration in the fields of education, health care, and the antipoverty programs. He shrewdly shied away from criticizing Johnson's Vietnam policies, and became a Democratic partisan by emphasizing the danger of the more reckless "solutions" to the conflict, such as "total bombing," that several Republican candidates had been advocating.[19]

On November 8, 1966, Democrats lost 47 House seats, reducing their margin to 248 to 187, three Senate seats, making the division 64 to 36, and eight governorships, for a 25-to-25 split of the states. Kennedy privately predicted that the Republicans would do even better in 1968: "I would think the Democrats are in for some difficulty in 1968," he wrote Anthony Lewis, "that is unless [Michigan Governor George] Romney is as stupid as he occasionally appears. I am sure if he handles it at all well he can get the nomination, and unless the President and his advisers show more wisdom about the Democratic organization than they have in the past, and most importantly are able to have a good deal more success with Vietnam than I anticipate—could very well win in 1968. (Please Burn)."[20] Kennedy had learned from his itinerant campaigning that Johnson's war, as well as his autocratic control of the Democratic National Committee, had become sources of discord among the leaders of state and regional Democratic organizations.

Throughout 1966 and 1967, Kennedy received information and advice from prominent antiwar activists, peace organizations, and Asia scholars. These materials deepened his understanding of the history and politics of Vietnam, and the role of the United States. By the end of 1966, his analysis of the war had become far more sophisticated. The entrenched warfare in Vietnam, and the Administration's apparent commitment to a military solution, confirmed some of the key criticisms set forth by the antiwar movement. The Cornell Southeast Asia specialist George Kahin continued to send Kennedy reports about the internal politics of the conflict. Kennedy read Kahin's studies with interest, and periodically asked him for suggestions.[21] He also carefully scrutinized the arguments contained in the book Kahin wrote with John W. Lewis, *The United States and Vietnam*, published in 1967.[22]

Antiwar groups, progressive policy institutes, and individual peace activists prodded Kennedy to take an ever stronger stand against the war. Marcus Raskin and Arthur Waskow of the Institute for Policy Studies periodically sent Kennedy Vietnam analysis papers, and stayed in contact with Walinsky.[23] The New Leftists Andrew Kopkind and Staughton Lynd also sent antiwar materials to Kennedy.[24] The Inter-University Committee for Debate on Foreign Policy, which included on its executive board the antiwar academics Douglas Dowd and Howard Zinn, sent Kennedy an eighty-two-page booklet, which presented a strong scholarly case for United States disengagement from Vietnam.[25] The defense expert Daniel Ellsberg dispatched to Kennedy his analyses of the war.[26] Throughout 1966 and 1967, Kennedy's two earnest young aides, Walinsky and Edelman, hardened their opposition to Johnson's Vietnam policies, and maintained an open line of communication with most of the major peace organizations. By sifting through the mass of information on Vietnam from a wide spectrum of opinion that flooded his office, Kennedy formulated his own analysis of the war.

In September 1966, the pediatrician and peace activist Dr. Benjamin Spock, whose books on child rearing influenced a generation, believed Kennedy to be "the only person who could lead this country back to peace and decency." Spock sent the senator a forceful appeal: "I want to express again my hope that you will save our country by advocating a foreign policy that is boldly different from Johnson's so that not only idealistic but bewildered people will have a standard and a person to rally around. . . . (I would be delighted to help line up clergy, academicians, writers and other intellectuals for a public appeal to you.)"[27] Spock feared that Johnson would "take the easiest and most perilous course of drastic further escalation."[28] The famous baby doctor challenged Kennedy to take a bolder stand against the war. He argued for U.S. recognition of the N.L.F., and a negotiated peace "as soon as the safety of our Saigon allies is assured."[29]

Dr. Spock's prescription for peace in Vietnam resembled the position Kennedy would advocate about five months later. However, Spock's point about assuring the safety of the Saigon government showed that even well-informed opponents of the war could overlook the thornier details complicating a political settlement, which Kennedy, given the hostility of the Administration and his prominent political role, could not gloss over. He offered to meet with Spock as soon as his schedule would permit. In the meantime, acknowledging the doctor's importance to the national Vietnam debate, Kennedy asked Richard Goodwin to meet with him in New York City.[30]

In early 1967, the *Village Voice* reporter and Kennedy partisan Jack Newfield set up a meeting with Tom Hayden and Staughton Lynd at Kennedy's apartment in the United Nations Plaza in New York. Hayden and Lynd were well-known New Left leaders, and vigorous opponents of the war. In December 1965, they had traveled together to Hanoi to start a dialogue between the American left and the North Vietnamese, and to secure the release of prisoners of war.[31] According to Newfield, Kennedy took an interest in Hayden's work in behalf of P.O.W.'s, and in organizing a black community union in Newark, New Jersey. He thought Hayden's experience might inform his own pet urban project, the Bedford-Stuyvesant Restoration Corporation.[32] It was evident to both Hayden and Lynd that Kennedy had been rethinking his position on Vietnam policy, albeit cautiously.[33]

The conversation during Kennedy's private meeting with the two New Leftists quickly centered on the war. "Both Staughton and I found Senator Kennedy sensitive and fair-minded in our discussion of Vietnam," Hayden wrote Edelman a few days later. "I was very impressed with his degree of concern and his willingness at least to explore drastic policy alternatives."[34] Hayden believed "the Communists" would jump at the chance to participate in elections, and that Kennedy should more forcefully push his own peace initiatives, and not wait for the Administration to spell out its negotiating terms. "The Senator agreed," Hayden concluded, "when we said rather baldly that lack of information [about negotiating terms] is a poor reason to murder Vietnamese."[35] Hayden and Lynd, like Spock, recognized Kennedy as the one national political figure who might be able to slow Johnson's course in Vietnam. They pressed him through a combination of rational argument and moral appeal to take a bolder public stand against the war.

Kennedy and his staff had been planning since December 1966 a European trip to meet with heads of state for talks on European affairs, Southeast Asia, and nuclear arms control. Derisively referred to as "Bobby's 'royal visit' to Europe" in some of Johnson's private correspondence,[36] Kennedy's trip coincided with the Administration's latest effort to appear interested in a negotiated peace in Vietnam.

In early February 1967, when Johnson temporarily halted the bombing of North Vietnam, and a four-day truce honoring the Tet lunar new year was in effect, Kennedy visited America's principal European allies. During his talks with British, French, and German heads of state, he gauged the depth of Western Europe's disagreement with the United States' course in Southeast Asia. He found that sentiment against the U.S. military conduct ran high. When he heard that Johnson had resumed the bombing of North Vietnam, and decided to pursue greater escalation, Kennedy believed the U.S. had yet again missed an opportunity to explore negotiations.

In Europe, Kennedy met with British Prime Minister Harold Wilson, German Chancellor Kurt Kiesinger, and Italian Premier Aldo Moro.[37] In Paris, he participated in two days of meetings with senior French officials, including President Charles de Gaulle, who had denounced the U.S. intervention. During his meeting with Kennedy, de Gaulle did not conceal his utter contempt for the ruling junta in South Vietnam, particularly for South Vietnam's nominal Premier, Air Vice Marshal Nguyen Cao Ky.[38] On February 1, Kennedy discussed Vietnam extensively with the director of Asian Affairs for the French Foreign Ministry, Etienne Manac'h, a diplomat with experience dating back to the French intervention in Indochina. The First Secretary of the American Embassy in France, and the United States' resident Vietnam scholar, John Gunther Dean, also attended the meeting, acting as an interpreter and keeping an eye on Kennedy's official visits in France for the Administration. Kennedy, who had been bombarded during earlier legs of his trip with numerous proposals for peace in Vietnam, nearly missed the fact that Manac'h had subtly informed him of a significant shift in Hanoi's position regarding negotiations.

Manac'h suggested that with a United States bombing halt in place, Hanoi might be willing to negotiate directly with the U.S., while the official status of the N.L.F. in South Vietnam was held in abeyance.[39] This stance was reportedly passed on to Manac'h by Mai Van Bo, North Vietnam's representative in Paris,[40] and was a departure from Ho Chi Minh's earlier demand that the N.L.F. be recognized as a legitimate political force in South Vietnam prior to the start of negotiations.[41] The leftist Australian journalist Wilfred Burchett had also reported a similar shift in Hanoi's position after he interviewed the North Vietnamese Foreign Minister, Nguyen Duy Trinh.[42] The delicate exchange between Kennedy and Manac'h at the United States Embassy in Paris marked the birth of the "peace feeler" controversy. It became the latest media-fueled debacle for Kennedy upon his return to the United States.

The day after Kennedy's Paris meetings, Secretary John Gunther Dean sent five cables to Washington covering Kennedy's conversations with French officials, including Manac'h and the socialist deputy François Mitterand.[43] Edward Weintal of *Newsweek* magazine, a diplomatic reporter with a reputation for breaking stories, probably obtained a copy of one of Dean's diplomatic cables. Weintal wrote in *Newsweek* that a "significant peace signal" came from Hanoi during the Manac'h meeting, which was "unveiled for the benefit of Robert F. Kennedy for reasons best known to the French."[44]

On February 6, 1967, the *New York Times* ran the story on page one. Kennedy appeared to be usurping the Administration's prerogative in international diplomacy by assuming the role of U.S. emissary, when his official status as a junior senator did not warrant it. After a search came up empty inside the State Department for the leaked cables, the White House suspected Kennedy, or someone close to him, had been the source of the Weintal story.[45] Kennedy flatly denied it. Dean had informed Kennedy's aide, Joseph Dolan, that one of the conversations, although not the one with Manac'h, was "highly classified and should . . . be treated as such."[46] When Kennedy returned to the United States, and journalists bombarded him with questions about the "peace feeler," he seemed baffled: "I return from Europe," he said, "hopeful about peace but without any 'feelers.'"[47]

Kennedy telephoned Johnson's appointments secretary, Marvin Watson, and asked for a meeting with the President to report directly on his trip, and clarify the peace feeler affair.[48] For public consumption, Watson insisted that

Kennedy state formally that he was "requesting" an audience with Johnson.[49] Although Kennedy's White House meeting was officially off the record, news of it caused a stir among the press. Eager to report news of any breakthroughs in the search for peace in Vietnam, or on the latest skirmish in the "Kennedy-Johnson feud," journalists grilled White House Press Secretary George Christian about the peace feeler at a press conference prior to the meeting. Christian said that Kennedy had not been representing the White House or the President on his trip. He skirted the question of whether Kennedy disrupted a "secret" diplomatic track which Secretary Rusk and National Security Adviser Walt Rostow had spoken of publicly while Kennedy was in Europe.[50]

Johnson sent Undersecretary of State Nicholas Katzenbach, who had served as a top aide to Kennedy in the Justice Department when he was attorney general, to meet Kennedy at his Senate office. Meantime, Rusk briefed Johnson twice that afternoon about Kennedy's purported peace efforts in Europe.[51] The President also huddled with several of his closest confidants prior to the meeting, including Rostow, Supreme Court Justice Abe Fortas, Marvin Watson, and his special assistant, Joseph Califano.[52] Kennedy and Katzenbach arrived at the White House together, and the meeting began at 4:34 P.M. in a room on the second floor. Only Kennedy, Katzenbach, Johnson, and Rostow attended the gathering, which lasted about an hour and fifteen minutes.[53]

The ensuing confrontation between Kennedy and Johnson that chilly winter day is described in several of the biographical works on Kennedy.[54] The common source for Kennedy's side of the story, since he subsequently dropped the subject, comes from what he told his press secretary Frank Mankiewicz and his legislative aide Peter Edelman upon returning to his office immediately following the meeting.

According to Mankiewicz, Kennedy had told Johnson at the meeting that the leaked diplomatic cable probably "came from your State Department," to which Johnson snapped, "It's *your* State Department!," insinuating that it was teeming with pro-Kennedy Easterners.[55] Ignoring the President's response, Kennedy went on to present a number of his suggestions about attaining peace in Vietnam. He argued for a permanent end to the bombing, and an expansion of the role of the International Control Commission to oversee a cease-fire and negotiations. Johnson listened intently and then said: "Well, I want you to know that I'm not going to adopt any single one of those suggestions because we're going to win the war, and you doves will all be dead in six months." Kennedy responded: "I don't have to listen to that"; he got up and walked out.[56]

Edelman said in a subsequent interview that Kennedy had been shaken following the meeting, and told him Johnson had been "very, very crude and angry." The President was in no mood to receive policy advice from his bitter political rival. When Johnson had growled, "You doves will be dead in six months," Kennedy took this to mean that the President believed the United States would win the war within the year.[57] The meeting with Johnson, Edelman thought, was what led Kennedy to give a new speech on Vietnam, because "after being treated that way, he felt he didn't owe Johnson a thing."[58]

When Kennedy walked out of the meeting, Katzenbach and Rostow tried to salvage the situation by asking him to tell the press, who were waiting in the West Lobby of the White House, that there had been no peace feelers at all during his trip. Kennedy refused. His uncertainty in the matter precluded such a definitive statement, but he agreed to say he had not brought home any new initiatives (which was true, since it was a State Department official who transmitted the message to Washington).[59] "I did not bring home any peace feelers," Kennedy meekly told the press.[60]

Responding to a question, Kennedy said that the general feeling among the European leaders with whom he spoke was that North Vietnam's position had loosened somewhat, but these matters were best left to the President. Although Johnson's abusive manner during the meeting angered him, Kennedy was diplomatic, and publicly closed ranks with the White House. He said his conversation with Johnson convinced him that the President was "dedicated to finding a peaceful solution to the struggle in Vietnam."[61] He later took pains not to blame Dean, the official who felt the heat for the purported leak. "I hope what has happened in the past two weeks has not caused you great difficulty," Kennedy told Dean in a handwritten note. "I am of course very sorry. If there is anything I can do either confidentially or in any other fashion, you will let me know."[62]

About an hour after Kennedy's acrimonious meeting with Johnson, the presidential correspondent for *Life* magazine Hugh Sidey asked the White House if he could spend a few minutes with the President to discuss the reported Vietnam peace feelers.[63] Johnson approved the interview, and Rostow helped him prepare for it. "We are certainly having mounted against us the most systematic and purposeful Communist psychological warfare operation since 1945," Rostow wrote Johnson, "designed to make us stand down the bombing of the North unilaterally."[64] In Rostow's view, Kennedy was little more than a Communist dupe.

Rostow advised Johnson to emphasize in his interview that despite the "psychological warfare offensive" from Hanoi, the Administration was ever vigilant in its "meticulous and total effort to make sure that nothing is missed" in the area of new peace initiatives.[65] He wanted Johnson to preempt the question Sidey would surely ask: How did Kennedy manage to pick up a peace feeler the Administration had overlooked?

On February 13, 1967, Johnson resumed the bombing of North Vietnam, thereby rendering moot any peace feeler from Hanoi. Thus ended the Administration's latest bombing halt, which began on February 7 and lasted five days and eighteen hours. Ho Chi Minh had made it clear on numerous occasions there would be no negotiations so long as American bombs rained over North Vietnam. The Administration concluded that Hanoi's position had never changed, and the brief excitement in the press over the status of negotiations arose from Kennedy's personal political ambitions. Kennedy responded to the news of the bombing, tactfully taking care not to single out Johnson for blame: "I deeply regret that the bombing of North Vietnam has resumed. Beyond that, it is most unfortunate that the truce period has gone by without greater progress being made by all of us on both sides toward a peaceful ending of this tragic war."[66]

The peace feeler incident once again demonstrated Kennedy's political vulnerability when he engaged in public scrapes over Vietnam with the Administration. Prowar editorialists excoriated him for usurping the president's prerogative in foreign affairs. The syndicated columnist Robert Allen denounced "the power-minded New York Senator" for his "aggressive head-line grabbing and anti-Johnson sharpshooting."[67] Allen, whose articles about Kennedy were passed on to the FBI's liaison to the White House, Cartha DeLoach, informed his readers (and the FBI) that Kennedy's "ever-busy publicity minions" had "leaked word" that the senator would soon deliver "a widely fanfared [sic] speech on the Vietnam war," advocating "a let's-be-friendly-with-Peking course."[68]

Other commentators either sensationalized Kennedy's clash with Johnson, or speculated that his stand on the war was merely part of an elaborate scheme to seize the Democratic presidential nomination in 1968.[69] One columnist close to Johnson, William White, argued that Kennedy's views on Vietnam had irrevocably placed him at the head of the domestic anti-Johnson forces.[70]

In the weeks between Kennedy's bitter meeting with the President on February 6 and his Vietnam speech on the Senate floor on March 2, it appeared that the U.S. had missed another opportunity for peace talks. In addition to Hanoi's softening of its line on negotiations, and Soviet Premier Aleksei Kosygin's promise, while meeting with British Prime Minister Harold Wilson in London, to aid in the peace process, Pope Paul VI and United Nations Secretary General U Thant also pressed Johnson to stop the bombing permanently and begin talks.

The time had come for Kennedy to risk the Administration's wrath with another Vietnam statement. Perhaps Kennedy was emboldened in part by a February 1967 Gallup poll naming him as the more popular choice for the 1968 presidential nomination among Democratic voters over Johnson and Hubert Humphrey.[71] Walinsky's original draft of the address went through about a dozen revisions. Given that this speech promised to be his lengthiest and most detailed statement on the war to date, Kennedy called for more comment than was his normal practice; the criticisms helped shape the tone of the final product. Those who critiqued multiple drafts included Peter Edelman, Arthur Schlesinger, Richard Goodwin, Theodore Sorensen, and the Harvard professors Richard Neustadt and Henry Kissinger.[72] His calling on Kissinger reveals the high degree of caution with which Kennedy broached the topic. The final version adopted many of the Administration's Cold War premises for pursuing the war, and was far less hard-hitting than the committed doves on Kennedy's staff desired. The perceived inadequacies of the speech sparked a strong private response from Walinsky and Edelman.

According to Walinsky, both Neustadt and Kissinger wished Kennedy would not make any comprehensive statement on the war.[73] Neustadt had argued that Kennedy's "position as a former member of the Administration," and "a major figure in the Democratic Party prohibit[ed] an honest speech about the war and what LBJ is doing." He was "deeply concerned" about a split between Kennedy and the President.[74] After Neustadt and Kissinger finished changing the speech, Walinsky believed, it dropped "between stools." He called it a "charade" that "the Administration really meant all that about peace and negotiations."[75] In a separate note to Kennedy, Walinsky wrote that nowhere did "the draft question any of the basic premises of the war, or the Administration's rationale," which he believed Kennedy should challenge.[76]

Edelman, the other young dove on Kennedy's staff, also criticized the watered-down version of the speech. "The draft is mushy," he wrote Kennedy, "and it looks like you are walking a tightrope."[77] In Edelman's view, Johnson's policy, despite public claims to the contrary, was in fact directed toward the "impossible" goal of "military victory." He could not see how Kennedy could avoid "stating that the Administration's policy is more and more clearly at variance with what it professes to be."[78] Edelman urged Kennedy to use the speech to "reinforce the utility" of his recent European trip, and said that if Kennedy went with the final draft he would be "trying to have it both ways, trying to please both sides."[79] For Kennedy, the speech was a delicate balancing act: he sought to criticize Johnson's Vietnam policy without taking on the Administration's false statements about its quest for peace or its public deceit about the nature and progress of the war that was then manifesting itself as a "credibility gap."

Edelman subsequently told an interviewer that Kennedy chose not to break free at that time from the "facade" of supporting the Administration's stated goals in Vietnam, because "he was convinced that it would not help end the war," and "that Lyndon Johnson was so insane that he would literally prolong the war simply because Bobby Kennedy was against it."[80]

Arthur Schlesinger had urged Kennedy to insert language into the speech deploring the Administration's apparent stand that "we cannot negotiate when we are behind because we are weak; and we cannot negotiate when we are ahead because, if we intensify the pressure, we can be even farther ahead at some later time."[81] Shirking the concerns of Kennedy's dovish advisers, the final version of his stop-the-bombing address left largely unscathed what Schlesinger called the Administration's vicious logic about the war. Neustadt and Kissinger had won out over Edelman and Walinsky.

It is clear from the comments scribbled across multiple drafts of the speech that Kennedy and his staff were well aware of the official lies and deception about Vietnam emanating from Administration sources. Kennedy, who penciled in changes of the speech well past midnight the night before he delivered it,[82] decided to avoid ventilating the issue at that time. Calling Johnson a liar would backfire; it would damage Kennedy's credibility, and his relations with Democratic insiders, as well as throw red meat to a national press corps awaiting any opportunity to exploit the Kennedy-Johnson conflict.

Members of Kennedy's staff floated a few trial balloons about the upcoming Vietnam speech to columnists and reporters to build an atmosphere of anticipation, and to focus national attention. The leaks inspired a premature rebuttal from James Farley, a Johnson loyalist and former chairman of the

Democratic National Committee. Farley condemned Kennedy's "soaring ambitions," and said: "Insulting, belittling, and interfering with the office of the Presidency is not the act of a mature citizen, let alone a United States senator."[83]

On March 2, 1967, despite anxiety surrounding the speech, when Kennedy pulled up in his car in front of the New Senate Office Building, instead of rushing inside he climbed aboard a bus filled with mostly African-American school children who were on a field trip to the capital. He joked with the children, invited them to visit, and then bounded into his suite of offices on the ground floor to prepare for the speech.[84] Later that afternoon, he allowed in half-a-dozen journalists to his private office to discuss the background of his address. "The President," said one reporter, "makes the charge that speeches like this do a disservice to our boys." Kennedy thought for a moment, and then replied: "You have to balance that against what you think does the greatest amount of good. I don't think we're going to end the war by military action."[85] In response to another question, Kennedy conceded that American public opinion leaned more to the hawkish side.

At 3:40 P.M. on March 2, Kennedy rose to speak on the floor of the Senate, with some twenty senators in the chamber, the largest gathering to hear a speech in several weeks. Senator J. William Fulbright lent his conspicuous presence, and he and the nineteen other senators listened intently.[86] Senate Majority Leader Mike Mansfield of Montana and George McGovern were in attendance. Senators Joseph Clark of Pennsylvania, Claiborne Pell of Rhode Island, Albert Gore of Tennessee, and Joseph Tydings of Maryland, all Democrats, along with the Republican John Sherman Cooper of Kentucky, added their support. Several senators who disagreed with Kennedy were there to listen, including Democrats Robert Byrd of West Virginia, Henry ("Scoop") Jackson of Washington, Frank Lausche of Ohio, and Gale McGee of Wyoming, along with the Republican Minority Leader, Everett Dirksen.[87] Charles Percy of Illinois and Edward Brooke of Massachusetts showed polite interest.

Cautiously, Kennedy outlined a comprehensive exit strategy for the United States in Vietnam certain to anger President Johnson. He took care to display deference to Johnson, and refused to suggest, as Edelman and Walinsky had argued, that the Administration's calls for a negotiated settlement had been disingenuous. "For years," he said, "President Johnson has dedicated his energies in an effort to achieve an honorable peace."[88] Kennedy's first words came out flatly, quietly, lost in the Senate din. But soon the chamber settled down, and the loudest sound, except for the senator's measured tones, was the turning of pages by people following the prepared text. Kennedy's wife, Ethel, sat with friends in the family section of the Senate gallery, and perhaps half of Kennedy's full-time Washington staff of thirty-two were there, some in the family gallery, most in the staff gallery. Mankiewicz and Walinsky roamed around the floor of the Senate; Edelman sat in the family gallery.

Kennedy offered a mea culpa for his and President Kennedy's role in decisions which helped produce the crisis in Vietnam: "As one who was involved in many of those decisions, I can testify that if fault is to be found or responsibility assessed, there is enough to go round for all—including myself." He grappled with the moral consequences of his past actions. But he also spoke of "the grave and painful responsibility borne by the President of the United States," and said that "nearly all Americans share with us the determination and intention to remain in Vietnam until we have fulfilled our commitments."[89] This last point was consistent with Johnson's stated policy.

Kennedy then criticized the war for "diverting resources which might have been used to help eliminate American poverty, improve the education of our children and enhance the quality of our national life." To those who believed the bombing of North Vietnam was necessary to show the South Vietnamese the depth of the U.S. commitment, Kennedy said that the 400,000 American fighting men in Vietnam were "a far more effective and continuing proof of our commitment and determination" than the bombing of the North.[90] The operative paragraph appearing midway through the speech, which Mankiewicz distributed as a separate press release, stated: "I propose that we test the sincerity of the statements by Premier Kosygin and others asserting that if the bombardment of the North is halted, negotiations would begin—by halting the bombardment and saying we are ready to negotiate within the week; making it clear that discussions cannot continue for a prolonged period without an agreement that neither side will substantially increase the size of the war in South Vietnam [either] by infiltration or reinforcement." Pertaining to a gradual disengagement of American troops, Kennedy proposed the following:

> An international group should be asked to inspect the borders and ports of the country to report any further escalation. And under the direction of the United Nations, and with an international presence

gradually replacing American forces, we should move toward a final settlement which allows the major political elements in South Vietnam to participate in the choice of leadership and shape their future direction as a people.[91]

By calling for an enlarged role for the United Nations and the International Control Commission following a permanent cessation of the bombing, Kennedy sought to remove the United States as an unrestrained unilateral military force in Vietnam. He wanted to use the reprieve of a cease-fire and bombing halt to shore up the flagging legitimacy of the United States in the eyes of the world community. And he once again offered his support for the inclusion of the N.L.F. in the political life of South Vietnam.

He suggested that the South Vietnamese government "begin its own discussion with the National Liberation Front. All the people of South Vietnam," he said, "Communist and non-Communist, Buddhist and Christian, should be able to choose their leaders, and seek office through peaceful political processes, free from external coercion and internal violence."[92]

In a twist of logic compatible with Johnson's position, Kennedy accepted the fiction that North Vietnam and the United States were equally responsible for the conflict; he placed most of the blame for the war on America's enemies in Vietnam: "the fault rests largely with our adversary," he said. Although he had clearly stated early in the speech that "the most powerful country the world has ever known" had "turn[ed] its strength and will upon a small and primitive land," he largely ignored the overwhelming power of the United States military and economic investment in South Vietnam, which was then predicted to total $20 billion for 1967. By accepting the Administration's reasoning on this point, Kennedy showed an unwillingness to acknowledge the United States' responsibility for the war commensurate with its power in Vietnam. It was an issue he could have raised without calling into question Johnson's sincerity in pursuing a negotiated settlement.

Kennedy took care neither to challenge the Administration's word, nor to hold Johnson personally responsible for the debacle. His ideas were not earth-shattering; Senator Wayne Morse of Oregon had advanced similar proposals. Nevertheless, Kennedy's speech resonated loudly inside the Oval Office. George Christian, Johnson's press secretary, remembered Johnson working himself into a lather after Kennedy's speech, while going over press clippings chronicling Kennedy's twists and turns on Vietnam policy over the previous year.[93]

During Kennedy's speech, Senator Henry Jackson distributed a letter from Johnson to the senators and reporters present, which called the bombing of North Vietnam "an integral part of our total policy which aims not to destroy North Vietnam but to force Hanoi to end its aggression."[94] Democratic hawks like Jackson, Lausche, and McGee demanded total loyalty to Johnson's Vietnam policy even if it meant dividing the party.

The day after Kennedy's speech, White House aide Fred Panzer sent Johnson the results of a Gallup poll to be made public two days later showing "pairings" of Kennedy with the two potential Republican presidential nominees in 1968: Michigan Governor George Romney and former Vice President Richard Nixon. The survey found Kennedy either tying or trailing the Republicans. Panzer interpreted the poll data for Johnson: "Apparently RFK is dropping off. As he takes a position to the left of the President on Vietnam, he is also taking himself out of the main stream of public opinion on the conduct of the war."[95] The fact that Kennedy's name was included at all in 1968 presidential polls angered Johnson.

To Panzer's glee, the poll indicated that Kennedy had failed to gain politically from his stop-the-bombing speech. It also revealed that despite the attacks from the left for failing to take a stronger stand, Kennedy would risk damaging himself in the eyes of the generally hawkish electorate if he pushed the issue too hard. If he had offered only an uncompromising indictment of the war at that time, he would have probably weakened his influence on national policy; he therefore refused to go beyond a carefully reasoned argument gently persuading the Administration to change course. In any case, Johnson flatly rejected Kennedy's relatively mild prescriptions for a negotiated settlement in Vietnam. Those who had faulted Kennedy for not coming out earlier with a more strident antiwar message, believing that such a bold move would galvanize the peace forces and rally the public to the cause, misread the popular sentiment of the period.

Johnson offered no direct rebuttal to Kennedy's speech, but he did try, as was his common practice, to divert media attention away from the young senator. The President gave two substantial speeches, held a lengthy press conference, hosted a Congressional reception, and made the headline-grabbing announcement that the Soviets had agreed to talk about limiting nuclear arms.[96] He even provided special buses for the press to follow him around that day.

The Administration's foreign policy specialists evaluated Kennedy's proposals. National Security Adviser Rostow sent Johnson a summary of an article from the Soviet newspaper *Izvestia* published in Moscow on March 4, 1967. The *Izvestia* report focused on the passages where Kennedy had shown "his solidarity with the purposes of American policy in Vietnam." The article, Rostow speculated, "might well have been written by the Soviets to convey a message to Hanoi" that Ho Chi Minh "should not fall into the trap of thinking that the Senator's speech will result in a change of U.S. policy."[97] Rostow, the ardent cold warrior, welcomed this Soviet interpretation.

In a secret memo to Johnson, Secretary of Defense Robert McNamara confirmed one of Kennedy's major claims: the bombing of North Vietnam prevented any progress toward peace talks. "The group [in Hanoi] favoring negotiations was in the ascendancy during the latter part of last year and was prepared to start negotiations in December," McNamara wrote, "but was deterred from doing so by our bombing attacks of December 13 and 14."[98] McNamara recommended suspending the bombing north of the 20th parallel to induce the Soviets to press the Democratic Republic of Vietnam (D.R.V.) to join in secret discussions with the United States. He also believed that further steps could be taken to reduce the bombing if negotiations proceeded satisfactorily.[99] Some of Kennedy's views on Vietnam had apparently seeped into the thinking of his friend McNamara.

Secretary of State Rusk, who believed that all of the previous halts in bombing had been dismal failures, interpreted Kennedy's speech for Johnson in a less conciliatory manner.[100] "The main difficulty with the Kennedy proposals," Rusk wrote, "is that Hanoi has made it clear that they would strongly oppose every essential point in them. The Senator's problem, therefore, is not with us but with Hanoi."[101] Rusk believed that a suspension of the bombing was "quite different from a permanent cessation," and warned that without some corresponding action by Hanoi, the U.S. would find itself "in a struggle that could last for years."[102]

Publicly, Rusk's response to Kennedy's speech was terse: "There is . . . no reason to believe at this time that Hanoi is interested in proposals for mutual de-escalation such as those put forward by Senator Kennedy."[103] Rusk's view illustrates the intransigence of the Administration's position on bombing North Vietnam: The U.S. would continue bombing until Ho Chi Minh agreed to negotiate. The reactions of Rusk and McNamara, as well as Johnson—who requested the transcripts of discussions among his foreign policy advisers leading up to the first bombing pause of May 11–17, 1965— show that Johnson and his chief Cabinet officers had at least listened to Kennedy's suggestions.[104]

In the Senate, Democratic hawks entered into the *Congressional Record* strong statements disagreeing with Kennedy's call for a cessation of the bombing. A few editorialists, such as Frank Conniff of the *World Journal Tribune* in New York City, hurled invective, calling Kennedy an exponent of Hanoi, and denounced his "irresponsible disparagement" of Johnson's position.[105]

The public's reaction to Kennedy's March 2 speech was mixed. Leaders of the antiwar movement generally welcomed his prescription for peace, but they, like Edelman and Walinsky, believed he had not gone far enough in confronting the Administration's embroidered view of Vietnamese political reality. Kennedy had also refused to rule out future military moves if the peace effort became derailed. He might have missed an opportunity to move mainstream opinion toward the peace movement's position. But the views Kennedy expressed at the time were wholly consistent with those of the principal doves in the Senate, including Fulbright who publicly backed Kennedy's proposals. Kennedy thanked Fulbright in a handwritten note: "both your presence and your comments added immensely to the day."[106]

Kennedy's speech might not have been sufficiently confrontational to satisfy the doves on his staff, but it earned him praise from the Vietnamese Buddhist leader Tran Van Dinh, the head of the Vietnamese Buddhist Association of the United States and Canada. "You have shown to the Vietnamese people both in North and South Vietnam," Dinh wrote Kennedy, that "you perfectly understand their problems and share their dreams. I am sure, at this moment, the students in Saigon, the intellectuals in Hanoi, the NLF cadres in the jungle are pondering over your speech. I am in full agreement" with "your proposal for a peaceful and honorable settlement of the war in my tortured homeland."[107]

Kennedy was not simply preaching to the converted when calling for peace in Vietnam; he could also appeal to centrists and even conservatives. Several Washington columnists sent Kennedy discreet notes in the days following his speech. Among them were Hugh Sidey, the presidential correspondent for *Life* magazine who had interviewed Johnson after the peace feeler episode. "You did a magnificent job," he wrote. "I don't even agree with your policy, (although I'm beginning to waver—I get the feeling lately the White House doesn't know where to go)."[108] The conservative political commentator Rowland Evans sent Kennedy a handwritten note the day after his speech: "Congratulations again on your speech in the Senate. You are absolutely right—keep at it! I consider Vietnam to be a blot on the United

States' record and the sooner it is stopped, the better."[109] These cordial notes, of course, could also be attempts by Washington journalists to flatter a potentially rich source.

On the morning of March 7, 1967, Kennedy appeared on NBC's *Today* show, where the hosts, Hugh Downs and Sander Vanocur, grilled him about Johnson and Vietnam. Illustrating the media's penchant for framing Kennedy's views as little more than crass political maneuvering, Downs and Vanocur opened the interview by skipping over the war issue altogether. Instead, they focused on the possible effects of his March 2 speech on his relations with President Johnson and the Democratic Party. Kennedy deflected this line of questioning: "I don't think really the question of personalities should enter into this matter," he said. "I think [the war] is of far greater importance. I know that President Johnson is a man of peace. I know that he wants to find an end to this struggle in Vietnam. I have perhaps some different ideas as to what should be done."[110] Kennedy was clearly uncomfortable discussing the politics of the speech, and tried to direct the discussion back to his call for a cessation of the bombing.

Downs and Vanocur were tenacious, however; they returned to Kennedy's political rivalry with Johnson later in the interview. This time Kennedy reiterated his belief that the Vietnam War was far more important than his domestic political standing and "transcend[ed] any loyalty to one's own political party." He then summarized the main points of his speech, and emphasized the lost opportunity for peace talks after the conciliatory statements of Soviet Premier Kosygin and other leaders. "I thought we were at a critical time. And before we take the final plunge to even greater escalation, I think that we should try negotiation. If we can't find the answer to it we can always go back to the war."[111]

Downs asked Kennedy the utterly premature and presumptuous question of whether he would accept the Democratic presidential nomination in 1968 if it were offered to him. Kennedy, taken aback, replied: "No, I mean, I'm going to support President Johnson, and I'm going to support Vice President Humphrey, and I would expect that the rest of the Democratic Party would do likewise. And I would be glad, if they feel it would help, I'll be glad to campaign."[112] Kennedy's reputation for being a tough political operator, earned when he had doggedly served the interests of his brother, had come back to haunt him years later when he tried to convince media pundits that his own political ambitions had nothing to do with his opposing Johnson's Vietnam policies. Throughout the spring and summer of 1967, Kennedy attempted some deft political tightrope walking by supporting Johnson's reelection, while at the same time raising fundamental criticisms about the President's handling of the war. It proved to be an impossible act to sustain.

About two weeks after Kennedy's speech, the White House released an exchange of letters between Johnson and Ho Chi Minh, hoping to bolster the Administration's position. However, a number of Congressional doves concluded that the famous Johnson-Ho letters proved North Vietnam's willingness to start negotiations in exchange for a permanent bombing halt. Kennedy issued yet another statement of regret: "I can only wish that we had seized the initiative publicly advanced by Premier Kosygin, and confirmed, it now develops, in the Ho letter, and halted the bombing in exchange for a beginning of negotiations."[113]

***

Given the political climate, Kennedy's call to stop the bombing was probably the strongest position he could take without damaging the Democratic Party for the 1968 elections and risking his own political future. According to a Harris poll taken just after Kennedy's speech, Americans opposed a halt to the bombing of North Vietnam by a four-to-one ratio, and gave Kennedy's peace proposals a paltry 15 percent approval rating.[114] Those who believed an even tougher stand against the war on Kennedy's part would strengthen his political voice and marshal the nation to demand peace were mistaken. Moreover, if Kennedy had charged Johnson with being disingenuous in his public call for unconditional negotiations, it would play up Kennedy's media image as a calculating political operator, and—in the intense Cold War atmosphere prevailing in wartime—probably damage his ability to influence national policy.

In March 1967, the peace movement was just beginning to open up the debate on Johnson's war aims. The following month, Martin Luther King, Jr. broke with the Administration on Vietnam, and abruptly ended his working relationship with the Johnson Administration on civil rights. King's move also estranged him from other black leaders who were unwilling to cross Johnson on Vietnam. The antiwar movement was in its infancy; a few large protests occurred in the spring of 1967, followed by an ambitious student volunteer program that summer, but significant demonstrations did not materialize until later that fall. Meanwhile, the U.S. troop commitment in Vietnam had doubled since early 1966, and was rapidly approaching 500,000.

Kennedy did manage to infuse into the national debate a re-evaluation of the U.S. military effort. His message stopped short of calling for a unilateral withdrawal of American forces, but its evenhandedness could potentially resonate with a cross-section of liberal and centrist opinion. By emphasizing negotiations over withdrawal, Kennedy hoped to maintain his role as a nationally recognized leader who opposed the U.S. course in Southeast Asia. He did not wish to play into the hands of his detractors, who saw his differences with Johnson as nothing more than political posturing.

With his March 2 address and subsequent public statements, Kennedy sought to rehabilitate the waning legitimacy of the United States in the eyes of the world community, which was increasingly horrified by the American military action in Southeast Asia. "I think our own country's split, and I think there's also been a decline of our own leadership around the world because of the war in Vietnam," Kennedy said on the *Today* show. "I found it in South America. I found it in Africa, and I found it just recently and most dramatically in Europe." If the Administration tested his proposals for peace and Hanoi blocked them, then "the world would know" that "it was not the United States that prevented finding a peaceful solution to the war in Vietnam. It was the other side."[115] An attempt at negotiations had become, in Kennedy's view, essential for the wider international leadership role of the United States.

The war divided the Democratic Party. When Kennedy and other Senate doves called for an end to the bombing as a first step toward peace talks, many Democratic senators had reached the opposite conclusion. Senator Jackson, the chairman of the Armed Services Committee, believed the bombing of North Vietnam "demonstrated that the Soviet Union cannot prevent the United States from bombing a brother Communist state."[116] He reasoned that the bombing was one of the only bargaining levers the U.S. possessed "to pressure Hanoi to de-escalate militarily and to negotiate."[117] Jackson's view reflected the Administration's line which most Democrats supported.

Kennedy confronted weighty political obstacles: if he came out too strongly against Johnson on the war, the Washington press corps would interpret it as a personal vendetta calculated to further his own presidential ambitions; if he remained too cautious he would be open to the charge of lacking the courage of his own convictions. These political limitations continued to plague him for a year after his stop-the-bombing speech.

Kennedy tried to remain within the parameters of the Administration's stated goals in Southeast Asia while providing a prescription for disengagement. At a time when a Harris poll showed that 67 percent of Americans favored continuing the bombing of North Vietnam,[118] he risked taking himself out of the mainstream debate if he advocated a "cut and run" policy, or attacked the false premises of a war that was generating a martial spirit among a significant sector of American society.[119] The peace movement had not yet succeeded in substantially swaying public opinion. However, in the months following Kennedy's speech, the movement made strides in opening up the debate.

With his March 2, 1967, stop-the-bombing address, Kennedy had accepted the Administration's stated goals in Southeast Asia, while providing a blueprint for disengagement. The Cold War logic of containment dominated the debate about U.S. actions in Southeast Asia, and Kennedy remained largely beholden to this logic. However, the comments by Kennedy and members of his staff on multiple drafts of the speech clearly show that Kennedy held no illusions about the weakness of the Saigon regime, or Johnson's lies and deceit regarding the progress of the war.[120] He chose to avoid confronting Johnson's mendacity at that time because he did not wish to contribute to bringing down a Democratic president with whom he generally agreed on domestic policy; nor did he wish to commit political hara-kiri. This state of affairs would change dramatically by the end of 1967.

3   At the Center of the Storm: Kennedy and the Shifting Political Winds of 1967

A story is told of a European revolutionary who, watching from a window and seeing the crowd running by, exclaimed, "There go the people—I must hurry and catch up with them, for I am their leader."[1]

Throughout 1967, Kennedy followed the advice of his more pragmatic counselors and refrained from leading into battle the antiwar forces of the Democratic Party. Despite his ongoing criticisms of the war, he remained cautious (some would say overly cautious) in acting on his convictions. In the name of party unity, and his own long-term political survival, he disavowed citizens' groups which called upon him to run for president in 1968, and he repeatedly said he supported President Johnson's reelection.

However, Kennedy's tactical retreat did not stop him from critically evaluating the United States' course in Southeast Asia. In August 1967, he condemned the South Vietnamese military for disrupting the upcoming "elections," which the Johnson Administration had preordained to be free and fair.[2] "There is mounting and distressing evidence of efforts to interfere with the free choice of the people," Kennedy said on the Senate floor a few weeks before the Vietnamese voting. "Candidates have been barred because their views were 'unacceptable,' though they were loyal citizens. Jails still contain prisoners whose only offense is opposition to the present government. The right of candidates to debate issues is restricted by press censorship. Their ability to campaign is hampered by harassment."[3] The Saigon military, Kennedy argued, was "moving to perpetuate its power regardless of the voting." He called for the United States to reaffirm its commitment "to the Vietnamese *people*—not to any government, not to any generals, not to the powerful and privileged few."[4] The sham of the September 3, 1967, elections, which barred from participation any group or individual remotely associated with the National Liberation Front, reinforced Kennedy's earlier calls for recognizing that body.[5]

The open-ended U.S. commitment to shoring up the South Vietnamese regime had led to a buildup in American troops to over 400,000.[6] President Johnson had brought the United States into a prolonged foreign conflict, which eventually sowed the seeds of dissension within his own party, particularly at the local level. The ideological contradictions among Democrats could not be glossed over indefinitely, and reflected a widening breach between the prowar leadership and ordinary voters. No matter how hard Kennedy tried to avoid it, events drove him into the center of the intraparty conflict.

In the spring of 1967, the New York political activist Allard Lowenstein, who had years of experience in the civil rights movement, responded to the emerging divisions within the Democratic Party by organizing a grassroots movement to "dump Johnson." Lowenstein's faith in the ability of activists to stop the Vietnam War through diligent grassroots organizing was contagious among white middle-class college students. His message was deeply inspiring to thousands of politicized young people who had their awareness of social injustice raised by participation in the civil rights and antipoverty struggles. Lowenstein attempted to harness the elements within the Democratic Party that opposed the war, and had been responsive to decentralized politics. He nearly single-handedly mobilized the peace wing of the party, augmenting it with thousands of foot soldiers from the college campuses.

By late 1967, a few of Kennedy's key advisers, sensing a shift in the mood of the country, mapped out for the senator an artful political strategy. Kennedy sought to maintain his political base among the growing number of peace Democrats without causing an irreparable rift with Johnson. It was a delicate balancing act. Lowenstein believed Kennedy the strongest potential antiwar challenger to Johnson in 1968, and therefore urged him to lead the "Dump Johnson" effort. But Kennedy refused; he saw it as folly to try to steal the nomination away from an incumbent president; nor did he wish to divide the party, upon which depended his own political future. On November 30, 1967, Senator Eugene McCarthy of Minnesota announced his entrance into the primaries as a peace candidate. Kennedy then tried to placate both McCarthy's supporters and the Johnson forces which controlled the Democratic National Committee (D.N.C.). This stance, which Kennedy's political professionals charted out to keep his options open, satisfied neither side.

Kennedy protected his own political base, and took great care that his decisions not erode the support of his core constituencies of working-class whites, African Americans, and Latinos. Many of his closest advisers believed that he might be faced with the choice of either challenging Johnson for his party's nomination in 1968, or passively witnessing his supporters either shift allegiance to McCarthy or simply drift away under four more years of Johnson or a Republican successor.

As the election year drew closer, the Johnson Democrats, who controlled all the levers of power of the Presidency and the D.N.C., relied heavily upon the upper echelons of the party hierarchy, and state and municipal political machines. It was in Johnson's interest to pursue a strategy of eschewing the primaries and piling up endorsements from powerful regional Democrats. This game plan, which largely ignored the large number of peace, antipoverty, and civil rights groups, might have been adequate in a less tumultuous year. However, by 1968, opposition to the war in Vietnam had mobilized a sizable number of citizens, polarized the party, and sparked a groundswell of anti-Johnson sentiment.

These widening divisions within the party pushed Kennedy into an untenable political position. Some of his friends and advisers believed that his only course was to break forcefully with Johnson, while others, whom Kennedy greatly respected, believed he must remain loyal to the President, and refrain from tearing the party apart. No one close to Kennedy doubted that Johnson would use all of the resources at his disposal to punish any rival.[7]

Kennedy regularly sought counsel on the changing political environment of 1967 from diverse sources, with often conflicting results. In 1966 and 1967, the contradictory advice from Kennedy's friends, advisers, and political analysts, as well as the Administration's reaction to the stirrings of peace Democrats, exposes a fateful rift between the party's leadership and its rank-and-file members.

Throughout 1967, Democratic peace activists criticized Kennedy for not breaking with Johnson and assuming a leadership role in the opposition. Yet the volatile political environment within which the New York senator had to maneuver created realistic political constraints which militated against accepting such a role. Torn between his deep misgivings about the war and his desire to become president someday, Kennedy spent most of 1967 boxed in by his critics from both the left and the right, and by his own cautious political instincts.

He had attracted talented people to his staff, such as the Pulitzer Prize-winning journalist Edwin Guthman, the former Peace Corps director Frank Mankiewicz (who became Kennedy's press secretary), and the gifted speech writer and campaign director Richard Goodwin. Some of Kennedy's advisers stayed with him from the time he had headed the Justice Department, some joined him when he became a United States senator, and still others were holdovers from his brother's presidency. One reason why Kennedy could attract an array of talented individuals was the fact that he was no ordinary junior senator; he had a realistic chance of someday becoming president of the United States. Most of Kennedy's aides and advisers designed political strategies which strengthened his chances for the Democratic presidential nomination sometime after Johnson's second term, most likely in 1972.

Kennedy maintained a balance among his advisers between what might be called the pragmatists and the idealists. The younger firebrands, such as speech writer Adam Walinsky and legislative assistant Peter Edelman, who were 30 and 29 years old respectively when they joined Kennedy's staff, prodded him toward a more open break with Johnson on Vietnam. The cooler, more conventional advice of Arthur Schlesinger, Jr. and Theodore Sorensen, both of whom had advised President John Kennedy, tempered the vigorous sentiments of his youthful aides. Kennedy depended on his "idea men," such as Schlesinger, Goodwin, and Sorensen, for direction and tutoring. Schlesinger, for example, could masterfully explain the pedigree of ideas that informed a particular policy debate, or map out the wider historical context of a political conflict. Yet when the situation required brutally frank, gloves-off political advice, Kennedy turned to two professional politicians: Frederick Dutton, a Washington lawyer, manager of campaigns, and a former adviser to President Kennedy; and Joseph Dolan, a skilled political operative and former Colorado state legislator.

Dutton freely offered Kennedy advice on a wide range of subjects including public statements, speech topics, hints for polishing his television persona, and for utilizing his Senate staff more efficiently.[8] In late 1967, when Dutton suggested an extended mission to test the political waters for a possible presidential run, Kennedy followed his advice;[9] when Dutton advised Kennedy to hand out "state by state assignments" to "a dozen trusted people" to monitor the changing political environment, Kennedy belatedly did so;[10] when Dutton, in knowing contradiction to Kennedy's own personal feelings, called upon him to publicly "fraternize" with Johnson, and maintain a public posture of "reticence" about his options for 1968, Kennedy did both, and took a good deal of flak from his antiwar supporters.[11] Throughout 1967, when it came down to brass-tacks political decisions, Dutton had Kennedy's ear.

In late 1966, Dutton had shared with Kennedy his belief that the Democratic Party was in trouble, and warned him to protect himself from the charge that he was contributing to the party's difficulties. The Democrats had lost forty-seven House seats in the midterm elections, not an inordinate number for a party in power, but Dutton believed the large troop escalations in Vietnam, and Johnson's autocratic style of party leadership, were taking their toll on the Democrats' chances in 1968. He warned his boss to be cautious in his criticisms of the Administration.[12]

However, Dutton saw the political climate as creating an opportunity for Kennedy: "The dominating aspect of the public scene right now seems to be the country's deep dislike for President Johnson's personality. That translates into wanting qualities of the spirit in their alternative choices."[13] If Kennedy played his political cards intelligently, Dutton believed, he could become this alternative choice for the nation, but only after Johnson had served out his second term.

Dutton felt that public speculation about Kennedy's prospects for running in 1968 was both premature and counterproductive. Under specific circumstances, he believed, Kennedy would have a good chance of winning for the party, but he warned against "even obliquely" flirting with the possibility. Dutton feared Kennedy could severely damage his long-term prospects if he challenged Johnson politically, thereby reinforcing his reputation for ruthlessness and opportunism. These labels had originated in the late 1950s during Kennedy's days as the chief counsel for the Senate Select Committee on Improper Activities in the Labor or Management Field, when he doggedly pursued the Teamsters Union boss Jimmy Hoffa. They were strengthened in 1960 when he served as John Kennedy's hard-nosed campaign manager. Despite the risks, Dutton told Kennedy he should not enter a "political cloister," but refrain from speculating on his possible candidacy in 1968 if the question is ever raised.[14] In Dutton's view, if Kennedy were to keep his options open and effective, this stance was politically imperative. The senator took to heart Dutton's dispassionate, professional advice.

In the aftermath of the Paris peace feeler incident, and Kennedy's attack on the Administration's war policies in March 1967, Dutton cautioned him not to become bogged down in tactical controversies with the White House. He urged Kennedy to avoid any "direct slugging match" with Johnson, regardless of the provocation. As for 1968, Dutton offered Kennedy a bitter pill: "If the President runs for re-election you will have to campaign for him whatever one's private views are." Dutton believed Kennedy would have to "minimize" his dissent within the party in order to "maximize" his own base for 1972. Virtually all of Kennedy's closest advisers saw 1972 as the earliest possible time for him to make a bid for the presidency. Dutton therefore warned Kennedy to avoid appearing too political, because an open conflict with Johnson could only give a negative impression. To protect his future political viability, Kennedy should bide his time despite his feelings about the war.

Dutton prodded Kennedy to "use an early opportunity to make some tangible gesture to the White House entirely on your own initiative." Kennedy's most influential political adviser advocated a tactical cease-fire with the President;[15] he did not welcome this idea, but Dutton thought it would be helpful.

The press had consistently interpreted any policy disagreements between Kennedy and Johnson as either a battle of wills between two bitter political rivals, or as part of a mutual personal vendetta. The high-level conflict naturally caused great concern among Kennedy's advisers. Kennedy forwarded a copy of the Dutton letter to his brother, Senator Edward Kennedy, for his comment.[16] Edward Kennedy, too, had become a voice calling for reconciliation with Johnson.

Kennedy sometimes forwarded particularly substantive letters from Dutton to his other key political aide, Joseph Dolan. "Joe, as usual I think he has some good points," he scribbled at the top of one Dutton letter.[17] On political matters, Dolan usually agreed with Dutton, as he did with the gesture to the White House idea, but he felt Dutton failed to pay serious attention to the possibility Kennedy might enter the 1968 presidential race.[18] Dolan suggested that Kennedy practice a little "backstopping" by "chiming in" with his own criticisms of Johnson's war policies only after other senators, such as J. William Fulbright, voiced their opinions. According to Dolan, Kennedy's "muted agreement in the background" could "slide by and avoid" the headlines exploiting the Kennedy-Johnson feud.[19] Dolan, like Dutton, believed Kennedy should remain cautious but keep his options open; a well-publicized conciliatory statement to Johnson in the spring or summer of 1967 would be a prudent first step.

About a week after Dutton's cautionary remarks to Kennedy, Milton Gwirtzman, an aide to Edward Kennedy, and a partner in Dutton's Washington law firm, fired off a memo to Kennedy specifically addressing "RFK-LBJ Problems." Gwirtzman wanted Kennedy, among other things, to ask George Gallup and Lou Harris "to kindly stop running you in their 1968 Presidential polls," because they gave the impression that he was a candidate for the presidency in 1968.[20] Despite the demonstrable link between Johnson's periodic drops in popularity and Kennedy's rise, these polls, Gwirtzman argued, complicated matters by annoying Johnson, and playing up the media-fueled personal rivalry.

Gwirtzman prescribed several concrete actions Kennedy might take to damp down the "feud" between himself and the President. One recommendation, which mirrored the advice of Dutton and Dolan, was for Kennedy to make a joint appearance with Johnson at a major event in New York, and use it as an opportunity to reiterate support for him.[21] Shortly thereafter, Kennedy began speaking positively about the President's reelection.

In early 1967, Joseph Alsop, one of the nation's most influential syndicated columnists, who had been a Kennedy family friend as well as a strong supporter of Johnson's Vietnam policies, offered Kennedy some unsolicited advice on his conflict with the President. It was a delicate time for Johnson, Alsop wrote, and went on: "You really must give more weight to the support of what people call the 'establishment' than I think you now do. . . . Adam's kids [Walinsky's grassroots political contacts] are wonderfully attractive and stirring supporters, but as an old uncle, I have to point out that they have neither the money nor the votes."[22]

Whereas Dutton, Gwirtzman, and Alsop pressed Kennedy to retreat from direct confrontations with Johnson, others whose opinions Kennedy valued and respected urged him to do just the opposite. The Harvard economist John Kenneth Galbraith, an opponent of the Vietnam War, privately pointed to Kennedy's "slight tendency" to "back down or hedge a bit . . . after taking a bold and right position." He had gotten that impression in February 1966 when Kennedy tempered his original suggestion about recognizing the N.L.F. Galbraith wrote that he got a similar sense of the senator's hedging when Kennedy periodically stressed his "affection for the President." He encouraged Kennedy to stand by his convictions: "With all . . . the people who are inviting you to be silent, discreet and serene you must be under terrible temptation to calculate or even be a trifle cagy. Don't. . . . It is fatal. . . . People will forgive mistakes but not an attempt, even partially successful, to outwit them."[23] Galbraith had identified the crux of Kennedy's dilemma: did not his own conscience dictate casting aside tactical political concerns?

Galbraith sensed a disingenuousness in Kennedy's support for Johnson while denouncing his war.

In the fall of 1967, when the historian Henry Steele Commager received an advance copy of Kennedy's book *To Seek a Newer World*, he, like Galbraith, urged him to break sharply with Johnson. Commager alerted Kennedy to the perils of his contradictory public stands: "Your materials lead, inevitably it seems to me, to a refusal to support President Johnson," he wrote. "If the situation [in Vietnam] is indeed as you describe it, you cannot consistently support the man chiefly responsible for it."[24] Kennedy, like the Democratic Party itself, as Commager had pointed out, was moving in two contradictory directions.

The discordant advice from people whom Kennedy greatly respected was difficult to sort out. He summed up his mood in a handwritten note to his friend, the journalist and author Pete Hamill, who was in Rome: "You have not missed anything back here in the United States either in Washington or New York. Everybody is mad at everyone else—and each week we keep turning the corner in Viet Nam."[25]

On June 3, 1967, Kennedy's political advisers finally prevailed in spurring him to make public amends with the President. The Senator's opportunity came when he was invited to introduce Johnson at a $100-a-plate Democratic State Committee dinner in Manhattan.[26] In his zeal to prove to New York Democratic power brokers that he was a team player, Kennedy gave Johnson, according to the *New York Times*, "perhaps the warmest endorsement the Senator has ever offered."[27] Outside the Americana Hotel that evening there were about 1,400 antiwar protesters, including a sizable group of "Reform" Democrats, among then Allard Lowenstein, who had organized legions of angry party members, and about sixty former Peace Corps volunteers. Some among the Peace Corps contingent held placards reading: "Stop bombing the schools we helped to build." Other protesters carried more extreme signs depicting Johnson in a Nazi uniform with the caption: "Wanted For Murder."[28]

On the stage inside the ballroom, with Johnson sitting directly to his left and Vice President Hubert Humphrey on his right, Kennedy began his introduction sandwiched between two of the most accomplished liberal politicians of the era. Citing Webster's dictionary definition of the word "greatness," he said it "could have been written for" President Johnson. "The height of his aim, the breadth of his achievement, the record of his past, and the promises of his future," Kennedy gushed, all showed that Johnson "came to lead this nation at a time of uncertainty and danger, pouring out his own strength to renew the strength and the purpose of all the people of this nation, and of the nation itself." Lyndon Baines Johnson, Kennedy continued,

> has gained huge popularity, but he has never failed to spend it in the pursuit of his beliefs or the interest of his country. He has led us to build schools, to clean the water, to recapture the beauty of the countryside, to educate children and to heal the sick and comfort the oppressed on a scale unmatched in history.
>
> In 1964 he won the greatest popular victory in modern times, and with our help he will do so again in 1968. With our help, he will have by his side the best Vice President since his predecessor, Hubert Humphrey.[29]

The 1,650 New York Democrats attending the formal gala were pleased with Kennedy's short speech; so were Johnson and Humphrey. Kennedy's kind words that evening made headlines across the country, and were widely interpreted to mean that he would actively campaign for the Johnson-Humphrey ticket in 1968 despite his opposition to the war. *Newsday* referred to Kennedy's "elaborate praise" as the "biggest boost" for the President during his New York visit. The *New York Post* called it "a surprisingly warm and unqualified endorsement."[30] Johnson referred to Kennedy's remarks that June evening on several occasions over the following year, and credited Kennedy with grasping the difficulties facing a president when personal popularity collided with controversial decisions.[31]

However, not everyone was as pleased with Kennedy's speech as Johnson and his New York City supporters. Walinsky tried, unsuccessfully, to persuade the *Village Voice* journalist Jack Newfield, who strongly opposed the war and was highly critical of Kennedy's comments that evening, that Kennedy's praise for Johnson was in reality a subtle exercise in irony.[32] Kennedy's friend, the journalist Jimmy Breslin, wrote that "only a very few thought they had detected this slight hint of put-on in Kennedy's speech." Breslin reminded his readers in his syndicated column that just a month earlier, as part of the Spring Mobilization, thousands of people had marched against the Vietnam War in New York City, and "Lyndon Johnson was a name marchers used only to frighten children."[33] Schlesinger wrote Kennedy a couple of weeks after the event: "I think you have made only one mistake [recently] and that is your remarks at the dinner in New York about LBJ. They seemed out of character, and that is one thing you must never do."[34]

After the event at the Americana Hotel, Kennedy rode in the presidential limousine with Johnson and former New York Governor Averell Harriman to attend the President's Club Grand Ball at the Waldorf-Astoria. This exclusive event was closed to the press, and only Democrats who made donations of $1,000 or more could attend. "The President seemed to be enjoying himself this evening," Johnson's daily diary recorded. "He danced the greater part of the evening and appeared to be having a delightful time."[35] Kennedy joined Johnson at his table. It was an elegant night of celebration, where the two powerful Democrats called a temporary truce. Kennedy seemed to have completely capitulated to Johnson.

Johnson's speech that night had been crafted to strike some early campaign themes for his reelection in 1968. He also spoke at length about the United States' support for Israel at a time when tensions in the Middle East were mounting (the Six-Day War broke out two days later). Kennedy recognized Johnson's ability to garner political support when facing crises abroad, and he strongly agreed with the Administration's support for Israel and with its broad Middle East policy. It made political sense for Kennedy to cool his criticisms of Johnson at a time when the President was facing the prospect of yet another foreign policy debacle, and followed an extremely popular course in the eyes of New York City Democrats. However, Kennedy's decision to offer such warm praise for Johnson surely cost him support among peace Democrats and, as Schlesinger would remind him, ran contrary to his own convictions about Vietnam. It also reinforced the notion, held by Kennedy's critics from the left, that political expediency would always supersede his moral opposition to the war.

Dutton had earlier written Kennedy: "Politics is so much a matter of vacuums, either you fill them or someone else will."[36] Ironically, Kennedy's calculated retreat from direct confrontations with Johnson, at the behest of Dutton and others, helped create just such a political "vacuum." Allard Lowenstein was determined to fill this void in leadership. Beginning in the spring of 1967, he devoted his formidable organizing skills to an effort to wrest the Democratic nomination from the incumbent president.[37]

The 1966 midterm elections had given little indication that the antiwar faction of the party was a force powerful enough to sweep an insurgent

Democrat into the White House in 1968.[38] But as the political ground continued to shift in 1967, Lowenstein sensed an opening. The Administration's Vietnam policies were beginning to cause significant divisions within the party, and he searched for a national figure willing to challenge Johnson in the primaries. The carnage in Vietnam had enflamed Lowenstein's moral outrage.

Lowenstein believed Kennedy, given his famous name and popularity, his opposition to the war, and his influence within the party, was the strongest potential challenger. In 1966, Lowenstein had become what he called a zealot for Kennedy when he accompanied the Senator on an unpublicized visit to a Queens veterans' hospital to meet wounded soldiers returned from Vietnam. "We went through that hospital," he recalled, "and it was very clear how deeply the war bothered him even before he made many public statements about it." According to Lowenstein, Kennedy "was the only man in the world who could have meant anything to those kids." Kennedy's compassionate interaction with these young war victims was, in the politically savvy Lowenstein's eyes, "just too genuine to ever have been artificial."[39] It was this type of shared experience that created a lasting bond between the two men.[40]

In 1967, Lowenstein witnessed the college campuses heating up over the war. He had worked closely with student activists and the civil rights veteran Reverend James Bevel to organize a Spring Mobilization Against the War, which produced the first large-scale antiwar demonstrations in New York City and San Francisco.[41] Lowenstein also played a role in organizing the Vietnam Summer project, modeled after the civil rights movement's Freedom Summer of 1964.[42] Vietnam Summer had about 30,000 student participants in 700 cities, who canvassed door-to-door against Johnson's war policies.[43] In October 1967, Lowenstein helped organize a series of Stop the Draft Week protests, which culminated in a march on the Pentagon by nearly 50,000 antiwar demonstrators.[44]

College students who actively opposed the war had access to an infrastructure for mass organizing that most citizens' groups, including labor unions, could only dream of: campus newspapers, radio stations, bulletin boards, sites for assembling, buildings to occupy, professors to tap for teach-ins, and so on. Lowenstein recognized the potential of these vast student armies for mobilizing campus resources. He worked to fuse the goal of stopping the war in Vietnam with a grassroots effort, driven by student power, to unseat the President.

From his nearly nonstop itinerant visits to college campuses around the country, Lowenstein observed first-hand the growing activism and commitment of young people. He dedicated himself to channeling this student energy toward the goal of defeating Johnson's renomination and stopping the war. In the words of his biographer William Chafe, "Lowenstein put himself at the head of an insurgent movement that pledged to accomplish radical ends through reformist means."[45]

What gave Lowenstein's Dump Johnson movement added strength was his successful galvanizing of various left-liberal Democratic organizations. By October 1967, "the movement achieved a momentum that even hardened politicians could no longer ignore."[46] Although college students were the foot soldiers, Lowenstein demonstrated that his movement could reach beyond the campuses. Influential Democrats from the anti-Communist Americans for Democratic Action (A.D.A.), one of whose board members was Lowenstein, explored peace candidate alternatives to Johnson. Other Democratic groups that energized the peace wing of the party, largely stemming from Lowenstein's activities, included the Coalition for a Democratic Alternative (C.D.A.), and the Conference of Concerned Democrats (C.C.D.). Eventually, liberal magazines such as *The New Republic* endorsed in cover-story editorials the Dump Johnson campaign.[47] By the fall of 1967, Lowenstein's efforts to organize the nascent dove faction of the party began to bear fruit.

The White House did not take Lowenstein's Dump Johnson movement or any other dissident Democratic activities lying down. The President's political aides closely monitored all of the significant gatherings of the increasingly disenchanted Democrats, including the A.D.A., the C.D.A., and the C.C.D. Johnson loyalists in the government and the D.N.C. threw dirt into the gears of as many renegade Democratic groups as possible. Working closely with the White House, D.N.C. leaders initiated a series of concrete steps designed to counter, or at least limit, the effects of the antiwar elements within the party, as well as the peace movement generally.

At about this time, the political scientist John Roche emerged as one of the most important of the intellectual advisers who met regularly with the President.[48] Roche had been a Brandeis University professor and a national chairman of the A.D.A. (1962–1965). About a month before an A.D.A. board meeting, Roche predicted that the antiwar faction would beat a strategic retreat, reflecting a "collective political understanding that attacks on the president will be the route to disaster."[49] At a September 1967 board meeting, the A.D.A.ers who remained loyal to Johnson pushed through a vote to repudiate any flirting with alternative candidates.[50] They also succeeded in squelching efforts to use the organization to elect anti-Johnson delegates to the Democratic National Convention, and even forced the A.D.A. to soften its criticisms of the Administration's Vietnam policies. By the time Johnson's allies were finished with the A.D.A., all that survived of its opposition to the war was the vague call to bind the party to a "peace plank" in its 1968 platform, which the Washington civil liberties lawyer Joseph Rauh promoted.[51] The Johnson people were confident they could kill the peace plank at the convention.

With regard to Lowenstein and his Dump Johnson effort, Roche, who was the President's point man at the A.D.A., explained to Johnson: "The late Allard K. Lowenstein was left a querulous, bitching, pleading casualty."[52] Roche shared with the President his relish that the A.D.A. now faced "a lovely intestine brawl between the peace nuts and the Rauh entourage." Roche promised "to stand (with my faithful thirty) on the sidelines, and throw some gasoline on the fire every time it threatens to die down."[53] He was confident that the syndicated columnists Rowland Evans and Robert Novak would repudiate in print the peace stirrings of A.D.A. board members.[54] Flushed with success, Johnson repeated this practice of dividing and conquering his critics in any organization tied to the party.

To counter the proliferating number of peace groups, with their full-page newspaper ads and mass mailings attacking the Administration, the White House created a citizens' committee of its own called the National Citizens' Committee for Peace with Freedom in Vietnam. This "nonpartisan" group functioned as a propaganda vehicle for Johnson's version of events in Southeast Asia.[55] It enlisted private citizens, Vietnam "experts," and former military and government officials to counter the arguments for disengagement that were then being voiced by antiwar liberals, particularly Senate doves such as J. William Fulbright, Frank Church, George McGovern, Eugene McCarthy, and Robert and Edward Kennedy. The former Illinois senator Paul Douglas headed the committee, which was announced with great fanfare on October 23, 1967, the day after the largest antiwar protest in Washington to date.[56]

Presaging Richard Nixon's "silent majority," the prowar Citizens' Committee stated in its initial press release that it spoke for "the great 'silent center' of American life."[57] The committee's most important endorsement came from former President Dwight Eisenhower. The organizers of this

Johnson vehicle, including Douglas, Roche, and presidential aide Harry McPherson, were careful to deny any explicit link to the Administration. "There are bound to be accusations that it is a White House 'front,'" Roche wrote Johnson. "I will leave no tracks. I can be remarkably invisible (I was in the West Wing for five months before the newspapermen knew about it)."[58] Roche worked behind the scenes to steer the "independent" committee in behalf of the President.

Within the Democratic Party, Johnson's political operatives and the leadership of the D.N.C. under Chairman John Bailey sought to enforce party unity. The D.N.C. marshaled its own youth contingent inside the Young Democrats (Y.D.) in an attempt to counter Lowenstein's student movement. Throughout 1967, officials at the highest levels of the D.N.C. followed closely the power struggles of the Young Democrats on a state-by-state basis, and knew the names and positions of the key players, all of whom were in their early twenties.

The President himself took an interest in the anti-Administration activities of the Illinois Young Democrats. He ordered Marvin Watson to press Chicago Mayor Richard Daley and Chairman Bailey to follow through with their efforts to influence the organization on his behalf.[59] In November 1967, the White House and D.N.C. took steps to quell the antiwar and anti-Johnson sentiments at the Young Democrats' national convention in Hollywood, Florida. The Administration's manipulation of the Young Democrats reflected its desire to counter the appeal among youth of Lowenstein's Dump Johnson movement. Lowenstein, the nation's most ardent advocate for replacing Johnson, perturbed the President's allies.[60] Some Johnson loyalists believed Lowenstein was working in tandem with Kennedy elements to squeeze Democratic organs in "a thinly veiled attempt to create a vacuum into which RFK could be nominated."[61]

One response from the D.N.C. in the battle for winning the hearts and minds of America's young people was to sponsor a pro-Administration Democratic Summer Intern Program. Designed to blunt the effectiveness of Lowenstein's Vietnam Summer, this youth project brought together "several thousand" college students with the aim of spreading support for Johnson's Vietnam policies. The Administration's partisans inside the D.N.C. called the program a great success.[62] Within the A.D.A., Young Democrats, and other Democratic organizations, Johnson and his political allies employed all available means to promote the war. They might endure criticism of

Vietnam policy, but any effort within the party to unseat Johnson would not be tolerated.

More ominous was the consideration Johnson's senior advisers gave to using the Federal Bureau of Investigation and "other intelligence" units to spy on the major organizations opposed to the Administration's war policies. Many of these groups were thought by his advisers to be linked to Kennedy. Johnson routinely ordered the FBI's liaison with the White House, Cartha DeLoach,[63] to conduct background checks on antiwar personalities, and even on citizens who merely wrote letters to the White House expressing disapproval of the war.[64] Presaging Nixon yet again, in the summer of 1967 Johnson's political operatives drew up a blueprint for a "Special Office" to secretly investigate and disrupt the activities of peace groups and individual activists. DeLoach coordinated the unit's activities with the FBI, the Justice Department, "anti-riot personnel," and federal prosecutors.[65]

In the fall of 1967, Johnson and his allies felt sufficiently threatened by the National Conference for New Politics (N.C.N.P.) in Chicago that they initiated moves to disrupt its activities. The N.C.N.P. was an endeavor, strongly New Left in its orientation, to unify peace and civil rights activists. The convention itself had featured Martin Luther King, Jr. as its keynote speaker, and sought to unify black and white political organizers who supported civil rights and opposed the war.[66] The goals of Johnson's Special Office were "to launch, coordinate, and carry on a political anti-guerrilla operation to thwart the long-range plan of the NCNP and other such groups making up the Black Power-Peacenik coalition."[67]

The Labor Day weekend N.C.N.P. gathering in Chicago's Palmer House ultimately brought together about 3,000 people from some 370 organizations, including representatives of the Committee for a Sane Nuclear Policy (SANE), Negotiations Now!, and Citizens for Kennedy.[68] It was the largest gathering of the American left since Henry Wallace's 1948 Progressive Party convention. FBI informants monitored the N.C.N.P. conference and reported to Johnson that those gathered "supported the idea of a ticket comprised of Martin Luther King for President and Dr. Benjamin Spock for Vice President." Adding to Johnson's paranoia, the informants failed to mention that King had made it clear he was not interested in running for president.[69]

In addition to the "anti-guerrilla operation" of the White House Special Office, FBI Director J. Edgar Hoover tracked the activities of individuals attending the N.C.N.P. through the Special Agent in Charge (S.A.C.) of the

FBI's Chicago office. The FBI agent reported to Hoover that "the group was dominated by communists."[70] Some of the same FBI operatives who had been charged with following the activities of Kennedy from the time he was attorney general had also kept Hoover apprised of the activities of the N.C.N.P.[71]

FBI informants told Hoover there were "many pro-Robert Kennedy liberals" participating in the conference "including a number of original organizers of the New Politics organization who were seeking a third party ticket as a means of weakening President Lyndon Johnson's campaign for re-election in 1968." The FBI saw this as an effort to "lay the basis for a Robert Kennedy 1972 campaign." The Bureau also was concerned that "[a] great deal of 'Kennedy money' was reportedly put into the NCNP."[72] The FBI, as well as Johnson's Special Office to combat the "Black Power-Peacenik coalition," had lumped together Kennedy and King with "communists" inside the N.C.N.P., and believed Kennedy financed the entire effort.

Johnson's Special Office also traced the sources of funding for peace groups and left-leaning African-American national organizations to discern whether or not they received funds from foreign or communist sources. The committee compiled detailed biographical information on the nation's principal antiwar and civil rights leaders.[73] In addition to the snooping of the White House, some of the President's closest advisers discreetly worked to use the Administration's influence over independent foundations and labor unions to "turn off the tap [of funding] to various anti-Administration organizations."[74] Johnson had gone on the offensive.

The efforts of federal law enforcement officials, working in coordination with the White House, monitoring and sabotaging the activities of citizens' groups, illustrates the level of the Administration's fear and suspicion regarding the peace movement. At that time, the FBI had also launched its infamous Counter Intelligence Programs (COINTELPRO), a series of domestic spying and sabotage operations targeting antiwar and black power organizations, as well as leaders such as Martin Luther King.[75] The FBI's charge that Kennedy and King were in cahoots with "communists" at a time when the United States was killing communists in Southeast Asia, along with the false accusation that "Kennedy money" backed it all, exemplifies the corrosive effects the Vietnam War had on domestic politics. Also, Johnson had apparently grown quite comfortable with using the FBI, as he did at the 1964 Democratic National Convention, to spy on his political enemies.

Meanwhile, members of Kennedy's staff began to stiffen their opposition to Johnson and the war. In late 1967, Walinsky and Richard Goodwin offered their views of the President and the fissures developing within the Democratic Party. Walinsky was perhaps the best informed person on the Senator's staff on issues pertaining to Vietnam, and he held strong antiwar sentiments. He informed Kennedy that his "deep personal dislike of Lyndon Johnson," had led him to "acquire the most dangerous of all prejudice: a vested intellectual interest in [Johnson's] failure." Unlike Dutton and Dolan, Walinsky could see no reason for Kennedy to remain on Johnson's good side. "The President of the United States is more than a reflection of his time, he shapes it," Walinsky wrote Kennedy, and added, "Our time, our America, is being shaped by an ignorant bully."[76] Kennedy offered no written response to Walinsky's anti-Johnson ruminations.

Walinsky argued to Kennedy that it was politically suicidal for him to remain loyal to Johnson in 1968. He agreed with Lowenstein and other Democrats active in the peace movement that Kennedy should be more openly confrontational with the President. Rather than muting his public criticisms of Johnson's Vietnam policies, Walinsky urged Kennedy to escalate them. He hoped Kennedy would run for president in 1968, and wanted him forthrightly to confront Johnson, instead of offering one conciliatory gesture after another.[77] The Senator's young speech writer had a compelling point: Kennedy could not make a credible bid for the nomination in 1968 if he remained loyal to Johnson up to the last minute.[78] Walinsky's constant advocacy of a direct battle with Johnson accentuated the split between the younger firebrands on Kennedy's staff and his more cautious pols.

At the age of 36, Richard Goodwin had already established himself as an experienced speech writer, political operative, and campaign organizer. He had been an invaluable aide and speech writer to both President Kennedy and President Johnson, and was credited with coining the terms Alliance for Progress, to describe President Kennedy's Latin America policy, and the Great Society to define Johnson's domestic agenda.[79] So skilled was Goodwin in the arts of speech writing and politics that rival Democratic politicians vied for his services.

In late 1967, Goodwin shared with Kennedy his analysis of the political picture. His critique of the U.S. military presence in Vietnam mirrored Walinsky's,[80] but was expressed (at least in writing to Kennedy) in terms far less contemptuous of Johnson.[81] Goodwin saw the Senator's political strength as directly proportional to Johnson's decline in popularity. The situation required neither reckless confrontation nor political retreat. The widespread hostility to LBJ resulting from the war and Johnson's leadership style, Goodwin concluded, meant that "few Democratic Party pros were loyal to LBJ or even liked him." Goodwin believed a significant number of party insiders might come around to Kennedy if he showed he was serious about seeking the nomination. "What have they got to lose," he wrote. "Johnson can't read you out of the Democratic Party, even if he wanted to"; he predicted it would be "an asset" if Kennedy forcefully opposed LBJ.[82]

Like Walinsky, Goodwin believed that Kennedy would suffer political damage if he continued to back Johnson's reelection. And if Johnson were reelected in 1968, Kennedy would have "quite a period of having to stay out of real opposition," which would further hurt his "image."[83] Should Kennedy decide to run, his chances of winning the Democratic nomination were slim: "We all use the figures one in five," Goodwin wrote, "but that's about as arbitrary as Vietnam body counts."[84] The tone of both Goodwin's and Walinsky's remarks to Kennedy reveal that by late 1967 the Administration had lost much of its legitimacy in the eyes of two of Kennedy's most important aides. Goodwin concluded his lengthy memo to Kennedy with an analogy summing up Kennedy's unique voice in national politics: "You are a strong, well-defined, controversial politician whose views are regarded as a direct emanation of character and personality. Most politicians are like piano players, and when they strike a wrong note only experts know. But you are the guy in the back row with the huge cymbals and when you clang them at the wrong place the whole auditorium jumps."[85]

In December 1967, many of Kennedy's closest friends and advisers took for granted that it would be disastrous for him to challenge Johnson for the nomination; others close to him believed just as strongly it would be disastrous if he did not. Political forces pulled Kennedy in contradictory directions, but he was too much the party loyalist, and too fearful of the potential backlash from party bosses, to make a final break with Johnson. Goodwin and Walinsky had clearly reached the point where their stands on Vietnam prevented them from following Kennedy in 1968 if it meant also remaining loyal to Johnson. Kennedy would have to make a choice.

Still, conventional political wisdom held that if Kennedy could weather the storm, and keep from burning bridges with Democratic power brokers, he would be in a good position to run for president in 1972. Johnson's second term would be over, thereby freeing him to take on Vice President Hubert Humphrey for the nomination without being accused of dividing the party.

He might then offer himself as a youthful alternative to what Dutton had called "the dull middle aged tone that President Johnson and Hubert have hanging like a pall over the country."[86]

* * *

Kennedy's periodic cozying up to Johnson cost him support among peace advocates, and sowed dissension within his own staff. The only concrete political move he made in preparation for 1968 was to ask Dolan to contact a cross-section of Democratic regulars to gauge the depth of intraparty antagonism caused by the war, and the disillusionment with Johnson's leadership.

The White House and the D.N.C. applied intense pressure on the A.D.A., the Young Democrats, and other organizations tied to the party to force them to march in lockstep behind Johnson on Vietnam. They also monitored and disrupted Lowenstein's Dump Johnson movement. The Administration's use of the FBI to track antiwar activists, and the creation of its prowar Citizens' Committee, showed how far the present Democratic leaders were willing to go to silence or confuse their critics.

The President's advisers saved their most vicious private ad hominem attacks for Kennedy and other Democratic doves whom they saw as a major threat. By the end of 1967, events on the ground in Vietnam, along with the opposition at home, had proven Johnson wrong when he had asserted in February 1967 that Kennedy and his dove colleagues would be "dead" politically in six months.[87] The doves were alive and well and growing in number.

When prominent public figures denounced the wanton destruction and waste in Vietnam, Johnson Democrats often responded by questioning their loyalty in wartime. The top Democratic leadership appeared to be ill-prepared for the moral depth of the intraparty opposition to the war. Appeals to rally around the flag began to ring hollow. The increasingly violent means the Administration employed in its attempt to subdue Vietnam conflicted fundamentally with its stated liberal goals of building a more just and humane society at home.

There was an epic struggle brewing for the soul of the Democratic Party over two visions of the future. One faction flowed in the direction of the Lowensteins of the party, toward grassroots organizing and movement-oriented politics, which sought to stop the war and ensure against future Vietnams. The other faction swirled around the Johnsons and Humphreys of the party, dedicated to liberal ideals but overly beholden to the political machines, and committed to an unpopular war. Kennedy was caught between these two groups, one inchoate and marginalized, the other well established and in power.

There were powerful cross-currents operating in American politics in addition to Vietnam which led to a climate of social unrest, such as the racially charged urban rebellions, but the war in Southeast Asia polarized the Democratic Party. As the consensus to wage war continued to dissipate, Kennedy, trapped in the middle, tried to depersonalize his policy disagreements with Johnson, and stave off destructive battles with the Administration.

4   "The Hottest Place in Hell": Kennedy, the Democrats, and the McCarthy Candidacy

With Johnson we lose. He has disillusioned all of us who transferred our faith from John F. Kennedy to him. We voted against Goldwater, but we find ourselves saddled with his foreign policy anyway. Johnson means defeat for the Democrats in '68.

But with Robert F. Kennedy, we have a candidate who can win. He has become a rallypoint for all who are appalled by this hateful war in Viet Nam. And his appearances throughout the country testify to the enthusiasm he can inspire not only in Democrats but also in many Republicans.[1]
—Citizens for Kennedy recruiting letter, June 27, 1967

The polarizing effects of the Vietnam War eventually thrust Kennedy into the center of a bitterly divided Democratic Party. When the pragmatic political managers around him, such as Frederick Dutton and Theodore Sorensen, urged him to publicly clarify his support for Johnson's reelection, Kennedy had acted on this advice, and alienated a sizable number of his antiwar supporters. In November 1967, Minnesota Senator Eugene McCarthy heeded Allard Lowenstein's call and entered the Democratic primaries as a peace candidate alternative to Johnson. By tapping the energy of college students and antiwar activists, McCarthy's candidacy demonstrated the potential power of youth activism in primary campaigns.

Kennedy tried to maintain a semblance of party unity without weakening the McCarthy movement or damaging his own political position. Those who looked to Kennedy to lead the antiwar Democrats, such as the organizers of the spontaneous Citizens for Kennedy groups, felt a tangible sense of frustration and betrayal. They believed the Senator had placed political expediency above his own conscience. Kennedy's aides closely watched the early rumblings of the McCarthy movement. By analyzing the efforts of McCarthy's supporters, they reached a new understanding of the potential electoral power of students and peace activists working at the grassroots. Kennedy's pols also recognized for the first time the usefulness of the Citizens for Kennedy organization, which by the end of 1967 had established dozens of small chapters all over the country.

The same month McCarthy announced his candidacy, Kennedy's book of essays, *To Seek a Newer World*, hit the bookstores, and it contained his most resolute critique of Johnson's war policies to date. Kennedy had sought comments from his advisers on multiple drafts, but was careful to make sure it was his own work, recalling the controversy his brother had faced about ghost writers for *Profiles in Courage*.[2] The timing of the publication of *To Seek a Newer World* helped keep Kennedy's political options open for 1968.[3] Fully one-third of the book was devoted to Vietnam. In it, Kennedy reiterated his February 1966 call for accepting the National Liberation Front in the political life of South Vietnam. He also expanded on the themes of his March 2, 1967, address, calling for an unconditional bombing halt, a reduction in the level of United States troops, disciplinary actions aimed at the Saigon government to curb corruption, and direct negotiations with Hanoi *and* the N.L.F.[4]

So devastating were Kennedy's passages about Johnson's war policies in *To Seek a Newer World*, that two antiwar organizations, the Committee for a Sane Nuclear Policy (SANE), and Clergy and Laity Concerned About Vietnam (CALCAV), distributed the Vietnam excerpts as antiwar pamphlets.[5] *Look* magazine, whose editorial staff had been generally sympathetic to Kennedy's views, also published the Vietnam essays.[6] Among national political figures of the 1960s, Kennedy remained a widely publicized voice of opposition to the war. Yet despite the dissemination of his views and his stature as a leading dove, another Irish Catholic politician rapidly eclipsed him.

Four days before McCarthy formally announced his candidacy, Kennedy told an interviewer on the television program *Face the Nation* that he supported the idea of a peace candidacy: "There would at least be a discussion," he said, "and one was desperately needed since there had been no real dialogue about Vietnam."[7] He believed that any debate about the war must come from within the Democratic Party, because the Republicans had contributed precious little to the national discussion on Vietnam, save for calls for greater U.S. military force. He favored the opening of a constructive debate that McCarthy's presidential candidacy promised.

Later in the same interview, Kennedy explained the awkward position the news media had thrust him in by constantly speculating about his presidential ambitions. He had repeatedly told the press that he was against challenging Johnson in the primaries because he did not wish to derail the social legislation the Administration successfully passed. Although his views on the war were generally very close to McCarthy's, Kennedy could not repudiate Johnson by running himself, he said, "because there are many of the things that President Johnson stands for in the domestic field that I also support."[8] When the journalists badgered him about whether he would run in 1968, Kennedy replied: "No matter what I do, I am in difficulty. I don't know what I can do . . . other than to try to get off the earth in some way."[9]

On November 30, 1967, McCarthy announced his entry into the presidential primary races. Kennedy's friend and colleague, South Dakota Senator George McGovern, believed Kennedy became "terribly distressed" at the news because he could foresee the trouble it was going to present to him.[10] McCarthy's supporters immediately asked Kennedy for an endorsement, and several dovish members of Congress urged him to do so. Kennedy refused. From the Kennedy camp's point of view, if Kennedy were to support Eugene McCarthy against President Johnson and McCarthy then lost—which he would—it would appear to the general public that the war and LBJ's conduct of it had been approved, and this would be very bad for the country.[11]

The political pressure continued to increase to the point where Kennedy could no longer credibly support Johnson in 1968 unless the Administration drastically altered its Vietnam policies. Neither could he throw his support behind McCarthy because his inevitable defeat, no matter how important symbolically, would only weaken Kennedy's standing in the party without gaining him anything. He was caught in a political double bind. Given Kennedy's pride and feelings of carrying the banner for his brother, he could not play second fiddle to any insurgent, especially McCarthy, who had supported Adlai Stevenson over John Kennedy at the 1960 Democratic convention. Kennedy clung to the belief that he must avoid splitting the party regardless of his personal feelings toward Johnson's leadership and the war. His friend Averell Harriman pointed out to him that he was obligated to protect the party from "the deadening hand" of the Republicans in 1968.[12]

There were other reasons why Kennedy declined to back McCarthy. Perhaps most importantly, he withheld his endorsement because he simply did not believe McCarthy would make a good president. According to Peter

Edelman, Kennedy thought McCarthy, in addition to being a lazy politician, was "less than totally honest in his politics on the Senate Finance Committee," and that he was a "lousy senator, willing to bend to special interests to finance his campaigns."[13] Moreover, McCarthy ran an essentially single-issue campaign that masked some of his past inconsistencies. After a little investigating, Dolan informed Kennedy that one "unhappy development resulting from the McCarthy candidacy is that liberals will research [the] McCarthy voting record, and will become disillusioned when they find out that he isn't all that liberal."[14]

Although McCarthy became a hero to segments of the New Left and the campus antiwar movement, he was on the wrong side of many important progressive issues. He had voted against an amendment to the Voting Rights Act of 1965 outlawing poll taxes; he sided with the National Rifle Association (N.R.A.) with votes against gun control; he rejected an amendment to a bill requiring members of Congress to disclose their financial assets; he voted against limiting draft extensions to two, rather than four, years; and he also voted against Edward Kennedy's motion to cut a wasteful defense appropriation for gratuitous rifle training, an N.R.A. pet project.[15] McCarthy earned a voting rating from the liberal Americans for Democratic Action of 62 percent in 1967, while Robert Kennedy's A.D.A. rating always stood at 100 percent.[16]

In addition, McCarthy had simply not shown up for key roll-call votes in the Senate on legislation relating to welfare, civil rights, and Social Security; he voted on vital Social Security legislation only two times out of eight.[17] President Johnson and his advisers noted that during the prolific 89th Congress, McCarthy missed 106 out of 259 roll-call votes during the first session, and 39 out of 238 in the second. In the 90th Congress, through November 21, 1967, McCarthy had missed 85 out of 274 roll calls.[18] Kennedy observed McCarthy in the Senate, and saw his languid leadership style as a severe detriment to any serious presidential bid.[19] Johnson and his advisers agreed with Kennedy; White House memos privately referred to McCarthy's "laziness" as "abominable."[20] Workaholics like Johnson and Kennedy had difficulty fathoming the more whimsical aspects of McCarthy's personality.

However, McCarthy had displayed great courage in stepping forward to challenge Johnson when no other Democratic leader dared; Kennedy, on the other hand, still publicly endorsed the President.[21] Because of his prominent seat on the Foreign Relations Committee, McCarthy was among the most influential critics of Johnson's Vietnam policies inside the Democratic-controlled Senate. His primary bid succeeded in creating political breathing room for the growing opposition, and loosened Johnson's suffocating stranglehold on the party. More than any other single political event of 1967, McCarthy's peace candidacy upped the ante for the antiwar faction of the Democratic Party, and greatly increased the pressure on Kennedy to match his words with deeds.

When considering a presidential contest, Kennedy operated under an entirely different set of political realities than McCarthy. From the time of President Kennedy's assassination, members of the press recognized his potential to attain the highest office in the land.[22] When he traveled abroad, foreign leaders received him as if he were a head of state, not a junior senator.[23] If Kennedy decided to run for president in 1968, or any other year, it would be to win, not to make a symbolic statement. He continued to stand by the conventional political wisdom that challenging Johnson would be foolish, and could cost him a future shot at the presidency.

The most daunting problem facing Kennedy was that he seemed to be standing still at a time when those opposed to the Vietnam War rallied around McCarthy. The peace wing of the party now had the proper vehicle around which to coalesce: direct primaries. Kennedy, a man of action, had chosen to watch from the sidelines, and it was a disillusioning time for his supporters. Kennedy remained frozen while the political ground shifted beneath his feet. His detractors denounced him for failing to either run himself or formally endorse McCarthy.

Within the Kennedy camp, McCarthy's entrance into the primaries ignited a sense of urgency. Kennedy's aides feared that McCarthy, at the very least, could cleave off a section of the Senator's youth base, and weaken his presidential chances for 1972. With McCarthy openly defying Johnson and challenging him in the primaries, Kennedy seemed to have one foot planted on each side of a widening fissure: McCarthy's followers demanded Kennedy stand by his principles and support their candidate; Johnson, in turn, demanded total loyalty.

Members of Kennedy's staff did everything they could to maintain his standing with mainstream Democrats without weakening McCarthy's intraparty challenge. If he failed to put distance between himself and the McCarthy movement, Kennedy would surely suffer the opprobrium of the D.N.C. and the party bosses. Yet if he appeared too distant from McCarthy and the peace elements within the party, he risked turning his back on tens of thousands of his own supporters. His dilemma became increasingly clear.

Shortly before McCarthy announced his candidacy, Dutton wrote Kennedy that he believed the Minnesotan's campaign could be useful to Kennedy. "McCarthy will cut into both your liberal and Catholic followings," he wrote, "but he loosens the situation up." Dutton hoped McCarthy's challenge might "intimidate" Johnson in a way similar to Estes Kefauver's cowing of President Harry Truman in the 1952 primaries. He told Kennedy that "a small flap" for McCarthy would be constructive for both him and the country.[24] Sorensen advised Kennedy to draft a statement on the McCarthy candidacy and then refer all questions back to it.[25] This tactical posture, he expected, would minimize the inevitable questions from the press about Kennedy's intentions.

Three days after he discussed with Kennedy the political efficacy of a "McCarthy boomlet," Dutton suggested having staff members collect full, up-to-date material on the "forty or so likely key Democrats in the 1968 national convention." Dutton also believed Dolan should "regularly call working-level Democrats for nuances about the various local scenes." Among the party stalwarts on Dolan's list were Chicago Mayor Richard Daley, Governor Harold Hughes of Iowa, the Speaker of the California Assembly, Jesse Unruh, Martin Luther King, Jr., Walter Reuther of the United Auto Workers (U.A.W.), Governor Warren Hearnes of Missouri, and Indiana Senator Vance Hartke. Dutton also urged Kennedy to meet with prominent out-of-towners at his home, Hickory Hill, and ask his friend Tom Watson of I.B.M., and Steve Smith, Kennedy's brother-in-law, to meet with Democratic leaders whenever they passed through New York City.[26]

Allard Lowenstein had organized the movement that made McCarthy's campaign possible, and thereby lit a fire beneath the feet of Kennedy's political professionals who now wished to assess the mood of the party. Kennedy's staff stepped up its contacts with state and local Democratic leaders, and carefully monitored the McCarthy organization and the D.N.C.'s response to it. Kennedy's people also tracked the operations of the McCarthy campaign through internal contacts.[27]

Some state-level Democrats worried that Kennedy might sooner or later endorse McCarthy, and confront them with a choice between supporting the incumbent President or a Kennedy/McCarthy challenge.[28] Kennedy's office sent out mass mailings to New Hampshire Democrats, who were then preparing for the earliest primary, scheduled for mid-March 1968, asking them *not* to endorse a Kennedy candidacy, because he would not run in

1968 and he supported Johnson.[29] Restating his endorsement of Johnson had its own political perils for Kennedy. "Those 'RFK supports LBJ' headlines hurt your friends around the country," Dolan wrote Kennedy. "You should try to always have anything you say about LBJ's candidacy closely coupled with something about neutrality in the McCarthy-LBJ fight."[30] Despite sound advice from his staff and some deft posturing on Kennedy's part, his public statements designed to maintain party unity in the face of the McCarthy challenge seemed to satisfy no one, least of all the Senator himself.

On November 30, 1967, Democratic delegates from forty-two states met at the Sheraton-Blackstone Hotel in Chicago for two days of intensive caucuses centering on McCarthy's primary bid. Harold M. Ickes, the son of President Franklin Roosevelt's Secretary of the Interior, served as the conference coordinator.[31] To the chagrin of McCarthy's staff, Lowenstein slipped into the role of keynote speaker at the largest public rally of the weekend. He had not been scheduled to speak, and did so only upon learning that McCarthy was running late. Lowenstein got carried away with his own oratory, and forced a perturbed McCarthy to wait an additional twenty minutes while he whipped the crowd into a frenzy. In his speech, Lowenstein assured the peace forces they would be triumphant. He also might have been venting his disappointment about turning over the reins of his Dump Johnson movement to McCarthy and his staff.[32]

Kennedy's longtime friend William Haddad forwarded a report to Kennedy from a participant at the Democratic conference, where McCarthy outlined the major themes of his campaign. More than 500 people had gathered to form a national organization to promote McCarthy's candidacy. According to the informant, Sandy Frucher, those assembled were "generally well scrubbed, intelligent, middle-class businessmen types," and were "rank and file party workers and minor party officials." The conference was certainly worth watching from Kennedy's standpoint, and Frucher mentioned that some of McCarthy's supporters correctly conjectured that Kennedy people had attended the event.[33]

Frucher reported that McCarthy had not anticipated the mainstream cast of characters at the conference, and some "pros" had "prepared him for a group of kooks, radicals, and 'Bobby agents.'"[34] There were serious weaknesses in the early McCarthy campaign. The underlying problem at the conference, in Frucher's view, was that McCarthy had no organization whatever, and to be a viable candidate relied on the organization that Lowenstein had built up on his own over the past three months. And many of McCarthy's supporters considered Lowenstein a "Bobby agent."[35]

When McCarthy stepped up to the dais after Lowenstein had finished his spirited speech, he spoke rather listlessly, according to Frucher, and rarely paused for applause. The report went on: "Many in the audience were disappointed by the content of the speech and many more by the way it was delivered." It was a less than animated way to launch a primary campaign designed to unseat an incumbent president for pursuing an unjust war. McCarthy left the impression "of being lazy and disorganized, and perhaps not serious about his own candidacy."[36] McCarthy's performance was a far cry from the clarion call against Johnson and the war the assembled Democrats had desired. Any "instant" campaign is bound to show signs of disarray, and McCarthy's was no exception. Yet many of the critiques of McCarthy following the conference were more a consequence of his anemic style of leadership in a time of heightened passions than of the gaffes to be expected in the launching of an ill-prepared campaign.

McCarthy's performance at the event was so uninspiring that a small "Dump McCarthy" movement immediately developed within the groups that had supported his candidacy, and led some people to call for renewed efforts to pull Kennedy into the race.[37] McCarthy, whom both Kennedy and Johnson believed to be a lackadaisical senator, showed signs of being a lackluster presidential candidate as well.

The White House and the D.N.C. both followed the Chicago gathering of peace Democrats closely. At President Johnson's request, his appointments secretary and fellow Texan Marvin Watson asked the D.N.C. to send several observers to the conference.[38] Johnson's informants described the participants as "middle-class, middle-aged and mild." The "Love-in set," a pro-Johnson participant wrote contemptuously, was absent from the gathering because it "felt that McCarthy lacked 'flower power.'"[39]

Seeking weaknesses in the McCarthy movement, the D.N.C. observers noted that only fifteen delegates at the conference came from Southern states, and that there were only about "a half-dozen Negroes in the total delegate body." The D.N.C. had accurately pinpointed a central flaw in McCarthy's campaign: its slender, white middle-class base. Johnson's people, like Kennedy's, believed that McCarthy delivered his keynote speech in "an ambling and offhand manner, almost as if McCarthy wished to make certain that there was no emotional demonstration."[40] In his speech—the full text obtained by the White House—McCarthy had invoked the legacy of President John Kennedy, and then contrasted it with the malaise that had set in since Johnson took power.

The potential hidden role of Kennedy elements in McCarthy's campaign weighed heavily on the minds of Johnson's political aides. There was "some speculation that Kennedy money, if McCarthy should win the first or second primary, would find its way into the Conference war chest," a Johnson informant reported. "The one unanswered question coming out of this conference is McCarthy's relationship to Robert Kennedy and the question of who will benefit from the McCarthy challenge." Johnson's observers knew that Lowenstein had looked to Kennedy before turning to McCarthy, and it was clear to them "that Senator Kennedy views McCarthy's candidacy at least with covert favor."[41] The White House and the D.N.C. displayed infinitely more concern over Kennedy's potential entry into the race, and his alleged behind-the-scenes efforts to help McCarthy, than over the Minnesota senator's campaign. Johnson partisans, who had earlier suspected Kennedy money behind the National Conference on New Politics, now also feared he was secretly bankrolling McCarthy's presidential candidacy.

Johnson's Democratic allies interviewed dozens of delegates and produced detailed reports about the gathering. The Johnson faction showed particular interest in the efforts of Dr. Martin Shepard, a founder of Citizens for Kennedy, who argued at the Chicago conference that "a McCarthy candidacy in New Hampshire would insure a Robert Kennedy candidacy in that state's primary."[42] One observer for the White House speculated that the only fear of the Kennedy people was that "McCarthy may trigger defections from their man."[43]

Johnson had asked Watson to search for a Kennedy hand behind the McCarthy challenge, but the President's trusted secretary found no sign of any direct or informal collusion between Kennedy and McCarthy. Watson informed Johnson that McCarthy himself denied that there was any collusion between them.[44] He attempted to reassure the President, who was obsessed with Kennedy's possible covert role in the campaign, that Administration officials saw no connection between the McCarthy campaign and any move by Kennedy for the Democratic nomination. Watson surmised that even if McCarthy maneuvered his way on to the ticket in 1968, a compromise could be reached to block Kennedy from being nominated: "In the event McCarthy were successful he could at least demand and get the Vice Presidential nomination, which would rule out Senator Kennedy from Presidential consideration, since both McCarthy and Kennedy are Catholics."[45]

Johnson's special consultant John Roche, who rapidly became one of the president's key political advisers, was more sanguine. He gleefully predicted that McCarthy would fail miserably in the Massachusetts primary, scheduled for April 30, 1968, after the Johnson forces "blitz[ed] the state." Roche assured Johnson that he would win handily "by at least 4 or 5 to 1." The Kennedys could do little to prevent McCarthy from being pummeled by the D.N.C. in Massachusetts because—in Roche's view—Teddy, like Bobby, ran solitary operations. In Roche's judgment, Massachusetts was "the ideal place . . . to politically obliterate McCarthyism."[46] To crush McCarthy, Roche advised the President to frame the differences between himself and the Minnesota senator "with the utmost simplicity: 'Which side are you on? McCarthy and the Vietniks? or L.B.J. and the soldiers in Vietnam?' "[47] Roche's hard-line perspective allowed no room for dissent, and Johnson's apparent acceptance of this view pointed to the fatal flaw in this rigid stand on the war: it essentially red-baited the Democratic opposition, and played to Johnson's paranoia. Roche shared his delight in the early stumbling of the McCarthy campaign: "Eugene McCarthy is doing so badly I am tempted to float the rumor that he is actually working for you to dispirit the 'peace movement.' "[48]

Another encouraging sign Roche noted was that at a recent meeting on Vietnam of the Massachusetts chapter of the A.D.A., "not one of the 'Kennedy intellectuals' turned up." Regarding Robert Kennedy's part in the McCarthy challenge, Roche wrote:

> The Kennedy role in this whole business is very complex. Ted is against it, but Bobby goes up one day and down the next.
>
> From one very reliable source, I have learned that Bobby has been feeling out old Kennedy people in Ohio, Indiana and Illinois to see if they would "go" if he blows the whistle. I'm told the answer is almost always the same: "It will wreck the party—you can't be serious."
>
> The real question therefore is: How *rational* is Bobby? And unfortunately, I am no psychiatrist. But I think a couple of real beatings for McCarthy in the early primaries would help him [Kennedy] keep his cool.[49]

Roche recommended to Johnson that he "take charge, get on those [primary] ballots, reorganize the DNC," and "break the backs" of his opponents.[50] It was sound political advice if Johnson desired to open the debate on the war, and go head-to-head with the McCarthy forces in the 1968 primaries. However, Johnson, sensing his own slip in popularity, had no intention of bloodying himself in a thirteen-state battle against a Democratic opposition staffed by thousands of college students and grassroots peace activists. Instead, he preferred to manipulate the D.N.C. and the party machinery from behind the scenes to "break the backs" of dissident Democrats. By the end of 1967, the polarization of the party had reached a new phase.

Beginning in September 1966, a handful of reform Democrats from Manhattan's West Side had organized Citizens for Kennedy/Fulbright '68. Dr. Martin Shepard, a 32-year-old psychiatrist, headed the group, which contacted thousands of people active in Democratic Party affairs. Shepard received a surprisingly enthusiastic response through placing ads in national magazines, and in the *New York Times*. Citizens for Kennedy/Fulbright '68 sent letters seeking support to nearly all of the delegates to the 1960 and 1964 Democratic National Conventions, and to hundreds of state and local party officials. An early recruit to the Kennedy-Fulbright cause was the former Democratic Congressman from Oregon, Charles Porter, a 48-year-old attorney who had served in the 86th Congress. Porter became a high-profile member of the group's coordinating committee.[51]

By August 1967, the grassroots Kennedy organization had obtained the signatures of fifty-four former Democratic convention delegates who publicly asked Johnson to retire for the good of the party. Later that month, Fulbright's name was dropped from the title, the group's literature explained, because it gave the impression they were promoting Fulbright as a vice presidential candidate, "when the name was merely symbolic of CFK's opposition to President Johnson and Secretary of State Rusk."[52]

Ten months after its inception, Citizens for Kennedy claimed a membership of 7,500 nationally, including thirty presidents of Young Democrat clubs. It had a full-time press secretary, a legal counsel, and a national coordinating committee. By the end of 1967, the organization had spontaneously blossomed nationwide, and like the antiwar movement itself, it functioned as a loose and decentralized collection of local civic groups.[53] Citizens for Kennedy soon had more than sixty active chapters (with ten in California and four in Illinois—the two states with the most affiliates), and it aggressively sought Kennedy delegates for the upcoming New Hampshire primary. Independent organizers established chapters in primary states such as California, Oregon, Indiana, Wisconsin, and South Dakota, and in the nonprimary states of Pennsylvania, Texas, Illinois, Oklahoma, Missouri, Nevada, New Jersey, Connecticut, Kentucky, Washington, and Florida.[54]

Like the antiwar movement, Citizens for Kennedy drew its life blood from volunteers, who held meetings in homes, churches, community centers, and union halls. Local chapters comprised the backbone of the national campaign, and they linked their support for Kennedy with issues facing their own cities and districts. Citizens for Kennedy promoted letter-writing campaigns, and by pooling small donations from hundreds of people purchased full-page ads in newspapers and magazines.[55] The group targeted labor unions, peace and civil rights organizations, and political clubs, as well as the college campuses. Citizens for Kennedy picked up steam on its own initiative throughout 1967 with each new escalation of the Vietnam War.

Looking to 1968, Citizens for Kennedy mailings said the Johnson Administration offered the American people "little but death abroad and disillusionment at home." Members promised to do everything in their power to oppose Johnson's renomination, and viewed Kennedy as "the only reasonable alternative" for Democrats who wanted "no wider war except the war on poverty" and wished to remain loyal to their party.[56] Citizens for Kennedy further predicted that if Johnson were the 1968 nominee, hundreds of thousands of Democrats would be forced "to bolt to the GOP or to abstain on election day." This outcome might lead to the defeat of thousands of Democratic candidates for Federal, state, and local offices.[57]

Citizens for Kennedy lobbied hard for an open Democratic National Convention where the final decision on the nomination might be contested with a groundswell of support for Kennedy. It called upon members of state and local Democratic Clubs to press their chapters into passing resolutions endorsing Kennedy, or at least to withhold their support from Johnson until the convention. In Texas, one local Citizens for Kennedy group went so far as to write letters to Johnson delegates asking them to "pretend to support Johnson and then vote for Kennedy once you get to the convention."[58] Tactics such as these infuriated Johnson's supporters. It is not surprising, therefore, that the White House and the D.N.C., through the use of informants within the national organization as well as in several state and local chapters, carefully tracked the activities of Citizens for Kennedy.

The D.N.C. routinely forwarded to the White House materials they obtained by signing on to Citizens for Kennedy mailing lists, so that Johnson's political advisers could see "the kind of junk" the organization sent out.[59]

Johnson once again abused his power over the FBI, and ordered the Bureau to keep a close eye on Kennedy's public statements about any group that was "promoting him for President."[60] Administration loyalists who had attempted to steer the Young Democrats away from opposing Johnson were particularly alarmed by Citizens for Kennedy's successful recruiting of the leaders of some Young Democrat chapters. If Citizens for Kennedy enlisted the Young Democrat leadership to join its cause, the coalition, one D.N.C. operative warned, "would be formidable."[61]

Throughout 1967, Kennedy repeatedly stated that he and his staff had no connection or interest whatsoever in Citizens for Kennedy. He had made clear that he preferred to see the group's organizers stop working in his behalf lest they divide the party, and spark the ire of Johnson and the D.N.C. Yet even while Kennedy wavered he, like Johnson, ordered his staff to trace the group's activities. Some of Johnson's advisers found it difficult to believe that Kennedy was not secretly encouraging the "draft Kennedy" campaign. Once again, banter about Kennedy money behind the effort surfaced in White House memoranda.

In the spring of 1967, Citizens for Kennedy had become so bothersome to Kennedy's standing with Democratic leaders that he was forced to send out letters to powerful party regulars clarifying his position. "I was elected Senator in 1964 for a term extending to January 1971," Kennedy wrote, "and have no future plans other than to serve New York State and the nation to the best of my ability as United States Senator." When it came to the grassroots movement that was prodding him to run, Kennedy added: "I am in no way associated with Citizens for Kennedy-Fulbright," and "have asked them to cease their organizational efforts on my behalf."[62]

John Seigenthaler, Kennedy's former assistant in the Justice Department and the editor of the *Nashville Tennessean*, was outraged at the contents of one D.N.C. newsletter that accused Kennedy of encouraging the citizens' group. "I think it is a disgrace to send out this sheet," Seigenthaler wrote Kennedy, "without a single word of explanation that you have rejected the support of Dr. Shephard [sic] and his group, and that you have announced total support for Lyndon Johnson in 1968. What the hell kind of operation are they running at the Committee?," he asked. "I think [Press Secretary] Frank M[ankiewicz] should call and raise hell with them about it."[63] Even when Kennedy made geniune efforts to distance himself from his grassroots supporters, the D.N.C., through tactless accusation and innuendo, pushed him to make the gulf even wider.

Other smaller citizens' groups sent newspaper and magazine articles to Kennedy indicating he was ahead in local opinion polls, or the winner in mock elections held at schools and colleges. These unsolicited articles, polls, and "election" results that flooded his office were signs of an evolving, as yet untapped national Kennedy movement.[64] However, in late 1967, even with the unfolding of the Dump Johnson campaign, and the proliferating Citizens for Kennedy chapters, a run for the presidency in 1968 appears to have been so far removed from Kennedy's thinking that he could still privately joke about it. "You had better get aboard or it's going to be too late," he wrote a friend, "There is one vacancy in the Cabinet and 4 Ambassadorships still left. Make a short statement for Stokely and say Ho Chi Minh is misunderstood—I'll be watching—Bob."[65]

Contrary to the inferences of Johnson's closest political advisers,[66] there is no evidence to suggest that anyone on Kennedy's staff gave open or hidden support to Citizens for Kennedy at this time.[67] Kennedy's political advisers initially viewed these groups simply as a nuisance that threatened to split the party and cast their man in the spoiler role. The organization's use of Kennedy's name on their mass mailings was cause for serious attention since it tended to generate headlines that angered Johnson and the D.N.C. The group's calls for Kennedy to run brought him only the wrath of Johnson Democrats (by far the most powerful party faction), disdain from McCarthy partisans, and bitter criticism from those who viewed his hesitation as either a display of cowardice or part of a Machiavellian scheme. It was not until the McCarthy campaign proved stronger than anticipated that the political professionals around Kennedy, such as Frederick Dutton, recognized the potential usefulness of these Kennedy for President chapters.

Opposition to the war in Vietnam had been the central unifying force behind Citizens for Kennedy, and it sought the strongest potential challenger to Johnson. "Either Lyndon Johnson must abandon his war in Vietnam," one Citizens for Kennedy pamphlet stated, "or the Democratic party must abandon Lyndon Johnson."[68] Other Democratic senators shared Kennedy's views, yet their opposition did not translate into a national citizen's organization calling upon them to run for president; in this respect, Kennedy was unique.[69]

The D.N.C. sought to thwart the "infiltration efforts" of Citizens for Kennedy, which were reportedly designed to press delegates to the 1968 convention to endorse a peace plank in the party's platform.[70] Informants tied to the D.N.C. regularly notified the White House, mainly through Marvin

Watson, about the overt links between Democratic officials and local chapters of Citizens for Kennedy. Observers kept Watson appraised about the activities of Citizens for Kennedy in California, Iowa, Missouri, New Hampshire, New York, Tennessee, Texas, and Washington, D. C.[71] Watson compiled detailed biographical data on the leaders of Citizens for Kennedy, while the D.N.C. sought to influence the fifty-four former Democratic delegates who had signed on to the group.[72]

The D.N.C. attempted to counter the effects of Citizens for Kennedy by sending out its own mass mailings to all of the former delegates and alternates to the 1960 and 1964 conventions, as well as to all current party officials nationwide. The letters denigrated the organization, and included a scathing article by the syndicated columnist and Administration shill Robert Spivak, attacking what he called the Fulbright-Kennedy crowd.[73] The response to the D.N.C.'s counteroffensive was disappointing; operatives reported that there had been no more than half a dozen acknowledgments of the mailing.[74]

One notably unfavorable response came from Senator Claiborne Pell of Rhode Island. Pell, who shared Kennedy's views on the war, was furious that the D.N.C. had distributed an attack piece against two senators.[75] D.N.C. Chairman John Bailey attempted to clarify the party's position in a subsequent mailing by pointing out that both Senator Kennedy and Senator Fulbright had disavowed "the so-called Kennedy-Fulbright movement."[76] By the fall of 1967, the D.N.C. felt the heat of the McCarthy challenge, and stiffened its resolve against all dissident Democratic groups. The Committee even denied Citizens for Kennedy the use of its Washington offices simply to hold a press conference.[77]

A few months before the New Hampshire primary, former Congressman Charles Porter, of the national coordinating committee of Citizens for Kennedy, vowed to mobilize nationally with or without the approval of the "candidate." Porter flatly predicted to the press that Kennedy would beat Johnson in New Hampshire even without actively campaigning. Members of the organization, according to Porter, would give Kennedy until the first of March 1968 to "shrug a shoulder or move an eyebrow" to signal them to forge ahead in New Hampshire.[78] In September 1967, the White House was furious at Porter's appearance on NBC News, where he promoted the Kennedy candidacy and attacked Johnson's leadership.[79]

The problems the "draft Kennedy" movement created for the New York senator were twofold: first, they led the press to subordinate Kennedy's criticism of the Vietnam War to a constant barrage of questions about whether he would run in 1968; and second, they fueled the worst suspicions of Kennedy's detractors, inside and outside the Democratic Party, who believed he was coyly promoting these grassroots efforts to further his own presidential ambitions. Although most political commentators considered Citizens for Kennedy an amateurish organization, its activities nonetheless captured the intense scrutiny of the D.N.C. and the White House.

To attempt to quell the controversy, Kennedy sent out yet another mailing on January 2, 1968, this time to his New Hampshire supporters, who were then seeking to become his delegates: "I am not a candidate for the nomination and . . . I have not authorized anyone to seek delegates on my behalf. I would therefore appreciate your ceasing your efforts in my behalf."[80] Kennedy's stance on the upcoming presidential election satisfied neither Johnson's supporters nor the growing number of disenchanted Democrats.

Dr. Shepard, who was the founder and co-chair of Citizens for Kennedy, wrote Kennedy later that month: "You are fond of saying the hottest place in hell is reserved for those who fail to act in times of great moral crisis. With villages burning and men risking their lives daily in this obscene war, I don't think it is asking too much of you to risk your political prestige by becoming an active Presidential candidate."[81] Shepard reaffirmed his group's plans to "carry Kennedy's banner" in New Hampshire, Pennsylvania, and South Dakota, and to place Kennedy's name on the ballot in the Wisconsin, Oregon, and Nebraska primaries. "Any attempt to take your name off the ballot in any of these states would seem to me inexcusable," he added. Shepard chose a powerful tack: his paraphrase of Dante's "hottest places in Hell" had become a staple for both John and Robert Kennedy. But setting moral appeals aside, Kennedy let party loyalty and conventional political wisdom prevail; through public statements and mailings, he continued to make it clear he was not interested in running for president in 1968.

Shepard's and others' attempts at moral suasion to prod Kennedy to action were not unfounded, given the increasingly moral tone of the Senator's criticisms of the war. In November 1967, for example, Kennedy told a national television audience: "We're killing South Vietnamese, we're killing children, we're killing women, we're killing innocent people because we don't want to have the war fought on American soil, or because they're 12,000 miles away and they might get to be 11,000 miles away." In the same interview, he pointed out that there were "35,000 people without limbs in South Vietnam," and "150,000 civilian casualties every year." "When we use napalm, when a village is destroyed and civilians are killed," he declared, "this is a moral obligation, and a moral responsibility for us here in the United States."[82] His failure to act on these convictions disillusioned and frustrated many of his supporters.

In late 1967, the Citizens for Kennedy groups finally caught Dutton's serious attention. He recognized the political potential of the "peace" and "volunteer Kennedy" organizations that were then mobilizing, and urged Kennedy to keep in close touch with them. This contact would allow Kennedy not only to keep informed on what they are up to, but also *"to help steer them when, and if, desirable."* Dutton suggested that Kennedy assign Schlesinger, Goodwin, or other "naturally inclined individuals" to the task, and prepare to harness the energy of these groups. Dutton was the first political professional close to Kennedy to point out to the Senator the latent usefulness of Citizens for Kennedy and other antiwar organizations in a 1968 primary bid.[83]

Operationally, Dutton stepped up contacts with Democratic regulars to assess the level of discontent with Johnson. He asked Kennedy to send copies of his major speeches on Vietnam, race relations, and other subjects to "all county chairmen, grass-roots 'club' leaders and union local heads." "These people are easily flattered by just a little recognition," he wrote, "and they make up a major part of any realistic political groundswell and convention delegate roster." The mailings would arouse some suspicion, he warned, but would be beneficial in the long run.[84]

Dutton also looked at the student movement in a new light, and thought it prudent "to keep track of the campuses and evoke a response there in the spring through student newspapers, etc." But the colleges were a "two-edged matter," Dutton wrote Kennedy, "because of the hostility of the older group towards the young, and the New Left's carping at you."[85] The Lowenstein movement and McCarthy's candidacy, which captured the imagination of thousands of young people, began to crack through Dutton's hard-boiled political pragmatism. The success that Lowenstein and his colleague Curtis Gans had in galvanizing peace and student organizations and mobilizing campus resources on behalf of the McCarthy candidacy made it appear that Kennedy's historical moment might quickly slip past him.

The McCarthy campaign enabled Kennedy to systematically test the political waters. At Dutton's suggestion, Kennedy sent Joseph Dolan on an extended fact-finding mission to gauge the extent of opposition to Johnson among Democrats. Contrary to the public statements of both Lowenstein and Kennedy, as well as to McCarthy's own intentions (yet suspected by some commentators at the time), the Kennedy camp used McCarthy's candidacy as a de facto stalking horse, whether McCarthy liked it or not.

Each time Kennedy was forced to publicly reiterate his support for Johnson's reelection it hurt him with the peace movement and Democratic doves. Yet pressed by the D.N.C. and party leaders, he continued to do so in the name of unity and took considerable flak for it. By demanding constant reaffirmations of loyalty, Johnson's allies forced Kennedy's hand recurrently to acknowledge the President as the true leader of his party. McCarthy's entrance into the race ignited the pro-Johnson and prowar forces among Democrats, who felt themselves increasingly under attack, and made the dividing line even more rigid.

Johnson fueled the intraparty divisions by publicly referring to his Democratic adversaries as the Kennedy-McCarthy movement.[86] By linking the two leaders, as if they were conspiring against him, Johnson drove a wedge between the two senators, and gave added credence to the stalking horse theory. In a single presidential utterance, Johnson prodded Kennedy to distance himself from McCarthy's candidacy, while at the same time implying that the McCarthy campaign functioned as little more than a front for Kennedy, which angered McCarthy's supporters.

To make matters worse, given Kennedy's role as a high-profile critic of the Vietnam War, prowar elements singled him out for jingoistic attacks. In late 1967, rightwingers set up an automated telephone line in the Washington, D.C., area for the sole purpose of red-baiting Kennedy. "Let Freedom Ring," an organization tied to the John Birch Society, offered citizens a free call-in service to receive information on Kennedy's latest acts of treachery. In addition to pouncing on Kennedy for "giving blood to the Viet Cong," the Let Freedom Ring recordings accused him of financing the Black Power movement, and advocating "Negro anarchy." Some of the far right's charges echoed the sentiments of the Johnson Democrats who saw Kennedy money behind virtually every act of dissent. Mankiewicz angrily responded to what he called the Birchers' vile and contemptible lies. "Some people take bicarbonate of soda after overeating," he told the *Houston Chronicle*. "These guys get on the telephone."[87] Despite his cautiousness, Kennedy had become a prime target of prowar forces both inside and outside the Democratic Party.

In mid-January 1968, on the final evening of a two-day regional conference of the D.N.C. in Salt Lake City, James Farley, a former chairman of the D.N.C. and a powerful New York Democrat, assailed Kennedy and other national figures who disagreed with Johnson's Vietnam policies. Although it was not Farley's first public jab at Kennedy retained in White House files, it was one of the most contemptuous public assaults on the Senator from a high-ranking Democrat.[88] Prominent Democratic officials, generally representing moderate party elements, attended the conference from Utah, Colorado, Arizona, Montana, Nevada, and Wyoming. The *Salt Lake City Tribune* summarized Farley's speech under the headline: "Doves Blistered by Farley; State Democratic Meeting Hears Scorcher." Johnson saved the text of Farley's address, and also kept a distilled version that featured each of his pointed attacks on some of the President's detractors.[89]

Farley saved his most bitter remarks not for McCarthy, who was then campaigning against Johnson in New Hampshire, but for Kennedy.[90] He tried to punish Kennedy and like-minded Democrats for their "disloyalty" by forcing them outside the discourse of civilized people. "I feel pity for the junior Senator from New York," he said. "I urge this young man . . . that he should not let himself open to the political ridicule aroused by the princelings of privilege weeping into their champagne buckets over the plight of the poor." Kennedy, Farley argued, had advocated "a Bay of Pigs run-out on a world wide scale." Farley was the keynote speaker at the Democratic banquet, and went on to say that he hoped "the junior Senator is no longer fellow traveling the Fulbright line, to the destruction of his country, his party and himself." Kennedy "comes close to the point of no return," Farley said, "when he declares that the President undermines the moral position of America in upholding the identical moral position of Presidents Truman and Eisenhower and of his own brother, President Kennedy, who solemnly promised the people of Viet Nam they would not be deserted."[91]

In contrast, Farley said, Johnson was a "patriot," and a "man of courage" who was "leading this nation to greatness."[92] Dolan's Democratic friends who attended the dinner told him that the banquet room grew still while Farley spoke about Kennedy, and that several people on the dais hung their heads as if ashamed to be listening; but no one left the table.

This type of vituperation coming from well-known Democrats only added to the atmosphere of divisiveness within the party. The Johnson wing not only refused to accommodate the emergent dove faction, but tried to silence and exclude it from the debate on the war. This strategy was doomed from the start. By going on the offensive against the peace Democrats, viewing them as anathema, the prowar leadership further weakened a party that was already facing a primary fight. Moreover, in the left-leaning political climate of the late 1960s, the venom of the prowar wing toward its intraparty critics disillusioned thousands of moderate Democrats, who at the very least expected a civil dialogue on the war.

By accusing Kennedy of "fellow traveling" with elements deemed "destructive" to the country, and advocating "a Bay of Pigs run-out on a world wide scale," Farley's rhetoric echoed the sentiments of the far right. The Democratic leadership's rigid adherence to the Administration's increasingly unpopular Vietnam policy, more than any other single factor, had poisoned the well of party unity.

The D.N.C. launched its own attack on Democrats identified with the peace wing of the party. Though individuals were not listed by name, antiwar leaders were the subject of ridicule in the D.N.C.'s mass mailings.[93] One Committee mailing denounced the "cheap carping and criticism of the President," and issued a warning against "the professional pessimists. The paid pollsters and pundits. The hucksters with their phony promises. The fast-talkers, sign-wavers, under-and-over-age 'Youth Leaders,' and militant marchers who thrive on discord and who say 'Do it our way—or else!'"[94] The letter closed with a pitch for donations and a final call to rally behind Johnson. The D.N.C.'s corrosive tone only served to further polarize the party, and revealed once again that the Committee operated as a vehicle for Johnson.

In another letter sent to registered Democrats, the D.N.C. proclaimed: "Citizens of the United States these days are paying close attention to what President Johnson says, and they realize now he has been right all along." The President's firm stand against his opponents at home and abroad, the D.N.C. claimed, had caused "the pendulum of public opinion" to "swing strongly his way." The Committee called upon all good Democrats to "stand up and speak for the President when he is being criticized."[95] As the New Hampshire primary approached, D.N.C. leaders grew more intolerant of criticism of the war. Like Farley's Salt Lake City speech, the timbre of the letters from the highest echelons of the Democratic Party mirrored the far right in its level of vitriol. Given that McCarthy's candidacy promised to bring the Vietnam issue to the forefront of Democratic politics, the party leadership's rigidity did not bode well. The Republicans, who offered little of substance to the Vietnam debate, could sit back and watch as their rival party tore itself apart.

Some rank-and-file Democrats found themselves alienated by the D.N.C.'s assault on the doves, and its calls to support the war. It was "a disgrace and an insult that such a letter went out from the Democratic National Committee," a constituent wrote Kennedy.[96] Another Kennedy constituent became so angry after receiving a prowar D.N.C. letter that he promised never again to support the Democratic Party because it was full of "lying politicians."[97] Ever the party loyalist even when the political efficacy of such a stand was becoming less evident, Kennedy wrote back: "Unfortunately, there is very little we can do about the content and taste of the letters the Committee sends out. . . . I hope your feelings about such a correspondence do not affect your faith in the Democratic Party."[98]

Johnson and the D.N.C. demanded a uniformity of opinion on the war among Democrats that was impossible given the opposition, especially at the state and local levels. As the outbursts of Democratic leaders against the war's opponents became more pointed, the intraparty debate became less civil. In this heated atmosphere, there was little room left for Kennedy to pursue his course of tactical compromise with both sides. The Johnson wing of the party felt the heat of the McCarthy challenge, and became even more extreme in its anticommunism and less tolerant of dissent. It appeared that some of the war's toxicities had leached into mainstream American political discourse. Compared to Farley's vengeful screed in Salt Lake City and the bitter letters from the D.N.C., Kennedy had been a paragon of decency and moderation.

In late 1967 and early 1968, the distinct rightward lurch of the Democratic leadership constrained the space that the peace wing had to politically maneuver. For Democrats who opposed the war and wanted to have their voices heard in national politics, there was no choice but to bring their views directly to the people in the primaries, and try to block Johnson's renomination. It was the Administration's stiff adherence to a disastrous policy in Southeast Asia which sparked both Lowenstein's Dump Johnson movement and the McCarthy primary challenge. As the election year 1968 began, Kennedy, who was still the dove figure who could mount the strongest challenge to Johnson, found himself trapped between party stalwarts who supported the war and controlled the political machines, and a Democratic opposition allied with the peace movement but backing a weak candidate.

* * *

Earlier in 1967, Joseph Dolan had speculated on the upcoming Senate races in 1968, and shared with Kennedy his fear that the President, the Administration, and the Republicans were in the process of waging a "pincers movement." The political squeeze, he said, left both incumbent and non-incumbent Democrats in an untenable position. Dolan's advice for them was to somehow demonstrate unequivocal support for the troops in Vietnam, without "swallow[ing] LBJ's war hook, line and sinker." It was a difficult balancing act, but these Democrats had to "separate themselves from the President" and his "present posture" of "put up or shut up." They had no choice but to run campaigns emphasizing their independence from Johnson and the Democratic leadership.[99] Thus, as early as the summer of 1967, it was evident that Johnson, who had exceedingly long coattails in 1964, would be a drag on many Democratic races in 1968.

Throughout 1967, Kennedy distanced himself from Johnson and the party leadership on the war while trying to maintain his political standing within the party. Given that he was not up for reelection until 1970, it was possible he might slip past the Democratic in-fighting of 1968. But Kennedy's antiwar views and rivalry with Johnson would not let him remove himself from the center of the intraparty conflict. The Democratic leadership's constant demands for loyalty to Johnson, along with groups like Citizens for Kennedy which challenged Kennedy to run, stripped him of the luxury of remaining outside the fray. Johnson's and the D.N.C.'s heavy-handed tactics to enforce unity backfired by pushing Kennedy in the opposite direction.

Kennedy remained cautious and professional even when fierce detractors like Farley evoked the name of his late brother to attack him. He disavowed the Citizens for Kennedy groups which urged write-in campaigns in New Hampshire and other primary states. By January 1968, some of Johnson's key advisers believed that Kennedy had come to the conclusion that he could not get the nomination, and that it would be "disastrous" for him to try.[100] John Roche summed up the situation for the President: "The point has been made to Bobby that if we go down, he goes down with us. He knows it (it is highly unlikely that any Republican elected in 1968 could be licked in 1972; by 1976 Bobby will be a grandfather). He has nowhere else to go and your victory is imperative to his plans for 1972."[101]

However, the opposition to the war within party ranks adversely affected the Johnson Democrats' position. In a trend that continued throughout the spring of 1968, the party leadership drifted ideologically closer to the Southern conservative bloc. Democrats from Southern states, such as the notorious segregationist Senator James Eastland of Mississippi, who chaired the

Judiciary Committee, had rarely cooperated with President Kennedy, and quickly soured on their fellow Southerner Johnson after his stands on civil rights in 1964 and 1965. However, when it came to anticommunism, these Southern Democrats, with a few notable exceptions,[102] were dependable supporters of the Vietnam War.

Johnson, feeling himself under attack from the doves, turned to the Southern wing of the party as well as to the Republicans for support. The President's stubborn adherence to his Vietnam policies created a curious set of tactical political alliances. The ensuing crisis stemmed partially from the spectacle of a liberal Democratic president pursuing a foreign policy with a distinctly right-wing odor, and it reflected the inherent ideological contradictions of Cold War liberalism.

5 The Collapse of the Myths:
Kennedy, Johnson, and the Tet Offensive,
January–February 1968

For the sake of those young Americans who are fighting today,
if for no other reason, the time has come to take a new look at the war in
Vietnam . . . stripped of deceptive illusions. It is time for the truth.
— Robert F. Kennedy, Chicago, February 8, 1968

In January and February 1968, a series of attacks in South Vietnam during the Tet lunar new year celebration showed that America's enemy could strike deep into the country's urban centers. The Tet Offensive belied the Johnson Administration's predictions that victory was at hand. It seriously undermined the arguments for continuing the war, and strengthened the resolve of the opposition. It also proved to be a crucial turning point, not only in the war but in President Johnson's political relations to his critics, both inside and outside the Democratic Party, and especially to Robert Kennedy. The offensive in Vietnam thrust Kennedy into a new and even more difficult political environment.

Throughout 1967, the Administration had targeted Congress for a public relations campaign on the Vietnam War. In hearings and in backroom meetings with Congressional leaders, Johnson and his advisers claimed that enemy strength had peaked, and the war was steadily moving in the United States' favor. In December 1967, Johnson declared that America's enemy had "met his master in the field."[1] With the launching of the Tet Offensive on January 30, 1968, Congressional mistrust of these rosy predictions began to grow in intensity. Tet seemed to confirm the public's worst suspicions, long held by peace activists, about the nature of the war and the Administration's duplicity in covering up the truth.

In the weeks following Tet, large numbers of American soldiers engaged in ferocious street battles. Johnson and members of his Administration downplayed the offensive's significance, but quietly debated a request for a 40 percent increase in American combat troops.[2] Countering Tet's effects on U.S. opinion proved difficult, given the extensive television coverage of the attacks that raged for weeks in Saigon, Hue, and dozens of smaller towns and cities. The Administration argued that the Tet Offensive, despite media images to the contrary, had been a devastating military defeat for the enemy.[3] However, the fighting exposed the weaknesses of the U.S.-backed Government of South Vietnam (G.V.N.), as well as the severe limitations of the Army of the Republic of Vietnam (A.R.V.N.). Johnson tried to manage the crisis by insisting that the offensive was of no significance in the wider war. This position gave opponents of the war, including Kennedy, new ammunition against U.S. policy. Following Tet, letters from American G.I.'s serving in Vietnam which contradicted Johnson's version of events inundated Kennedy's office.

In early 1968, Kennedy witnessed some of the more dovish members of his staff depart to work against Johnson in the upcoming elections. He also saw a large segment of his constituency flock to the peace candidacy of Senator Eugene McCarthy. The Tet Offensive precipitated the moment when Kennedy could no longer support Johnson's reelection.

The heightened political rivalry between Kennedy and Johnson had at its core a foreign policy crisis. Kennedy's support for Johnson's domestic agenda kept him from making his final break with the incumbent president. The enemy offensive, and the U.S. response, ultimately set off a chain of events that produced a reevaluation of American war aims in Vietnam. The Administration's reaction to Tet further polarized the Democratic Party, and stirred up Congressional animus. Events on the ground in Vietnam shifted the momentum of the struggle, and placed new constraints on Kennedy's political choices.

On the night of January 30, 1968, the Tet lunar new year festivities began in Vietnam. There was a temporary truce in place which allowed thousands of people to visit relatives for the holidays. The movement of civilians, and the setting off of fireworks at nightfall, provided excellent cover for the N.L.F. and the People's Army of Vietnam (P.A.V.N.) to prepare to launch a series of well-planned assaults on urban centers. The N.L.F. and P.A.V.N. left untouched no symbol of the American presence in South Vietnam, and hit virtually every significant military and political target throughout South Vietnam. Fierce attacks blistered the country from the ancient imperial capital of Hue in the north to the southern town of Ben Tre in the Mekong Delta, where it became necessary, in the words of one American Army Major, to destroy the town in order to save it. The N.L.F. and P.A.V.N. assaulted 36 of the 44 provincial capitals, and hundreds of smaller targets throughout South Vietnam. They successfully held for a time large swaths of five of the six major cities, 64 district capitals, and 50 hamlets.

When the largest attacks first broke out, South Vietnam's President General Nguyen Van Thieu declared a nationwide state of martial law. He banned all public gatherings and demonstrations, instituted stricter censorship of newspapers and periodicals, and ordered closed all places of entertainment. In the same announcement in which he imposed martial law, Thieu also stated: "The general offensive attempt of the Communists has been completely foiled."[4] Thus, America's allies in Vietnam had dismissed the offensive as a failure the moment it began. The Johnson Administration reached the same premature conclusion. Because there had been no general uprising, the Administration proclaimed Tet a United States victory. "How ironic it is," Kennedy noted wryly in his first post-Tet address, "that we should claim a victory because a people whom we have given sixteen thousand lives, billions of dollars and almost a decade to defend, did not rise in arms against us."[5]

For most Americans who followed the war on television, it was the N.L.F. seizure of the United States Embassy in the heart of Saigon that was the single most spectacular event of the Tet Offensive. N.L.F. raiders on a suicide mission gunned down six American guards, and set up grenade launchers and large-caliber machine guns on the embassy grounds. They pinned down American Military Police (M.P.'s) for six-and-a-half hours with galling automatic weapons fire. Officials in Washington ordered the securing of the embassy the top priority. After a helicopter tried to land on the embassy roof to retrieve a wounded Marine only to be driven off by a hail of bullets, General William Westmoreland, the commander of all United States forces in Vietnam, decided to wait until dawn before attempting to retake the compound.[6]

Prime-time television news programs in the United States featured dramatic footage of American M.P.'s firing machine guns and grenade launchers at their own embassy. The decorative fish ponds and white concrete planters of the landscaped embassy grounds provided an idyllic backdrop for a bloody battle. The N.L.F. sappers were prepared to fight to the death, and the dramatic visuals were perfect for television. When the fighting finally subsided, the bloody, bullet-ridden corpses of fifteen N.L.F. guerrillas were strewn about the estate, their exhausted weapons lying by their sides.[7] The United States Embassy seal, proudly displaying the American eagle, lay blasted among debris at a bombed-out side entrance of the embassy. To some observers, the scene at the U.S. Embassy was an appropriate metaphor for the entire American war effort in Vietnam. Millions of Americans agreed with Eugene McCarthy, who said while campaigning in New Hampshire: "Only a few months ago we were told that 65 percent of the population was secure" in Vietnam. "Now we know that even the American Embassy is not secure."[8]

On the morning of January 31, 1968, when the earliest wire service reports of the Tet Offensive began trickling into the United States, Kennedy was in Washington, D.C., talking to a group of fifteen of the country's most influential political columnists. At the off-the-record National Press Club breakfast, Kennedy called the Vietnam War "one of the great disasters of all time for the United States."[9] Yet he also told the journalists that he would not oppose Johnson for the presidency in 1968 "under any conceivable circumstances."[10] When he made his final statement in the form of a press release, Frank Mankiewicz, in an effort to keep Kennedy's options open, prevailed upon him to change the word "conceivable" to "foreseeable."[11]

At the breakfast, Peter Lisagor of the *Chicago Daily News* handed Kennedy a fresh snippet of U.P.I. wire copy he had pulled from the teletype which reported the greatest enemy offensive of the war. The Senator skimmed the story, and muttered with a strong dose of irony, "Yeah, we're winning."[12] The next day, the *New York Times* praised Kennedy for placing "prudence . . . over passion. Those admirers who expected Senator Kennedy to lead an anti-Vietnam crusade within the Democratic party regardless of the personal cost misread their man. . . . When it comes to crucial decisions of politics and career, [Kennedy] remains an old pro."[13]

Kennedy's latest public endorsement of Johnson's reelection, on the opening day of the Tet Offensive, might have impressed Washington political commentators, but it eroded his stature in the eyes of the war's opponents. He rapidly lost support among the peace forces while McCarthy gained. As Kennedy attempted to differentiate between courage and self-destruction, some of his most talented staffers began drifting toward the McCarthy campaign. His key Vietnam speech writer, Adam Walinsky, considered giving notice shortly after Tet so that he could work full time against Johnson. Joseph Dolan, Kennedy's key political operative, along with his legislative aide Peter Edelman, spoke of requesting sabbatical leaves for the duration of the 1968 campaign.

Mankiewicz decided to bide his time and wait for the "unforeseeable."[14] Kennedy's most skilled speech writer, Richard Goodwin, departed in mid-February to become a pivotal force in McCarthy's New Hampshire primary campaign. Kennedy, who had been Allard Lowenstein's first choice to head the effort to unseat Johnson, now watched peace activists rally to a rival candidate who was even attracting members of his own staff. McCarthy ran away with Kennedy's once sizable youth constituency, and it was uncertain if he could ever get it back.

For weeks, General Westmoreland's forces faced guerrilla warfare in Saigon and other cities of South Vietnam. In a television broadcast, General Thieu urged his armed forces to "act ruthlessly" in clearing out the N.L.F. from occupied urban centers; they did not disappoint him.[15] American Marines battled ferociously to retake the citadel of the city of Hue, and provided some of the most lasting images of the entire war. The lavish use of American firepower, designed to keep U.S. casualties low, cost at least 8,000 civilian lives, and made refugees out of most of the city's 135,000 residents.[16]

The Americans and their South Vietnamese allies eventually succeeded in recapturing all of the cities lost during Tet. There were nearly 4,000 American soldiers killed in nine weeks of heavy fighting, and more than 14,000 wounded, the largest number of Americans killed in Vietnam in so short a period.[17] Saigon troops also suffered high casualties. In the months following Tet, retribution against the N.L.F. took a heavy toll. Everywhere in South Vietnam, many of the most able and experienced N.L.F. cadres, administrators, and combat leaders had exposed themselves, and were hunted down and killed or taken prisoner by the end of 1968.[18] The North Vietnamese government privately acknowledged that the offensive failed in its military objectives; but it succeeded in transforming the political landscape of South Vietnam.[19]

It was the "success" of the "post-Tet accelerated pacification program" which led the Johnson Administration to declare Tet an American military victory. However, the U.S. military's counteroffensive left destruction in its wake, including the massacre at My Lai and the creation of hundreds of thousands of new refugees. It caused greater political instability for General Thieu, and demonstrated that the war was far from over. Despite the Administration's praise for the performance of the A.R.V.N., its losses were the smallest proportionately among the major combatants.[20] While A.R.V.N.

casualty rates remained static in the months following Tet, American casualties increased by 500 percent.[21] After Tet it became clear who did most of the fighting for the Thieu regime.

In places like Hue in the north, Can Tho, My Tho, and Ben Tre in the Delta, and the Cholon and Nhonxa sections of Saigon, American firepower pounded into rubble rows and rows of homes and small businesses. For the United States and its allies these were Pyrrhic victories. The generous application of American bombing and shelling bred resentment among the civilian population, thereby further weakening the already tenuous political legitimacy of the South Vietnamese government. "The widespread use of artillery and air power in the centers of cities may hurt us far more in the long run than it helps today," Kennedy warned.[22]

One incident of the Tet Offensive that Kennedy condemned was Brigadier General Nguyen Ngoc Loan's summary execution of a suspected N.L.F. guerrilla. An NBC camera crew filmed General Loan, the Chief of the National Police of South Vietnam, as he casually drew his snub-nosed revolver, placed it to the right temple of his hapless, grimacing victim, and quickly squeezed the trigger.[23] While Loan reholstered his pistol, the barefoot young man, hands bound behind his back, recoiled from the bullet, and slowly collapsed backwards onto the pavement. Associated Press photojournalist Eddie Adams tripped the shutter of his camera just as Loan pulled the trigger; he captured a sequence of photographs of the macabre spectacle, and along with it a Pulitzer Prize.[24]

On February 3, 1968, about twenty million American television viewers watched General Loan's curbside execution on the *Huntley-Brinkley Report*.[25] This act seemed a stunning testimony to the brutality of the United States' allies in South Vietnam. Kennedy asked the State Department to clarify its position on the General Loan incident. The Assistant Secretary of State for Congressional Relations, William Macomber, Jr., wrote back, "General Loan has said that to his certain knowledge the Viet Cong concerned had been personally responsible for the wanton killing of the families of South Vietnamese policemen and soldiers, and that he shot him in the heat of battle." Secretary Macomber tried to reassure Kennedy that the United States and the Government of South Vietnam both adhered to the relevant protocols of the Geneva Convention on the treatment of prisoners of war which explicitly forbid such executions.[26]

The Director of Central Intelligence, Richard Helms, also excused General Loan's cavalier killing of a prisoner of war. In a letter to Johnson, Helms wrote there was "ample historical precedent for giving summary justice to enemy soldiers working behind the lines on military missions in civilian clothes."[27] Neither Loan's widely-known corruption, nor his practice of shooting prisoners, tarnished his credibility in the eyes of Johnson's military chiefs.[28] General Earle Wheeler, the Chairman of the Joint Chiefs of Staff, suggested to a member of Congress that Loan's "act was performed more in a flash of outrage" than in cold blood.[29] Four days after Loan's nationally televised act of murder, in a meeting of the National Security Council, Wheeler called him a valued ally and intelligence source.[30]

Kennedy had been privately pursuing the release of P.O.W.'s on behalf of their family members since the beginning of 1966. He received an urgent telegram from a worried wife of an American prisoner of war in Vietnam who was concerned about the potential effects of Loan's atrocious behavior. "How can the United States allow public executions of the Viet Cong?" Gaylee Thorness of Sioux Falls, South Dakota asked. "My husband is a prisoner of war in North Viet Nam and I am concerned for his treatment. What has happened to Americans, do we no longer value the ideals that my brother died for in World War Two and we thought my husband fought for in this war? How can we condone these executions? I urge you to stop them. Is there any hope that peace negotiations can still be salvaged?"[31] The P.O.W.'s wife was justified in her concern; the N.L.F. had issued a stern warning following the Loan episode that "appropriate measures" would be taken if America's allies continued to execute prisoners.[32]

In his first speech after the Tet Offensive, Kennedy addressed the damaging effects of General Loan's brand of military "justice" on America's standing in the world : "Last week a Vietcong suspect was turned over to the Chief of the Vietnamese Security Services, who executed him on the spot—a flat violation of the Geneva Convention on the Rules of War. Of course, the enemy is brutal and cruel, and has done the same thing many times. But we are not fighting the Communists in order to become more like them—we fight to preserve our differences. . . . The photograph of the execution was on front pages all around the world—leading our best and oldest friends to ask, more in sorrow than in anger, what has happened to America?"[33]

Kennedy's outrage seemed more in accord with the public's revulsion over Loan's action than the Administration's self-serving apologetics. Surely, if a North Vietnamese equivalent of a General Loan had executed an American flier for participating in the killing of civilians from the air, the Administration would have denounced it as yet another example of the enemy's depravity.

Kennedy became reclusive while the Tet Offensive dominated the news. He made no public appearances, failed to attend committee meetings, and did not return phone calls. According to Jack Newfield, Kennedy "spent hours moping and pacing alone" in deep contemplation.[34] Holed up in his Senate office, he closely followed the offensive as it unfolded, and evaluated the Administration's spin on events. He drifted away from his pragmatic political advisers such as Dutton, Sorensen, and Edward Kennedy, all of whom advised him not to run in 1968, and moved closer to the younger firebrands around him, like Edelman and Walinsky, who called upon him to follow his conscience.

At this time Arthur Schlesinger tried to give Kennedy some gentle encouragement. "I know how hard these last weeks have been for you," he wrote, "I am sure that the decision you reached was the only one in the circumstances." He urged Kennedy to "go no further than you have in taking yourself out of things," because "given the uncertainty of events and fortunes these days, the situation may take a new turn by the spring and unconditional declarations of non-candidacy might be an embarrassment." Schlesinger made it clear that he was not "trying to open questions which have been settled." Yet he forwarded to Kennedy a statement from a graduate student at the City University of New York entitled "Reflections of a 22-Year Old on Senator Kennedy in January 1968." This short essay, which Schlesinger apparently believed represented the sentiments of many young people, poignantly implored Kennedy to run for president in 1968.[35]

The Tet Offensive confirmed Kennedy's worst fears about the Saigon regime. The killing of civilians and looting by U.S. allies was a discouraging sign. Long before Tet shattered the illusion of an imminent U.S. victory in Vietnam, influential peace groups, many of them linked to religious institutions, looked to Kennedy for leadership on the war. Organizations such as the Fellowship of Reconciliation, Clergy and Laity Concerned About Vietnam, and the American Friends Services Committee voiced their opposition to what they saw as an immoral war. These and other peace groups bombarded Kennedy's office with their mailings, and sent dozens of letters of support whenever he criticized Johnson's war policies. Kennedy paid close attention to the stirrings of the religious left, which he knew had wider influence in American society than its secular counterpart.

Kennedy's daily mail included obituaries of men killed in the war, and letters from clergy who were pained by the large number of funerals they were forced to perform. In Vietnam, the Catholic bishops had called for a peaceful settlement, and a significant cross-section of Catholics at the parish level in the United States were actively working for peace.[36] The Vietnamese Buddhist poet and leader Thich Nhat Hanh had achieved some success in bringing together Catholics and Buddhists inside Vietnam who opposed the United States intervention; Hanh had also met with Pope Paul VI.[37] The Pope himself had called for peace in Vietnam, and the war ran contrary to the progressive social gospel of Vatican II. Kennedy, who was known as a devout Catholic, could not help but be moved by these appeals from persuasive sources.

In addition to religious groups, secular antiwar organizations such as the newly formed Vietnam Veterans Against the War (VVAW), the Committee for a Sane Nuclear Policy (SANE), and the Women's Strike for Peace also sent their materials to Kennedy, and asked him for guidance and support.[38] In January 1968, courageous individuals whom the Senator greatly admired such as Martin Luther King, Jr., César Chávez, Benjamin Spock, John Kenneth Galbraith, and Allard Lowenstein were all active opponents of the war. Kennedy had been highly critical of the Administration's Vietnam policy since the earliest escalations; now the Tet Offensive pushed him to take his opposition to a higher level.

From the Americans serving in the military in Vietnam, Kennedy received dozens of letters. Judging from the overall tone of the correspondence just after Tet, the soldiers who wrote Kennedy were not flushed with optimism after their victories in the field. They generally sound somber, angry, and disappointed with their government for placing them in such a confusing wartime environment. "Grunts" and officers alike decried the level of corruption among their South Vietnamese allies, and complained bitterly about the A.R.V.N.'s lack of motivation to fight. Many of them confessed their own misdeeds or wrote of atrocities committed by their fellow Americans. Kennedy received a relatively small number of letters from American servicemen who supported the war, but many of them also expressed discontent with Johnson's policies.[39]

Some of these letters from Vietnam represented commonly held sentiments. An Army medical officer, Michael Orr, was so disgusted with what he saw in Vietnam that he sent Kennedy all of his medals and outstanding service decorations "in hope some day" he would "give them back to L.B.J."[40]

"Most of us know we are not being told, or ever have been told the truth about Viet Nam. Mr. Kennedy, I know you can't stop the war in one day," the Army medic concluded, "but I do know you will work for the good of the people, not for the good of L.B.J. as L.B.J. himself is doing today."[41] Letters such as these confirmed the level of bitterness many servicemen had come to feel toward their commander in chief. The fact that they chose Kennedy to confide in reflects his role as a trusted advocate of peace.

Richard Klingenhogen, a recent Vietnam veteran who put in his year of service as the "Chief Computor" for an artillery battery, wrote Kennedy: "As I see it, the South Vietnamese people are primarily interested in our money and goods. They steal everything they can get their hands on and resale [sic] it to the G.I.'s at black market prices in their villages." About the progress of the war, the former artillery man wrote: "No place in Viet Nam was ever really secure. We were just 45 miles directly north of Saigon, and it wasn't once that we didn't lose a few A.P.C.'s [Armored Personnel Carriers], men, or tanks when we ran a convoy to Saigon for ammo and supplies." As for the performance of the South Vietnamese soldiers, the veteran continued: "The local ARVN troops are very poor. One night we accidentally landed three eight inch rounds no more than 150 to 200 meters from an ARVN outpost, and they never even heard them explode." "Something has to be done soon," he went on, "for too many Americans are losing their lives and not knowing why."[42]

In the early days of the Tet Offensive, Gabriel Mannheim, a U.S. Army Specialist 4, wrote Kennedy from Vietnam: "One can very easily identify the places where the Army has been, because the only thing we leave behind us is dust and mud. We kill everything that was living on the land prior to our occupation. I realize that is the price of war. . . . Most of us count the days we have left, before we go home, and every day is one closer to home. When a soldier goes out on a mission he is happiest if he does not make contact with the enemy. He is out there on two missions, one is that which was told him by the officer in charge, the other is his own, which is to stay alive. And the latter one is more important to him. This is in direct contradiction to our previous wars, where every mission brought the war closer to its end."[43]

The Tet Offensive clearly illustrated to American fighting men in the field that the United States was in for a long and tough struggle. Those who witnessed first-hand the attacks, as well as the woefully inadequate response of most A.R.V.N. units, disagreed with the Administration's contention that the enemy had suffered a defeat. Had Tet truly been a U.S. victory, one might expect an echo of measured optimism among American troops in Vietnam. Instead, there is only despair.

One letter Kennedy received during his post-Tet period of introspection was intimately connected to the offensive. A veterinarian from the town of Delevan in upstate New York forwarded Kennedy a letter that his younger brother had written him from Vietnam about a week before Tet. The brother, Warrant Officer Dwight Arthur Dedrick, was a 22-year-old helicopter pilot. On January 31, 1968, the first day of the attacks, Dedrick was shot down and killed near Hue; he was one of the early American victims of the offensive. "The war is not going very well and I just can't understand it," the young man wrote six days before his death. "I think too many people have a great misconception of the war and the wealth of the U.S. . . . . I don't think the people back home realize that the U.S. is capable of losing because they have never tasted defeat before, but, believe me, if things don't change and change soon, we are going to get our backs broke."[44]

Elsewhere in the letter Dedrick wrote, "The NVA [North Vietnamese Army] have moved tanks into the Khe Sanh area, can you imagine, damn tanks. I just know that they don't let stuff like that get back to the States and I don't know why." Young officer Dedrick's last letter home reflected the malaise that engulfed a large number of American servicemen in Vietnam in early 1968. Since the letter was forwarded by the brother of the deceased soldier, it also could have been a painful reminder to Kennedy of family bonds that can be violently severed in an instant.

Kennedy responded personally to an American officer who had written him shortly after Tet; their exchange stands out as a poignant link between the death of President John Kennedy and the war in Vietnam. On November 25, 1963, Marine Corps Captain Samuel Bird of Wichita, Kansas, had been the commander of the military pallbearers at President Kennedy's funeral. About eighteen months later he was sent to Vietnam. On his birthday, January 27, 1966, the day before he was to be transferred out of combat, Captain Bird was severely wounded, and became paralyzed. He sent Kennedy a Christmas card in December 1967; attached to it was a Polaroid snapshot of the young officer, his life irrevocably altered by the war. The photograph shows Captain Bird sitting in the backyard of his parents' modest suburban home; mounds of snow and ice are seen in the background. Dressed smartly in his Marine Corps Blues, the disabled captain smiles proudly for the camera, medals on his chest, his thin limbs delicately draping his wheelchair.

"I hope you are coming along well," Kennedy wished the young officer in a handwritten note. "I was delighted to hear you were able to go home for Christmas."[45] The picture was a testimony to the war's waste of America's most precious asset: the courage and self-sacrifice of its young men.[46]

While the Tet Offensive exposed on the nightly news the underlying myths of the war, Kennedy contemplated his role in national affairs. The enemy offensive, and the Administration's response to it, made it clear that he could not support Johnson's reelection. The President had campaigned for Kennedy in New York in 1964 when he ran for the Senate, and Johnson would undoubtedly expect him to return the favor in 1968. This he could not do. McCarthy's campaign gained momentum from the events in Vietnam, and pulled the antiwar forces further away from Kennedy. At some point during this period of intense self-reflection, Kennedy realized the time had come for him to run for president of the United States.

The Tet Offensive unraveled the bipartisan consensus on waging the war, and exacerbated the divisions within Johnson's foreign policy inner circle. Most Republicans remained committed hawks; Senator John Tower of Texas dismissed the offensive as the "death rattle" of an already defeated foe.[47] Others, however, began reconsidering their support. The Republican senator from South Dakota, Karl Mundt, a ranking member of the Foreign Relations Committee, had been a strong supporter of the war. But after he heard Secretary of State Dean Rusk portray Tet as a U.S. victory on *Meet the Press*, the conservative senator started to waver.[48] Other hard-line senators, such as John Stennis of Mississippi and Henry "Scoop" Jackson of Washington, both of the Armed Services Committee, began for the first time to see the limitations of a policy that insisted on pursuing a military victory.[49]

Tet confirmed the long-held suspicions of Senator J. William Fulbright, the chairman of the Foreign Relations Committee, about the Administration's public deceit concerning the true nature of the war. Fulbright sent a letter on behalf of the committee to Secretary of Defense Robert McNamara asking him some very tough questions.[50] Other committee members, such as Senate Majority Leader Mike Mansfield of Wyoming, Frank Church of Idaho, and Eugene McCarthy looked forward to formally questioning Secretary of State Rusk and other senior officials.[51]

President Johnson viewed the Tet attacks as part of a coordinated challenge on the part of the Communists. He was deeply concerned about the possibility of a Dien Bien Phu style defeat at the United States Marine base at Khe Sanh. He saw the Tet Offensive as directly related to the increase in skirmishes along the border between North and South Korea, and the North Korean's seizure of the U.S.S. *Pueblo*.[52] Johnson also became increasingly suspicious of the press, and of his domestic opponents both in Congress and in the wider society.[53] "There seems to be a great effort to discredit this government and its military establishment," he told his foreign policy advisers in early February.[54] He warned Congressional leaders about "sympathizers and 'agents of the enemy' in this country working against us."[55]

From the moment the offensive began, Johnson entertained the notion that it was the American news media, with their unbalanced reporting, which plucked defeat from the jaws of victory for the United States. The day the offensive began he blamed the press for souring the public's impression of the war, even though only a week earlier he had praised it for its balance.[56] "You won't hear much in the press about how bad the enemy's bombing in Saigon was last night," Johnson bitterly complained during a meeting with Congressional leaders. "All we hear about is how bad our bombing is." "Measure your statements before you make them," he cautioned, because "the greatest source of Communist propaganda . . . is our own statements."[57]

Johnson disparaged what he believed to be the public's misperception about Tet, telling his foreign policy planners: "I do not share the view that many people have that we took a great defeat. Our version is not being put to the American people properly."[58] Yet it was precisely the flaws in the Administration's public explanation of Tet that the news media could not ignore. The media were simply reflecting the Administration's own obfuscations about the state of the war, and the contradictions between its portrayal of events in Vietnam and what was really happening on the ground.[59]

In his first formal press conference following the Tet attacks, Johnson used a familiar tactic: he implied that most Americans would agree with his view of Tet if they had access to White House intelligence information, which naturally had to remain secret due to "national security." The enemy offensive, he said, was "just like when we have a riot in a town or when we have a very serious strike, or bridges go out, or lights—power failures and things." He continued: "They have disrupted services. A few bandits can do that in any city in the land. . . . I think we know that the march on the Pentagon can tie up things here. I think we can see what happened in Detroit. I think we can see what happened in Saigon. . . . The fact that people's morale may be suffering, and they may be having difficulty doesn't keep them from breaking glass windows or shooting folks in a store or trying to assassinate somebody. That goes with it. That is part of the pattern."[60]

Given his apparent commitment to a military victory in Vietnam, Johnson had little choice but to attempt to diminish the significance of the offensive. In the process, he drew disturbing parallels between a peace demonstration in Washington, D.C. in October 1967, the riots in Detroit's black neighborhoods of July 1967, and the largest Communist offensive of the Vietnam War. In mid-February, Johnson sought political refuge in the military, telling servicemen at a breakfast aboard the U.S.S. *Constellation*: "You fellows have acted so marvelously to it all while others have thrown themselves down in the streets. You belong to a big group—an honored group. Nobody likes to go to war, or die; everybody is scared to die."[61]

Privately, Johnson's military chiefs reported that the Army of the Republic of Vietnam had been "mauled," and that the United States had to act promptly to prevent the A.R.V.N. from falling apart. General Wheeler expected that the American and South Vietnamese armed forces would be in what he called an "emergency situation" for at least three months following Tet.[62] He also questioned whether the G.V.N. [Government of South Vietnam] was strong enough to stand up to another wave of attacks.[63] Secretary of State Rusk wondered aloud at one foreign policy gathering whether the A.R.V.N. might not require as much as six months to "get back in shape" following Tet.[64] These concerns were in marked contrast to the Administration's public claim that Tet had been an unmitigated U.S.-South Vietnamese victory.

While South Vietnam's cities exploded in heavy fighting, Kennedy's close friend Secretary of Defense McNamara appeared before Congress. He insisted that his computerized "hamlet evaluation system" had determined that "67 percent of the people of South Vietnam live under allied military protection and some form of continuing G.V.N. administration." He also contended the U.S. was succeeding in "ferreting out the hidden Vietcong infrastructure," and there had been "encouraging progress" in the "political arena" as well.[65]

But despite the quantitative data that Defense Department computers spit out for public consumption, McNamara knew the armed forces of South Vietnam had taken a beating during Tet. At a meeting of the Joint Chiefs shortly after the offensive began, McNamara had suggested moving American troops into rear areas in South Vietnam so they could prod the A.R.V.N. into fighting more aggressively; then they might begin to reclaim the countryside. This suggestion sparked a terse reply from Army Chief of Staff General Harold Johnson, who said: "Mr. Secretary, there are no rear areas in Vietnam anymore."[66] President Johnson decided to send General Wheeler to Vietnam, where he could meet with General Westmoreland, assess the situation, and try to make sense out of "Westy's" highly ambiguous troop requests that were then trickling into Washington in the form of confusing and seemingly contradictory cables.

Both the Director of Central Intelligence Richard Helms and the hardline Deputy Defense Secretary Paul Nitze believed the A.R.V.N. had developed a serious problem with desertions after Tet. Wheeler flatly denied this charge upon his return from Vietnam: "there were no A.R.V.N. desertions," he declared unequivocally.[67] C.I.A. Director Helms was concerned not only about desertions, but with "defections" of soldiers from the ranks of the South Vietnamese armed forces to the enemy. The C.I.A. predicted an increase in defections because, Helms said, "the Viet Cong and North Vietnamese have treated the people in the countryside rather decently." The United States therefore had to be ready to "confront the possibility of desertions" from the A.R.V.N. to the N.L.F.[68] Helms's private suggestion contradicted the military as well as the Administration's public stance. There were also serious disputes between the C.I.A. and the Pentagon over the numerical estimates of enemy strength. Helms questioned the Joint Chiefs' optimistic numbers after Tet: "I am not sure how accurate they are," he cautioned, "I worry about those figures on casualties and enemy strength being used."[69]

In the weeks after Tet, Clark Clifford, whom Johnson was bringing in to replace Robert McNamara as Secretary of Defense, increasingly became the voice of reason among Johnson's foreign policy planners. He quickly reached the conclusion that there had been serious intelligence failures prior to the Tet attacks. "Our people were surprised by the twenty-four attacks on the cities," he said at a meeting of the President's Senior Foreign Affairs Advisory Council. "God knows the South Vietnamese were surprised with half their men on holiday." Clifford continued: "On the one hand, the military has said we had quite a victory out there last week. On the other hand, they now say that it was such a big victory that we need 120,000 more men."[70] Just four days earlier, Johnson had fumed at Senator Robert Byrd of West Virginia when he suggested there had been flaws in American intelligence prior to the attacks.[71]

General Wheeler promoted a plan that would modify the existing restrictions, imposed by Johnson and civilian defense officials, on the bombing of Hanoi, Haiphong, and other cities in North Vietnam. Johnson had resisted bombing population centers in the past; now Wheeler attempted to use the crisis of Tet to push through changes in U.S. bombing policy that proponents of an unrestrained air war had long advocated.[72] Wheeler expressed his frustration that the bombing of North Vietnam had never produced the United States' maximal military goal: the end of North Vietnamese support for the insurgency in the South. Nor did the bombing successfully interdict the flow of arms, men, and supplies from North Vietnam to the forces fighting the United States in the South. In what would become a recurring theme during the war policy debates among Johnson's advisers after Tet, Wheeler denounced the atrocities of the enemy while in effect planning his own. Tet had sparked an internal debate among Johnson's advisers that laid bare the contradictions of U.S. policy; had this debate been carried out publicly, it would have added strength to Kennedy's February 8, 1968 speech in which he interpreted the offensive as a total disaster for the U.S. war effort.

* * *

The military and political effects inside South Vietnam of the Tet Offensive widened the gap between Johnson's civilian and military advisers.[73] Departing Secretary of Defense McNamara grew more skeptical of the capabilities of the A.R.V.N., and of the competence of the Saigon government. General Wheeler called for loosening the existing restraints on the air war, which he knew would lead to increases in civilian casualties.[74] National Security Adviser Walt Rostow, the most dedicated hawk among Johnson's civilian advisers, advocated taking advantage of the enemy's apparent exposure with Tet by invading North Vietnam[75] (a half-witted notion given the fact the U.S. and its allies could not even hold most of the territory in the South). Secretary of State Rusk was in the unenviable position of having to go before the Fulbright Committee and sell to an increasingly skeptical Congress the idea that Tet was indeed an American victory. Incoming Secretary of Defense Clifford would say later that the pressure became so intense between Johnson and his advisers during the sixty days following Tet that he felt the government itself might come apart at the seams.[76]

Kennedy understood that Tet was in no way a "victory" for the United States. Postwar revisionism aside,[77] the success or failure of the United States' war effort in Vietnam depended upon the political viability, even popularity, of the Republic of South Vietnam's governing institutions and leaders. Tet severely weakened the Saigon regime's ability to legitimately govern. Compartmentalizing the war into separate "military" and "political" categories might have been useful to the technocrats inside the Defense Department, but it was an artificial distinction inside Vietnam. Kennedy would speak about this discrepancy in his comprehensive post-Tet assessment. For the Tet Offensive pushed Kennedy into taking on his role as the national leader of the peace Democrats. As the nation grappled with the limitations of American power in Southeast Asia, Kennedy prepared to make his final break with Johnson and the party leadership.

6 The Breaking Point: Kennedy Responds to Tet, February 8, 1968

> No war has ever demanded more bravery from our people and our Government—not just the bravery under fire or the bravery to make sacrifices—but the bravery to discard the comfort of illusion, to do away with false hopes and alluring promises.
>
> —Robert F. Kennedy, Chicago, February 8, 1968

Eight days after the Tet Offensive began, Kennedy spelled out its significance in a speech that stands out as one of the most eloquent indictments of the Vietnam War given by any public figure of the 1960s.[1] It was Kennedy's first major Vietnam address since March 2, 1967 and his words reached a wide audience. The speech marked Kennedy's final break with Johnson, and freed him from the obligations of party loyalty which shackled him to the prowar Democratic leadership. All of Kennedy's subsequent speeches on Vietnam, with varying nuance and emphasis, restated the major conclusions of his post-Tet analysis.

Kennedy's assessment of Tet combined deep concern for the lives and safety of American combat troops in Vietnam with an unequivocal denunciation of the war. Like the major spokespersons of the peace movement, he argued that the best way to end American casualties in Southeast Asia was to end the war. However, unlike many elements within the antiwar movement, Kennedy refrained from challenging the dominant national symbols of patriotic duty, as well as the central tenets of the Cold War. In doing so he attempted to shield himself from the attacks of prowar commentators who already questioned his "loyalty." The framing of Kennedy's post-Tet address gave it the potential to resonate loudly with a cross-section of Americans.

Kennedy's prescription for peace was consistent with the Administration's stated foreign policy goals of spreading democracy and countering adventurism. More importantly, he injected into the language of dissent a strong dose of patriotism. At a time when the louder elements of the antiwar movement and the New Left openly called for a National Liberation Front victory, Kennedy's critique embraced the left's goal of ending the war but stayed within mainstream ideological parameters. He and other Democratic doves recognized that in opposing U.S. Vietnam policy they would have to remain critical of the Soviet Union and China to be taken seriously by a majority of Americans.[2] Kennedy sensed in the weeks following Tet that the broad middle class was turning against the war, and he helped push it along. The New Left criticized him for stopping short of rejecting the Cold War and for failing to denounce U.S. imperialism, but his analysis of the war registered with a much wider audience as a result.[3] Kennedy's blueprint for disengagement from Southeast Asia, unlike that of the New Left, could appeal to political and foreign policy elites.[4]

Kennedy stated clearly that if the regime of Nguyen Van Thieu and Nguyen Cao Ky ultimately fell as a result of the Tet attacks or after an American troop withdrawal, there would be no love lost on his part. This stand contrasted markedly with the views of President Johnson and Vice President Humphrey, whose commitment to the South Vietnamese junta remained so solid that both leaders constantly apologized to the public for its ineptitude, corruption, and brutality. Kennedy's unequivocal denunciation of the Saigon government was forceful and straightforward; those who held to the belief that his disagreement with the Administration rested solely on tactical grounds were grossly mistaken.[5]

In early January 1968, prior to the Tet Offensive, Edward Kennedy had traveled to South Vietnam as the chairman of the Senate Judiciary Committee's Subcommittee on Refugees and Escapees. The Massachusetts senator returned with new evidence of widespread corruption within the Saigon government and the refugee relief agencies it administered. Upon his return from Vietnam, Edward briefed his brother fully, and confirmed Robert's long-held suspicions about the Thieu regime.[6] Edward Kennedy's trip to Vietnam and his subsequent report sparked great concern among Johnson's Southeast Asia specialists both in Saigon and Washington, who immediately produced an orchestrated "refutation" of his findings.[7] This first-hand account from Vietnam by the Kennedy from Massachusetts brought his and his brother's opposition to the war to a new level. Robert Kennedy picked up some of the themes of his brother's report in his own post-Tet assessment.

The significance of Edward Kennedy's trip to Vietnam was threefold: first, it marked a turning point in both his and Robert Kennedy's relations with the Administration and the prowar Democratic leadership; second, it widened the debate over the existing United States military strategy in Vietnam, with its high toll in civilian destruction, which the peace movement had been publicizing for years; and third, it shone a media spotlight on the regime's corruption and the plight of ordinary Vietnamese, thereby strengthening the position of those who opposed the war on moral grounds.

Neither the Johnson forces nor the political press allowed Robert Kennedy to voice his dissent free of speculation about his ulterior political motives. The constant discussion in the media about Kennedy's presidential ambitions, his rivalry with Johnson, and his role as the unofficial heir to President Kennedy's legacy all combined to produce an air of anticipation for his post-Tet address.

Kennedy's February 8, 1968, appearance at the annual Book and Author luncheon in Chicago had been scheduled to promote *To Seek A Newer World*, and for purely political reasons he had planned to speak on a subject other than Vietnam.[8] But four days before the luncheon he decided to speak instead on the Tet Offensive. "Johnson can't get away with saying it was really a victory for us," Kennedy told Walinsky.[9] It would be the kind of antiwar speech that Walinsky and Goodwin had been readying themselves for over a year to write for the Senator. He gave them the green light, and they seized upon the Chicago forum to express their deep revulsion to the war. Walinsky quickly worked up a draft, and he and Goodwin polished it together.[10]

Kennedy reviewed two alternative versions of the speech, and without exception chose to retain those paragraphs which contained the most pointed criticisms of the Administration's war policies.[11] Kennedy's post-Tet address went far beyond his March 2, 1967 speech in attacking Johnson's position.[12] By combining support for the troops with a passionate appeal for coming to terms with the reality of the U.S. intervention, he attempted to extricate from the prowar forces their putative monopoly on "patriotic duty" in time of war. Kennedy, who made only minor revisions of the final draft, employed imagery reminiscent of the spirit of sacrifice that characterized the nation during World War II. He called on Americans' higher sense of national purpose, and challenged them to press their government to withdraw from the conflict. He displayed a remarkable faith in the ability of ordinary citizens to recognize and understand the bitter truth about the war, and to take action to force their government to change course.

On the morning of the luncheon, Kennedy met with Chicago Mayor Richard Daley, who was at the time the most powerful municipal politician in the Democratic Party. The Irish Catholic Mayor's political base in Chicago—mainly white working-class people of diverse ethnic origins—was similar to the Kennedys' bases in Boston and New York. Daley had been a good friend of Joseph Kennedy, the patriarch of the Kennedy clan, who in 1945 became one of Chicago's most influential landlords when he purchased the enormous Merchandise Mart.[13] Mayor Daley also had been a key supporter in John Kennedy's successful 1960 presidential campaign to the point of raising suspicions of vote-rigging in Cook County.[14] Daley not only had ironclad control over the Chicago patronage system and the Illinois Democratic delegation, his importance in national politics was augmented by the fact that he would host the 1968 Democratic National Convention that August. Powerfully affected by the death of a close friend's son in Vietnam, Daley watched uneasiness with the war grow among his core constituents. The Mayor welcomed Kennedy's decision to use his speaking engagement in Chicago to step up his criticisms of the war.[15]

Daley told Kennedy that he had tried to explain to Johnson that the war issue had become so damaging that he had little hope of being reelected unless he changed his policies.[16] Kennedy shared his belief with Daley that Johnson would remain committed to his course in Vietnam because the war had become a matter of honor to him, to which Daley replied: "There comes a time when you must put your honor in your back pocket and face realities."[17]

The morning Kennedy spoke in Chicago, newspapers reported that N.L.F. main force units and P.A.V.N. regulars had overrun a Marine base at Langvie, east of Khe Sanh; it was the first use of tanks in the war by the enemy. Large swaths of the Cholon district of Saigon were still engulfed in flames, and the suburbs to the south and west of the capital passed between A.R.V.N. control by day and N.L.F. control by night. Convoys of military vehicles bringing supplies to embattled American troops drove into cleverly deployed ambushes on every major road. American air strikes, napalm, and artillery pummeled the city of Hue into rubble, as television reporters clung to the belts of Marines who fought ferociously to reclaim ruins.[18]

"Our enemy savagely striking at will across all of South Vietnam," Kennedy opened his remarks, "has finally shattered the mask of official illusion with which we have concealed our true circumstances, even from ourselves." He dismissed the Administration's repeated claims that a U.S. military victory was in sight. "Those dreams are gone," he said. Although the "Vietcong will probably withdraw from the cities," the enemy had clearly demonstrated, in Kennedy's view, that "half a million American soldiers with 700,000 Vietnamese allies, with total command of the air, total command of the sea, backed by huge resources and the most modern weapons, are unable to secure even one city from the attacks of an enemy whose total strength is about 250,000."[19] "At one time," he added, alluding to calls for a change in U.S. military strategy, "a suggestion that we protect enclaves was derided. Now there are no protected enclaves."[20] The audience, which included Mayor Daley and his minions in the Chicago Democratic machine, sat enraptured as Kennedy's words grew in drama and intensity.

The first "illusion" Kennedy wished to dispel was "that the events of the past two weeks represent some sort of victory. This is not so," he said. Given that "thousands of men and arms were infiltrated into populated urban areas over a period of days, if not weeks" prior to Tet, and "few, if any, citizens rushed to inform their protectors of this massive infiltration," the Administration had "misconceived the nature of the war." By attempting "to solve by military might a conflict whose issue depends upon the will and conviction of the South Vietnamese people," Kennedy concluded, the United States had sown the seeds of its own failure in Vietnam.[21]

This last statement led Kennedy to the second illusion: "that we can win a war which the South Vietnamese cannot win for themselves." This idea was similar to a point Edward Kennedy had raised the month before, one which Administration officials condemned, when he emphasized the internal nature of the conflict, inseparable from Vietnam's history and politics.[22] Yet the "wise and certain counsel" that the United States could not fundamentally alter Vietnam's historical course, Robert Kennedy argued, had "gradually become an empty slogan, as mounting frustration led us to transform the war into an American military effort." Kennedy had questioned the Administration's moves to Americanize the war as far back as 1965; now he finally denounced the war outright.

Kennedy then turned to the corruption and ineptitude of the South Vietnamese government. Borrowing from his brother's refugee report, he singled out the rampant organized graft in Saigon as one of the key reasons behind the failure of the Thieu regime to win popular support. "Every detached observer," he said, "has testified to the enormous corruption which pervades every level of South Vietnamese official life." Hundreds of millions of dollars were being "stolen by private individuals and government officials," at the same time the American people were "being asked to pay higher taxes to finance our assistance effort." The tragic end product of the regime's criminality, Kennedy said, "is not simply the loss of money or of popular confidence; it is the loss of American lives." The notion that the United States wasted billions of tax dollars in Vietnam could reach a wide swath of American voters who might disagree with Kennedy on most other issues.

At several points in the speech Kennedy stressed the centrality of the political nature of the struggle in South Vietnam: "Political and economic reform are not simply idealistic slogans or noble goals to be postponed until the fighting is over," he said. "They are the principal weapons of battle." The U.S.-backed Saigon government failed miserably at winning the hearts and minds of the Vietnamese because "people will not fight to line the pockets of generals or swell the bank accounts of the wealthy." Kennedy forcefully took on the Administration's contention that the Republic of South Vietnam had a viable mass base: "We have an ally in name only. We support a government without supporters. Without the efforts of American arms that government would not last a day."[23]

The third illusion Kennedy countered was the belief that "the unswerving pursuit of military victory, whatever its cost" was "in the national interest of either ourselves or the people of Vietnam." For the Vietnamese, he said, "the last three years have meant little but horror." The country had been "devastated by a weight of bombs and shells greater than Nazi Germany knew in the Second World War," and "whole provinces have been substantially destroyed." He cut through the staid euphemisms of Johnson's technocrats that were designed to hide the human suffering wreaked by U.S. policy.[24]

The fourth illusion was "that the American national interest" was identical with "the selfish interest of an incompetent military regime." He assailed the Administration's public relations campaign to portray General Thieu as a freely elected democrat. He flatly rejected Johnson's claim that the United States had a vital interest in propping up Thieu as a defense against the spread of Asian Communism. The only thing the United States gained in the bargain, Kennedy argued, was a debilitating land war in Asia. "We are told," he said, "that the battle for South Vietnam is in reality a struggle for 250 million Asians"; however,

> the war in Vietnam does not promise the end of all threats to Asia and ultimately to the United States; rather, if we proceed on our present course, it promises only years and decades of further draining conflict on the mainland of Asia—conflict which, our finest military leaders have always warned, could lead us only to national tragedy.

Kennedy dismissed the "domino theory," which posited that if one nation fell to communism dozens of its neighbors must follow. The other Asian "dominoes," he said, faced no substantial threat from the collapse of the Thieu regime. Nor should U.S. prestige rest upon the success or failure of a corrupt military junta. This stand, consistent with the tenets of the Cold War while refuting the logic of falling dominoes, allowed Kennedy to reach a broad constituency, and perhaps even influence elite opinion.

Kennedy argued that United States interests would be best served by a policy of disengagement. The American promise to South Vietnam had been largely fulfilled:

> We have an interest in maintaining the strength of our commit-
> ments—and surely we have demonstrated that. With all the lives and
> resources we have poured into Vietnam, is there anyone to argue that
> a government with any support from its people, with any competence
> to rule, with any determination to defend itself, would not long ago
> have been victorious over any insurgent movement, however assisted
> from outside its borders?

As he did with the domino theory, Kennedy struck down the Administration's assertion that U.S. "credibility" in the eyes of the international community was at stake in Vietnam. From the time of his trip to Europe in February 1967, he had understood this was not the case. In fact, the opposite was true: the spectacle of U.S. military might in Southeast Asia was leading important allies to question U.S. motives in world affairs.

The fifth and final illusion which Kennedy addressed was Johnson's apparent belief that the United States possessed the power to "settle this war in our own way and in our time on our own terms." "Such a settlement," he said, "is the privilege of the triumphant; of those who crush their enemies in battle or wear away their will to fight. We have not done this, nor is there any prospect we will achieve such a victory." In Kennedy's view, the tenacity of those who fought against the United States, coupled with the corruption of the junta, had swept away any hope of a decisive U.S. military victory. The time for a peace settlement had arrived. The United States could no longer harden its terms "every time Hanoi indicates it may be prepared to negotiate."

In a conciliatory gesture, Kennedy went on to contextualize the conflict, making it clear that he was not placing the blame for the failures of the war solely on Johnson's shoulders. "For twenty years," he said,

> first the French and then the United States have been predicting victory in Vietnam. In 1961 and in 1962, as well as 1966 and 1967, we have been told that "the tide is turning"; "there is 'light at the end of the tunnel,'" "we can soon bring home the troops—victory is near—the enemy is tiring." Once, in 1962, I participated in such predictions myself. But for twenty years we have been wrong. The history of conflict among nations does not record another such lengthy and consistent chronicle of error. It is time to discard so proven a fallacy and face the reality that a military victory is not in sight, and that it probably will never come.[25]

By conceding that he had been a participant in the search for a military victory in Vietnam back in 1962, and by including 1961 and 1962 in his "chronicle of error," Kennedy proved his willingness to attest to his own role and the role of President Kennedy in meddling in Vietnam's internal affairs and laying the foundation for the war. As he had done in March 1967, Kennedy accepted his share of the blame, admitted his error, and then sought to correct it. It might have come too late to satisfy his critics, but Kennedy's mea culpa showed that, in contrast to Johnson, he believed stopping the war was more important than maintaining a facade of personal infallibility.[26] The admission made Kennedy more vulnerable to the constant charges from the war's supporters that his conversion from hawk to dove had been politically motivated.

Concluding his February 8 address, Kennedy reiterated his call for disengagement, and expressed a deep empathy with the American troops: "The best way to save our most precious stake in Vietnam—the lives of our soldiers—is to stop the enlargement of the war," and "the best way to end casualties is to end the war." He continued: "This is a great nation and a strong people. Any who seek to comfort rather than speak plainly, reassure rather than instruct, promise satisfaction rather than reveal frustration—they deny that greatness and drain that strength. For today as it was in the beginning, it is the truth that makes us free."[27] With that, Kennedy finished his remarks, and members of the press and his Democratic colleagues broke into sustained applause. Those present sensed that a burden had been lifted from Kennedy's shoulders; he had crossed the Rubicon by finally repudiating Johnson.

After reading a press release of Kennedy's speech, the influential Washington columnist and Kennedy family friend, Joseph Alsop, who had written countless articles supporting the Administration on Vietnam, left a message with Kennedy's secretary Angie Novello.[28] Alsop informed her that he had spoken to three important friends in the hours following Kennedy's address, "none of them particular friends of Lyndon Johnson," and each of them had told him that "after that speech they were compelled to regard Bobby Kennedy as a traitor to the United States."[29]

Later that afternoon, when excerpts of Kennedy's remarks appeared in every major newspaper, including a lengthy, sympathetic page-one analysis by Tom Wicker of the *New York Times*, President Johnson sent the following quotation from John Stuart Mill to Dean Rusk, Robert McNamara, Clark Clifford, and the Joint Chiefs of Staff:

War is an ugly thing, but not the ugliest: the decayed and degraded state of moral and patriotic feeling which thinks nothing worth war is worse. . . . A man who has nothing which he cares about more than his personal safety is a miserable creature who has no chance of being free, unless made and kept so by the exertions of better men than himself.[30]

The President might not have believed Kennedy exuded a decayed sense of patriotism, requiring the exertions of better men, but the rift between the two most powerful Democratic leaders had clearly entered a new phase after Kennedy publicly exposed the war's "illusions."[31] In their private correspondence with Johnson, White House aides openly referred to Kennedy's analysis of the war as "aiding the VC psychological offensive."[32]

Johnson ordered his staff to dig up newspaper clippings dating back to 1962 that quoted Kennedy's earlier hard-line views on Vietnam. He then had them passed along to sympathetic journalists who attacked Kennedy in print for being a hypocrite on the war.[33] Yet Kennedy had publicly admitted he had been wrong about Vietnam, something Johnson never brought himself to do.[34]

The first powerful Democrat to denounce publicly Kennedy's latest Vietnam criticisms was Johnson's close friend and confidant, Texas Governor John Connally. Connally blasted Kennedy at a Jefferson-Jackson Day Dem-

ocratic fundraiser in Atlanta. The New York senator's views had "a detrimental effect on the whole attitude of people in this country," he said, "and
[an] even more disastrous effect insofar as Ho Chi Minh and the Communist
world are concerned." Kennedy's "words and his actions have been a source
of discord in this country," Connally declared.[35]

The same day Kennedy's speech made headlines, White House Press
Secretary George Christian treated C.I.A. Director Richard Helms to a steak
lunch, and asked him on behalf of Johnson to write a response. After Tet,
debate about how to proceed in Vietnam had intensified among Johnson's
foreign policy advisers; the President wanted Helms's comments to counter
Kennedy, and to defend the Administration's upbeat interpretation. Helms
worked up a relatively polished draft that afternoon and sent it to the White
House. He argued that Kennedy's Chicago address contained "a minimum
of fact and a maximum of tone, attitude and innuendo." Using a precision
in dissecting text befitting a lawyer, Helms questioned the very definitions
of the words "victory" and "secure," and said Kennedy used "conjuring
tricks" to change the meaning of these words.[36]

Helms posited that since the Communists took "a very great gamble" by
launching the Tet Offensive in the first place, it made more sense to con-
clude that "Hanoi believed the long-term pre-Tet trends" were not running
in the Communists' favor. In Helms's view, the attacks themselves were
"perhaps the best testimonial to the over-all validity of our basic assessment
of what was happening in South Vietnam."[37] The Director of Central Intelligence tried to give the White House a counterargument to Kennedy's
devastating Chicago speech. Yet the best he could muster was to argue that
the enemy's ability to launch a country-wide offensive, holding dozens of
cities, in some cases for weeks, was in fact, a testimonial to the Administration's cheery declarations of U.S. military and political progress in South
Vietnam.

While the White House grasped at straws to refute Kennedy's post-Tet
critique of Vietnam policy, Kennedy received widespread support from
many members of Congress, religious and secular peace activists, scholars,
private citizens, and American servicemen in Vietnam. Pennsylvania Democratic Senator Joseph Clark read Kennedy's speech into the *Congressional
Record*. "The Nation is accustomed to viewing with a special significance
the comments of the junior senator from New York on Vietnam," Clark said,
and Kennedy's Chicago speech "justified those expectations."[38] Two days
after Kennedy spoke, Senator J. William Fulbright sent him a handwritten

note: "Your speech in Chicago was very effective, one of the best I have seen by anyone. I do believe the country is beginning to respond—is beginning to recognize the peril into which we have been led."[39]

A cofounder of the new antiwar group, Vietnam Veterans Against the War (V.V.A.W.), Carl Rogers, wrote Kennedy's aide Jeff Greenfield: "As an organization we are in complete agreement with the views expressed so strongly by Senator Kennedy" in Chicago.[40] Rogers also thanked Greenfield for the assistance of Kennedy's staff in helping the V.V.A.W.'s organizing efforts in Washington, D.C. Many other antiwar groups including Clergy and Laity Concerned About Vietnam, the Women's International League for Peace and Freedom, the Fellowship of Reconciliation, and the freshly assembled Business Executives Move for Vietnam Peace, stepped up their contacts with Kennedy's office in the weeks following his Tet speech.[41]

American servicemen in Vietnam as well as recent veterans of the fighting also wrote Kennedy offering their support; many of them urged him to run for president. "I appreciate what you are trying to do," wrote a recently retired Navy veteran who had spent ten months in Vietnam.[42] "I am deeply interested in your views of the current situation," wrote an American Marine whose tour of duty in Vietnam was to end in 45 days.[43] A U.S. Army private wrote Kennedy: "Your remarks were buetiful [sic]. Spoken like a true compatriot. I was too young to vote for your brother, I supported Johnson and was betrayed, I'm old enough to vote now. If you keep talking like that strong 'Kennedy' conviction, I will vote for you, and so will a great majority of 'The Boys.' Please Run."[44]

Another serviceman, Army Specialist John Allan, wrote Kennedy, "as an American presently on active duty in Vietnam, I wholeheartedly support your position and hope you maintain the courage and conviction to bring this message across to the American people. Our country needs your leadership badly." The soldier continued:

> Almost every night the men that live in the hutch I do end up debating the pros and cons of this senseless war. . . . It certainly is time we shattered the illusions of the present administration and let the South Vietnamese play a greater role in this war including participation by the Viet Cong in the political life of their country.
>
> As a Democrat I can not vote again for President Johnson and all the influence I can bring upon my friends, relatives, and others will be stated that way. Our efforts toward peace have not been great

enough nor has the President been willing to face the reality of real sound, constructive, negotiations. Senator Kennedy, this nation needs you—A Statesman.[45]

The letters to Kennedy from peace groups, active duty servicemen, and Vietnam veterans show that the lines of opposition had hardened after Tet. It became more difficult for the Administration to question the "patriotism" of its opponents (as Johnson often did),[46] especially when the criticism came from those who were doing the fighting. In his Chicago address, Kennedy dissented against the war in ideological terms intelligible to people across the political spectrum.

* * *

Kennedy's stature in American politics empowered him to indict the Administration's Vietnam policies at a time when prowar mouthpieces, Democrat and Republican alike, routinely called into question the loyalty of the war's opponents. Kennedy's words cut through the official fog of lies and deception which hid the true nature of the war. "Our nation must be told the truth about this war," he said, "in all its terrible reality, both because it is right—and because only in this way can any administration rally the public confidence and unity for the shadowed days which lie ahead."[47] Far from a reckless political exercise designed to foment discord, as Governor Connally claimed, Kennedy's call for peace attempted to come to terms with what he saw as a failed and misguided adventure in Southeast Asia. Had Kennedy remained silent after Tet, his acquiescence would have greatly strengthened the hand of Johnson and other prowar leaders who argued it was a U.S. military victory.

In his Chicago address, Kennedy called upon Americans' highest ideals while pointing to the harsh realities of the war. He asked the American people to accept the idea that the only truly courageous course for the United States in Vietnam was to get out. In contrast, former Vice-President Richard Nixon, who on the same day Kennedy spoke in Chicago announced he would seek the Republican presidential nomination, offered only deliberately vague and self-serving platitudes about the war.[48]

In the weeks following Kennedy's Chicago speech, the CBS News anchorman, Walter Cronkite, who had supported the war from the start, drew a conclusion similar to Kennedy's. On February 27, Cronkite said in a special report to an audience of millions: "The only rational way out . . . will be to negotiate, not as victors, but as honorable people who lived up to their pledge to defend democracy, and did the best they could."[49] Cronkite, like Kennedy, spoke a language that appealed to the middle class.[50] After viewing Cronkite's report, Johnson knew he had lost mainstream America on the war.[51] Some among Johnson's inner circle blamed the television networks for spreading "anti-U.S. propaganda."[52]

With his Tet address, Kennedy's contempt for General Nguyen Van Thieu and Air Vice Marshall Nguyen Cao Ky became crystal clear; he believed the United States had wasted too many lives propping up their regime. His stand was in marked contrast to the kid gloves with which Johnson treated the Saigon government. Understandably, the Republic of South Vietnam's permanent observer mission at the United Nations issued a shrill press release following Kennedy's Chicago address, bitterly denouncing his "irresponsible ignorance" of Vietnam.[53] Kennedy had rejected the legitimacy of the junta in Saigon, just as millions of Vietnamese and Americans had, and this furnished an opening for other politicians to reach the same conclusion without sounding overly defeatist or unpatriotic.[54] Kennedy was the most powerful national figure to draw a line against the Administration's efforts to put forth the most flattering image of the Thieu regime.

The thrust of Kennedy's latest appraisal of the war stripped him of the facade of supporting Johnson's reelection in 1968. He was the most powerful national figure to speak out so strongly against Johnson's Vietnam policies. More than any other politician, including McCarthy, Kennedy could divide the party to the point of vanquishing the Democrats' hopes for 1968. He had the ability to galvanize the peace forces into a far more formidable voting bloc than either McCarthy's primary campaigns or any single component of the antiwar movement. As a former Cabinet officer and presidential adviser, he also had the potential to influence elite policy opinion. His final break with Johnson might not have come early enough to satisfy his detractors from the New Left, but Kennedy strengthened and legitimized dissent.

In early 1968, a volatile moment had been reached in American politics and society. Tens of thousands of families from every corner of the country had sons in Vietnam.[55] Kennedy carefully combined a devastating critique of the war's "illusions" with strong support for the American servicemen. The antiwar movement often lacked this essential linkage. The patriotic nature of Kennedy's dissent on the war helped him reach a wide audience, while maintaining his ties to his core working-class constituency.

7 Fifteen Days in March: Kennedy Challenges Johnson, March 1968

These are not ordinary times and this is not an ordinary election. At stake is not simply the leadership of our party, and even our country, it is our right to the moral leadership of this planet.
— Robert F. Kennedy announcing his candidacy for the presidency, March 16, 1968

The weeks following Kennedy's February 8 speech witnessed a marked unraveling of the Democratic Party. The Johnson Administration's claim that the Tet Offensive was an American military victory worsened the President's credibility gap and galvanized opposition in dozens of Congressional districts. Kennedy no longer supported Johnson's reelection, but he hesitated to enter the presidential race himself. He reassessed his political strength as Eugene McCarthy's New Hampshire primary campaign gathered momentum, assisted by the skilled management of Richard Goodwin, who, disgusted at Johnson's Vietnam policy and fed up with Kennedy's indecisiveness, concluded he could do more to stop the war by assisting McCarthy; he joined McCarthy's campaign in mid-February.[1] Opposition to the war and Johnson's leadership had entered a new, critical phase, and crystallized among Democrats nationwide.

The Democratic Party not only experienced serious divisions over Vietnam, but also found itself torn between two seemingly irreconcilable factions: the organizational leadership, cemented in the Johnson Administration, of municipal machine bosses and high-ranking labor unionists on the one hand; and a profusion of grassroots community groups staffed by rank-and-file activists on the other. This intraparty struggle would decide the fate in national politics of the hundreds of newly formed citizen organizations of the 1960s.

In the years leading up to 1968, Kennedy had carefully cultivated favorable ties to federal, state, and local Democratic figures. His celebrity and family name had earned him a reputation as one of the party's most successful fund-raisers. Tickets sold briskly at his speaking events, and unlike appearances by Johnson and Humphrey, where the Democratic National Committee routinely claimed 50 percent of the proceeds, Kennedy allowed the local committees to keep the lion's share of the receipts.[2] Through his speaking engagements on behalf of Democratic candidates, Kennedy built up political patronage at the local level.

Starting in January 1968, Kennedy's key political operative, Joseph Dolan, had been quietly canvassing prominent Democratic politicians about Kennedy's possible entrance into those primaries in which Kennedy could become an eligible contender. Dolan contacted leaders in every section of the country, including the conservative South.[3] In February, he shifted from asking generic questions about one's political proclivities to asking far more concrete, technical questions about each state's often eccentric bylaws for selecting delegates, and quirks in primary eligibility. Dolan sought ways to ensure that the selection process remained fluid and noncommittal. The goal was simple: discourage as many Democratic delegates as possible from making ironclad endorsements of Johnson as the nominee.[4]

Occasionally Dolan relayed to Kennedy synopses of political advice he garnered in the course of his surveys. On March 10, 1968, two days before the New Hampshire primary, Dolan wrote Kennedy in a kind of shorthand that "friends" believed he should "wait another month or two. War is going worse. Johnson is so proud that when he sees McCarthy doing well and war deteriorating, he'll . . . keep his plans to himself till he gets to the Convention, then try to give it to Humphrey." Dolan speculated that a showing of 35 percent or better for McCarthy in New Hampshire, "could deliver a stunning upset, win some delegates, and move *your cause* forward substantially."[5] Whether McCarthy liked it or not, Dolan aimed to make use of his New Hampshire campaign as a "stalking horse" for Kennedy.

In the heat of the New Hampshire primary, the presidential adviser John Roche identified for Johnson the "three great assets" of the McCarthy dissidents: "inertia on the part of pro-Administration people" who viewed primaries as "trivial"; the "crusading zeal of the anti-war young"; and "the organizational talents of the Communists and the hemi-demi-semi-Communists who have been out of circulation (and making money) since Henry Wallace."[6] However, Roche's main worry was Kennedy. He proposed that Johnson press Kennedy for an endorsement by inviting him "with due respect and plenty of publicity" to a meeting of New York Democrats convened to prepare a pro-Administration delegate slate; Johnson agreed, and ordered Marvin Watson to "get it done."[7]

Texas Governor John Connally took on the task for Johnson of sounding out other Democratic governors. Connally's contacts on behalf of the President mirrored Dolan's efforts on behalf of Kennedy. The party was being probed by two powerful opposing forces. Anticipating Kennedy's entrance into the race, Connally sought to gauge the effects such a move might have on delegates to the Democratic National Convention. "If Bobby Kennedy gets into this," Missouri Governor Warren Hearnes warned Connally, "they will undermine you with your delegates. They will steal them or buy them."[8] The White House took steps to thwart efforts to field alternative delegate slates in the upcoming primaries in New York and other states. Reports trickled into the Oval Office that Kennedy had been handing out P.T.-109 tie clasps at his recent appearances, a gesture reminiscent of past campaigns by John Kennedy that was interpreted as a sign he would run.[9] Johnson loyalists speculated that Kennedy might soon ask McCarthy "if he wouldn't rather be Secretary of State than United States Senator."[10]

On January 25, 1968, McCarthy had chosen to open his New Hampshire campaign by appearing at the same location John Kennedy used in launching his 1960 presidential bid. In case anyone missed the symbolism, McCarthy stood next to a bust of President Kennedy, and effusively praised the fallen leader.[11] Old photographs of Senator McCarthy with President Kennedy permeated his campaign literature. The peace candidate's invocation of the memory of John Kennedy shows that for most people then the late President was still a source of inspiration, and not usually associated with laying the foundations for the Vietnam War.

Two days before the primary, the wire services reported that Robert Kennedy had given McCarthy's campaign "a late-hour lift," by indirectly upbraiding the Johnson forces for questioning McCarthy's loyalty. Kennedy denounced the Johnson campaign's radio and newspaper advertisements which stated that a McCarthy victory would be "greeted with cheers in Hanoi."[12] Other pro-Johnson radio spots attacked "peace-at-any-price fuzzy thinkers who say 'Give up the goal, burn your draft card and surrender.'"[13] Kennedy told an audience in Des Moines at a dinner honoring Iowa Governor Harold Hughes, who was running for the Senate, that McCarthy was "setting forth his honest views on what is best for our nation, just as President Johnson is carrying out policies which he believes are best for our nation.

The motives of neither should be impugned." He then paid McCarthy a high compliment by comparing the criticisms of the Minnesota senator to similar charges "made in 1960 against President Kennedy."[14]

Roche, who had rapidly risen to become President Johnson's resident intellectual, analyzed the political landscape: "Bobby Kennedy's latest flutter indicates to me the vital importance of locking-up delegates in the *non-primary* states," he wrote. "Bobby is playing a *convention* strategy," and now that "Goodwin is taking over as McCarthy's campaign manager," Kennedy's "crowd will help Gene" in the hope "enough votes can be picked up to block first-ballot nomination."[15]

The day New Hampshire voters went to the polls, Kennedy traveled to Delano, California, where he attended a Catholic service with United Farm Workers (U.F.W.) leader César Chávez. Chávez's health had been seriously weakened by his twenty-five-day hunger strike. Kennedy broke bread with Chávez, whose fast had been a moral appeal to friends and foes alike to refrain from violence in settling their differences in the midst of a long and bitter farm workers strike and boycott. It was clear to Chávez, and to many of his followers during the visit, that Kennedy had already decided to run.[16] In California, Kennedy also met with Democratic officials who had long been urging him to challenge Johnson, including the powerful Speaker of the Assembly, Jesse Unruh, who had prepared a tentative Kennedy delegate slate for the state's June 4 primary.

On March 12, 1968, McCarthy stunned Johnson and his political advisers in New Hampshire by capturing 42.2 percent of the Democratic vote to Johnson's 49.4 percent. An additional 5,511 Republican write-in votes for McCarthy meant that in the overall tally he trailed the President by a scant 230 votes.[17] Publicly, Johnson dismissed McCarthy's victory as "insignificant"; "New Hampshire is the only place," he scoffed on election night, "where candidates can claim 20 percent as a landslide, 40 percent as a mandate, and 60 percent as unanimous."[18] Despite his public nonchalance, Johnson ordered his staff to produce a detailed analysis of the New Hampshire vote, paying particular attention to his campaign's mistakes, and to the voting data on Catholics and organized labor.[19]

Presidential aide Fred Panzer, who wrote an assessment of the election, reported to Johnson that the "Hanoi is listening" slogan, which Kennedy criticized, had hurt his campaign. There also had been a "lack of leadership" of the pro-Administration forces. Panzer detected a Kennedy hand in New

Hampshire: "McCarthy's total has been heavily inflated by pro-Kennedy contingents," he wrote. "Since New Hampshire Democrats are heavily Irish Catholics," he reasoned, "they would tend to vote the Irish name and back the Kennedy choice."[20] Kennedy, of course, had not endorsed McCarthy.

After New Hampshire, Arthur Schlesinger, who had previously supported Kennedy's running in 1968, apparently changed his mind. He wrote Kennedy that since McCarthy had established himself "as the symbol of the opposition to Johnson and the war," Kennedy should avoid going against him in the primaries. If Kennedy jumped into the race after New Hampshire, Schlesinger argued, he would "appear a spoiler, trying to run off with Gene's marbles after he had the courage to open the game." One of Schlesinger's fears was that entering the race after McCarthy's New Hampshire triumph "would revive the theory" of Kennedy "as a ruthless political opportunist." On the other hand, Schlesinger wrote, "since it is McCarthy who has assumed the onus of party-splitting," the situation gave Kennedy freedom of maneuver. Schlesinger then offered the unrealistic advice that Kennedy stay out of the primaries but emerge at the convention "as the only hope" after McCarthy amassed enough anti-LBJ delegates.[21]

Kennedy paid scant attention to Schlesinger's middle-of-the-road approach. If he risked being labeled a spoiler by running in the remaining primaries after McCarthy's New Hampshire victory, then he surely would be labeled a super-spoiler if he waited to snatch up McCarthy's delegates at the convention. Kennedy understood that his only realistic course of action was to go head to head against Johnson in the remaining primaries. He would have to make acquiring delegates more difficult for the President in the hope of blocking a Johnson coronation at the Chicago convention.

The youthful volunteers for McCarthy, motivated by their strong desire for peace in Vietnam, proclaimed their candidate's victory a repudiation of the war. However, a well-publicized poll of New Hampshire voters conducted by Lou Harris showed that as many hawks as doves voted for McCarthy. Harris estimated that had the war been the central issue, McCarthy would have received only 22 percent of the vote. New Hampshire's Democratic voters were more anti-Johnson than antiwar. Moreover, McCarthy's appeal, in Harris's words, was primarily among the "egghead, affluent, suburban vote." In his syndicated column, Harris contrasted McCarthy's relatively limited New Hampshire constituency with Kennedy's broader national strength among lower income groups.[22]

Two days after the New Hampshire primary, Roche warned Johnson that he could not afford to play a passive role while the party split apart. "Your troops need a standard to rally around," he declared. "The longer you put off announcing your intentions for 1968, the worse the morale situation gets and the more the opportunists start canvassing their options."[23] Although Roche believed Johnson need not actively campaign—he pointed out that Franklin Roosevelt had not even gone to the convention in 1944—he wanted him to at least announce his intentions for reelection.[24] He goaded Johnson to seize the initiative and show strong leadership before Kennedy stepped forward.

In order to discern the level of pro-Kennedy sentiment, the White House systematically surveyed Democratic members of Congress, governors, and other party leaders. The results of the canvass on behalf of the President revealed that support for Johnson among Congressional representatives held, but just barely. Evidence surfaced that the fissures had widened, and that a tough intraparty battle was brewing. Party officials generally toed the Administration's line, but could not mask the emergent regional and ideological divisions.

Kennedy searched for a way to allow Johnson to heed the calls of the peace wing of the party and shift direction in Vietnam, without his having to challenge the president's nomination. Theodore Sorensen promoted this strategy. Sorensen had been one of President Kennedy's most trusted speech writers, ghost-writers, and political advisers, and he vehemently opposed Kennedy's running in 1968. After a quick evaluation of the delegate hunt, Sorensen concluded that an attempt to unseat Johnson not only would fail, but also snuff out the Democrats' hopes in the general election in November. There still remained the slim possibility that the party could overcome its divisions on the war, which had been confirmed by McCarthy's strong showing in New Hampshire, and reunite behind the President.

Sorensen wanted to try almost anything to dissuade Kennedy from entering a race which he viewed as far too politically dangerous. He hoped that forming a presidential commission on Vietnam comprised of personnel acceptable to both Johnson and Kennedy, and charged with redirecting United States policy, might salvage the situation. The commission idea, which Chicago Mayor Richard Daley first proposed to Kennedy in early February, might mollify dissident Democrats, Sorensen believed, and prevent Kennedy from running. Sorensen, with Daley's backing, prevailed upon

Kennedy to make a final effort at reconciliation with Johnson and the Democratic leadership before seeking the nomination himself.[25]

Mayor Daley saw the commission as a last-ditch effort to shore up party unity in a volatile election year. Out of respect for the Illinois power broker, Kennedy pursued the matter even though he had doubts about its success. He was in no position to ignore the wishes of a Democratic politician as powerful as Daley. Kennedy referred to Daley as "the ball game" if he were to enter the race, and understood that he had to demonstrate to the would-be kingmaker his willingness to go the extra mile before launching a campaign to unseat Johnson.

Senator Edward Kennedy had miraculously stayed on Johnson's good side (his work on the refugee subcommittee notwithstanding), and he was given the task of broaching the commission idea to Administration officials. On March 13, 1968, shortly after the evening news reports of McCarthy's impressive showing in New Hampshire, Edward Kennedy telephoned Secretary of Defense Clark Clifford at his home, and shared his brother's deep concern about Vietnam, as well as about Johnson's attitude toward the crisis in the cities. When he conveyed Robert's desire to discuss Vietnam with the Defense Secretary, Clifford made himself available the following day. There are conflicting versions of the confidential meeting on the morning of March 14 between Sorensen, Kennedy, and Clifford and the meeting later that day between Johnson and Clifford.[26]

The next morning, as Robert Kennedy and Sorensen were on their way to Clifford's Pentagon office for the eleven o'clock meeting, Kennedy kept asking, according to Sorensen, "How do I know that the announcement of a commission would really mean any change in policy?"[27] At the gathering, Clifford gave both Kennedy and Sorensen the distinct impression that he too favored a reevaluation of Vietnam policy. He also shared his belief that the situation would improve with respect to negotiations within the next five months.

According to Clifford's account, which he prepared for Johnson, Kennedy informed him that Daley, Sorensen, and his brother Edward had come up with a proposal. Sorensen then laid out the Daley commission idea, and gave Clifford a list of those who might serve. These were former Ambassador to Japan Edwin Reischauer, Yale President Kingman Brewster, Defense Department official Roswell Gilpatrick, former aide to President Kennedy Carl Kaysen, Senators Mike Mansfield, John Sherman Cooper, and George Aiken, and Generals Lauris Norstad and Matthew Ridgeway.[28]

Clifford quickly changed the subject to politics, and outlined to Kennedy the pitfalls of trying to take the nomination from Johnson. He described the Truman campaign twenty years earlier when Truman, like Johnson, seemed to have been deserted by a large segment of his own party, only to come back and win the election. Clifford said, according to the account he prepared for Johnson, that he believed the possibility of Kennedy's defeating the President for the nomination was zero. He also warned Kennedy that he was "making a grave mistake if he assumed that the situation in Vietnam would be the same in August of this year as it is now."[29] Johnson could end the war at any time, and pull the rug out from under his opponents. The Secretary of Defense told Kennedy that "a number of factors" would "remain under the President's control, such as the decision as to when to start negotiations." Clifford cautioned Kennedy that he "would be grievously disappointed as events transpired in the next five months." He plainly hinted that the Administration was already in the process of reevaluating the United States position, with or without a special commission. Kennedy said he had considered these elements, but "still felt he would have to run unless President Johnson would agree" to appoint the commission.[30]

Later that afternoon, Johnson summoned Clifford to the White House, where he mulled over the Daley proposal with two of his closest political advisers, Supreme Court Justice Abe Fortas and Vice President Hubert Humphrey. When the Secretary of Defense arrived, they discussed the matter at length, and formulated several reasons for rejecting outright the commission plan. Johnson instructed Clifford to call Sorensen and Kennedy, and inform them of his decision. Clifford's own account of the conversation indicates that Kennedy was more than willing to modify the proposal to make it more acceptable to Johnson.[31]

Clifford told Kennedy that no matter what compromises he was willing to make, Johnson disliked the arrangement because it would be considered a "political deal," and therefore he rejected it. But the Daley-Sorensen-Kennedy plan for a commission to reevaluate Vietnam policy was, of course, a political deal. It was a final effort to pull Democrats together under Johnson's leadership before Kennedy felt obliged to make a move that could severely damage the party. Certainly, the status quo was no longer tolerable; something had to give. Johnson's rejection of the proposal was a direct slap in the face to Daley. At that time, the President had apparently concluded that he either did not need Daley, or could sufficiently control him at the convention. The war had become a source of personal honor to Johnson, regardless of its political costs.

Kennedy could now turn to Daley and truthfully say that he had done all he could to implement his plan. A few days later, when the substance of the confidential meetings became known and reporters asked Daley about Johnson's repudiation of the Vietnam commission, he barked: "No comment."[32]

It was the White House that broke the story, reneging on its agreement to keep the meetings confidential, and telling CBS News that Kennedy had issued an ultimatum, and demanded that Johnson appear on television to announce that "a complete revision of the U.S. war was needed." A White House press release claimed that when Clifford presented the plan, Johnson's immediate reaction had been a definite No; but this was not the case.[33] Johnson also gave *Time* magazine's Hugh Sidey information about the confidential meeting that cast Kennedy in the worst possible light.[34] Johnson's version of events reinforced all of the old stereotypes of Kennedy as a ruthless opportunist. Internal White House memoranda confirm what Kennedy's aides claimed at the time, and the President denied: it was Johnson who first broke the confidentiality agreement.[35] His handling of the episode made all of the participants appear almost ridiculous.

In truth, Secretary Clifford had serious private misgivings about the war, which he had called a "sinkhole" in one gathering of senior foreign policy advisers about a week before the meeting with Kennedy.[36] After the conference with Kennedy and Sorensen, Clifford, despite his changing view of the war, felt that his public silence would be the best policy regarding the commission discussions. Meanwhile, the White House gave to the press an account crafted to cast Kennedy in the role of a usurper of presidential authority.[37] As was the case in February 1966, when Kennedy first suggested recognizing the National Liberation Front, he was once again publicly burned for accepting at face value statements about Vietnam made privately by Administration officials who refused to bring their private and public views of the war into alignment.[38]

Johnson ordered the White House special counsel DeVier Pierson to pass on to Sorensen his official reasons for rejecting the commission proposal. Pierson transmitted the following objections: first, the President was already open to consultations "with anyone in or out of government who could provide useful advice," which made a commission superfluous; second, a publicly announced commission would have an encouraging "psychological" effect on Hanoi; and third, it would have the appearance of a political deal "demeaning" to both Johnson and Kennedy.[39]

Pierson's transcript of his telephone conversation with Sorensen, which he prepared for Johnson, shows Sorensen reacting with deep disappointment to the news of Johnson's squashing the commission:

SORENSEN: I really thought that Clifford believed this was a desirable approach. He seemed to feel that the commission would be a sensible way to enable the President with dignity to explore reasonable alternatives to our present policy.

I had hoped that the commission would be an alternative to having Senator Kennedy enter the race and divide the party making it difficult for whoever is nominated in August to win.

PIERSON: I agree it would have that effect. The President knows that a contest for the nomination will be divisive and make it harder for the party this fall. That's why we've appreciated your efforts to keep that sort of thing from happening. . . .

SORENSEN: But it just won't work that way. You see, I had a hard time convincing Bob that even a commission would have enough impact. When we first discussed it, he did not think it was enough to have real meaning on our policies. . . . [But] when we left Clifford's office the senator agreed that it was a promising prospect. Now, you say that even this is too much.[40]

Pierson said that Johnson had made up his mind and could not be swayed, to which Sorensen replied, "Well, I appreciate your confirming this. I guess Bob will run now. I suppose I'll have to change hats." "Change hats?," Pierson asked. "Yes," Sorensen replied, "I'll have to put on my campaign hat. I'm sure you understand I'll have to help Bob if he runs."[41] Sorensen, who had been an informal adviser to both Johnson and Kennedy, would now withhold his services from the White House.

Johnson spurned the last chance to include the Democratic Party's peace wing in the campaign of 1968. It was a long shot, but the party might have displayed a degree of unity by ventilating the Vietnam issue in a constructive manner. Two days later, Sorensen wrote Johnson: "I regret very much that the Commission idea proved unacceptable . . . As you can understand, I have an obligation to do all I can to assist Senator Kennedy; but I hope we can remain in touch whenever that will serve the best interests of our country and party."[42]

After Johnson leaked his highly biased version of the meeting, Kennedy issued a strongly worded press release attacking his decision: "I am surprised that the traditional rules of confidence governing White House conversations are no longer respected by the White House itself, but their version of conversations which have taken place over the past few days on the subject of Vietnam once again fall so short of the truth that I believe the American people are entitled to the facts."[43]

Keeping Daley's role in the commission affair hidden (Kennedy referred to the Mayor only as "a Democratic political leader who is a friend of mine, and supporting President Johnson for reelection"), he described the meetings: He had made it clear, Kennedy said, that if the commission "were more than a public relations gimmick, if both the President's announcement of the commission and its membership signaled a clear-cut willingness to seek a wider path to peace in Vietnam, then my declaration of candidacy would no longer be necessary."[44] Kennedy's press release describing the Clifford meeting is consistent with Clifford's own private memorandum to the President.[45] Kennedy's list of names of people to serve on the commission matches the list Clifford sent to Johnson, save for one name: Robert Kennedy's, which appeared on Clifford's list but not on Kennedy's own.[46]

Kennedy's statement went on to say that it had become unmistakably clear "that so long as Lyndon B. Johnson was President our Vietnam policy would consist of only more war, more troops, more killing and more senseless destruction of the country we were supposedly there to save." What angered Kennedy was not so much Johnson's rejection of the commission, which he understood was the President's prerogative, but rather Johnson's decision to go public with such a self-serving and misleading description of the confidential meeting. "This incident reveals in the sharpest possible terms," he said, "why the American people no longer believe the President and the White House; why the credibility of our political leadership has been so critically eroded, and why it is clear that the only way we are going to change our policy in Vietnam is to change Administrations in Washington."[47] With that, the only thing left for Kennedy to do was to attempt to wrest the nomination from the incumbent President.

Johnson's flat dismissal of the Vietnam commission came at a time when appeals for Kennedy to run had intensified. On March 9, a friend from California, John Stewart, had written Kennedy, "I realize if you choose to run a lot of good men will be pulled down with you and the party will be split, but the country will know the truth." He continued:

> When President Kennedy wrote "Profiles of Courage" he spoke of men who sacrificed their own political careers for what they believed to be the good of the nation. That time is here Senator. . . . There are many of us, as you know, who will drop everything to aid this stand. The time is now and you're the only one who can do it. The answer, however, lies in your own heart.[48]

Kennedy hinted that he had made up his mind in his handwritten reply, "Thank you for the letter. I appreciate what you said—I shall see what I can do—Best Bob."[49] Some of Kennedy's other friends wrote him at that time urging him to run, including the sportswriter Dick Schaap, who was working on a biography of Kennedy, and James Whittaker, the first American to climb Mt. Everest, who had accompanied Kennedy on his climb of Mt. Kennedy in Canada in 1965.[50] In early March, Dolan urged Kennedy to "immediately start trouble for Johnson in the Texas delegate selection process."[51]

On March 13, Kennedy set forth his views on running in a handwritten letter to Anthony Lewis of the *New York Times* in London. "The country is in such difficulty and I believe headed for even more that it almost fills one with despair," he wrote.

> I just don't know what Johnson is thinking. But then when I realize all of that I wonder what I should be doing. But everyone I respect with the exception of Dick Goodwin and Arthur Schlesinger have been against my running. My basic inclination and reaction was to try, and let the future take care of itself. However the prophecies of future doom if I took this course made to me by Bob McNamara and to a lesser extent Bill Moyers plus the politicians' almost unanimously feeling that my running would bring about the election of Richard Nixon and many other Republican right-wingers because I would so divide and split the party, and that I could not possibly win—all this made me hesitant—I suppose even more than that. . . .
>
> So once again—what should I do?
>
> By the time you read this letter both of us will know.

If I am not off in the California primary Ethel and I will be coming to Ireland at end of May. Why don't you join us? The Irish government is dedicating a memorial to President Kennedy on his birthday May 29th—you look a little Irish and it would be good for your black soul—and maybe mine also.[52]

On March 15, Kennedy's time of indecision officially ended when he sent out telegrams to powerful Democrats around the country notifying them of his imminent entrance into the race: "I want you to know before my public announcement that I have decided to seek the Democratic Presidential nomination. Running in harmony with Senator McCarthy, I shall campaign not in opposition to any person but in support of new policies of hope and reconciliation. At home, in Vietnam and around the world. Fully aware of the deep divisions already present in our party, I earnestly seek your thoughtful consideration, counsel and support."[53]

Also on March 15, Richard Goodwin, who, like Sorensen, had strong ties to Kennedy, and whose personal loyalty to Kennedy would eventually require him to leave the McCarthy campaign when Kennedy entered the race, took a night flight with Edward Kennedy to Green Bay to meet McCarthy, who was preparing for the Wisconsin primary. The two men did not arrive at McCarthy's hotel until three in the morning on March 16, and a groggy McCarthy came out to greet them. According to Goodwin, McCarthy and his wife Abigail were "seething about RFK's anticipated entry," and the Minnesota senator "seemed totally disinterested" in talking politics. Given Goodwin's close friendship with Kennedy, McCarthy understood that he would, sooner or later, offer his services exclusively to Kennedy.[54] In addition to constituting a personal gesture to McCarthy on the part of the Kennedy camp, the purpose of the meeting, Goodwin later wrote, was to try to work out "a postponement of the confrontation between Kennedy and McCarthy, hopefully working out a plan where the anti-Johnson forces could work together, at least till the California primary which everyone accepted as the crucial place of decision."[55]

The conversation lasted only twenty minutes. McCarthy would continue on his own path regardless of Kennedy's decision. The press was poised to report the contacting of McCarthy as yet another instance of Kennedy flexing his political muscle. But McCarthy told reporters he had "appreciated the effort" that Kennedy had taken in sending his brother to meet him before the announcement. "It was a courtesy on the part of Robert Kennedy," he said, "and nothing of substance was discussed, there was no offer of any concession to me and no request of any concession from me."[56]

When prominent Democrats began receiving word of Kennedy's intentions, Johnson's supporters inundated the White House with calls and telegrams. Marvin Watson spoke with several key Democrats, including Governor Harold Hughes of Iowa, who told him that "the Kennedy thing had them whip-sawed out there."[57] One of the White House's favorite anti-Kennedy journalists, Robert Spivak, suggested to members of Johnson's staff that John Connally denounce Kennedy's entry into the race as part of "a long and proven record of treachery" that not only "stabb[ed] the President in the back, but also McCarthy." Johnson aide Larry Temple believed Connally would relish the hatchet-man role, but advised against using him because the Governor's already famous anti-RFK image would limit his public effectiveness.[58]

On March 15, Presidential aide Fred Panzer compiled for Johnson the results of an unreleased Gallup poll which paired Kennedy and the President among various voting blocs. The poll showed that among those who either believed the Vietnam War had been a mistake or that it was not going well Kennedy beat Johnson in every category. It is clear from Panzer's summary that the White House was far more concerned with Kennedy than McCarthy. "Of the two doves," Panzer wrote Johnson, "Bobby is the one with the claws. He hurts far more than McCarthy."[59]

On Saturday morning, March 16, 1968, Johnson's worst nightmare came true.[60] Robert Kennedy entered the chandeliered, Corinthian-columned Senate Caucus Room and opened with the identical words that John Kennedy had used in 1960: "I am announcing today my candidacy for the presidency of the United States." Inside was a throng of more than four hundred people, including old political pros from John Kennedy's inner circle, the nation's preeminent political commentators, family, friends, his wife Ethel, and nine of his ten children. "I run to seek new policies," he continued, "policies to end the bloodshed in Vietnam and in our cities; policies to close the gaps that now exist between black and white, between rich and poor, between young and old in this country and the rest of the world."[61] Reconciliation among the races and ending the war would be the themes of Kennedy's campaign.

Although Kennedy stressed stopping the bloodshed in Vietnam early in his statement, he went on to point to other issues involving poverty and race. "We've seen the inexcusable and ugly deprivation which causes children to starve in Mississippi, black citizens to riot in Watts, young Indians to commit suicide on their reservations because they have lacked all hope and they feel they have no future, and proud and able-bodied families to wait out their lives in empty idleness in eastern Kentucky."[62] Kennedy, the "opportunist," had expressed in his announcement speech a deep compassion for the plight of poor whites in Kentucky and Native Americans on reservations, two largely disfranchised groups which could help him little politically.

"I do not run for the Presidency merely to oppose any man, but to propose new policies," he said. This statement drew audible snickers from a few members of the press corps in light of the epic battle between Kennedy and Johnson that reporters had been fueling for years. Never a confident public speaker, Kennedy paused and glanced up from his notes, then continued, "I do not lightly dismiss the dangers and the difficulties of challenging an incumbent President." He then contrasted his willingness to enter the primaries with Johnson's reluctance to announce his own candidacy. Kennedy said that he and McCarthy were "campaigning to give our forces and our party an opportunity to select the strongest possible standard bearer for the November election, to insure that my candidacy must be tested beginning now, five months before the convention and not after the primaries are over." He added that his decision "reflect[ed] no animosity or disrespect toward President Johnson" who had "served President Kennedy with the utmost loyalty," and had been "extremely kind" to members of Kennedy's family "in the difficult months which followed the events of November of 1963."[63]

In the press conference which followed his announcement, Kennedy refused to be blamed for the deep divisions that plagued the Democratic Party in early 1968. "What has divided the party," he said, "is not me, not Senator McCarthy, but the policies that are being followed by the present administration. I would hope that before this is finished and completed, before the convention is over, that we can unite the party and have the strongest possible candidate with the candidates having presented their views across this country and in the primaries."[64]

In response to the inevitable charge of opportunism from a reporter, Kennedy explained his predicament: "I am not asking for a free ride, I have got five months ahead of me as far as the convention is concerned. I am going to go into the primaries. I am going to present my case to the American people. I am going to go all across this country. I believe in that system of going in and having one's self tested before the American people, I am willing to do that. The people will be the judge."[65]

In Wisconsin, McCarthy maintained a blasé attitude toward Kennedy's entrance. At a press conference, he agreed that Kennedy had not been responsible for dividing the party: "I don't see that the entrance of Senator Kennedy in any way changes [the state of the party]. If there is a split, it is there anyway, and I don't see his coming in as having a serious effect by way of widening the split or splitting the party in any way."[66]

Johnson had no comment on Kennedy's decision, and opted to leave Washington after watching videotapes of Kennedy's speech and press conference on the White House's closed circuit television channel. He spent the remainder of the weekend planning strategy with some of his political advisers at his ranch in Austin. His staff wired to the LBJ Ranch the complete transcripts of both Kennedy's speech, and his and McCarthy's press conferences.

Although the Administration offered no formal response to Kennedy, Vice President Hubert Humphrey gave a speech that afternoon in French Lick, Indiana, the first primary state in which Kennedy would campaign. He presented what would become a recurring theme of the Administration's defense in the face of Kennedy's challenge. Regarding the war, Humphrey said, "the success of aggression in Vietnam would lead to wider and far more dangerous aggression throughout all of Southeast Asia." He said the Administration was undertaking an "intense review" of Vietnam policy, but he had faith that "most Americans know that there can be no true and lasting peace in Vietnam, or Southeast Asia, until militant and powerful Communist forces are convinced that aggression will not pay."[67] The Democratic leadership stood by Johnson and the war. Humphrey quoted President Kennedy, which he rarely did, and likened Robert Kennedy's primary campaign to the 1948 election where President Harry Truman prevailed over both the Dixiecrats and Henry Wallace's progressives. "We fought and we won," he intoned, adding the inanity: "America has not lost its way. America is on its way."[68]

When Kennedy entered the race, Harold "Barefoot" Sanders, Johnson's close associate from Texas who acted as his Congressional liaison, undertook a comprehensive survey of Democratic members of Congress. With the assistance of Marvin Watson and other White House staffers, Sanders sought to discern the level of intraparty dissent which Kennedy's candidacy exemplified. The Johnson White House had polled Congressional sentiment on specific pieces of legislation in the past, but the timing and nature of Sanders's assessment set it apart. It provided Johnson with a clearer understanding of the effects of Kennedy's challenge on the party and his own political standing. It was the most thorough canvass ever taken by the Administration focusing on Johnson's political strength among Democrats. McCarthy's role is barely mentioned in Sanders's report, and is cited only in relation to Kennedy.

Sanders and his staff called nearly every Democratic Representative to determine the mood of the party now that it faced a three-way race. He also expressly sought out their advice on how best to thwart Kennedy in their respective states or districts. The White House and the D.N.C. had received word that there were serious worries among Democrats about the effects of Kennedy's entrance. "The Kennedy people are playing hard ball with respect to obtaining delegates' support," a representative from New York reported, "and are willing to finance Kennedy delegates' slates against all opponents."[69] Members feared that if they spoke out too soon for Johnson's reelection, Kennedy would throw his weight behind peace candidates in their own primaries.[70]

Sanders learned that the Viva Kennedy groups of Latinos which the John Kennedy campaign had formed in 1960 were now revitalized, and becoming "noisy" in Texas, California, and the Southwest.[71] Of particular concern were the activities of Kennedy's people in enlisting the support of former Peace Corps volunteers and local community leaders associated with the newly created voluntary organizations such as VISTA and Head Start, and programs administered by the Office of Economic Opportunity (O.E.O.). Kennedy's early campaign had begun aggressively organizing people who were connected with the myriad federal antipoverty programs to utilize their grassroots power.[72] In Johnson's home state, Spanish-speaking antipoverty personnel worked for Kennedy, and it was reported that "the VISTA people have constantly attacked the President's friends and supporters."[73] Johnson witnessed his archrival tap into groups that he hoped to use for his own reelection as a kind of federal patronage system.[74] The White House paid particular attention to anti-Johnson activities among O.E.O. employees and others working in the community action programs.[75]

In the South, Sanders reported a tremendous outpouring of support for Johnson among Democrats, who were nearly universal in their contempt for Kennedy. "Kennedy cannot make any inroads in the South," concluded one Southern Democrat.[76] A few politicians from the old Confederacy told Sanders they would vote for the third party presidential candidate, Alabama Governor George Wallace, if Kennedy won the nomination.[77] North Carolina Democrats reported that if Kennedy won the nomination the state would go Republican.[78] Southern Democrats were nearly unanimous in their belief that Kennedy's entry boosted support in their region for Johnson. Said one North Carolina Democrat, "The only thing that could have made them madder and done me more good would have been an announcement by Ho Chi Minh."[79] "That lousy hypocrite," another Southerner said of Kennedy, "will risk the future of the Democratic Party to further his own pip-squeak ambitions."[80]

Sanders summed up the Southern situation: "Obviously, the net result of their [Kennedy and McCarthy] candidacies has been to help the President in the South," he wrote, "Since both are considerably to the left of the President, the President becomes a more attractive alternative to the Southerners than heretofore. . . . The McCarthy-Kennedy effort makes it easier for them to support the President publicly."[81] However, Sanders suggested avoiding the overt endorsements of Southerners because, he wrote Johnson, "it would leave the public impression that that is where most of your support is centered."[82]

Sanders also believed it would be unwise for Johnson to "make a public race as to who can get the most Congressional endorsements"; it was in Johnson's interest not to press Democrats who were facing divided loyalties. The prudent course of action would be to allow members of Congress to "remain quiet and take no position." A strong showing of support for Johnson, especially from Southern conservatives, would surely backfire. Sanders warned: "We must be careful between now and the convention to avoid the appearance that our support comes only from the South, Southwest, and the big city machines."[83]

In a follow-up memo to Johnson entitled "The Goal," Sanders laid out a strategy for the 1968 campaign: "For the preconvention campaign we move to the left to dilute the Kennedy-McCarthy support among liberals who are the base of the Democratic party in the North, Northeast and Far West and who will influence the delegations from those areas." The President should play it quietly until after the primaries were over, and then crush his opposition at the convention. "For the post-convention campaign," Sanders went on, "we may have to move to the right to pick up . . . the middle and lower middle class voters who are better off financially than ever and who are concerned about crime and inflation in addition to Vietnam."[84]

In Sanders's view, Kennedy was "the chief threat at the convention" as well as the key "preconvention problem." Johnson could not afford to overreact, but neither could he neglect "nursing" the delegations that appeared to be in his camp. "Delegates must be buttoned up so tight," Sanders wrote, "that even if we lose in California, Wisconsin or Oregon, they will stay hitched."[85] He urged Johnson to announce his candidacy, and create the impression that a "smooth-running, dedicated organization" functioned nationally in behalf of the President, even though at that time it was nonexistent. An announcement of candidacy from Johnson, Sanders believed, would thwart Kennedy's attempt to control delegates that were caught in the middle of the squabble.[86]

Sanders's survey also showed that Johnson Democrats outside the South, particularly in New England, the Northeast, and the Far West (where Johnson was weakest), greeted the new political situation with trepidation. Others displayed strong evidence of conflicting loyalties. A Rhode Island representative, for example, said his only course would be to "remain uninvolved" in the primaries in his own state or risk "stir[ring] up the pro-Kennedy forces." A Democratic member of Congress from Maine shared his feelings of split loyalty because he felt "indebted to the Kennedys who have helped raise considerable money at fund raisers."[87] One member of the New York Congressional delegation said that if he came out for Johnson, "Bobby will run people against him and win."[88] Other pro-Administration Democrats expressed concerns about planned appearances by Kennedy at Democratic fundraisers, and sought ways of breaking off the engagements even if they had been booked long in advance.

Regarding the war, some Democratic members of Congress reported to Sanders and his staff that since the Tet Offensive there had been a "tailspin loss" of public support for Johnson's Vietnam policy. Democrats from the North and Northwest complained about the political effects of promoting the Administration's view of Tet. A member of the Washington state delegation said that his credibility had been severely damaged "by claiming that the Communists did not win in the Tet offensive when the people believed that they did win." A Democrat from Minnesota, McCarthy's and Humphrey's home state, said that "statements that we won the Tet offensive when we did not" hurt him and the state Democratic leadership.[89] The senior Congressman from Florida, New Dealer Claude Pepper, voiced his strong support for the President, and his worries about his state's delegation. Pepper said that "more people dislike Kennedy than the President," but he also suggested Johnson make some progress towards negotiations in Vietnam before the election.[90] Representative Tom Foley of Washington expressed his view that it "would be disastrous if Kennedy's entry would force the President to polarize his position toward the hawk side and people would get the impression the President is not flexible toward peace."[91]

A Pennsylvania representative told Sanders there was "a definite credibility gap," and "that the overwhelming number of voters believe that the Administration lies about what is going on in Vietnam, and what the real objectives are."[92] A few cited the negative local political effects of General Westmoreland's request for additional troops.[93] Even Democrats who strongly supported the Administration's Vietnam policies admitted that their mail had dramatically turned against the war in recent months, and "the preponderance is for us to get out."[94] One prowar Democrat from North Carolina called the war an "albatross around our necks."[95]

Congressman Lee Hamilton of Indiana suggested that Johnson offer a "bombing pause soon," or some "other act of equivalent significance" preferably "after some victories on the ground." He believed Secretary of State Dean Rusk should resign because he had become a "political liability." However, Hamilton added that he was "disgusted" with Kennedy "for dividing the party this way," and predicted that Kennedy would lose the Indiana primary. He also said he had talked with Sorensen who agreed with him that "it had been a mistake for Bobby to get in the race," but Sorensen "had to stand by him."[96] With Kennedy's entry, Johnson could no longer count on the support for the war of many vulnerable political allies.

The rising Democratic star, Massachusetts Congressman Thomas "Tip" O'Neill, reported to the White House that he had spoken with Edward Kennedy and Kenneth O'Donnell in Boston, saying "Bobby was crazy to think about running" because "he was the most unpopular man on the Hill." O'Neill said that the three politicians "commiserated on what a lousy position Bobby had catapulted all of us into"; O'Neill's bitterness surfaced when he added that Kennedy viewed him as "just another goddam Boston politician."[97]

After days of frantic phone calls to almost every Democratic member of Congress, Sanders reported to the President the results of his survey:

So far we count 160 Democratic Congressmen supporting the President. This includes (1) those who have expressed public support, (2) those who have expressed private support but will be publicly neutral for the present, and (3) those who will be neutral but who state that they will not support either Kennedy or McCarthy.[98]

However, Sanders expected "defections" to Kennedy from members of the Massachusetts and New York Congressional delegations. "The reputation for high pressure tactics belong[s] with the Kennedys," he wrote, "and we should leave it with them. Many of these Congressmen who are privately for us but publicly neutral want to avoid primary contests at home. If they are pressed to make a public choice now as between the President, McCarthy or Kennedy, many will refuse to do so—and the resulting psychological impact is bad."[99] Johnson, then, could no longer count on open support from members of his own party. He approved a plan for the newly-formed National Committee for Johnson/Humphrey to schedule a series of "semi-weekly get-togethers for Democratic Congressmen in groups of twenty to twenty-five, mixing out-right supporters with those who are in the doubtful category."[100] The hope was to persuade the fence-sitters by showing them Johnson was still the true boss of the party.

When Kennedy announced his entry into the race, the polarization of the Democratic Party reached a new stage. All of the latent regional, personal, and ideological divisions surfaced. The Southern wing and its prowar soulmates from other states rallied behind the besieged Johnson; the left wing, gaining strength from the waxing dove faction, moved toward Kennedy or McCarthy. Most Democratic politicians outside the South chose to withhold their endorsements until they could sense which way the political winds were blowing. Johnson's partisans in the South were ordered to hold their fire, lest it become embarrassingly apparent where his last bastion of support now resided. If the White House's canvass confirmed anything, it was that Kennedy's power inside the party was formidable.

Meanwhile, there had been an outpouring of support for Kennedy among Democratic regulars, particularly in California where Jesse Unruh earnestly assembled a network of county chairmen and state coordinators. He announced that "more than 24,000 California Democrats have signed nominating petitions" for Kennedy, and that it had been "clearly demonstrated that Senator Kennedy's candidacy is the spark which the Democratic Party has so badly needed over the past few years."[101] Unruh's early assistance was crucial to Kennedy's chances in the pivotal California primary.

Kennedy hastily put together a crack team of political operatives, including Dick Tuck, a legendary campaign manager with a reputation for trickery, and John Kennedy's former advance man Jerry Bruno, widely known as "the best in the business." On March 22, the *Washington Post* reported that the Kennedy campaign had enlisted "prominent individuals from 26 key fields representing the broad power structure of America." The campaign had divided up tasks based on subcategories of targeted voters including: Returning Peace Corps Volunteers, Clergy, Writers, Entertainers, Lawyers, Senior Citizens, Labor, Academics, Public Employees, Law Enforcement Officials, and current and former Public Officials. African Americans and Puerto Ricans comprised a separate list, and there was a category called Nationalities which would target the Irish-, Polish-, Italian-, and Mexican-American communities.[102] Soon the campaign had a Youth and Student Division, a Press Division, a Volunteer Division, a Speechwriters' Division, a Research Division, a Grass-Roots Division, and other specialized staffs.[103]

On the morning Kennedy announced his candidacy, members of his and Edward Kennedy's Senate staffs met to plan strategy, and to divide responsibilities. Dolan handled scheduling for the first days of the campaign, which brought the candidate to New Jersey, New York, Kansas, Wisconsin, and California.[104] In addition to the members of his own staff, Kennedy drew on the talents and experience of his and John Kennedy's old friend, Sorensen, his brother-in-law Steve Smith, former Presidential aide Kenneth O'Donnell, President Kennedy's former press secretary, Pierre Salinger, and other experienced political managers who had been instrumental in guiding John Kennedy to victory in 1960. The fame and infectious confidence of Kennedy's campaign directors, who knew how to win a presidential election, intimidated even some of the most cynical and detached members of the press.[105]

Johnson and his advisers had their hands full. On March 18, two days after Kennedy made his announcement, nearly one-third of the House of Representatives, a total of 132 members—91 Republicans and 41 Democrats—joined in sponsoring a resolution calling for an immediate Congressional review of United States policy in Southeast Asia.[106] Kennedy's attempt to form a presidential commission on Vietnam, which Johnson rejected outright as an "ultimatum," now seemed like a moderate step. On his own initiative, Johnson requested that the Senior Advisory Group, known as the "Wise Men," which in practice functioned much like a presidential commission, assist him in an internal reevaluation of Vietnam policy.

Among those in the Senior Advisory Group were Dean Acheson, the secretary of state under President Truman; Undersecretary of State George Ball; McGeorge Bundy, special assistant to Presidents Kennedy and Johnson; Douglas Dillon, the secretary of the treasury under President Kennedy; Cyrus Vance, the deputy secretary of defense; Arthur Dean, the chief Korean

War negotiator; John McCloy, the high commissioner to West Germany under President Truman; General Omar Bradley, the World War II commander and first chairman of the Joint Chiefs; General Matthew Ridgeway, the Korean War commander and later NATO commander; General Maxwell Taylor, the chairman of the Joint Chiefs under President Kennedy and later ambassador to Saigon; Robert Murphy, a senior career ambassador of the Truman-Eisenhower period; Henry Cabot Lodge, Jr., formerly a senator and twice ambassador to Saigon; Abe Fortas, an associate justice of the Supreme Court and a close friend and adviser to Johnson; and Arthur Goldberg, Ambassador to the United Nations.[107]

The last time the so-called Wise Men had met was in November 1967, when they had nearly unanimously spurred Johnson to push for a military victory in Vietnam. That same month, Johnson decided to ease his Defense Secretary Robert McNamara, who privately had been raising questions about the military's strategy, out of the Cabinet. He appointed McNamara head of the World Bank.[108] Clark Clifford, who was brought in as Defense Secretary-designate before McNamara's actual shift to the World Bank, had been committed to the United States position in Vietnam, but his attitude slowly began to change when he realized the depth of the military's own confusion about how to proceed.

Perhaps more importantly, Clifford, who had years of Wall Street experience, saw that the U.S. commitment to South Vietnam had fiscally overextended the nation. In March 1968, stock markets became jittery as the first signs of the devastating inflation of the 1970s began to peek through. Rampant speculation in gold seriously weakened the dollar in international currency markets.[109] On the day Kennedy announced his candidacy, the London gold market was closed to check the massive drain.[110] When the Wise Men met on March 25 and 26, the three months since their previous meeting had witnessed the Tet Offensive, a request for 206,000 additional troops splashed across the front page of the *New York Times*, and a potentially serious economic crisis. This time the majority of the group called for a policy of deescalation with negotiations, which was not dissimilar to what Kennedy had been calling for since March 1967. The policy elite had moved away from Johnson and closer to Kennedy. Johnson was floored by the volte-face of his most important body of Vietnam advisers. Someone had "poisoned the well," he complained. He ordered the military and intelligence officials who had briefed the Senior Advisory Group to give him the same briefings they had given the Wise Men; during their presentations Johnson's expressions and body language clearly showed he was unhappy and unimpressed with their bleak appraisal of the war.[111]

The instability of the stock and currency markets; the beginning of inflation; the refusal of Wilbur Mills, the chairman of the House Ways and Means Committee, to push through a bill increasing taxes to pay for Vietnam; and the general sense of unease with Johnson's ability to manage the war all contributed to a shift away from the Administration among business elites. Many of the Wise Men, along with Clifford, represented corporate and financial interests, and showed lukewarm support of Johnson's domestic agenda. The divisions gripping the Democratic Party greatly magnified big business's disquiet with the progressive direction in which Johnson had led the federal government. The mismanagement of the war led to economic instability. Kennedy made it a campaign issue with a sharp public statement on the gold crisis which explicitly linked it to Johnson's Vietnam policies. On March 26, feeling the pressure, Johnson growled to the Joint Chiefs of Staff: "I don't give a damn about the election. I will be happy just to keep doing what is right and lose the election. . . . Most of the press is against us. . . . We have no support for the war. This is caused by the 206,000 troop request, leaks, Ted Kennedy and Bobby Kennedy."[112]

During the last two weeks of March, Johnson evaluated the state of his Presidency: He had the results of Barefoot Sanders's canvass showing that his principal sources of support were now conservative Southerners and right-wing Democrats from other regions. Mayor Daley was a wild card given his exasperation with the war, and his fear that Johnson would bring Illinois Democrats down with him in November. The latest polls predicted that Johnson would lose to McCarthy in the Wisconsin primary scheduled for April 2. The Wise Men had rendered their surprising verdict with a call for deescalation; the military wanted far more troops than Johnson could possibly deliver. Business elites were displaying a vote of no confidence in his leadership. Congress had scuttled his latest tax bill. The long, hot summer of 1967, which saw in Detroit the most destructive riot in U.S. history, promised an even worse summer in 1968 with the further deterioration of race relations and Johnson's apparent rejection of the recommendations of the National Advisory Commission on Civil Disorders (the Kerner Commission). Martin Luther King, Jr. was organizing a massive Poor People's March on Washington. Outside the White House, college students held vigils and chanted "Hey, Hey, LBJ! How Many Kids Did You Kill Today?" The latest Gallup poll showed that Johnson's public approval rating was in rapid decline.[113] And Robert Kennedy was running a fifty-state, high-powered presidential campaign that challenged the loyalties of thousands of Democrats nationwide.

Johnson sought advice from some close friends about whether he should seek reelection. On the afternoon of March 31, Governor Connally, who regularly counseled Johnson, sent a message to the White House: "If the President feels he should not run, the announcement should be made now. Every day he waits compounds the problem because of the additional people asked to help in the campaign." Connally recognized that it was "a personal decision that only the President should make," but, he advised, "there should be no more 'agonizing reappraisals.'"[114] That evening at 9:00 P.M. Eastern Standard Time, Johnson addressed the nation from the Oval Office. Speech writer Harry McPherson worked up a draft of the speech, and with the input of Clifford and others they softened its originally hard-line tone on the war in each subsequent version.

The President defended his Vietnam policies, and announced the U.S. would limit its bombing of North Vietnam to the area just above the demilitarized zone. He recapped the destructive effects of the Tet Offensive, but still adhered to the view that it had been an American victory. He said he would send another 13,500 support troops to Vietnam, which would bring the number to the preapproved total of 525,000. The United States faced "the sharpest financial threat in the postwar era," he said, "a threat to the dollar's role as the keystone of international trade and finance." Johnson tacitly admitted that the war had been a drain on domestic programs, and that a peace settlement would "permit us to turn more fully to our tasks at home." He still believed that "America's security" was at stake in Vietnam, and that Hanoi "should be in no doubt of our intentions," and "must not miscalculate the pressures within our democracy in this election year."[115]

After reaching the end of his prepared statement, the teleprompter went blank, and Johnson added his own peroration:

I have concluded that I should not permit the Presidency to become involved in the partisan divisions that are developing in this political year.

With America's sons in the fields far away, with America's future under challenge right here at home, with our hopes and the world's hopes for peace in the balance every day, I do not believe that I should devote an hour or a day of my time to any personal partisan causes or to any duties other than the awesome duties of this office—the Presidency of your country.

Accordingly, I shall not seek, and I will not accept, the nomination of my party for another term as your President.[116]

Johnson's announcement surprised the nation. Marvin Watson telephoned all of the Cabinet officers, and a few dozen key Democrats around the country, to get their reactions. Several members of the Cabinet, such as Secretary of Labor Willard Wirtz, had missed the coda of Johnson's speech, and were stunned by the news that the President had decided against running for reelection.[117] About a hundred antiwar activists gathered outside the White House, some wearing Kennedy and McCarthy buttons, and sang: "We *Have* Overcome."[118]

In a brief press conference later that evening, Johnson said that he had been thinking about not running since November 1967 "when General Westmoreland was back here." He said he had discussed it with McNamara in August 1967, and more recently with Clifford, Rusk, Connally, and some staff members including Press Secretary George Christian. His decision, he assured the press, was irrevocable. "Did Senator Kennedy's entry into the race have anything to do with the timing of your announcement?" a reporter asked. Johnson replied: "Well, it added to the general situation I talked about that existed in the country."[119]

On the evening of March 31, Kennedy sat in a commercial airplane on the tarmac of La Guardia airport in New York City, having just arrived from a campaign event in Phoenix, Arizona. At about 10:00 P.M. a flustered John Burns, the chairman of the New York State Democratic Party, rushed aboard. "The President is not going to run," he blurted out to everyone on the plane. "You're kidding," was Kennedy's initial response. On the way to his apartment at the United Nations Plaza, Kennedy wondered aloud to Richard Dougherty of the *Los Angeles Times* whether "he'd have done this if I hadn't come in."[120] Kennedy's nemesis had removed himself from the battle, and left a curious void that ironically created new political obstacles. The minute the President's speech ended, Edward Kennedy and other senior campaign personnel contacted key Democrats seeking support now that Johnson was out of the race.[121] At 11:43 that evening, Kennedy sent the President a telegram:

> First of all, let me say that I fervently hope that your new efforts for peace in Vietnam will succeed. Your decision regarding the Presidency subordinates self to country and is truly magnanimous. I respectfully and earnestly request an opportunity to visit you as soon as possible to discuss how we might work together in the interest of national unity during the coming months. Sincerely, Robert F. Kennedy.[122]

Kennedy huddled at his Manhattan apartment with his close friends and advisers, including Dutton and Sorensen, revising campaign strategy well into the morning.[123] Johnson's abrupt pullout dramatically transformed the political landscape, and illustrated the depth of the crisis facing the Democratic Party.

Although Johnson was no longer a candidate, Kennedy's request for a meeting with him had sparked a bitter initial response: "I won't bother answering that grandstanding little runt," Johnson reportedly said.[124] Following the results of the Wisconsin primary, which showed the President had received less than a third of the vote, he agreed to meet Kennedy. The meeting was the first face-to-face encounter between the two leaders at the White House since the acrimonious exchange of February 1967, when Johnson predicted that Kennedy and other Democratic doves would be "politically dead" in six months. It was Johnson's political life that now seemed to be coming to an end. This time, Kennedy brought Sorensen with him. Johnson was accompanied by National Security Adviser Walt Rostow, who had been present at the February 1967 meeting, and Charles Murphy, a former counsel to President Harry Truman who served as an aide to Johnson, and was a well-respected Democratic insider.

On the morning of April 3, 1968, the so-called unity meeting began with Johnson speaking at length about the war in Vietnam, at times pointing to a large map which Rostow held up for him. Perfunctorily, he clarified the Administration's position on limiting the bombing of North Vietnam to below the 20th parallel, which had caused some misunderstanding in Congress and in the press. Making a point of showing deference, Kennedy thanked Johnson for explaining the details of the bombing pause, saying he had been a bit "confused" himself. Kennedy told Johnson his March 31 speech had been "magnificent," and apologized for not maintaining closer contact with him.[125] Now that the two men sat at the same table, and conferred directly, the atmosphere in the room became subdued, even warm, as both politicians sought common ground.

The President then went on to extol the improvements of the Thieu regime, and spoke about other foreign policy crises facing the United States in Asia and in the Middle East. In what had become vintage Johnson, the President blamed the monetary crisis on the news media and Congress's refusal to pass his tax bill. The New York Times story of March 10, which first reported the 206,000 troop request, he said, "cost the nation a billion dollars in gold."[126]

Listening patiently, Kennedy did not interrupt Johnson's soliloquy. Sorensen jumped in at one point to compliment McPherson for writing a fine speech for the President for March 31. Johnson paused briefly, and then spoke at some length about a half-dozen foreign policy emergencies. As he concluded his rather nervous remarks, Johnson said he would ask his press secretary, George Christian, to tell the news media that he and Kennedy "did not go into politics" at the meeting.[127]

At this point, Kennedy respectfully asked Johnson if he could broach a sensitive topic: "Can I ask about the political situation?" he said. Johnson gave a quick nod, and Kennedy expressed what had been on his mind all along: "Where do you stand in the campaign? Are you opposed to my effort and will you marshal forces against me?" he bluntly asked.[128] Johnson responded, saying he wanted to keep the Presidency out of the campaign. "I will tell the Vice President about the same things I'm telling you," he said, "I don't know whether he will run or not. If he asks my advice, I won't give it." Although his position "might change at any time," Johnson assured Kennedy that he would "stay out of pre-convention politics. I am no king maker," he added, and he had "not talk[ed] to Daley about this in Chicago."[129] Johnson then launched into yet another lengthy monologue about how he had not wanted to run for president in the first place in 1964, and that he viewed his Presidency as a continuation of President Kennedy's legacy. The President said he would be willing to meet with Kennedy as events unfolded, and would offer similar briefings to McCarthy and Nixon.

Sorensen asked Johnson if members of the Administration were "free to take part in pre-convention politics and support candidates." Sorensen had in mind Lawrence O'Brien, a former John Kennedy confidant who served as Johnson's postmaster general, as well as a few other politically savvy Administration officials who could help Kennedy. Johnson replied that he had to give it some thought, and no one pressed him for an answer. Kennedy's political ties to officials inside virtually all of the Cabinet departments dating back to his brother's administration had long been a source of deep concern for Johnson and his inner circle.

Kennedy shared with Johnson his desire to speak with him at a later date before he endorsed another candidate. Johnson agreed: "If I move; you'll know," he said. He then heaped lavish praise on the late John Kennedy. "As President Kennedy looked down at him every day from then until now," Johnson said, the late President "would agree that he had kept the faith."[130] He told Kennedy he believed the press had exaggerated their personal antagonisms, and that he did not hate him or dislike him, and still regarded himself as carrying out the Kennedy/Johnson partnership.[131] The encounter concluded on a hopeful note with handshakes all around, and wishes of good will. Rostow recorded that there was "a real chance of influencing the campaign to minimize vindictiveness and devisiveness [sic]."[132]

Johnson had scheduled another meeting with Vice President Humphrey right after Kennedy and Sorensen left the White House. Despite the President's assurance to Kennedy that he would stay out of preconvention politics and offer Humphrey no political advice even if he asked for it, Johnson not only coached Humphrey and gave him detailed advice, but urged the Vice President to announce his candidacy right away. He also promised his strongest support. Humphrey, out of a sense of loyalty, hesitated in announcing his candidacy too soon after Johnson withdrew. It was not a question of personal loyalty, Johnson assured him. Anything Humphrey chose to do was consistent with his March 31 speech, he insisted.[133]

Johnson warned Humphrey that should he decide to run he should "bear in mind that the heart of the matter lay not with the Southerners who, in the end, might well support him, but with the following six states: New Jersey, Pennsylvania, Illinois, Michigan, Ohio, and Indiana." In Johnson's political calculus, Humphrey had to focus his attention on these states if he was to defeat Kennedy. He said he "did not know where Daley and [New Jersey Governor Richard] Hughes and others would come out." But he thought it was possible that "in the end, Daley and Hughes would go with Kennedy."[134] Not only was the Kennedy campaign squeezing Johnson from the grassroots, it was also stripping away the support of some of the most important Democratic machines. Although political prognosticators gave

Kennedy long odds for winning the nomination, the President privately conveyed to Humphrey that he was in for a tough fight.

Any good will that Kennedy had generated by the "unity meeting" with Johnson had quickly evaporated. Johnson had immediately pushed Humphrey to use brass knuckles in his fight against Kennedy. When press reports of the April 3 meeting appeared, Johnson exploded in anger, and blamed Kennedy and Sorensen for leaking the story. (Johnson apparently considered such leaks a presidential prerogative.) During a subsequent courtesy call from Eugene McCarthy, when the subject of Kennedy came up Johnson simply sat back in his chair and silently drew a finger across his throat in a slow slitting motion.[135] The implication was clear. Johnson planned to employ all of the levers of power of the presidency and the party apparatus to bar Kennedy from the nomination.

* * *

Kennedy's run for the Democratic nomination in 1968 was far more than a personal clash between two political rivals, or an "opportunistic" bid by a zealous young senator. His entry into the race was a manifestation of the centrifugal forces that pulled the Democratic Party apart. His decision brought to a head the contradictions and divisions that had been building within Democratic ranks since Johnson's earliest escalations of the Vietnam War.

Kennedy's entry created the most explosive situation in Democratic politics in decades. He attempted to harness the grassroots examples of participatory democracy, originating from the civil rights and antiwar movements, to serve his own political interests as well as the electoral benefit of the party. The party needed an infusion of new blood, and when Kennedy finally entered the race, he placed hundreds of Democratic officeholders and party officials in a delicate position. A difficult burden fell on Democrats from Massachusetts, Connecticut, New York, New Jersey, Indiana, Illinois, Michigan, and California, all states in which Kennedy had helped dozens of candidates in past elections. Democrats across the country owed Kennedy favors, some large, others small, and he now cashed in his political chips.

Kennedy became a lightning rod for the ideological, organizational, and regional divisions inside the Democratic Party. Although his candidacy brought these fissures to the forefront of American politics, it did not create them. The party suffered from a serious malady, and Kennedy's new role as a presidential candidate was more a symptom than a cause. In a bizarre tactical alliance, representatives of both the right and the left attacked Kennedy as a ruthless opportunist for entering the race when he did. He was willing to split the party in an attempt to cleave off its right wing, put an end to the bipartisan war that had so damaged its credibility, and harness and strengthen its grassroots electoral base. It was a gamble with the highest of political stakes, a battle for the heart and soul of the Democratic Party.

When Johnson withdrew from the race, a few political commentators attributed his decision to the polls which predicted a devastating loss in the April 2 primary in Wisconsin.[136] Others have credited McCarthy's stunning performance in New Hampshire with ultimately knocking Johnson out of the 1968 presidential race.[137] But it was Kennedy's entry that pushed Johnson over the edge. In 1968, Doris Kearns, who was a young aide to the President, told William Vanden Heuvel that Johnson "said it several times that McCarthy never scared him one whit." In Kearns's view, Johnson had felt no competition whatsoever with McCarthy, but the competition with Kennedy "was very real."[138] Kennedy entered the race, in part, because the McCarthy campaign had revealed the extant divisions within the party, but had made little progress in influencing those Democratic power brokers who distanced themselves from the Administration.

The New Hampshire results, Kennedy's entry into the race, and the findings of Barefoot Sanders's canvass all pointed to Johnson's political vulnerability. His mandate of 1964 had all but vanished. Moreover, viewed as a whole, the events of March 1968 paint a picture of the nation's dominant political party on the verge of breaking apart. Johnson's decision to withdraw when he did was a wise one. It prevented a humiliating public repudiation of his leadership in the last months of his term. This move did not mean he would refrain from working hard to pass on the mantle to his handpicked successor, Hubert Humphrey.

FIGURE 1   Robert F. Kennedy with his brother, President John F. Kennedy, outside the Oval Office. Serving his brother's political career had been the defining element in Robert Kennedy's life up to November 22, 1963. *The John F. Kennedy Library.*

FIGURE 2   President Lyndon Johnson had Lawrence O'Brien, who was a Kennedy family friend and Johnson's special assistant at the time, send this photo of the signing of the Community Health Centers Act Amendments in 1965 to New York Senator Robert F. Kennedy as a friendly gesture. The conflict between Kennedy and Johnson would eventually tear the Democratic Party apart. *The John F. Kennedy Library.*

FIGURE 3 Kennedy in his Senate office with his two young aides, Peter Edelman and Adam Walinsky. Edelman and Walinsky would become important voices on Kennedy's staff calling on him to take ever stronger stands against the war in Vietnam and against Johnson's leadership. *The John F. Kennedy Library.*

FIGURE 4   Kennedy visiting wounded Naval veterans returned from Vietnam at the U.S. Naval hospital in St. Albans, Long Island, December 16, 1966. This kind of direct contact with the young war victims had a strong and lasting impact on Kennedy. *The John F. Kennedy Library.*

FIGURE 5   The launching of the *U.S.S. John F. Kennedy* from the Drydock in Newport News, May 27, 1967. It was a rare and solemn moment of prayer where Johnson and the Kennedy family gathered to honor the memory of President John F. Kennedy. Present are Robert and Ethel Kennedy, Rose Kennedy, Edward Kennedy, and Jacqueline, Caroline, and John F. Kennedy, Jr. *Newport News Drydock Comapany*

FIGURE 6 Robert, Edward, and Joseph P. Kennedy at a 1967 World Series baseball game. The elder Kennedy had been severely disabled by a stroke in 1962 which left him paralyzed and incapable of speech. *The John F. Kennedy Library.*

FIGURE 7   Kennedy relaxing at a Paris cafe in February 1967 while he was on a European tour where he received the controversial "peace feeler" from Hanoi. France-Soir

FIGURE 8   A cartoon summing up Johnson's obsession with Kennedy's criticism and political challenge. *The John F. Kennedy Library.*

FIGURE 9   Kennedy breaking bread with United Farm Workers Union founder Cesar Chavez, who had fasted for 25 days in the name of nonviolence, on March 10, 1968. *George Ballis.*

FIGURE 10   Kennedy and Chavez, March 10, 1968. Kennedy called Chavez "a great man" and "an heroic figure of our time." A close personal friendship developed between the two leaders between 1966 and 1968. *George Ballis.*

FIGURE 11   Kennedy with Chicago Mayor Richard Daley. Daley was Kennedy's most powerful informal ally among Democratic power-brokers he would need if he were to wrest the 1968 presidential nomination from the party leadership. *The John F. Kennedy Library.*

FIGURE 12   Kennedy is here caught expressing his frustration while campaigning in Oregon in May 1968. He became the first Kennedy to lose an election after a string of 26 consecutive victories. The Oregon loss on May 28, 1968 had the effect of energizing Kennedy's supporters in the California primary scheduled for June 4, 1968. *Helene Berinsky.*

FIGURE 13   Kennedy on the stump in 1968 addressing one of many large gatherings. *Black Star/Shapiro*

FIGURE 14 Kennedy receiving a daisy from a supporter in New York City while on the campaign trail. *Helene Berinsky.*

FIGURE 15 A typical
street scene from South-
Central Los Angeles
during Kennedy's 1968
primary campaign.
Rachel Scott

FIGURE 16 Kennedy campaigning in the African-American neighborhoods of Los Angeles. Blacks and Latinos would prove the pivotal force in Kennedy's victory in the California primary. *The John F. Kennedy Library.*

8 Civil Rights and the Urban Rebellions: Kennedy, King, and the Politics of Race, 1965–1968

> What we need in the United States is not division; what we need in the United States is not hatred; what we need in the United States is not violence or lawlessness; but love and wisdom, and compassion toward one another, and a feeling of justice toward those who still suffer within our country, whether they be white or they be black.
>
> —Robert F. Kennedy, Indianapolis, Indiana, April 4, 1968

On February 29, 1968, the National Advisory Commission on Civil Disorders presented its report to President Johnson. Johnson had appointed the commission, headed by Illinois Governor Otto Kerner, to analyze the causes of the riots of 1967 in African-American urban centers. The report described twenty-four violent outbursts in twenty-three cities, provided profiles of eight, and identified the underlying social conditions that produced the massive uprisings in Detroit and Newark the previous summer. In an often-quoted statement, the Kerner Commission said that America was becoming "two societies, one black, one white—separate and unequal." The body also concluded that reversing these trends required "a commitment to national action—compassionate, massive and sustained, backed by the resources of the most powerful and the richest nation on this earth."[1] Johnson ignored the report for nearly a month, refused to accept a bound copy, and denied the commission members the customary courtesy of a formal White House presentation.[2]

Kennedy cited Johnson's apparent rejection of the commission's findings as a major reason for entering the presidential race. "The Report of the Riot Commission has been largely ignored," he said in his announcement speech.[3] Nine days after Kennedy's entry, Martin Luther King, Jr. told the annual convention of the Rabbinical Assembly that he was discouraged that "the President himself has not made any move toward implementing any of the recommendations of that Commission."[4] Kerner and the other members called for forming partnerships between federal, state, and local governments and the private sector and community leaders to rebuild impoverished urban communities. These proposals were similar in content and spirit to programs that Kennedy had long advocated.[5]

In the election year 1968, the Republican Party exploited for its own electoral benefit the emergent "white backlash," which had registered in national opinion polls since Barry Goldwater's 1964 presidential campaign. The African-American political gains of the 1960s, along with the riots in the cities, raised racial tensions nationally and created a climate ripe for partisan exploitation. Race-baiting in the 1968 presidential campaign became most flagrantly identified with Alabama Governor George Wallace, who prepared to run as an independent, but it was also integral to Republican front-runner Richard Nixon's "Southern strategy." In early 1968, Kennedy and King sought to counter the political influence of racist appeals.

In late March 1968, while Kennedy campaigned heavily, Martin Luther King, Jr. devoted his formidable organizing talents to a drive to bring the nation's poor people to Washington, D.C., for a series of massive nonviolent demonstrations. King's Poor People's Campaign attempted to unify African Americans and poor whites in pressing the Administration and Congress to enact a $30-billion-a-year domestic "Marshall Plan" to alleviate poverty. His call for federal assistance mirrored the Kerner Commission's recommendations. King hoped the march on Washington would sustain the momentum of the civil rights movement by broadening its goals to include wider class grievances. He also searched for a nonviolent alternative to the wave of riots that had ripped through black neighborhoods in the preceding years. Although King understood the underlying social causes for the urban uprisings, he believed they were misguided as forms of political protest.[6]

Kennedy and King moved toward an informal political alliance that could be mutually beneficial. The two leaders, King's assistant Andrew Young later explained, "continued down parallel paths of opposition to racism, poverty, and war."[7] Kennedy desperately needed the African-American vote if he was to win the primaries, sidestep the Democratic hierarchy, and ultimately take the nomination from the Administration's candidate-in-waiting, Vice-President Humphrey. If Kennedy was successful, King would be in a position to negotiate with a chief executive who was greatly indebted to the black vote.

The Democratic leadership's apparent swing to the right on the war emboldened conservatives within the party. Kennedy's campaign organization sought to pull the party away from these elements, exclude its prowar, segregationist faction, and move the grassroots activism of the period toward building a new progressive coalition. Large-scale participation and support from African Americans in the Democratic primaries was essential to Kennedy's winning the nomination. The campaign aggressively reached out to blacks, and was active in every region of the country including the Deep South, where a significant number of whites despised Kennedy. One of the overarching aims of the entire campaign became bringing together low-income whites and African Americans wherever possible.

Five years earlier, back in 1963, when Medgar Evers, the chairman of the Mississippi office of the National Association for the Advancement of Colored People (N.A.A.C.P.), was assassinated and and then, only five months later, President John Kennedy was killed, an enduring friendship developed between Robert Kennedy and Medgar Evers's brother, Charles. Charles Evers took his brother's place as the head of Mississippi's N.A.A.C.P., and helped Kennedy win black support in his 1964 New York Senate campaign.[8] Evers came to view Kennedy as the only leader who "offered the nation some hope of bringing the races together."[9] In 1968, Evers worked long hours for Kennedy's presidential campaign in the South and in California. "You should continue to gather steam and go all the way," he wrote Kennedy during the campaign. "I am with you 100 percent."[10]

Although Kennedy had been criticized by some prominent blacks while he was attorney general for not moving quickly and actively enough on civil rights, by the end of the summer of 1963, after prodding by activists, he had repeatedly demonstrated his commitment to the cause of African-American equality. During his Senate years Kennedy assiduously forged strong and enduring bonds with dozens of African-American leaders that transcended conventional politics. For example, after Kennedy attended a memorial service for Medgar Evers at Arlington National Cemetery, Clarence Mitchell, the veteran civil rights leader and director of the Washington, D.C., bureau of the N.A.A.C.P., wrote him a note of appreciation for his "unassuming and quietly sympathetic" appearance at the service. The Senator's presence outside the glare of the press, Mitchell wrote Kennedy, was "one of the many reasons why you hold a place of honor in the circle of public men." "The presence of you and your children," he added, "softened the edge of our sorrow because you, too, bear the weight of a great loss."[11]

In March 1966, Kennedy had visited the Universities of Mississippi and Alabama to speak at racially integrated student-organized events. The students welcomed him back to the scenes of intense racial conflict where his efforts as attorney general had been instrumental in integrating both campuses.[12] Governor George Wallace, a longtime Kennedy detractor and one of the nation's most famous and unapologetic opponents of racial integration, was part of the same forum as Kennedy and also spoke at the state university, though on a different day. Kennedy did not shy away from sparring with the Alabama governor on his home turf. Despite some blustering from Wallace and his supporters, Kennedy's appearances in Alabama had the effect of strengthening the local mobilization of black civil rights activists and their liberal white allies.

Kennedy received an enthusiastic welcome at both the University of Alabama and the University of Mississippi. In his remarks at both campuses, he issued a call to rise above racial hatred, and work together to make the South a more just place for all its citizens. "Negroes must be as free as other Americans," he said, "free to vote and to learn and to earn their way, and to share in the decisions of government which shape their lives." He saw no room for compromise on the issue of equal rights for blacks. "We know we must make progress," he emphasized, "not because it is economically advantageous; not because the law says so; but because it is right."[13]

In June 1966, Kennedy had traveled to South Africa at the invitation of the National Union of South African Students (N.U.S.A.S.). There he met with the "banned" Nobel Peace Prize winner Chief Albert Luthuli, and toured the black township of Soweto. He had been in South Africa when James Meredith, the young civil rights activist who had been the first black ever to attend the University of Mississippi, was shot while embarking on his solo March Against Fear in Mississippi. Before an audience of 7,000 at the University of Witwatersrand, Kennedy stressed the parallels between the racial oppression of South African apartheid and the brand of racism Meredith faced in the American South.[14] Upon his return, he wrote a cover story for *Look* magazine entitled "Suppose God Is Black," drawing on the experience of his trip.[15]

In April 1967, at the urging of Marian Wright, who staffed Mississippi's office of the N.A.A.C.P.'s Legal Defense and Education Fund, Kennedy had returned to Mississippi as a member of a Senate subcommittee on poverty. He met with the N.A.A.C.P. leader Aaron Henry; the head of the Mississippi Freedom Democratic Party (M.F.D.P.), Fannie Lou Hamer; Charles Evers; and Oscar Carr, a wealthy white planter who became an ally of the civil rights movement. They took him through the muddy backroads of the impoverished Mississippi Delta, "one of the worst places [I have] ever seen,"

Evers later said.[16] Wright described the scene at one hamlet they visited: "I was very moved by what Bobby Kennedy did when we went to visit [a black family] in Cleveland, Mississippi," she recalled. "Without cameras . . . we went inside a very dark and dank shack. It was very filthy and very poor. There was a child sitting on a dirt floor, filthy." Kennedy "got down on his knees and he tried to talk to the child and get a response." The malnourished little girl, who was not quite two years old, lay listlessly in Kennedy's arms as he sat rocking her back and forth. He then became angry, Wright remembered, and she "knew that somehow he would be a major force in trying to deal with hunger in Mississippi for children."[17]

Kennedy's maturing awareness of the plight of African Americans during his Senate years was not limited to the South. On August 12, 1965, just five days after Johnson had signed the landmark Voting Rights Act, the Watts-Willowbrook section of South-Central Los Angeles exploded into six days of violence, including widespread acts of arson and looting. When order was finally restored, thirty-five people had been killed, twenty-eight of them black; 900 were injured, and more than 35,000 had been arrested. Twelve thousand National Guardsmen were sent in to quell the disturbance.[18] Racism, poverty, and abuses by local law enforcement officials were the focus of black anger. The Watts rebellion showed Kennedy and the nation the depth of despair in African-American urban communities outside the South.

While the National Guard battled blacks in Watts, Kennedy told reporters that he believed it was pointless to demand African Americans obey the law when they reacted to conditions that would lead any group to lash out at their oppressors.[19] He advocated massive federal assistance to the cities for job training in black urban areas, especially targeting young people. In an offhand remark in the same interview, Kennedy said he believed civil rights leaders, by focusing their attention almost exclusively on the South, had neglected the problems of poverty and racial discrimination that existed in the North and West. This notion resonated powerfully with Martin Luther King, Jr.; "Kennedy's words ate at him," Andrew Young later recalled.[20]

In the wake of the riot, King toured the damaged streets of Watts, and was met with hostility from Los Angeles Mayor Sam Yorty. Yorty, who was a right-wing Democrat and a Kennedy foe, dismissed King's charges of police brutality as ridiculous, and rejected his proposal for a civilian review board to oversee the Los Angeles Police Department.[21] King left the city frustrated, saying that the white leadership of Los Angeles displayed "a blind intransigence and ignorance of the tremendous social forces which are at work here."[22] Kennedy subsequently toured Watts, met with local black leaders, and reached the same conclusion from the rioting as had King. Both King and Kennedy had elicited hostility from L.A.'s white power structure. After seeing Kennedy's stand on the riot, the African-American Democratic state senator from the Watts area, Mervin Dymally, became a strong supporter, and was a Kennedy delegate during the California primary.[23]

While Watts burned, Kennedy addressed the New York State convention of the Odd Fellows to speak out on the issues raised by the rebellion. He singled out unacceptable levels of black unemployment as the primary cause of the uprisings. He praised the accomplishments of the Southern civil rights movement, but added, in a statement that echoed the sentiments of civil rights activists: "It is one thing to assure a man the legal right to eat in a restaurant; it is another thing to assure he can earn the money to eat there." Kennedy argued that the riots arose, in part, from the government's inability to "directly affect the wide margins between Negro and white unemployment rates."[24]

With regard to the apparent disrespect for the law the outbreaks revealed, Kennedy explained that for blacks the law meant "something different" than it did for whites. "Law for the Negro in the South," he said, "has meant beatings and degradation and official discrimination; law has been his oppressor and his enemy. The Negro who has moved North has not found in law the same oppression it meant in the South. But neither has he found a friend and protector." The law, Kennedy said, does not protect blacks "from paying too much money for inferior goods," or "from having their furniture illegally repossessed"; it did not "protect them from having to keep lights turned on the feet of children at night, to keep them from being gnawed by rats." Nor did the legal system "fully protect their lives—their dignity—or encourage their hope and trust in the future."[25]

This strong critique of racism in the American legal system from a former attorney general legitimized those who focused on the underlying social and economic causes of the riots. Kennedy showed an empathy with blacks' frustrations at a time when the right wings of both major political parties were calling for increased repression under the guise of "law and order." From 1965 to 1968, both King's and Kennedy's interpretations of unemployment and poverty as the primary causes of the civil disorders remained essentially unchanged, and were consistent with their initial assessments of the Watts riot.[26] They both also firmly believed that as forms of protest the riots were counterproductive.

Although Kennedy's brief tenure in the Senate granted him relatively little time for building a legislative record, he succeeded in inserting his views into the national debate on poverty, civil rights, and the explosive race relations in the cities. He served on the Senate's Labor and Public Welfare Committee, and on two subcommittees that dealt exclusively with domestic poverty: the Subcommittee on Manpower, Employment, and Poverty, and the Subcommittee on Migratory Labor. Kennedy's work on these committees established him as one of the Senate's most outspoken allies of African Americans, workers, and the poor.

He sponsored or cosponsored amendments to the Economic Opportunity Act of 1964 that increased spending on antipoverty programs. He amended the Civil Rights and Voting Rights Acts to strengthen their provisions against discrimination in housing, and to streamline laws so blacks could more easily register to vote in the South. As a member of the District of Columbia Committee, he introduced bills to establish a community college and college of arts and sciences, another bill requiring landlords to repair substandard rental housing, and a provision to allow for eventual home rule in the overwhelmingly black District.[27]

In January 1966, Kennedy had clarified his views on poverty in three lengthy speeches which set the stage for him to present comprehensive legislation to deal with urban unemployment.[28] In October, he called for a massive increase in federal aid to provide jobs for inner city blacks; he sponsored amendments to several acts passed by the 89th Congress in the areas of health, education, and welfare to increase the federal commitment to urban blacks. "No Government program now operating," he said in the fall of 1966, "gives any substantial promise of meeting the unemployment crisis affecting the Negro of the cities."[29] In 1967, he cosponsored the Emergency Employment Act, which proposed allocating $2.8 billion for the rapid creation of 200,000 jobs, with another 250,000 jobs earmarked for the following year in African-American communities.[30]

Kennedy had toured the Bedford-Stuyvesant section of Brooklyn on several occasions, and believed it a good site for putting into practice an attempt at a self-sustaining, private/public partnership in rebuilding an impoverished community. It was a neighborhood of over 400,000 people, 84 percent black and 12 percent Puerto Rican, living in disintegrating brownstone tenements, amidst abandoned buildings and trash-strewn vacant lots. The program required grassroots community participation at every level of planning and development.

The rough-and-tumble Democratic politics of New York City made initiating the project a difficult task. Kennedy invited the New York Republicans Senator Jacob Javits and Mayor John Lindsay of New York City to assist in the planning and implementation of the program. He had attached an amendment to the Economic Opportunity Act of 1966 that successfully wrested $7 million in federal start-up funding for his Special Impact Program in Bedford-Stuyvesant. He hoped this pilot program might serve as a model for similar projects throughout the nation. In December 1966, at a public school in "Bed-Sty," Kennedy outlined the goals, structures, and requirements for the endeavor.[31] The overarching goal was to create sustainable, well-paying, skilled jobs for the community, by attracting private investment in partnership with federal, state, and local government.

Under Kennedy's direction, two nonprofit public-interest corporations were formed, one to manage the rebuilding of the physical infrastructure of the area, the other to enlist private sector investment in job training and job creation. The chairman of the Bedford-Stuyvesant Renewal and Rehabilitation Corporation was the local Judge Thomas Jones. The Development and Services Corporation included private sector executives, and Kennedy friends such as former Secretary of the Treasury Douglas Dillon, and Thomas Watson of I.B.M.

"We are all in this together," Kennedy told the community gathering, which also included Senator Javits and Mayor Lindsay. "Today on this platform and in this room, there are Democrats and Republicans, white and black, businessmen and government officials, rich and poor, and people from every part of this varied community. This is a unique effort—the only one of its kind and scope in the country. We have to show that it can be done. We are going to try, as few have tried before," he said, "not just to have programs like others have, but to create new kinds of systems for education and health and employment and housing. We here are going to see, in fact, whether the city and its people, with the cooperation of government and private business and foundations, can meet the challenge of urban life in the last third of the twentieth century."[32] Kennedy and his staff then produced a comprehensive program to try to apply the principles of the Special Impact Program nationally. By using the same kind of tax incentives and guarantees the federal government gave corporations that invested abroad, Kennedy wanted to prod capital to invest in domestic poverty zones.[33]

In 1967, Kennedy introduced two highly complex bills which had taken his legislative aides Peter Edelman and Adam Walinsky about six months to prepare and required the substantial rewriting of the nation's tax law. The first bill, the Urban and Rural Employment Opportunities Development Act, provided, among other initiatives, tax incentives for private industry to invest in poverty areas based on provisions similar to those of the Foreign Investment Credit Act, which was designed to fuel American investment in underdeveloped nations. The second bill, formerly known as the Urban Housing Development Act, furnished benefits including tax credits and low-interest loans to firms which agreed to construct low-rent housing in poverty areas under specific conditions, stipulating that they employ workers from the local community. These acts sought to institutionalize on a federal level some of the programs that had been implemented in Bedford-Stuyvesant.

Despite Kennedy's efforts, and the Johnson Administration's antipoverty programs (which were beginning to buckle under the fiscal constraints of the Vietnam War), the riots in urban black communities continued to intensify in the years following Watts. In 1966, there were 53 outbursts of violence in 44 cities for a total of 92 days; in 1967, there were 82 outbursts in 71 cities over a period of 270 days; and by the end of 1968 there had been, in that one year, 155 outbursts in 106 cities lasting over 286 days.[34] In the summer of 1967, the largest of the riots of the 1960s broke out in Detroit. After the task of restoring order proved beyond the capacity of Michigan's National Guard, Republican Governor George Romney turned to President Johnson for troops. Johnson sent in the 82nd Airborne. When it was over, there were 43 dead, about 1,000 people injured, 7,000 arrested, and $50 million in property destruction.[35]

The riots produced a response from the Johnson Administration in the form of some increased aid to the cities. But after the summer of 1967, the emphasis on repression and social control overshadowed ameliorative federal action.[36] The Administration shifted its attention from alleviating black poverty and creating jobs to allocating funds for training local police forces in riot control. In early 1968, Johnson had publicly compared the Detroit rebellion to the Tet Offensive in South Vietnam.[37] (He also privately shared with his foreign policy advisers his reluctance to send more troops to Vietnam "because of the possibility of civil disturbances here in the U.S.")[38] By 1968, Johnson rarely spoke of building a Great Society anymore, and along with his snubbing of the Kerner Commission, revealed he had moved toward law-and-order solutions to social problems. Following the Detroit riot, Kennedy called for a freeze in spending on the Vietnam War in order to divert $2 to $4 billion to emergency poverty assistance. Kennedy's advocacy of a shift from guns to butter caught the suspicious eyes of the Director of the Federal Bureau of Investigation, J. Edgar Hoover, who sensed a hidden communist influence.[39]

Kennedy's call for programs and provisions such as a negative income tax, family and children allowances, income supplements, and a guaranteed annual income, sought to move beyond race-specific federal antipoverty programs.[40] He seriously discussed solutions to the problem of urban poverty that would cost the federal government $100 billion.[41] Throughout 1967, he moved steadily toward class-based solutions to poverty designed to give people the opportunity to work, while maintaining a floor below which the poor of all races could not fall.

By the time of the 1968 presidential primaries, Kennedy had garnered strong political support among African Americans in Detroit, Chicago, Los Angeles, New York, and other cities. His presidential campaign aggressively recruited poverty workers associated with the earlier Great Society programs. Kennedy's staffers went so far as to refer to the riots and civil disturbances in black communities as "civil rights indicators," which could ultimately help Kennedy win black support.[42]

The goals and practices of the Kennedy campaign represented the polar opposite of what became known as the Republicans' Southern strategy. In March 1968, Richard Nixon emerged as the GOP front-runner after winning the New Hampshire primary, and he carefully positioned himself to take advantage of the rifts within Democratic ranks that the Administration's handling of the war, and its efforts in favor of civil rights, had created. Although Nixon's views on race relations were far more moderate than the overt bigotry of Wallace, he nonetheless saw an opening to exploit the white uneasiness with perceived black political gains. Nixon's so-called Southern strategy had nationwide implications, since it fueled white backlash tendencies everywhere, especially in places where blacks and whites lived in relatively close proximity due to similar economic class conditions.[43]

The success or failure of this strategy depended upon the use of subtle (and not-so-subtle) codes, which framed the policy debates about crime, welfare, integration and other issues. These codes were designed to play on white fears of black demands, and drive a wedge between whites and African Americans, with a particular interest in dividing low-income people generally. Crime, poverty, and the riots were to be associated in the public mind as arising from afflictions that African-American communities brought upon themselves. In early 1968, in exchange for Southern support, Nixon worked out a deal with Republican state chairmen from the South, promising to roll back federally mandated desegregation, and to appoint "strict constructionist" Justices to the Supreme Court if he were elected president.[44] In contrast, Kennedy's campaign strategy, which also had clear political implications for race relations nationally, had been built upon years of cultivating ties with African-American civil rights leaders, with the clearly stated goal of fostering equality, integration, and racial solidarity.

The task of directing Kennedy's own Southern strategy fell on John Seigenthaler who, as the editor of the *Nashville Tennessean*, and a lawyer who had served as Kennedy's administrative assistant at the Justice Department, was highly knowledgeable about civil rights and Southern politics.[45] Seigenthaler was a valuable ally in the attempt to win Kennedy supporters in the South and border states. At a time when Wallace and other segregationists were fanning the flames of the white backlash, and black separatism was on the rise among the youth contingent of the civil rights movement—most notably within the Student Non-Violent Coordinating Committee (S.N.C.C.)—the Kennedy campaign managed to make modest progress in bridging the racial divide even in the Deep South.[46]

In Mississippi, the Kennedy campaign gained political support from some of the former members of the Mississippi Freedom Democratic Party (M.F.D.P.), which had tried unsuccessfully to field an alternative delegate slate independent of the Democrats' regular segregationist delegation at the 1964 Democratic National Convention.[47] The campaign also showed some success in winning the support of Mississippi Democratic leaders who had been part of the regular Democratic delegation in 1964.[48]

Postwar social and economic trends in the South, including urbanization and industrialization, made possible a loose political alliance of progressive business elites, liberal whites, and large numbers of newly franchised African Americans.[49] These groups became the Kennedy campaign's main targets in the South. Through bringing together a minority of white liberals and a majority of African Americans (thousands of whom could potentially vote for the first time because of the 1965 Voting Rights Act), the campaign hoped to create racially integrated delegations throughout the South that were independent of the formal Democratic Party organization.[50] Kennedy capitalized on the identity crisis afflicting the Southern wing of the party after a decade of civil rights victories for blacks.

The campaign also sought the support, wherever possible, of regular Democrats who opposed the party organization's handpicked candidates.

The goal was to peel off Democratic officials and fence-sitters. It was in Kennedy's political interest to demand aggressive enforcement of the provisions of the Voting Rights Act to extend the franchise to as many blacks as possible in the South. The campaign also ran its own voter registration drives among Southern blacks. In Mississippi, the Kennedy campaign pulled together an integrated state delegation headed by the leader of the Young Democrats Hodding Carter III, Oscar Carr, Charles Evers, and the veteran S.N.C.C. activist Lawrence Guyot.[51] These and other civil rights leaders in Mississippi subsequently formed an independent Kennedy for President committee.[52]

Similar to the M.F.D.P., the Kennedy campaign's overall goal for Mississippi, according to one campaign memo, was to create "a liberal and biracial Democratic coalition to supplant the traditional segregated party."[53] Compared to Nixon's presidential campaign strategy, the Kennedy campaign's goal might be called a reverse Southern strategy. If the campaign fostered biracial political alliances in Mississippi, it could repeat that strategy elsewhere in the country.

In Alabama, when it became apparent that Wallace was attempting to take over the Democratic electors for his newly formed American Independence Party, his action led a group of Democrats to sponsor their own slate, and seek sanctuary inside the Kennedy organization. Members of this alternative Democratic group, which was estimated to represent at least "95 percent of the Negro political strength," provided the Kennedy campaign with canvassers who were experienced civil rights organizers.[54]

On March 21, 1968, just five days after Kennedy announced his candidacy, he traveled to the heart of Wallace country.[55] Before an audience of 9,000 at the University of Alabama's Tuscaloosa campus (where five years earlier Wallace had stood in the schoolhouse door to block the registration of two black students, Vivian Malone and James Hood), Kennedy called for racial equality and reconciliation. "We have to begin to put our country together again," he told the integrated audience. "So I believe that any who seek high office this year must go before all Americans: Not just those who agree with them, but also those who disagree; recognizing that it is not just our supporters, not just those who vote for us, but all Americans, who we must lead in the difficult years ahead. And this is why I have come at the outset of my campaign, not to New York or Chicago or Boston, but here to Alabama."[56] In Alabama, as in Mississippi, the Kennedy campaign showed early success in attracting the support of members of the regular Democratic delegation.[57] The campaign fought Wallace in his own backyard, and aggressively sought to build biracial coalitions.

In the spring of 1968, Martin Luther King, Jr. dedicated himself to a similar set of objectives. "The primary Negro political goal in the South," he wrote, "is the elimination of racism as an electoral issue." African Americans and lower-income whites, King hoped, "will develop an alliance that displaces the Wallaces and with them racism as a political issue."[58] Regarding the 1968 elections, King wrote that one of his goals was to mobilize the African-American vote to "undermine the Congressional coalition of Southern reactionaries and their Northern Republican colleagues."[59] King was committed to stopping Nixon's Southern strategy in its tracks, and Kennedy shared this goal.

Kennedy had strong support among northern blacks as well. Just after he announced his candidacy, the African-American Congressman John Conyers of Michigan told the campaign that he was "four-square" behind Kennedy's candidacy. Conyers wanted "to do all he could to help," and believed Kennedy had "an excellent opportunity to line up substantially all the Michigan delegation."[60] Conyers and the singer Harry Belafonte were two people whom King and the Southern Christian Leadership Conference (S.C.L.C.) used behind the scenes to "secure influence" with Kennedy without having to make a formal endorsement.[61] The Democratic leaders of two of Detroit's thirteen districts, which were 75 percent African American and the site of the summer's riot, declared themselves uncommitted to the national ticket to remain open to joining the Kennedy cause.[62]

Mayor Richard Hatcher of Gary, Indiana, the second black ever elected mayor of a northern city, also supported Kennedy. In 1967, he had won his mayoral election against the Gary political machine by a tiny 1,300-vote margin. The national news media closely followed the election because of its racial overtones. Kennedy had campaigned for Hatcher, and provided the black mayoral candidate with the services of his experienced political operative, Dick Tuck, to assist in the campaign.[63]

On the afternoon of March 31, 1968, prior to Johnson's withdrawal from the race that evening, King flatly told the press: "I cannot support President Johnson for reelection." King and other S.C.L.C. leaders met later that day with Representative Conyers and Mayor Hatcher, important young black politicians and strong Kennedy partisans. They discussed creating a national commission of inquiry to examine the policy positions of the presidential candidates. King followed the S.C.L.C.'s practice of withholding endorsements of any political candidates in national elections, but his strong private preference was clearly for Kennedy, who he said would make a "great president."[64]

King's close friend and executive assistant of the S.C.L.C., Andrew Young, reflected later that spring on King's perceptions of Kennedy: "There was a strange attitude of both admiration and caution in Martin's conversations about Bobby," Young wrote in response to an interviewer's query. King "was extremely impressed" with Kennedy's "capacity to learn, to grow, and to deal creatively in any given situation."

> He felt inadequate in his "political" actions and saw Bobby as a man of both moral courage and a keen sense of political timing. . . . He admired Bobby's blend of "crusader" and realistic politician. . . .
>
> Although Martin was a long time giving up on Lyndon Johnson, he always placed a great deal of hope in the fact that Bobby was a force to be reckoned with and stood in the wings as a "beacon of hope" for the poor, the black, the young and the otherwise alienated idealists of our nation.

Neither King nor Kennedy could have profited by "an overt relationship, and both avoided any direct association." Yet, in Young's view, "a distant camaraderie which needed no formal tie or physical link" developed between the two men, "a genuine spiritual brotherhood which leaped across the widest chasms of our time—a bridge across lines of race, class and geography which nevertheless led them to [a] common faith [and] hope."[65]

Kennedy and King both had repeatedly criticized the disproportionate number of African-American servicemen who fought in Vietnam. It was the key reason why Kennedy opposed college draft deferments, which he considered demonstrably discriminatory against blacks, Latinos, and poor whites. Kennedy deplored the number of African Americans killed in Vietnam. "Negroes, 11 percent of the population," he said, "suffer 22 percent of all combat deaths in the jungles of Vietnam."[66] King also noted this discrepancy. "There were twice as many Negroes as whites in combat in Vietnam at the beginning of 1967," he wrote, "and twice as many Negro soldiers died in action in proportion to their numbers in the population."[67]

Like Kennedy, King had been cautious in formulating his opposition to the war. Given his deep gratitude for Johnson's commitment to civil rights, King carefully crafted his antiwar views, and did not wish to risk his working relationship with the President. King waited until April 1967 to break with Johnson, and when he finally repudiated the war, King, like Kennedy, suffered attacks by the press and many former political allies.

When King criticized Johnson on the war, Roy Wilkins, the president of the N.A.A.C.P., and Whitney Young, the head of the Urban League, both sharply disassociated themselves from King and the S.C.L.C. Other prominent African Americans openly criticized and distanced themselves from King, including the diplomat Ralph Bunche, the former baseball star Jackie Robinson, and Senator Edward Brooke of Massachusetts. The N.A.A.C.P. went so far as to pass a resolution explicitly denouncing any attempt to link the civil rights and antiwar movements. Prominent journals such as the *Washington Post*, the *New York Times*, and *Life* magazine flayed King for his stand against the war, and his break with Johnson as detrimental to the cause of civil rights.[68] By 1968, King, like Kennedy, was attempting to unite not only proponents of the civil rights movement, but those who supported civil rights *and* opposed the Vietnam War.

King and Kennedy also shared some bitter enemies. In addition to the hatred both leaders could evoke in extreme anti-Communists and white supremacists, they also sparked the antagonism of the federal law enforcement establishment. The FBI's harassment of King is well documented.[69] Kennedy himself had played a role in the FBI's surveillance of King when he was attorney general, and in 1962 had authorized Hoover's request for a wiretap on King and his aide Stanley Levison, who Hoover believed was a communist. It was an egregious violation of King's and Levison's civil liberties that Hoover later used to embarrass Kennedy during the presidential campaign. However, Kennedy's cooperation with the FBI in 1962 while he was attorney general did not prevent the ever-suspicious Hoover from planting informants inside Kennedy's regional campaign organizations, and keeping a close eye on the candidate's public appearances.[70]

King believed a massive march of poor people on the nation's capital could broaden the civil rights movement, and bring about a class coalition that crossed racial lines. He believed that by building bridges to the white poor and working-class the movement might gain greater political strength in an election year, and give greater visibility to the issue of poverty. He said the protest march would be "a Selma-like movement on economic issues," referring to the demonstrations in Alabama that helped win passage of the Voting Rights Act.[71] King called for new federal programs that "go beyond race and deal with economic inequality, wherever it exists." He hoped that the white poor could be engaged in the struggle, and forge a "powerful new alliance."[72]

King's Poor People's Campaign and Kennedy's presidential campaign both fought uphill battles, but they moved in the same general direction, toward a class-based, multiracial coalition. King reached out to lower-income whites from his primary base among African Americans; Kennedy tapped blacks from his primary base of lower-class and working-class whites. "As we work to get rid of the economic strangulation that we face as a result of poverty," King wrote, "we must not overlook the fact that millions of Puerto Ricans, Mexican Americans, Indians, and Appalachian whites are also poverty stricken. Any serious war against poverty must of necessity include them."[73]

The election year presented an opportunity to organize the nation's poor, and breathe new life into the nonviolent civil disobedience of African Americans and their allies. The lure of electoral politics might then attract the thousands of young people, black and white, who had begun to embrace and romanticize violent tactics for social change. King designed the campaign to mobilize poor people, build on the past successes of the civil rights movement, and, most importantly, keep the issues of race relations and poverty on the front burner in a year which promised a pivotal election.

With the Poor People's Campaign, King said he wished to "transmute the rage of the ghetto into a positive constructive force." There must be "a radical re-ordering of priorities," he explained, including "a de-escalation and final stopping of the war in Vietnam, and an escalation of the war against poverty and racism here at home." He sought the help of the antiwar movement in making the Poor People's Campaign a success, by linking poverty with the waste of resources on the war. He promised to bring a core group of "about 3,000 people to Washington," including the entire impoverished hamlet of Marks, Mississippi.[74]

The poor people and their allies planned to occupy the public spaces of Washington for "at least sixty days, or however long we feel it necessary," King promised. He hoped it would be reminiscent of the 1963 March on Washington. He said the campaign would culminate on June 15 in a massive rally. "We want to provide an opportunity once more for thousands, hundreds of thousands of people to come to Washington," he said. "We hope that all of our friends will go out of their way to make that a big day, indeed the largest march that has ever taken place in the city of Washington."[75]

The Poor People's Campaign was not only a bold attempt to unite the Northern and Southern black rights movements, but also, as King had said explicitly on several occasions, to forge a class-based movement was his ultimate goal.[76] It was an enormous gamble, and the movement suffered some serious setbacks, but King believed that a new class coalition was the next, and possibly only, logical step left for the maturing civil rights movement of the late 1960s. Robert Kennedy strongly supported the hopes and objectives of King's Poor People's Campaign.[77] Like King, he viewed the march as a positive alternative to riots, one that could reassert the efficacy of nonviolent direct action and pull the debate away from the politics of racial division and "law and order" of the Wallaces and Nixons. Given Kennedy's uphill climb to win the presidential nomination, King's mass mobilization of blacks and lower-income whites could help him politically.

In addition to Marian Wright, the Kennedy campaign's most direct link to the Poor People's Campaign was through the antipoverty researcher and democratic socialist Michael Harrington. Harrington first received national recognition in 1962 with publication of his influential book on poverty, *The Other America*, which President John Kennedy had praised.[78] He served on the S.C.L.C. research committee that was responsible for drafting the policy demands of the Poor People's Campaign.[79] He also actively campaigned for Kennedy in Indiana and California.[80] Harrington called Kennedy "one of the most compassionate and conscientious of men with regard to the ghettos."[81]

In late March 1968, against the advice of some of his closest advisers, King took time out from organizing the Poor People's Campaign to travel to Memphis to help with a month-long strike of the city's 1,300 African-American sanitation workers. He felt obliged to his old friend in Memphis, Reverend James Lawson, who had been a pivotal figure in the early days of the civil rights movement and who asked King for his assistance in the struggle against a recalcitrant local white power structure in Memphis. On March 28, King led about 9,000 people on a march through downtown Memphis. The demonstration quickly degenerated into violence after young blacks at the rear, some of whom were probably agents provocateurs, began smashing windows and fighting with police. When the riot was over, one black youth had been shot and killed by police, sixty people were injured, and 4,000 Tennessee National Guardsmen had closed off the central city. The Kennedy campaign closely followed these events in Memphis.[82]

The news media, encouraged secretly by the FBI, lambasted King for not being able to control the demonstration.[83] In Washington, conservative members of Congress called for denying King permits to bring the Poor People's Campaign to the capital. If King could not prevent violence at a relatively small march in Memphis, they argued, how could he prevent violence from occurring at a demonstration many times that size in the nation's capital? The *Wall Street Journal*, showing how strongly Kennedy had become identified with the demands of the Poor People's Campaign, suggested that Kennedy would lose votes in the primaries if the Washington protest turned violent: "Might there be a sharp reaction against him as the man whose speeches helped stir the rioters?" the editors asked.[84]

On Sunday, March 31, 1968, in a sermon in Washington's National Cathedral, King promised to bring to the nation's capital "the tired, the poor, the huddled masses." He said all they were asking for was what the Declaration of Independence had promised all Americans: life, liberty, and the pursuit of happiness.[85] King had lofty intentions for the march, but it was uncertain whether he could deliver. The demands included Congressional enactment of a full-employment plan, a guaranteed annual income, and construction funds for at least 500,000 units of low-cost housing each year.[86] The early organizing for the campaign was slow and arduous. King contemplated calling it off on more than one occasion, and twice was forced to postpone its opening date.

A few days after his Sunday sermon, King returned to Memphis to redeem the movement, and make another attempt at a peaceful march through the downtown streets. The fate of the Poor People's Campaign depended on his ability to prove to the nation that he could keep his protests from turning violent. He also felt obligated to the sanitation workers and their supporters, who had condemned the violence of the previous demonstration as the handiwork of a tiny minority of young people.

On April 3, 1968, a night of hurricane-force winds and severe storm warnings throughout the South, King spoke to an audience of about three thousand who crammed into the Masonic Temple in the black part of Memphis. He was pained that the media had only focused on the violence of the previous protest. The press, he said, "very seldom got around to mentioning the fact that one thousand, three hundred sanitation workers were on strike, and that Memphis is not being fair to them. . . . We have an opportunity to make America a better nation," he said. "And I want to thank God, once more, for allowing me to be here with you."[87]

That stormy evening, King once again demonstrated his mastery of the art of oratory, closing his prescient, emotion-filled speech:

> . . . Like anybody, I would like to live a long life. Longevity has its place. But I'm not concerned about that now. I just want to do God's will. And he's allowed me to go up to the mountain. And I've looked over. And I've seen the promised land. I may not get there with you. But I want you to know tonight, that we, as a people will get to the promised land. And I'm happy, tonight. I'm not worried about anything. I'm not fearing any man. Mine eyes have seen the glory of the coming of the Lord![88]

The following day, April 4, 1968, just before 6:00 P.M., King, his brother A.D. King, and some aides, prepared to leave the black-owned Loraine Motel. On the second floor, King emerged from room 306, and walked on to the balcony. A loud report like that of a car backfiring reverberated through the courtyard. An uncommonly accurate shot fired from a high-powered rifle ripped through King's neck, and within the hour the black spiritual leader had bled to death. He was 39 years old.

Kennedy heard the news of the shooting just before boarding a plane in Muncie, Indiana, to fly to Indianapolis. He was scheduled to kick off the formal opening of the Indiana Kennedy for President headquarters at a rally in the heart of the poorest black neighborhood of the city.[89] In Indianapolis, Kennedy learned that King was dead. Although word of the assassination had not yet reached those waiting to attend the Kennedy rally at the Broadway Center Outdoor Basketball Court, there had been news reports of rioting in a few black communities across the country. The Republican mayor of Indianapolis, Richard Lugar, concluded it was too dangerous for him to go through with the planned gathering and avoided the area. The chief of police advised Kennedy not to go because he expected violence as soon as the news of the shooting became known. The police offered only to escort the Senator and his entourage to the edge of the black neighborhood.

Even before King's assassination, there had been reports that the crowd at Kennedy's scheduled appearance in the black section of Indianapolis might become unruly. On April 3, the FBI's Special Agent in Charge (S.A.C.) in Indianapolis reported to the Bureau's headquarters that "the Kennedy rallies scheduled for April 4 in Indianapolis might be subject to some violence simply to embarrass Senator Kennedy." (Whether or not this refers to deliberately planted agents provocateurs is unclear. Substantial portions of the memo, obtained under the Freedom of Information Act, have been blacked out.) The heavily censored memo closes with a promise to "advise the Bureau concerning any information of interest that might develop concerning the scheduled rallies in the Negro neighborhoods of Indianapolis on April 4."[90]

After sending his wife Ethel ahead to a nearby hotel, Kennedy rode in silence to the site. His car became separated from his advisers and the press bus. When the rest of the motorcade caught up, one of his aides rushed up with some suggestions for talking points; Kennedy just crumpled the notes, and stuffed them in his pocket as he climbed onto a flatbed truck which served as a makeshift stage. He specifically requested that he not be introduced. Floodlights, rocking back and forth in the cold and blustery wind, provided the only illumination. Speaking extemporaneously, his voice anguished, Kennedy addressed the crowd of about one thousand African Americans.

"Ladies and Gentlemen, I am only going to talk to you just for a minute or so this evening because I have some very sad news for all of you," he began. "I have bad news for you, for all of our fellow citizens, and people who love peace all over the world and that is that Martin Luther King was shot and killed tonight." Those gathered, most of whom had not yet received word of the news, let out an audible gasp followed by screams of "No! No!" Kennedy briefly paused, then went on. "Martin Luther King dedicated his life to love and to justice for his fellow human beings, and he died because of that effort.

"In this difficult day, in this difficult time for the United States, it is perhaps well to ask what kind of a nation we are and what direction we want to move in. For those of you who are black—considering the evidence there evidently is that there were white people who were responsible—you can be filled with bitterness, with hatred, and a desire for revenge. We can move in that direction as a country, in great polarization—black people amongst black, white people amongst white, filled with hatred for one another.

"Or we can make an effort, as Martin Luther King did, to understand and to comprehend, and to replace that violence, that stain of bloodshed that has spread across our land, with an effort to understand with compassion and love.

"For those of you who are black and tempted to be filled with hatred and distrust at the injustice of such an act, against all white people, I can only say that I feel in my own heart the same kind of feeling. I had a member of my family killed, but he was killed by a white man. But we have to make an effort in the United States, we have to make an effort to understand, to go beyond these rather difficult times." Kennedy had never before referred to his brother's assassination in a public address. He then recited a line from a poem that had consoled him after President Kennedy's death.

"My favorite poet," he said, "was Aeschylus. He wrote: 'In our sleep, pain which cannot forget falls drop by drop upon the heart until, in our own despair, against our will, comes wisdom through the awful grace of God.'

"What we need in the United States is not division; what we need in the United States is not hatred; what we need in the United States is not violence or lawlessness; but love and wisdom, and compassion toward one another, and a feeling of justice toward those who still suffer within our country, whether they be white or they be black.

"So I shall ask you tonight to return home and say a prayer for the family of Martin Luther King. But more importantly, say a prayer for our own country, which all of us love—a prayer for understanding and that compassion of which I spoke.

"We can do well in this country. We will have difficult times; we've had difficult times in the past; we will have difficult times in the future. It is not the end of violence; it is not the end of lawlessness; it is not the end of disorder.

"But the vast majority of white people and the vast majority of black people in this country want to live together, want to improve the quality of our life, and want justice for all human beings who abide in our land.

"Let us dedicate ourselves to what the Greeks wrote so many years ago: to tame the savageness of man and make gentle the life of this world.

"Let us dedicate ourselves to that, and say a prayer for our country and for our people."[91]

The assassination of Martin Luther King, Jr. for thousands of African Americans meant also the end of nonviolence as a principle and tactic. Indianapolis remained quiet that night after Kennedy's remarks, while rioting spread through the black neighborhoods of 110 cities. When the wave of violence passed, there were 39 deaths, 2,500 injuries, and tens of millions of dollars in property damage. Despite the rioting in Pittsburgh, Chicago, Philadelphia, Washington, D.C., and other cities after King's assassination, a Kennedy contact reported at that time that the black communities all over the country were "firmly behind the candidacy of RFK," and the "tremendously competent ghetto leadership will make a great contribution to the campaign."[92]

Kennedy canceled his campaign events and phoned King's widow, Coretta Scott King, in Atlanta. At her request, he asked Mankiewicz to arrange for the slain civil rights leader's body to be flown from Memphis to Atlanta. Most air carriers, fearing the notoriety on the night of violence, refused to take on the task. In the early morning hours, a private plane was chartered from a Kennedy friend. Kennedy sent his African-American assistant, Earl Graves, and a group of young staffers to assist Coretta King. He also had three telephones installed at her residence the night of the assassination to deal with the barrage of incoming calls, and his staff set up a bank of phone lines in the West Hunter Baptist church in Atlanta for the King family's use.[93]

The FBI's Atlanta office sent Director Hoover a teletype marked "urgent" notifying him that Kennedy had supplied phones for King's widow. "This is a Negro Baptist church," an informant reported, "staffed by people employed by Senator Kennedy. Kennedy allegedly installed phones for use of the King family, relatives, and friends, and members of [the] Southern Christian Leadership Conference for their convenience in handling funeral arrangements, and the crowd expected to be in Atlanta for King's funeral." The FBI's Special Agent in Charge in Indianapolis also reported directly to Hoover the details of Kennedy's impromptu eulogy for King. The reports, which have large sections blacked out, came from two FBI informants, one inside the S.C.L.C., the other inside the Kennedy campaign.[94]

Hoover, who had routinely called Kennedy a "liar" and other epithets in the margins of internal memoranda,[95] sent the S.A.C. in Indianapolis a personal note of appreciation for his "thoughtfulness in keeping me apprised of events in the Indianapolis area," while Kennedy campaigned there.[96] Hoover and his Bureau, in addition to shamelessly harassing King, had been involved in efforts to "thwart" the "Black Power-Vietnik Coalition" of which the Kennedy campaign in their eyes had apparently become part.[97]

Black leaders in Cleveland prevailed upon Kennedy not to cancel a previously scheduled speaking engagement for the night of April 5, and to use the occasion to speak about violence in America. On the night King was killed, Kennedy stayed up late in his room in the Mariott Inn, Indianapolis, with his aides, Walinsky and Greenfield, to work on the next night's speech via telephone with Sorensen, who was in New York.[98] In Cleveland, Kennedy told a City Club audience: "We calmly accept newspaper reports of civilian slaughter in far-off lands. We make it easy for men of all shades of sanity to acquire whatever weapons and ammunition they desire." He then pointed to another form of violence that was "just as deadly destructive as the shot or the bomb in the night. This is the violence of institutions; indifference and inaction and slow decay. This is the violence that afflicts the poor, that poisons relations between men because their skin has different colors. This is the slow destruction of a child by hunger, and schools without books and homes without heat in the winter."[99]

The strong association between Kennedy and King in the public mind is illustrated by some of the letters Kennedy received from blacks in the aftermath of King's assassination. For example, on April 6, 1968, four African-American combat soldiers wrote Kennedy from their post on the frontlines in Vietnam. The black servicemen, all from the Deep South, expressed their feelings to Kennedy after hearing the news of King's death. Their letter is transcribed here as it was written:

Our home are Mississippi and Tennessee, we heard on the radio about Rev. Martin L. King was shot and kill yesterday in Tennessee and we don't feel good about it.

We are think why are we fighting so hard to kill the Viet Cong when they have not done anything to us. Yet back in the State our Leader are been kill like the Viet Cong over here.

If we do have to fighting why can't we fight back in the State where we can help our Self. Over here we are not help our self. Now we are about to agree with C Clay who refused the draft into the U.S. Army.

When he said, "why must we free the Vietnamese people when we don't have freedom in our own States." This prove Clay was right and if nothing don't be done about this right away then all Negroes should refuse to come in the army.

Now we hope to hear from you about this problem, because we are fighting harder than the other and we would love to come home to that same freedom as the other.

Good luck in your presidential election we are for you because we know you will help everybody.

Your Truly
From Viet-Nam
Sgt. Gilleglen "and other"[100]

In the days following King's death, Kennedy received other letters of support from bereaved blacks. The leadership of the National Association of Colored Women's Clubs sent Kennedy a telegram supporting his "plea for continued nonviolence in pursuing the cause, and the course which Dr. Martin Luther King loved and served so well."[101] A black women's group in New Haven, Connecticut, which had begun a nonviolent protest and boycott "as a memorial to Doctor King," sent Kennedy a telegram asking him for assistance against attacks from "white gangs." The African-American women's group informed the Senator that the police refused to protect them even though white hoodlums had brandished guns and hospitalized two of their members.[102]

On April 7, 1968, Robert and Ethel Kennedy, Marian Wright and Peter Edelman, and a small group of local officials, children, and citizens walked through the riot-torn neighborhoods of the nation's capital. A Washington, D.C., city councilman, Reverend Walter Fauntroy, recalled the scene: "The stench of burning wood and broken glass were all over the place. We walked the streets. The troops were on duty. A crowd gathered behind us, following Bobby Kennedy. The troops saw us coming at a distance, and they put on their gas masks, and got the guns ready, waiting for this horde of blacks coming up the street. When they saw it was Bobby Kennedy, they took off their masks and let us through. They looked awfully relieved."[103] This incident may be enough to suggest what Kennedy's role in the weeks following King's murder would prove to be. People who hoped to keep King's legacy of nonviolence alive now looked to Robert Kennedy for leadership.

Two days later, King's funeral was held at Ebenezer Baptist Church, where King's father had first begun his ministry.[104] Robert and Ethel Kennedy met with Coretta King to express their condolences. Most of the presidential contenders attended the funeral, including Humphrey and Nelson Rockefeller. Richard Nixon arrived to shouts of "politicking" from the crowd; Johnson sent flowers and a card.[105] McCarthy originally did not want to attend the funeral, and relented only when his campaign manager, Blair Clark, insisted that he go.[106] Inside the church, McCarthy sat directly behind Kennedy, allowing for a rare wire-service photo of the two of them together. The thousands of blacks who walked with King's coffin, placed atop a mule cart, after the service showed a nearly tangible warmth for Kennedy as he joined them for the five-mile journey from the church to another service at Morehouse College, King's alma mater. King's final destination was the South View Cemetery, a modest hillside graveyard founded in 1866 by six blacks who were fed up with carrying their dead to the "colored" area through the rear gates of the municipal cemetery.[107]

* * *

Although Johnson continued to fight for civil rights legislation, such as the Fair Housing Act outlawing racial discrimination in housing, which he signed into law in the wake of King's death, his commitment to stay the course in Vietnam undermined his support among civil rights activists at the local level. King's stand against the war split the movement, as the leaders of the more mainstream civil rights groups refused to break with the Johnson Administration. In the final year of his life, King had toured the country denouncing the Administration for spending hundreds of thousands of dollars for each enemy killed in Vietnam, while spending less than $100 on each American living in poverty. Johnson, King argued, had sacrificed the Great Society in the jungles of Vietnam. During his presidential campaign, Kennedy framed his criticisms of the war, as well as of the shamefully unjust treatment of blacks and other minority groups in the United States, in terms nearly identical to King's.

Like King, Kennedy believed that the federal government had an obligation to use its power to redistribute wealth downward as a means of helping the poor:[108] "In my judgment it is imperative that we lessen the gulf which divides those who have and those who do not. I do not believe our nation can survive unless we are able to accomplish a change which brings with it an acceptable way of life for all. If one segment of our society is impoverished, it impoverishes us all."[109] Like King, Kennedy was dedicated to working within democratic institutions to make them more responsive to the needs of the nation's least fortunate citizens.

With King's death, the progressive wing of the Democratic Party, which Kennedy sought to revitalize, was denied its most important link to the grassroots civil rights and antiwar movements. Kennedy no longer had his most influential informal ally in combating the politics of racial division that Wallace and Nixon were then fomenting. Thousands of King's supporters looked to Kennedy, despite the color of his skin and his social station, as the inheritor of King's legacy.

The Kennedy campaign showed that it could galvanize support among working-class whites despite the exploiting of white backlash, and the coded race-baiting of the Republicans. Kennedy challenged the right's political strength among low-income whites, the bloc of voters supposedly most susceptible to racist appeals. The year 1968 witnessed the birth of the Republicans' racist Southern strategy, and the Kennedy campaign sought from the start to blunt its force.

Kennedy walked a careful line on the race issue during the rest of his campaign. He sometimes shifted the tone of his stump speeches, especially before white conservative audiences in Indiana and Nebraska, to emphasize his law-and-order credentials as a former attorney general. The black rioting had become a real concern in many white communities, and Kennedy tried to cool the paranoia which had led to a measurable increase in the purchase of guns in the white suburbs. Kennedy's calls for maintaining the integrity of African-American urban communities by spending federal dollars to rebuild existing neighborhoods, without integrating the races, could be interpreted by whites to mean that blacks should be confined to their traditional neighborhoods.

Yet transcending racial antagonism in an election year took more than trying to placate both sides with calls for racial harmony; it required a sustained effort to organize a multiracial coalition of the lower classes. The Kennedy campaign attempted to bridge the racial divide even in the Deep South. The comprehensive programs Kennedy outlined for creating employment and rebuilding the riot-torn cities could only succeed politically if backed by a strong biracial alliance.

The candidate who emerged for the Democratic Party organization, Vice President Hubert Humphrey, given his public defense of the Administration's unpopular Vietnam policies, had great difficulty getting support from local activists and rank-and-file party organizers. Humphrey's position on the war led him to become highly dependent upon the party's largely prowar national and regional machines, and the party cadres lacked the flexibility to reach out effectively to the newly formed grassroots groups that looked to the Democrats for national leadership.

In 1968, neither Humphrey nor McCarthy were up to the task of mobilizing a broad-based progressive coalition with ties to both the peace and civil rights movements. Humphrey was a deservedly well-known champion of African-American civil rights, but he was beholden to the hierarchical party machinery and Johnson's unpopular war; McCarthy was a consistent voice for peace in Vietnam, but he possessed a far smaller political base than either Humphrey or Kennedy, particularly among African Americans and low-income whites. The Kennedy campaign sought to unite the peace and civil rights wing of the party, while influencing regular and machine Democrats wherever possible. Although it was an uphill battle, Kennedy possessed the organization, the mass base, the money, and the flexibility to make a highly credible challenge to the Democratic leadership for the 1968 presidential nomination.

9   Building a Coalition: Kennedy and the Primaries, March 16–May 28, 1968

So I come here today . . . to ask your help: not for me, but for your country and for the people of Vietnam. . . . I ask you, as tens of thousands of young men and women are doing all over this land, to organize yourselves, and then to go forth and work for new policies, work to change our direction.
—Robert F. Kennedy, Kansas State University, March 18, 1968

During the first two weeks of his campaign, Kennedy traversed the nation, visiting sixteen states that held nearly 800 of the 1,300 delegate votes needed to secure the Democratic presidential nomination. On March 16, 1968, the day he entered the race, a Gallup poll among rank-and-file Democrats showed his standing to be as strong as that of the incumbent president.[1] Still, Kennedy received warnings from friends in the party that Johnson might hold a "control bloc" of votes at the Democratic National Convention scheduled to begin on August 26 in Chicago. The campaign feared the Johnson/Humphrey forces might be able to secure the nomination on the first ballot by marshaling a collection of Southern, border, and Midwestern state delegations yet to be chosen.[2]

To counter the strength of the national Democratic organization, as well as that of the Administration's handpicked candidates at the state and local levels, Kennedy sought backing outside formal party structures. A March 25, 1968, memo to the campaign headquarters in Washington, D.C., summarized this strategy:

The existing and potential popular support for RFK's positions and candidacy is located in places, communities, and individuals that do not normally select or affect the choice and positions of delegates — in youth, in the ghetto, the poor, and in the great mass of idealistic people found in every stratum of society. The challenge they, and we, face is to forge this variegated potential into a cohesive force so powerful that it can perform the unprecedented feat of unseating a

President from his party's nomination, despite the fact that he has at his disposal the full power of patronage of the traditional party structure, of political inertia, and of an appeal to unity in a time of war.[3]

The tone and style of Kennedy's campaign was tuned to the passions that years of war and civil rights struggles had inflamed. The "frenzied" throngs that crushed the candidate at campaign stops created a frightening spectacle. Responding to the emotion of the crowds, Kennedy intensified his rhetoric, making him, according to one observer, "a force on the stump seldom seen in American national politics."[4] Kennedy, like Martin Luther King, Jr., also aroused the passions of his more unstable detractors: there was a bomb threat at a campaign stop in Salt Lake City, an attempted assault at an Oregon school, and a man on a rooftop with a rifle spotted just before the start of a Kennedy motorcade in Lansing, Michigan.[5] Risky incidents such as these were the price paid for a campaign that sought to channel the energy of the social movements of the period and relied heavily on the direct participation of ordinary people.

The campaign broadened its focus beyond the six primary elections Kennedy had entered, and pursued a fifty-state "continental" strategy. The candidate spent almost as much time in nonprimary states as he did in primary states, cashing in past political favors and letting his presence be known to party officials who would ultimately choose the victor at the convention. The campaign pressed members of state delegations to refrain from endorsing any candidate until the convention, and blocked wherever possible the attempts by state party organizations to impose the unit rule, which severely limited the freedom of delegates to change their votes once they committed to a candidate.[6] Given that Kennedy's ultimate political fate would be decided in Chicago, the campaign also openly pursued a "convention" strategy—meaning that the goal was to bring a bandwagon to the Windy City. Meantime, Kennedy generated public enthusiasm and media exposure, while making wise political moves behind the scenes to influence mainstream party officials.

In contrast, Eugene McCarthy had originally cast his presidential race as a largely symbolic protest against the Administration's Vietnam policies, morally courageous but with admittedly little chance of success.[7] "It's nonsense to set my mind on the presidency," he had said a few weeks after announcing his candidacy, "The challenge [is] on the issue—that's the important thing.

I'm testing the system."[8] McCarthy also refused to participate in the unrewarding yet vital work of personally urging Democratic officials to risk their political futures by joining his cause. He was known to cut speeches short or refuse altogether to appear at party gatherings, for no better reason than an indifferent mood.[9]

On April 27, 1968, Vice President Hubert Humphrey formally announced his entrance in the race—after he had safely ducked all of the deadlines for entering the primaries. Kennedy publicly challenged him to visit the primary states and defend the Administration's record. Humphrey was the clear front-runner, backed by the Democratic National Committee and the Johnson Administration, and he refused to engage either Kennedy or McCarthy. Instead, he focused on quietly lining up delegates and securing endorsements from big labor leaders and party stalwarts, without campaigning. Humphrey thereby cut off a meaningful dialogue between the party's national leadership and its increasingly mobilized irregulars at a time when Democrats faced their most severe divisions in two decades.

Unlike Kennedy and McCarthy, Humphrey's dependence on formal party structures, and his public identification with the increasingly unpopular Vietnam War, severely restricted his ability to enter the arena of grassroots, community-based politics. The Vice President's decision to rely almost exclusively on the Administration and the party machinery instead of breaking free of Johnson, along with his attempts to skirt the war issue altogether, might have reflected conventional wisdom given his advantages as the organization's candidate, but it thrust him into the role of apologist for the Administration's Vietnam policies.

On Sunday, March 31, 1968, a lengthy piece by the journalist Richard Reeves appeared in the *New York Times Magazine* that referred several times to Kennedy's campaign organization as a "well-oiled machine." The lateness of Kennedy's entry, and his hastily-assembled staff, did not stop Reeves from portraying the campaign as a juggernaut.[10] It was the kind of media exposure that reinforced complacency among Kennedy's supporters while energizing his opponents, and was a view Republican newspapers also promoted.[11] In reality, the early Kennedy campaign bore little resemblance to a machine, well-oiled or otherwise.

Kennedy had wavered up to the moment he announced, and when he finally entered the race his aides scrambled to assign tasks on a temporary basis.[12] During the first weeks of the campaign, the candidate traveled to previously scheduled appearances on regular commercial airline flights, causing logistical nightmares and mayhem at airports. Arthur Schlesinger, reflecting the general disarray of the early campaign, wrote "Help! Help! Help!" in a March 23 memo, complaining about the lack of an adequate research division, and asked, "Is anyone in charge of anything anywhere?"[13]

Yet despite these early difficulties, Kennedy doggedly pursued party officials, and adhered to a grueling campaign schedule. His belated entry finally freed him from his earlier caution and restraint. He began emphasizing the horrors of the war, the moral outrage of the world's most powerful nation devastating a small country, and the bitter divisions of the American people. In speech after speech, Kennedy blamed Johnson for the failures of the war and the erosion of peace at home. He forced Democratic leaders across the nation to make a choice they had hoped to avoid: either defend Johnson's Vietnam policies or endorse a viable alternative. Kennedy's speeches during the first weeks of the campaign drew the sharpest line yet between himself and the Administration.

On March 18, 1968, at an appearance scheduled prior to his becoming a candidate, Kennedy homed in on the war in a speech before about 14,000 students and faculty at Kansas State University in Manhattan, Kansas. He called Johnson's Vietnam policy "bankrupt," and "deeply wrong"; the Administration's "only response to failure," he said, had been "to repeat it on a larger scale. I am concerned that at the end of it all," he told the college audience, "there will only be more Americans killed; more of our treasure spilled out; and because of the bitterness and hatred on every side in this war, more hundreds of thousands of Vietnamese slaughtered; so that they may say, as Tacitus said of Rome: 'They made a desert, and called it peace.'"[14]

Kennedy ratcheted up the level of intensity of this address by quoting the American Army officer who had told reporters after wiping out the village of Ben Tre that it had been necessary to destroy the village in order to save it. "Where does such logic end?" he asked. "If it becomes 'necessary' to destroy all of South Vietnam in order to 'save' it, will we do that too? And if we care so little about South Vietnam that we are willing to see the land destroyed and its people dead, then why are we there in the first place? Can we ordain ourselves the awful majesty of God to decide what cities and villages are to be destroyed, who will live and who will die, and who will join the refugees wandering in a desert of our own creation?"[15] It was a potent speech that whipped the students into a kind of collective frenzy.

Three days later, at Vanderbilt University in Nashville, Tennessee, Kennedy assailed Johnson by name as responsible for the bitter divisions plaguing American society. In Los Angeles that weekend, in a statement that members of the press were quick to criticize as below the belt, he said that by turning to violence to solve what was essentially a political conflict in Southeast Asia, Johnson had "call[ed] upon the darker impulses of the American spirit."[16] It was tough talk that drew a few "demagoguery" charges, but Kennedy remained impassive, and gained widespread approbation from those whose resistance to the war had been uncompromising.

By 1968, the years of antiwar organizing and riots in the cities had thrust Vietnam and racial discrimination to the center of the American political debate. Kennedy was now freed to fuel the intraparty schism by pouring his heart and soul into fighting against the direction in which Johnson had led the nation since the assassination of President Kennedy. He seized the opportunity to voice his most forceful stands yet on the war and the deteriorating race relations. He sharpened his stand on Vietnam and on racism at a time when Humphrey and the Democratic leadership either glossed over these crises or ignored them completely.

Strategically, the Kennedy campaign sought to tap the remnants of the political infrastructure which had allowed John Kennedy to win the nomination in 1960. It also actively recruited volunteers who had served in the Peace Corps, an enduring legacy of President Kennedy's. The campaign sent out mass recruitment mailings to Peace Corps and VISTA volunteers, and to antipoverty workers, asking them to join the campaign.[17] Young members of the Peace Corps, including the future United States senator Paul Tsongas, offered to serve as volunteers.[18] The campaign, which also recruited directly at Peace Corps training centers outside the United States, provided an outlet for idealistic young people to be active in shaping their nation's future.

The Youth and Student Division of the Kennedy campaign had as one of its overall goals organizing "a massive voter registration/education drive with a national impetus," and consciously used Allard Lowenstein's 1967 Vietnam Summer as its model.[19] The campaign looked to the peace movement for examples of effective mobilizing at the grassroots. There was an intense effort to "plug into local community action programs," and draw off existing networks of activists that had been built up throughout the 1960s, often with the direct support of federal and state government dollars. "There are thousands of on-going programs both government and otherwise," an internal campaign memo stated. "It is quite possible that skillful Kennedy supporters can work with the leaders of these groups and interest them" in joining the campaign in a variety of capacities.[20] The strategy called for working directly with Native Americans, Latinos, African Americans, college students, and peace activists at the local level.

Kennedy's advisers learned valuable lessons from McCarthy's New Hampshire campaign. Through tapping into existing networks of young community organizers at the local level, they hoped to spur participation and generate excitement that could translate into primary victories. The campaign challenged the Democratic leadership by using the primaries to take the struggle for the nomination directly to the people. Kennedy wished to bypass formal party structures wherever possible, and take advantage of community action programs the party had promoted or sponsored.

This strategy depended for its lifeblood on people from church and civic groups locally organizing volunteers, setting up phone banks, and canvassing neighborhoods. Like the McCarthy campaign, the Kennedy organization attempted to fuse with citizens' groups, and embrace the social and political activism of the period. The mobilized citizenry opened the debate, and provided the mass base for a presidential candidate who in less polarized times might be considered too far to the left to make a serious bid for the presidency. In 1968, Kennedy's indictment of the Vietnam War, and his support of the goals and tactics of King's Poor People's Campaign, arose from an organic connection to the peace and civil rights movements. If he prevailed, the election of 1968 promised to be a turning point for the nation and for the Democratic Party.

Kennedy's turning to the social movements of the 1960s as a source of foot soldiers for his presidential ambitions led to some uneasiness among turf-conscious members of the New Left. The fear was voiced in New Left circles that Kennedy might "co-opt" the movement, dilute its demands, and offer the illusion of radical reform without substantive change. This co-optation thesis, first articulated by Robert Scheer in the February 1967 issue of *Ramparts*, was rehashed when Kennedy entered the presidential race.[21] "The Kennedy people have raised co-optation to an art form," Scheer wrote. "They have hooked onto the mood of crisis and, as with everything else, come to use it." Kennedy stood "a good chance of co-opting the current mood of dissent," he argued, "with a few choice phrases that appeal to weary liberals, frustrated student radicals and teenyboppers."[22]

Others linked to the New Left took the co-optation thesis a step further. Members of the Progressive Labor Party (P.L.), for example, denounced "Kennedyism" as a "liberal offensive against the anti-war movement," and labeled Kennedy, John Kenneth Galbraith, J. William Fulbright, and Martin Luther King, Jr. "stooges of imperialism."[23] In the months leading up to Kennedy's decision to run for president, there also had been confrontations between chiefs of the Students for a Democratic Society (SDS) over the Senator's leadership role. The SDS cofounder and leader Tom Hayden recalled a January 1968 meeting to plan demonstrations at the Democratic National Convention, where an SDS leader accused him of "leading this movement either into co-option by the Kennedy forces or into repression and violence."[24] These concerns reflected Kennedy's appeal among leftists, and rested on the assumption that the antiwar movement was better served working outside the structures of electoral politics than wasting its time trying to influence members of Congress or helping peace candidates. Yet nearly all of the prominent leaders of the national peace movement, including Benjamin Spock, William Sloan Coffin, David Dellinger, and King, had publicly rejected this premise.

The New Left was divided on Kennedy's place in the "movement."[25] When the campaign began to hit its stride, the leftist journalist Andrew Kopkind called Kennedy an "agent of national renewal."[26] Regarding the concerns of some activists about co-optation, Kopkind placed the blame back on the New Left itself. Leading organizers, he argued, had neglected to mobilize their political base, and thereby allowed their efforts to "evaporate into the Kennedy phenomenon."[27] In Kopkind's view, the left had to "up the ante," and press Kennedy to broaden the reforms he advocated.[28] Hayden later recounted the awkward position his openness to Kennedy's candidacy had posed for him. In his view, it was a "waste of energy" to fight "the McCarthy people for their double standards, and the SDS people for reducing everyone to meaningless opportunists."[29]

By 1968, the most important single organization at the national level for the peace movement was the National Mobilization Committee to End the Vietnam War (known as "the Mobe"). The Mobe consisted of a loose coalition of some twenty antiwar groups representing dozens of ideological orientations.[30] Aside from its ability to periodically organize impressive demonstrations (as it did in April and October 1967), the Mobe, given its conflicting political tendencies, had great difficulty functioning as an umbrella organization for the antiwar movement. It is highly unlikely that Kennedy or anyone else could have co-opted such an intrinsically diverse and variegated social phenomenon.[31] Moreover, it was the nation's religious left, which opposed the war on moral grounds—most notably Clergy and Laity

Concerned About Vietnam (CALCAV), and the Fellowship of Reconciliation (FOR)—that had perhaps the strongest appeal at the local level. Organized clergy for peace held far greater legitimacy and popular support than did any of the secular groups identified with the New Left.[32]

Kennedy's campaign was neither a product of the New Left nor beholden to its influence to a high degree. However, in the late 1960s, Kennedy's dedication to pluralism and peace, and his focus on class inequality, led him down a parallel path. Sometimes the New Left's emphasis on decentralized political power crept into Kennedy's speeches. In March 1968, he formulated a critique of American society surprising in its similarity to some of the currents of thought that were rippling through the New Left at the time: "Our Gross National Product now soars above $800 billion a year," Kennedy told an audience in Des Moines, Iowa. "But that counts air pollution and cigarette advertising, and ambulances to clear our streets of carnage. It counts the special locks for our doors and jails for the people who break them. It counts the destruction of our redwoods and the loss of natural wonder to chaotic sprawl. It counts napalm and nuclear warheads and armored cars for the police to fight riots in our cities. It counts Whitman's rifle and Speck's knife, and television programs which glorify violence to sell toys to our children."[33]

The New Left had articulated a devastating critique of United States imperialism abroad and racism at home.[34] But any "left" worthy of the name, if it was to move from theory to long-term political praxis, had to transcend the boundaries of the college campuses and make inroads into the progressive wing of organized labor.[35] Workers in the United States, organized and unorganized, looked to the Democratic Party for political expression, and Kennedy's base among progressive unionists far exceeded anything the New Left could muster.

The A.F.L.-C.I.O.'s political arm, the Committee on Political Education (COPE), gave Kennedy its highest rating for his voting record and initiatives favorable to labor. "Where unions are strong, the cause of progress and social justice is advanced," a Kennedy campaign flyer stated, "and where unions are weak, the whole society suffers."[36] Although Kennedy was a popular figure among unionists nationwide, the A.F.L.-C.I.O.'s President George Meany and other labor leaders steadfastly backed the Johnson Administration, even while its popularity plummeted. By 1968, whether it emanated from ideological belief, or was a sign of gratitude to Johnson for his progressive social agenda, or a political quid pro quo, Meany and the A.F.L.-

C.I.O. leadership became some of the nation's most vociferous promoters of the Vietnam War.

When Humphrey announced his candidacy, Meany gave him access to the levers of power of the nation's largest labor union. Along with Senator Walter Mondale (who filled Humphrey's former Minnesota Senate seat), and Senator Fred Harris of Oklahoma, Meany served on the national "Humphrey for President" committee. By 1968, Johnson's drop in popularity made it uncertain whether Meany and other pro-Administration labor leaders could deliver the votes of their rank and file. Organized labor became the object of intense competition between Kennedy and Humphrey. The Kennedy campaign aggressively pursued the unions at the local level, while Humphrey obtained largely top-down endorsements. (The middle-class limitations of McCarthy's political base left him largely outside the fray.)

Kennedy's major lever against Humphrey and the Democratic leadership in the unions was his close association with the United Auto Workers (U.A.W.) and its leader Walter Reuther. The U.A.W. had functioned as the "spine" in several states for John Kennedy's 1960 presidential race, and became a pivotal force in Robert Kennedy's primary campaigns.[37] Walter's brother, Roy Reuther, in addition to his U.A.W. activities, had been an organizer for César Chávez's United Farm Workers union. In early 1968, when Roy Reuther died of a heart attack, Kennedy had been the only outsider to sit with the Reuther family at the funeral.[38] The campaign consciously built on Kennedy's established ties to the Reuthers and the U.A.W.'s leadership.

However, the Johnson Administration applied acute pressure on U.A.W. leaders to back Humphrey, even though many of its locals, representing tens of thousands of workers, moved toward Kennedy. Walter Reuther was cautiously noncommittal. The day after Kennedy announced his candidacy, Reuther urged his political, regional, and field representatives to "make no statement and take no position because of the particularly fluid political situation."[39] Kennedy recognized, as did Humphrey and his political allies, that the U.A.W. was pivotal in states such as Illinois, California, and especially Michigan. In Michigan, the nation's center for automobile production, the makeup of the Democratic delegation to the national convention was almost totally dependent upon which way the U.A.W. turned.

Aides to President Johnson predicted that the U.A.W. would dominate the outcome of at least three Congressional races in Michigan, a staunchly Democratic and unionized state. The Johnson/Humphrey forces worried about

Reuther's openness toward the Kennedy candidacy. The Pro-Administration Michigan Congressman John Dingell informed the White House that he considered Reuther "the key to the Michigan delegation," and pressed Johnson and Humphrey "to line him up early and keep him lined up."[40]

When Johnson was still in the running, Reuther had "ducked" Humphrey's telephone calls on behalf of the President; to Johnson's aide James Rowe, Reuther's aloofness "meant trouble." After talking to Michigan's Democratic leaders, Rowe advised Johnson to call Reuther himself, and not allow him to hide behind the autonomy of the locals. The Administration forces concluded that Michigan would have "a 'Favorite Son' delegation," but whether it would be "pro-LBJ or weak-LBJ" would "depend on Reuther."[41] Kennedy subsequently was given an added boost in the state when he received the endorsement of Detroit Mayor Jerome Cavanaugh, who promised his "full and active support" for Kennedy.[42]

In Indiana, on April 25, 1968, about a week before Democrats went to the polls in the state's primary, the U.A.W.'s Marion County Citizenship Council, which included the Indianapolis area, voted at its regional convention to endorse Kennedy. The Indiana U.A.W.'s backing of Kennedy was an exercise in participatory democracy. Unlike Meany's A.F.L.-C.I.O., which forbade autonomous state conventions, the U.A.W. left the decision up to a vote of its local members. The Council represented thirteen unions with about 25,000 members. Elwood Black, Chairman of the Council, and President of U.A.W. Local 550, speaking for the union, made the following statement: "We met tonight and officially endorsed Senator Robert F. Kennedy as a candidate for the Presidency. The reason for our endorsement was the fact that we thought he could best present the UAW program more effectively than the other candidates. His record in the Senate has been 100 percent in favor of labor and civil rights legislation. We feel Senator Kennedy can best achieve the hopes and aspirations of the people we represent."[43]

The U.A.W. gave the campaign a boost among workers throughout Indiana, Illinois, Ohio, and Michigan who looked to it for leadership, whether formally belonging to the union or not. It also bolstered the efforts in Kennedy's behalf in California, where the union leader Paul Schrade organized U.A.W. members for that state's primary scheduled for June 4. Kennedy's endorsements from autonomous U.A.W. locals contrasted sharply with Humphrey's labor backing, which almost exclusively came from the leadership. Kennedy's labor support, unlike Humphrey's, had a decidedly grassroots flavor, untainted by the perception of dependence upon labor bosses who presided over rigidly hierarchical organizations.

In Indiana, Kennedy's union activists braced for a tough battle; Humphrey's supporters in organized labor were well financed and mobilized. The A.F.L.-C.I.O. distributed some 270,000 pamphlets supporting the Administration candidate against Kennedy. There were reports that COPE people in several primary states acted as advance men for Humphrey to get out the labor vote.[44]

In Oregon, the executive board of the A.F.L.-C.I.O., representing about 50,000 members, spoke out for Humphrey in the state's upcoming primary.[45] Without allowing rank-and-file members to participate in the decision, the union took out full-page ads for Humphrey in Oregon's major newspapers. Humphrey's labor record was easily as strong as Kennedy's, and he deserved union support. However, the union leadership's heavy-handed tactics in support of the Vice President, devoid of meaningful input from its members, caused tensions between the leaders and the rank and file.

Cecil Tibbit, who was the chairman of the Oregon United Labor for Kennedy, and the financial secretary for U.A.W. Local 492, rebuked the practice of top-down endorsements in a terse press release: "I regret most strongly that this action was taken without benefit of an endorsing convention at which the rank-and-file of the labor movement could have had a vote and a voice in the selection of labor's candidate."[46] Many local union leaders recognized that their members did not want a blanket endorsement of a candidate who still supported the Vietnam War, and they resented Meany's and other leaders' moves to stifle debate.

Kennedy's staff analyzed poll data which showed that rank-and-file unionists believed the war had been a mistake.[47] The Kennedy camp never accepted the notion, disseminated by some political commentators, that working-class people favored the war. In December 1967, a Gallup poll revealed that 49 percent of union families disapproved of Johnson's Vietnam policies, although they gave the President an overall approval rating of 55 percent.[48] Michigan Senator Philip Hart had warned the White House that it would "make life easier" for him and his Democratic colleagues with their predominantly working-class constituencies if "we could find a way to get out of Vietnam."[49] An internal campaign memo rejected the idea that working people were war hawks, noting that they had been the "strongest supporters of President Kennedy."[50]

George Meany and other A.F.L.-C.I.O. leaders were staunch anti-Communists, and vigorous supporters of Johnson's war policies. The union's stand on Vietnam often contradicted the views of the rank and file. The union's glossy monthly magazine, the *American Federationist*, regularly featured triumphant stories about how the union helped organize the "Vietnamese Federation of Labor," and achieved great gains for workers in South Vietnam by backing the Administration's war policies.[51] The union's leadership had grown so close to the Johnson Administration that it began functioning as a propaganda vehicle for the war.

However, there were signs that the A.F.L.-C.I.O.'s local support for the Administration was beginning to crack under the uneasiness with Vietnam. In late 1967, 523 A.F.L.-C.I.O. union leaders from thirty-eight states had formed the Assembly for Peace, to vent rank-and-file disagreement with its leadership's prowar views.[52] Kennedy received letters from union leaders around the country who dissented from Meany's endorsement of Humphrey and opposed their union's support for the war. For example, Wayne Glenn, the vice president of the International Brotherhood of Pulp, Sulphite and Paper Mill Workers, who had been a delegate to the 1956 Democratic convention, wrote Kennedy: "I think George Meany is off base letting the war have any influence on our choice of candidates. George Meany is so far removed from the rank and file members he does not even understand their thinking anymore. Your Labor record is excellent . . . I believe you are the Democrats' best hope of winning the Presidency. We should nominate the strongest vote getter, and that is you."[53]

From the start of his campaign, Kennedy sought to exploit the discontent among working Americans with Johnson's Vietnam policies. He made an effort to keep them in the party, despite the Administration's apparent disregard for the lives of thousands of their sons.[54] The Vietnam War was being fought by working-class kids, which produced a volatile set of conflicts within Democratic ranks. Because draft deferments for college students functioned in a demonstrably racist and classist manner, Kennedy, unlike McCarthy, opposed them, which cut into his support on the campuses and among middle-class youth generally, but was popular among working families.[55]

The rift within organized labor over Vietnam led Kennedy to go on the offensive against the war in speeches before working-class audiences. In mid-May 1968, he told the national convention of the U.A.W. in Atlantic City: "This nation must adopt a foreign policy which says, clearly and distinctly,

'No more Vietnams.' We cannot and we must not take as our mission the suppression of disorder and internal upheaval everywhere it appears. We cannot send American troops to assume the burden of fighting for corrupt and repressive governments all the way around the globe, governments unable or unwilling to gain the support of their own people in their own nations."[56] By shrewdly focusing on the illegitimacy of the Saigon regime, Kennedy could better get his antiwar message across to working people who might have sons in military service, but questioned the overall worthiness of the stated U.S. goals in Vietnam.

On May 7, Democrats in Indiana would go to the polls, and a loss for Kennedy there, in his first primary, could stop the campaign in its tracks. Some of Kennedy's aides believed Indiana could do as much for their candidate in 1968 as West Virginia had done for John Kennedy in 1960, when he finally put the religion question to rest. A notoriously conservative state, Indiana was a difficult first primary for an East Coast liberal. The March 28 filing deadline forced Kennedy's hand; against the advice of his more cautious advisers, he decided to throw his hat in the ring. When Sorensen told Kennedy that Indiana was a gamble, he replied: "the whole campaign is a gamble."[57]

The Indiana Young Democrats, whose president was a staunch Kennedy partisan, easily secured the 5,500 signatures needed to put Kennedy's name on the ballot.[58] A few thousand college students were bused into the state from Ohio, Kentucky, Illinois, Wisconsin, Michigan, and as far away as New York and Maryland, to help with the campaign. They contacted hundreds of thousands of homes, and practiced "issues canvassing" to discern the level of voter discontent with the war and the Administration. Seeking out Kennedy supporters among Hoosiers was difficult, an organizing letter warned volunteers; it required "long bus rides with peanut butter sandwiches and cold floors," and "an occasional door slammed in one's face, scattered curse words, and a lot of walking."[59]

Kennedy's advisers and campaign workers knew they faced a tough battle. Schlesinger wrote Kennedy that Indiana was "a middle-class, small-town, suburban state, fearful of challenge, seeking consolation and reassurance." In his view, "Indiana Democrats in the main do not want to be summoned to the barricades, and told they have to do great things to meet great crises." Kennedy's problems in Indiana, therefore, depended "less on content than on style"; Schlesinger advised him to "be low-key."[60] This kind of advice appears to have registered; Kennedy subsequently began emphasizing his law-enforcement experience as attorney general. He also sometimes framed the debate on the war in nationalist terms that highlighted its waste of tax dollars, and unnecessary American involvement.

In early April, after McCarthy's successful Wisconsin primary, where he won 56.2 percent of the vote,[61] Richard Goodwin left the McCarthy campaign and returned to work for Kennedy as a key adviser and campaign strategist. Goodwin had been instrumental in McCarthy's victories in New Hampshire and in Wisconsin, and he was convinced that Kennedy could make the strongest challenge against the Administration. Goodwin also wished to honor a long-standing personal friendship with Kennedy. Lawrence O'Brien, the political expert who helped steer John Kennedy to victory in 1960, resigned his Cabinet post as Johnson's Postmaster General to dedicate his formidable political skills to the Kennedy campaign. The value of Goodwin's and O'Brien's political acumen was illustrated by the fact that both McCarthy (in the case of Goodwin), and Humphrey (in the case of O'Brien), had offered them key positions in their own campaign organizations.

By mid-April, after Goodwin and O'Brien came aboard, the campaign gathered momentum. With Sorensen, Dutton, Dolan, Kenneth O'Donnell, Schlesinger, Pierre Salinger, Steve Smith, and the "Young Turks"—Walinsky, Edelman, and Greenfield—Kennedy had assembled a highly skilled campaign staff that blended experienced pragmatism with youthful idealism. The candidate embodied both these strains.

To counter the Indiana Democratic party's control of a powerful patronage system, the campaign turned to the grass roots: rank-and-file Democrats, unionists, community organizers, youth and students, and peace activists. The Indiana primary revealed in microcosm the transformation of the party that Kennedy hoped to accomplish nationally.

Democratic Governor Roger Branigan, who made the incredible claim that Vietnam was not an issue in the primary, ran as a stand-in for Johnson and Humphrey. Governor Branigan's campaign avoided the war, race relations, and virtually any other substantive issue in favor of playing to Hoosiers' ingrained chauvinism and xenophobia. He portrayed himself as a hometown boy besieged by big-money city slickers and carpetbaggers from the Eastern Establishment. He ignored, wherever possible, the fact that he was himself a Harvard Law School graduate and a corporate lawyer worth several million dollars.[62] Branigan's state party chairman, Gordon St. Angelo, ran an old-style patronage system where some 7,000 state employees were required to tithe 2 percent of their salaries into party coffers, producing a tight, dependable political base highly disciplined against bolting.

Although Indiana's two senators, Vance Hartke and Birch Bayh, were both dovish liberal Democrats, Kennedy's aides warned him that too stridently denouncing the war could hurt him in the state. Prowar sentiment ran high in Indiana, a state strewn with war memorials; Indianapolis was the site of the American Legion's national headquarters. A leading Indiana Democrat claimed that less than one-fifth of the state's residents wanted the United States to pull out of Vietnam without first attaining a military victory.[63] Kennedy's strategy was to build a coalition among working-class whites, and the state's 9 percent African-American population.

Eugene Pullium, a conservative Republican from Arizona, owned the state's two major newspapers, the *Indianapolis Star* and *News*, and both were dedicated to throttling Kennedy at every turn. Given Branigan's role as the "stop Kennedy" candidate, it is not surprising the Republican newspapers threw their editorial and political support behind him. The *Star* went so far as to run a front page story attacking Kennedy for fomenting "racism" following a speech he had given at the Indiana University Medical School. Kennedy had told the overwhelmingly white audience that African Americans fought and died in Vietnam in disproportionate numbers to their population.

The northern part of Indiana, Lake County, which stretched westward until it blended into greater metropolitan Chicago, provided Kennedy with his strongest base. There were many large blue-collar neighborhoods, including the cities of Hammond and Mayor Richard Hatcher's Gary. In 1964, Lake County had also included backlash areas where the segregationist George Wallace won 30 percent of the Democratic primary vote. According to one campaign memo, Kennedy student canvassers had produced results that seemed "too good to be true" in Lake County, but they had accurately confirmed that some former Wallace supporters now backed Kennedy. Kennedy's law-and-order message, selectively applied, had its desired resonance in conservative working-class districts; his Catholicism helped in this area as well. However, the campaign predicted that the Wallace crossover phenomenon would not bring many votes.[64]

It was in Lake County where the Branigan machine fought the hardest against Kennedy. Democratic officials who were part of the patronage system frightened the first busloads of students who came to work for Kennedy with threatening talk about court injunctions against their activities; Kennedy campaign literature often "accidentally," and inexplicably, disappeared in Lake County. Local officials were uncooperative in checking voter registration or in other bureaucratic necessities. In the days leading up to the voting, some polling stations were shuffled from site to site to disrupt the teams of amateurs who were getting the vote out for Kennedy. The campaign had to assign people to monitor every polling booth in the state starting at 4:30 in the morning on the day of the election.[65] To make matters worse, Kennedy surveys in Indianapolis and other cities revealed a well-financed Republican crossover vote for McCarthy. Kennedy staffers carefully watched the polls "so that the challenge procedure" could be "geared up if the number of crossovers mount[ed]."[66]

Kennedy spent the early days of the Indiana campaign with motorcades and speaking engagements in the populated urban centers, and then shifted his attention to rural areas and small towns. To tackle the problem of the state's reflexive conservatism, the campaign deployed the most traditional of stump tactics: the whistle-stop train tour. Two weeks before the election, the candidate embarked through rural Indiana on a six-car train, called the Wabash Cannon Ball, filled with staffers, volunteers, and reporters.[67] Kennedy used the homey tour to compete in rural and small-town Indiana against Branigan, the "native son" candidate, who had focused much of his attention outside the cities.

In the cities, the Kennedy campaign saturated the foreign language press, and ran 116 foreign language radio spots in Gary, Hammond, South Bend, and Chicago, which focused primarily on people of Polish, Croatian, Slovenian, Hungarian, and Spanish descent. The campaign also ran a lengthy advertisement in dozens of small foreign language newspapers, and in two weeklies aimed at African-American and Jewish readerships.[68]

Kennedy spent the last day of the campaign in a nine-hour motorcade through northern Indiana. When the chain of cars reached the Gary city line, Tony Zale, the former middleweight boxing champion from Gary who was a hero to Eastern European immigrants who worked in the steel mills, joined Kennedy along with Richard Hatcher, Gary's thirty-four-year-old African-American Mayor. They climbed into Kennedy's open car, and stood on either side of him for an hour while the car slowly pushed through the clogged streets. The three of them, standing on the back seat of the convertible, clung to each other's waists, and symbolized the kind of alliance that Kennedy hoped to forge.[69] The scene was a testimony to the Senator's ability to bring together working-class whites and African Americans in a city often plagued by violent racial strife.

In nearby Chicago, Mayor Richard Daley could not ignore the display of biracial support Kennedy received in the cities of Gary, Hammond, and other parts of Lake County. Kennedy had campaigned heavily in the Polish-American working-class districts of South Bend, and Daley was already aware of the candidate's popularity in the Polish wards of Chicago.[70] The Catholic Polish-American communities in the Windy City had admired Kennedy from the time of his well-publicized 1964 trip to Poland. He also had the public support of Jacqueline Kennedy's brother-in-law, Prince Stanislaw Radziwill, whose resistance to the Communist government of Poland made him a popular figure.[71] The outpouring of support for Kennedy in Lake County was precisely the kind of thing Kennedy wanted Daley to see.

The Kennedy campaign planned "maximum get out the vote activities" in populated areas across Indiana. Larry O'Brien drew up the blueprint for getting out the vote. These activities focused on areas of Kennedy's greatest strength, "among blue collar workers, Negroes, some ethnic groups, some Catholic elements, etc."[72] O'Brien had devised a series of commonsense efforts in the final days of the campaign, such as receptions where volunteers could meet Robert or Edward Kennedy, to energize the nearly fifteen thousand block captains. These local volunteers were responsible for making sure that likely Kennedy partisans made it to the polls.

On May 6, 1968, the final day of the campaign, just minutes before the courts in Indiana closed, the American Legion secured an injunction against Kennedy, his campaign committee and advertising firm, and Time-Life Broadcasting. The injunction aimed to stop a half-hour television spot which featured a short clip of Kennedy speaking before an audience of American Legionnaires, who donned their Legion hats with emblems in clear view. A Republican judge granted the injunction on the grounds that the campaign had illegally used the insignia of the American Legion for political purposes.[73] The film had been prepared for broadcast on the evening before the election, and had not been shown before. Kennedy, himself a member of the American Legion, was taken aback by the court's action. At ten o'clock on the eve of the election, he and his lawyers managed to secure a special hearing of the Indiana State Supreme Court. After some argument, they succeeded in getting the injunction lifted, but not in time to use the ad. Kennedy issued a press release saying that the members of Post Number 34 of the American Legion "gave permission in writing to appear in a political broadcast on my behalf. Presidents, Governors and thousands of political candidates have appeared before Legion meetings, as candidates, wearing their Legion caps proudly. I do not know what motives inspired this unusual legal action, but whatever they may be, I am hopeful its final disposition will not impair the free expression by American veterans of their questions on public issues, and their concern for their country."[74]

Despite the obstructionism of the state Democratic organization, the American Legion, and the open vituperation of the Pullium newspapers, Kennedy won the Indiana primary. He got 328,118 of the 776,513 votes cast, or 42.3 percent. Branigan got 238,700, or 30.7 percent, and McCarthy received 209,695, or 27 percent.[75] A precinct breakdown showed that roughly nine out of ten African Americans who voted in the primary cast their votes for Kennedy, and that he attracted more than the usual number of blue-collar whites, even in neighborhoods considered white backlash sites.[76] He carried the seven counties that Wallace had won in 1964. Kennedy prevailed in these backlash neighborhoods by successfully conveying the message that the interests of whites would be served by the black demands for social justice. Both groups could be uplifted, he argued, by programs that honored labor and assisted the poor. Finally, Kennedy's law-and-order credentials made it clear that he had little tolerance for rioting, and his Catholicism was a plus in these communities as well.

Kennedy won the election because white workers and African Americans registered and voted for him in large numbers. One of O'Brien's early estimates found that one African-American district in Gary gave Branigan 16, McCarthy 52, and Kennedy 697 votes. But Kennedy's appeal was not limited to these groups. He carried nine of the eleven congressional districts, and all the major cities except Bloomington and Evansville. He won seventeen of the twenty-five rural southern counties. He only lost two of the counties in which he had campaigned personally in the last two weeks.[77] Although the Indiana results did not confirm the emergence of a broad new coalition, they pointed the way toward bridging the racial divide, even in a conservative state with a bipartisan, organized, and hostile right wing. With the win in Indiana, Kennedy had sealed control of 63 Democratic delegate votes on the first ballot at the Democratic National Convention.

In Washington, D.C., the Democratic primary was held the same day as Indiana's, and Kennedy beat the slates backing Humphrey by 62.5 percent to 37.5 percent.[78] This gave him another 23 convention votes from the largely African-American District. The head of Kennedy's slate, Reverend

Channing Phillips, and his running mate Flaxie Pinkett, became D.C. Democratic National Committee members;[79] D.C.'s Kennedy delegation also included the relatively militant Colin Carew.[80]

With Indiana and D.C., Kennedy had captured 86 delegate votes, and
the campaign swung into motion. To the candidate's chagrin, some of the
major newspapers and television networks interpreted his victories as relatively meaningless.[81] McCarthy, with whom Kennedy shared a split-screen
television interview the night of the election, reinforced these sentiments
by telling reporters it did not really matter who came in first, second, or
third.[82]

Seeing the difficulties ahead, Kennedy's friend Anthony Lewis, who was
then the chief London correspondent for the *New York Times*, wrote him
after the Indiana victory: "You gave me a hard night. I see very little relief
for you in the indefinite future. Perhaps now, as Indiana starts things rolling,
you can give the public one thing I think it is lonesome for. That is hope."
Lewis went on to share with Kennedy his belief that only by ending the war
could he begin to lead a "revival of faith" among Americans in the "natural
decency" of their country.[83] Kennedy had established himself as a viable
challenger for the nomination. But whether or not he could successfully
lead a polarized nation, as Lewis pointed out, depended on his ability to
end the war, and move the country beyond the racial crises of 1968.

On the evening of his victory in Indiana, Kennedy had a casual conversation with a group of friends and journalists, including David Halberstam
and Jack Newfield. "I like Indiana," he said. "The people here were fair to
me. They gave me a chance. They listened to me. I could see this face, way
in back in the crowd, and he was listening, really listening to me. The people
here are not so neurotic and hypocritical as in Washington or New York.
They're more direct. I like rural people, who work hard with their hands.
There is something healthy about them. . . . I loved the faces here in Indiana,
on the farmers, on the steelworkers, on the black kids."[84] Now Kennedy had
to find out if he could count on the same degree of equanimity from the
voters in Nebraska.

Following the Indiana primary of May 7, the Kennedy campaign had one
week to prepare for the Nebraska election, where 23 delegate votes were at
stake. Like Indiana, Nebraska had all the earmarks of a tough state for an
East Coast, urban liberal. Its primarily rural population was Republican in
orientation. In 1960, it had given John Kennedy his second lowest vote, and
Nixon the largest majority of any state.[85] "The state is very conservative,

including the Democrats," Dolan wrote Kennedy, "In a sense Nebraska thought Barry Goldwater was a radical."[86] However, the campaign possessed a base from which to work. Theodore Sorensen and his brother Philip were native Nebraskans, and Philip had served as the state's lieutenant governor. In 1966, he had won the party's nomination for an unsuccessful gubernatorial bid. He maintained the vestiges of his own state campaign machinery, which he passed on to Kennedy, and was closely tied to many of Nebraska's important Democratic officials and community leaders.

As he did in Indiana, Kennedy vigorously toured the state, starting in the population centers around Omaha and then fanning out to the rural areas. It was a well-organized and efficiently run campaign, showing that Kennedy had strong appeal even in the Corn Belt. One week of campaigning was a short period in which to establish oneself as a presidential candidate, but the total number of registered Democratic voters in the state was smaller than Indiana's three-quarters of a million; the Democratic vote in Nebraska was slightly over 150,000.[87] Pat Lucey, a Kennedy political adviser from Wisconsin, managed the Nebraska campaign, and his operation reached every registered Democratic voter in the state at least four times with literature and telephone calls.

McCarthy, following his defeat in the Hoosier state, had downplayed the significance of the loss. But he also decried "the Kennedys" for "poisoning the well in Indiana."[88] The remark reflected a growing bitterness on McCarthy's part. He claimed that the Kennedy campaign had deliberately misrepresented his Senate voting record, making him appear less liberal than he truly was.[89] He vowed that Nebraska would be a more important race than Indiana, and then, according to the journalist Jules Witcover, "dawdled his way through a few days," and "left Nebraska on the critical last weekend" of the campaign.[90] As McCarthy himself expressed it in his memoir: "Nebraska happened on the way west."[91]

The blue-collar and black populations were relatively small in Nebraska, but Kennedy, building on his experience in Indiana, set out on a strenuous personal campaign to register and mobilize the state's African Americans and lower-income whites. While campaigning in the Nebraskan countryside by train and by bus, he outlined the provisions of his proposed Rural America Community Services Act to attack the problem of rural poverty by providing federal aid for development, and social services in remote areas. On May 10, in Beatrice, Nebraska, he made the offhand remark that he and Ethel might want to settle in the town someday with their "eleven children," which sent reporters dashing to the telephones to report the news that the candidate's wife was pregnant yet again.

On election day, as in Indiana, Kennedy had not only succeeded in getting out African Americans in large numbers, who gave him about 85 percent of their votes, but he also apparently tapped into a rural populist sentiment. He won 24 of the 25 counties where he had waged a personal campaign, and carried 88 of the state's 93 total counties. He got 52 percent of the vote to McCarthy's 31 percent.[92] The African-American and blue-collar base centered in Omaha gave him his strongest single showing; he won 60 percent of the working-class vote, and swept all the counties with concentrations of Polish-, Czech-, German-, and Scandinavian-Americans. He carried every city in the state with a population of more than 7,000. Mayor Daley took notice, telling reporters he believed Kennedy's Nebraska performance was "a very impressive victory." An impressive victory was exactly what Kennedy had hoped for.[93]

Even though McCarthy came from a farm state and had served as a member of the Senate Agriculture Committee, Kennedy carried 80 of the 86 rural counties, with a total vote in all farm counties of 60 percent. A Kennedy campaign press release, keeping the focus on Humphrey instead of McCarthy, pointed out that Kennedy and McCarthy, "the two candidates who have consistently called for new directions in America life," accumulated a total of 84 percent of the state's Democratic vote.[94] Johnson and Humphrey write-ins together totaled only 15 percent, and Humphrey's paltry 8 percent was far below what his supporters predicted he would receive.

The Kennedy campaign could now turn its attention to other tasks at hand. McCarthy had announced early on that he would not actively compete in the South Dakota primary scheduled for June 4. Senator George McGovern of South Dakota, himself up for reelection, campaigned for Kennedy and gave generously of his own organization. When McCarthy and Humphrey visited the state, McGovern stayed officially uncommitted, which proved politic. (Yet when Kennedy came to Sioux Falls on April 16 McGovern said that he would make "one of the three or four greatest presidents in our national history.")[95] McGovern's stance of halfhearted neutrality allowed him greater political breathing room with Democratic power brokers while he faced his own reelection. Privately, he shared his mailing lists with the Kennedy campaign, and discreetly exchanged useful political information.[96]

Huron, South Dakota, was the birth place of Hubert Humphrey, and it was presumed that he and McCarthy would be strong candidates in the state, since they both came from neighboring Minnesota. Although overshadowed by the intense campaigning in Oregon and California, the South Dakota primary was an important indicator of Kennedy's political appeal in the largely rural backyard of his two Minnesotan opponents. Kennedy's South Dakota effort was another efficiently run campaign by Pat Lucey.

About a month before the voting, Sorensen had spoken with McGovern, and reported back that the Senator was "friendly and optimistic about our chances."[97] Lucey believed that "a large percentage of the vote for RFK" in South Dakota, "was vital in order to underline the importance of California. A small vote in D.C. with a large vote in Indiana," he explained, "would have been of little help to us."[98] Thus, the object of the national campaign was not simply to pursue the delegate hunt, as it was called in the news media, but to pay attention to the symbolism of each primary victory as an indicator of Kennedy's ability to win the popular vote. It was imperative to impress upon the party bosses that Kennedy could win, and win big.

The only minority in South Dakota Kennedy could tap for support was the small population of Native Americans spread throughout the western part of the state. Kennedy had one of the best records in Congress on Native American issues, and was one of the few public figures who took time to speak out against the conditions of poverty, the alcoholism, and the suicide rates on the reservations. The campaign registered nearly a thousand Native Americans, and distributed transcripts of Kennedy's remarks before the Senate on the living conditions on the reservations.[99] Kennedy reached out to Native Americans in South Dakota even though, given their lack of voting strength, it was far from politically expedient. On May 23, a tribal gathering was held at which the executive director of the Agency for American Indian Affairs gave Kennedy a solid endorsement.[100]

In South Dakota, the campaign focused on radio instead of television, ran shorter print ads than it did in Nebraska, targeting some seventy-two weeklies in the state, and kept media costs down.[101] The campaign was frugal, and relied heavily on volunteers, belying the hostile press reports in Republican newspapers that claimed Kennedy was buying his victories. As election day neared, the campaign sent in the "Kennedy girls," as they were sometimes called, Jean Smith, Joan Kennedy, and Patricia Lawford, to make a final push. The campaign was primarily interested in using South Dakota "as a selling point to delegates from other states."[102] Kennedy won handily, beating McCarthy by 50 percent to 20 percent; Humphrey only managed to garner 30 percent of the vote.[103] All in all, the well-organized campaign in South Dakota was an exemplary one. Tapping into the McGovern network, and the state's relatively small population, freed Kennedy to focus most of his attention on Oregon and California.

Shortly after he announced his candidacy, Kennedy had received reports from Oregon that the McCarthy supporters there were very well organized, especially on the college campuses, and were "quite resentful of RFK's entrance into the race" and intended to work hard to counter the Kennedy efforts.[104] The campaign had been given sufficient warning about the potential difficulties it faced in Oregon, but the "well-oiled Kennedy machine" that Richard Reeves had described in late March was ill prepared to address them. In charge of running the state operation was the Oregon Congresswoman Edith Green, who had been a John Kennedy loyalist since 1960.

On April 1, a field report to the Kennedy campaign headquarters in Washington, D.C. from the Oregon Youth and Student Division stated: "Edith Green's people seem to have no organization, no budget, and not much activity."[105] On April 19, another report said in shorthand: "Eugene [Oregon]: disaster—nothing going—no headquarters—far behind, strong McCarthy."[106] About a week later, yet another memo reported that Green had "really cut herself off from [the] party by supporting RFK," and the cities leaned toward McCarthy while the countryside was for Johnson and Humphrey.[107] The *Eugene Register Guard* wrote that "many top Democrats in the state" were "asking, 'Where's the Bobby Kennedy organization?'"[108] On April 26, when William Vanden Heuvel arrived in Portland, he noted that there were just two phones and four desks in the headquarters, and wrote: "It was clear to all of us that the campaign was at a standstill."[109]

From the start, the Kennedy Oregon campaign was plagued with organizational glitches that allowed McCarthy to take the early offensive in organizing the state. Oregon had the characteristics of a state where McCarthy would do well. Thousands of Senator Wayne Morse's supporters had been early critics of the Vietnam War, and helped McCarthy from the moment he announced his candidacy. Oregon also lacked the base of poor whites and minorities that had given Kennedy his edge in Indiana and Nebraska.

To make matters worse, the Kennedy campaign had to gain control over a few loose cannons in Oregon who were making embarrassing statements to the press. For example, an unpopular Democratic politician who ran for state office tried to win points by "passing himself off as Chairman for Kennedy in Oregon." Another Oregon politician, Representative Sid Leiken, without authorization from the campaign, called himself the "co-chairman for the Kennedy forces," and boldly asserted to the press: "We thought we would win the Oregon primary before the announcement [of Johnson's withdrawal]; now we got it in the bag."[110] This kind of political grandstanding from supposed allies made the professionals on Kennedy's staff cringe.

The New York senator's mass base in Oregon was thin at best. One observer called Kennedy's visit to an oscilloscope plant in Corvallis the candidate's "confrontation with the 'great white silent majority.'"[111] The difficulty facing Kennedy in Oregon, the reporter continued, was that "more often than not" he was "talking to affluent people who have never seen a ghetto, an Indian reservation or a coal camp in eastern Kentucky."[112] The McCarthy forces had done a good job organizing the young people on the two main college campuses, in Eugene and Portland. When Kennedy landed at the airport in Eugene, there were twenty-two placards waved by the crowd, twenty for McCarthy and two for Ronald Reagan.[113] The number of Oregonian Kennedy volunteers was so unimpressive that the campaign quickly brought in a contingent of about seventy experienced canvassers who had worked in Indiana and Nebraska.[114]

Since McCarthy had already lined up the antiwar vote, the Kennedy campaign scrambled for an issue, any issue, that might register with Oregon's Democratic voters. Campaign staffers diligently combed Oregon's major newspapers, searching for any grievance or problem that Kennedy might use to garner local support.[115] The candidate's uncompromising stand on gun control hurt him among members of the rural white working class, who were employed largely in the timber industry and valued hunting as a pastime; his zealotry in the 1950s, when he was the young counsel for the Senate Rackets Committee investigating the Portland Teamsters Union for corruption, affected his ability to win the support of labor leaders and unionists. As the campaign grew more desperate, it even tried to ally itself with a tiny, marginal group of University of Oregon students, SDSers, and members of the Black Student Union, who planned a mini-Poor People's March on the state capital.[116]

Kennedy eventually sent in O'Brien and other professionals, but even his political miracle workers could not salvage the situation. When hard pressed in the last weeks of the campaign, the Kennedy forces were convinced that there simply were too few minorities and poor whites in the state to forge a semblance of a "have-not" coalition. The campaign tried to counter its dismal position by focusing on another potentially aggrieved group: white, middle-class women.

Edith Green, who was in charge of the state campaign, had won her last Congressional election with 67 percent of the votes. Kennedy made a few blatant appeals to female voters, including a call for a woman to be named to the American peace negotiating team then meeting in Paris. "They're the ones who have to give their husbands," he said. "They're the ones who have to send their sons. They're the ones that are making such a great sacrifice in addition to the men in Vietnam."[117] Organizers brought in Mrs. Arthur Schlesinger, Mrs. John Bartlow Martin, and Rose Kennedy to try to stir up support among suburban women. "The presidency is a tremendous responsibility, even greater than when Jack was in the White House," the matriarch of the Kennedy clan told an admiring female audience of about 300 at a Eugene hotel.[118] But all these efforts proved of no avail.

Shifting their attention away from the campaign's inherent difficulties in Oregon, Kennedy staffers closely monitored the McCarthy campaign, and found it was drifting into the role of a de facto "stop Kennedy" force. The Kennedy camp recognized it was losing the state; McCarthy was putting up a tough fight. Reports came trickling into the Kennedy headquarters that McCarthy officials encouraged canvassers to concentrate their animosity not on Humphrey, Johnson, or even the war in Vietnam but on Kennedy, including "pretty nasty" briefings on "how to handle the 'Kennedy' question."[119] McCarthy ridiculed Kennedy publicly, and attacked his advisers and even his dog.[120]

On May 21, McCarthy gave a filmed interview to Metromedia Television News while on a chartered plane flying from Klamath Falls to Coos Bay. He hinted that he would support Humphrey for the nomination if the Vice President modified his position on the war. When a reporter commented that Kennedy aides believed McCarthy's only role after his defeats in Indiana and Nebraska was to block Kennedy, McCarthy replied: "Sometimes the spoiler role is pretty effective. I think I've been more constructive in this campaign than anyone else. You can say that Bobby spoiled it for me by coming in. I'm not interested in the Vice Presidency on anybody's ticket, or being Secretary of State or the Ambassador to the United Nations."[121] This last statement was widely interpreted to mean that McCarthy planned to fight Kennedy to the bitter end at the convention.

McCarthy's apparent cozying up to Humphrey sent temporary shock waves through his own organization. Young volunteers were alarmed to hear their candidate, whose stance of political purity was one of his main selling points, consider backing the emissary of an Administration openly identified with the bloodbath in Vietnam. The following day, McCarthy backed away from his original statement. He first insisted he had been misquoted, (though his words were caught on film), and then he "clarified" his position, claiming to be "absolutely neutral" between Humphrey and Kennedy.[122] But the incident exposed the fact that McCarthy's visceral distaste for Kennedy had led him away from his original purpose: stopping the war.

McCarthy's stance was made all the more intolerable to peace activists by the fact that Humphrey and his more hawkish allies, in the heat of the campaign, had actually hardened their support of the war. In March 1968, Humphrey disagreed with Kennedy's charge that the war was "immoral," saying that "the success of aggression in Vietnam would encourage wider and far more aggression," and therefore such a view was "both hard to understand and insupportable by fact."[123] Out of personal pique, McCarthy had centered his attention on destroying Kennedy, who was the Democratic Party's most powerful and credible voice opposing the Administration's course in Southeast Asia. The McCarthy organization, which had begun as Allard Lowenstein's Dump Johnson movement, with the goal of ending the war, had become, by the Oregon primary, one dedicated to putting an end to Kennedy's chances of being president. In Portland, students printed handbills with the newspaper article containing McCarthy's remarks, along with an open appeal to McCarthy supporters to join the Kennedy cause.[124]

On May 24, McCarthy announced that his campaign had purchased a half hour of Portland television time for the following evening, and sent a telegram inviting Kennedy to debate him. After his Indiana, District of Columbia, and Nebraska victories, Kennedy, perhaps unwisely, had played the conventional front-runner role, and had ducked McCarthy's previous calls to debate. His position was that any debate without the presence of Humphrey, who was a declared presidential candidate, would only cost him without gaining him anything, except giving McCarthy added exposure (hence McCarthy's eagerness to debate).

The polls showed that Kennedy had clearly failed to electrify Oregonians, and McCarthy could very well beat him; McCarthy's debate challenge set off alarm bells among Kennedy's advisers. Except for Edith Green and Frederick Dutton, most people on Kennedy's staff with access to the candidate urged him to debate McCarthy. The younger staffers, especially Adam Walinsky, who could annoy the Senator at times with his persistent pressure, goaded him to accept McCarthy's offer. When Lucey, Vanden Heuvel, and Salinger weighed in on the side of his young speech writers, Kennedy deferred to O'Brien. Ever the pragmatist, O'Brien concluded that the debate did not matter one way or another to the outcome of the Oregon primary; he chose to remain neutral.[125] Kennedy decided not to debate.

As Kennedy had done months earlier when he balked at entering the presidential race, he once again decided to err on the side of caution. On May 25, he wrote McCarthy: "I regret that you did not also invite the Vice President, who is an announced candidate for President, and who found time yesterday to campaign in the state of South Dakota, where, like Oregon, he is not entered on the Presidential ballot." Kennedy continued:

> Both of us have traveled throughout the state of Oregon. I have answered questions at every stop from any citizen who had an inquiry. Many of the questions were asked by your supporters.
>
> The real struggle in 1968 is between those candidates who espouse change and the candidate who stands for the status quo. . . .
>
> I have already sent word that in the event the Vice President decides to accept this invitation I will be pleased to change my campaign schedule in any way necessary to join in a truly meaningful discussion of the important issues facing this nation in 1968.[126]

McCarthy's formal challenge came just three days before the voting, and O'Brien was probably correct that it would not have affected the results either way. But Kennedy's decision not to debate was a boon for McCarthy, allowing the Minnesota senator once again to show courage in contrast to Kennedy's supposed "opportunism." Kennedy's refusal soon took on the distinct flavor of a major tactical blunder. As the May 28 election grew closer, it became clear that Kennedy, once again, should have heeded the advice of the young firebrands on his staff.

In the final days of the Oregon campaign, McCarthy became increasingly bitter in his jabs at Kennedy. "Bobby threatened to hold his breath unless the people of Oregon voted for him," he said on several occasions.[127] His campaign ran false ads claiming that Kennedy had supported the war right up to the moment he decided to run for president. McCarthy also belittled the intelligence and education level of the average Kennedy voter: "The polls seem to prove that he is running ahead of me among the less intelligent and less well-educated voters of the country. On that basis, I don't think we're going to have to apologize or explain away the results in the state of Oregon."[128] McCarthy's supercilious snipes at Kennedy's constituents seemed to confirm that the "peace" candidate was losing sight not only of his original purpose but also of the common ground the two candidates shared.

On May 27, the day prior to the voting, an advertising agency working for McCarthy flooded Oregon's radio stations with a commercial that altered the results of a Lou Harris poll taken a few days earlier. The McCarthy radio spots asserted that the Harris poll predicted Kennedy would lose to Nixon in November if he were the nominee. In reality, the poll showed Kennedy beating Nixon 42 to 40 percent, and McCarthy losing to Nixon 39 to 40 percent. Vanden Heuvel fired off an angry telegram to the McCarthy campaign director in Oregon damning the ads, and exposing their falsehoods.[129] Pierre Salinger followed up with a stinging press release in behalf of Kennedy, confronting McCarthy about the misleading commercials. Salinger said that he had spoken personally with Harris in his New York office, and "he confirmed the total inaccuracy of Senator McCarthy's last day radio appeal to the voters of Oregon." It was the first time the Kennedy campaign had "found it necessary to protest what is clearly false and misleading advertising in behalf of Senator McCarthy." The timing of the radio spots on the eve of the election, and the McCarthy campaign's attempt to quietly pull them after Kennedy's people made them a public issue, in Salinger's view was "a clear admission on their part" that the ads "contain[ed] precisely the falsehoods" that were brought to the news media's attention.[130]

The Kennedy campaign took care not to blame McCarthy personally for the spots, and instead chose to refer only to his advisers. But neither did the Kennedy spokespersons allow McCarthy to pass off the advertisements as an innocent mistake. "Senator McCarthy's advisers are aware of the inaccuracy of the commercial," Salinger declared, "and are rushing it in at the last possible moment to prevent us, and Mr. Harris, from effectively setting the record straight." The fact that it was a "saturation spot" also suggested that McCarthy's aides "intend[ed] to make the most of what they know to be a wrongful appeal to the voters of this state."

Salinger took the issue a step further by pointing out that the problem might have arisen because a week earlier McCarthy had brought "a new campaign director into Oregon." According to Salinger, the new director, Thomas Finney, had been a member of the Central Intelligence Agency, a former law partner of Secretary of Defense Clark Clifford, and "very close" to Humphrey. "I state categorically," Salinger continued, "that Mr. Finney's 11th hour emergence in this campaign, and this sudden and re-grettable switch in advertising tactics, has more the purpose of advancing Mr. Humphrey's campaign than that of Senator McCarthy."[131] Salinger, who was known to have a flair for the dramatic, had not exaggerated the Finney affair. A key executive director of McCarthy's own campaign had resigned in disgust over Finney's appointment, citing complaints similar to Salinger's, and switched his support to Kennedy.[132] McCarthy's shift in tone toward his peace candidate opponent was now accompanied by a shift in tactics as well.

On election day, May 28, Robert Kennedy, after a streak of twenty-six victories, became the first member of the Kennedy family to lose an election. The Kennedy campaign in Oregon never hit its stride, and fought an uphill battle from the start. Edith Green had neither the political muscle with the state Democratic organization nor the mass base to put together a significant coalition of forces for Kennedy. She failed to deliver even her own district.[133] The suburbanites and young people flocked to McCarthy; some labor union-ists peeled off from the mainstream party leadership to back Kennedy, but not in large enough numbers to make a difference. And there were simply not enough African Americans and poor people to sweep the primary from below, through registration and get-out-the-vote drives, as Kennedy had done in both Indiana and Nebraska. The result was a disappointing 38.8 percent for Kennedy to 44.7 percent for McCarthy; Johnson and Humphrey between them won about 12 percent.

In his post mortem, Vanden Heuvel concluded that in Oregon the Ken-nedy organization had failed to tap into Senator Morse's network of sup-porters. Morse was the former dean of the University of Oregon, which became a McCarthy stronghold.[134] McCarthy had simply beat Kennedy to the punch in organizing Oregon's peace voters. Kennedy's original hesitancy about entering the race had sealed his fate in Oregon. Vanden Heuvel had estimated that there were only 20,000 African Americans in the entire state, who lived in more integrated communities than in most states; there also barely existed any other "identifiable ethnic group."[135] In addition, the Dem-ocratic political structure was far looser than in New York or Indiana: "The State Committee and county leaders either do not exist or have little or no influence." A large percentage of undecided voters went to McCarthy, an outcome that a Kennedy-McCarthy debate might have helped prevent. The size of Kennedy's traveling entourage worked against him in small towns, as did Kennedy's turning up late at virtually all of his campaign appearances. "Oregon was clearly a state where a stop-Kennedy movement had the realistic promise of success," Vanden Heuvel lamented.[136]

At a final gathering of Oregon campaign workers at the Benson Hotel in Portland, Kennedy took personal responsibility for the failure, and blamed himself for not being able to communicate with the voters of Oregon. He insisted on sending McCarthy a congratulatory telegram, which was a professional courtesy that McCarthy never gave Kennedy. When asked how it felt to be the first Kennedy to lose, after twenty-seven elections, Kennedy quoted Abraham Lincoln's joke about the man who was being ridden out of town on a rail: "If it wasn't for the honor of the thing, I'd rather have passed it up," he said. He accepted defeat gracefully, which may have surprised McCarthy and those of his supporters who had portrayed him as a child willing to "hold his breath" until the voters handed him the state. The Oregon loss, Kennedy conceded, would make it extremely difficult for him to deal with the delegations from the nonprimary states at the national convention: "They will use Oregon as an excuse for not supporting me," he said.[137]

McCarthy and his followers celebrated wildly in a grandiose setting a couple of blocks away from where Kennedy stayed.[138] "In Indiana we found our mistakes, and in Nebraska we found theirs," McCarthy told his jubilant supporters at the close of his victory speech. "In Nebraska I said that many wagons got to the Missouri, but the real test began when they crossed and started up the Oregon Trail. Here we have shown who had the staying power, who had the strength and the commitment. We had better horses, the best wagons, and the best men and women. Now the second test is California. California, here we come!"[139]

Politically, the people who truly had cause to celebrate were Humphrey and those who comprised the pro-Johnson wing of the Democratic Party. McCarthy's victory was their victory too. Kennedy's prowar detractors gleefully declared that the Kennedy phenomenon was finished. Press reports quoted some of Humphrey's backers, who predicted that if McCarthy handily beat Kennedy in Oregon, it might create enough momentum to stop him in California, thereby knocking him out of the race for good. Kennedy held no press conference the night of the Oregon loss. Back in his hotel room, a reporter asked him if he thought the Oregon defeat had hurt him, which evoked from the candidate a disbelieving gaze: "It certainly wasn't one of the more helpful developments of the day," he said.[140]

* * *

In the primary season of 1968, there was no shortage of political ironies. In New Hampshire, Eugene McCarthy had wrapped himself in the image of President John Kennedy, and gave speeches about how the country had been better off "five years ago." In Oregon, while sparring with Robert Kennedy, he held the late President personally responsible for the Vietnam War.[141] In Indiana, there had been the spectacle of a staunchly conservative newspaper chain advancing the cause of the New Dealer Hubert Humphrey in the Democratic primary; and Indiana's A.F.L.-C.I.O. had joined forces with the state's ferociously antilabor Republican papers in promoting Roger Branigan over Kennedy.

In South Dakota and Oregon, the McCarthy campaign ran full-page advertisements and printed leaflets calling on Republicans to cross over to vote for McCarthy. The campaign also formed a Republicans for McCarthy organization, which sought donations from members of the G.O.P. and boasted that over 5,000 Republicans had voted for McCarthy in New Hampshire. "This is not the year to worry about party loyalty," a Republicans for McCarthy ad proclaimed. "It's the year to worry about everything but."[142] McCarthy encouraged crossovers, and emphasized his attractiveness to Republicans while defending his record as a quintessential liberal.[143] His campaign employed the curious tactic of actively recruiting Republican voters in conservative states to help "remake" the Democratic Party into a more "progressive" and "responsive" institution.[144]

Hundreds of members of the Democratic state delegations who had endorsed Humphrey were open and committed hawks, such as Representative W. R. Poage of Texas, who asserted that "the Viet Cong receives more effective support from those in Washington who question our determination than from those in Moscow who supply rockets."[145] Yet this fact did not prevent McCarthy from running his campaign in a way that threatened to strengthen the party's prowar delegations at the expense of those Democrats who called for ending the Vietnam War. Kennedy increasingly became the object of McCarthy's wrath, at a time when Humphrey still openly supported the twisted logic of the Administration's Southeast Asia policy.

Kennedy's Oregon loss demonstrated that his candidacy depended to a large degree on the mobilization of minorities and the poor. It was further proof that the campaign gave pragmatic political form to a coalition of "have nots." Kennedy illustrated in the primaries that he could put together victories in states with a significant black community—even when it was small in proportion to the state's overall population—by generating enthusiasm, increasing participation, and swelling the ranks of Democratic voters. In Oregon, Kennedy lost because the campaign was not competently managed and because there were relatively few blacks and poor people in the state.

Ironically, the loss may have done Kennedy some good by erasing the juggernaut label and the illusion of the "well-oiled Kennedy machine" that Richard Reeves had described, and by mitigating the triumphalist predictions in the press.. The Oregon defeat, by demonstrating that he could lose an election, energized Kennedy's supporters in California. Black community leaders, progressive labor unionists (mostly associated with the U.A.W.), and César Chávez with his small army of dedicated activists all redoubled their efforts in the wake of the Oregon loss.

Like Johnson, Humphrey was dogged by antiwar protesters at his public appearances, and more often than not Democrats at the local level were bitterly divided over his defense of the Administration's Vietnam policies. Despite his liberal record, Humphrey's stand on Vietnam undermined his ability to communicate with a polarized and politicized electorate.[146] Kennedy's success in going to the grass roots reinvigorated the Democratic Party at a time when the Administration's candidate had great difficulty overcoming the divisions caused by the war. Kennedy's Oregon defeat had been a setback, but it was not fatal.

Meanwhile, despite Humphrey's solid record on civil rights and labor, he traveled around the country giving vacuous speeches about "the happiness of human opportunity."[147] Humphrey's blithe rhetoric largely rang hollow to a Democratic electorate embittered by years of war and polarization, and heavily influenced by movement politics. Nationally, Richard Nixon's coolly exploited "politics of discontent" seemed to have far more ideological resonance than Humphrey's calls for "happiness and joy."[148] Both Humphrey and Nixon wanted McCarthy to finish Kennedy off, and McCarthy, in his increasingly scornful and personalized battle against Kennedy, did everything in his power to work toward this end. These contradictory political trends crystallized in the California primary race.

10 California: Kennedy's Last Campaign, May 1–June 6, 1968

I cannot believe that the Democratic Party will nominate a man whose ideas and programs have been so decisively rejected. Yet the Vice President apparently believes he can win the nomination without once submitting his case to the people.

—Robert F. Kennedy, Ambassador Hotel, Los Angeles, California, June 4, 1968

Shortly after Kennedy's failure in Oregon, Janet Lee Auchincloss, the mother of Jacqueline Kennedy, wrote a comforting letter: "This defeat might be a help to your campaign, instead of a bitter blow. Somehow the first defeat or setback makes you a more sympathetic figure—and people will admire the courageous and graceful way you acknowledge it."[1] It was far from certain whether her upbeat assessment would prove accurate. Prior to his Oregon shipwreck, Kennedy had told reporters that if he lost any of the primaries, he no longer would be a "viable" candidate. On June 4, 1968, California's Democratic voters would go to the polls in their state's primary and make the final decision on Kennedy's viability.

California was the most important testing ground for Kennedy's ability to win delegates, and hence the nomination; a loss there would stop his campaign in its tracks. If he produced a victory, the 174 votes of the California delegation in the winner-take-all primary would place him in a far stronger position going into the convention. A win in the Golden State was essential if Kennedy was to use his primary victories to impress upon Democratic power brokers that he was the only candidate who could win for the party in November.

The state was well known for its schizophrenic politics that seesawed back and forth between conservatives and liberals. Despite Ronald Reagan's 1966 gubernatorial victory (and his jockeying for the Republican presidential nomination in 1968 in what the press had dubbed a noncampaign), registered Democratic voters outnumbered Republicans by over a million.[2] The notion that California represented a microcosm of the nation had been repeated in the news media so often it had become a cliché. In 1968, more than 10 million people called California home, making it the most populous state in the union. It was also the most ethnically and racially diverse, with large numbers of Asian Americans, African Americans, and Latinos. Californians were employed in all of the significant sectors of the economy, including agriculture, manufacturing, and high-technology industry. For the first time ever, computers would tally the results of a presidential primary.

Kennedy had strong political allies within a segment of the state's Democratic Party, with Assembly Speaker Jesse Unruh leading the way. Unruh had been a consistent voice encouraging Kennedy to enter the race, and a constant source of optimistic predictions for his chances in California. Unruh's organization gave Kennedy a base from which to influence state and local Democratic officials. Unruh also introduced reforms in the Assembly making it easier for delegates to jump from one slate to another.

In California, during the 1966 midterm campaigns, Kennedy had cultivated political alliances with Democrats at the local level. He had stumped the state for candidates, many of whom had little chance of winning, and had been an important fund-raising guest speaker for many local contests. When he entered the presidential race, he immediately won the support of not only the group around Unruh, but of dozens of prominent Democrats who had served in the administration of the liberal former Governor Edmund "Pat" Brown.[3]

What emerged in California was a tough three-way race among Kennedy, Humphrey, and McCarthy. Humphrey had the favor of the pro-Administration Democratic organization, which had been weakened by Unruh's defection but still controlled the party coffers. McCarthy, as he had demonstrated in Oregon, was a force on the college campuses and popular with independents, Republicans, and swing voters in the middle-class suburbs. Kennedy's strength lay primarily with the state's minority populations, and with low-income and working-class whites.

Representing the forces allied with President Johnson and Vice President Humphrey was a slate headed by California's Attorney General Thomas Lynch. On March 31, 1968, when Johnson surprisingly removed himself from the race, the Lynch slate was thrown into disarray and suffered some significant defections to the Kennedy camp. For example, two days after Johnson's announcement, California Representatives John Tunney and Robert Leggett announced in Washington that they were seizing the opportunity to leave the Lynch slate and join Kennedy.[4] The day after Johnson withdrew, reports surfaced in the *Los Angeles Times* and other California newspapers that McCarthy supporters were moving to the Kennedy camp.[5] Kennedy successfully peeled off other former Lynch delegates, including one who became the state-wide vice chairman of the California Kennedy for President campaign.[6] These shifts of allegiance strengthened Kennedy's chances, and reflected the new political environment following Johnson's withdrawal.

On April 3, 1968, the same day Kennedy and Johnson conferred in the White House, high-level members of the Lynch delegation met in Sacramento to plan their response to the President's withdrawal; they decided to wait and see if Humphrey needed them or, possibly, to draft Johnson.[7] The delegation was eventually reconfigured into a weaker slate of candidates representing Humphrey, whose name was not on the ballot but who formally declared his candidacy on April 27.

After discerning that Unruh's people had failed at the tasks of voter registration and neglected to organize blacks and Latinos, Kennedy sent in his own campaign team. The parallel Kennedy organization worked within Democratic Party structures, cultivated ties with party officials wherever possible, and jealously guarded its financial and tactical autonomy. Like John Kennedy's primary campaigns of 1960, which had relied on organizations outside formal party networks, Robert Kennedy's 1968 campaign had a high degree of independence and flexibility.

But Kennedy's strongest sources of support were to be found outside both the party institutions and the Unruh machine. His most significant political bases in the state were located in the Latino, African-American, and white working-class districts, concentrated heavily in the Los Angeles area but dispersed in other cities as well, particularly in the San Francisco Bay Area. He also cultivated ties to the Asian-American communities of Los Angeles and San Francisco, with the assistance of March Fong who later became California's secretary of state. Kennedy had demanded that his staff concentrate great attention on organizing white working-class neighborhoods, the inner cities, the barrios, and migrant farm worker communities.[8]

As with all the other primaries in which Kennedy was a candidate, central to the campaign's California strategy was to register and get to the polls as many minorities and low-income whites as possible. Kennedy's political aides had assessed McCarthy's strength in the suburbs, and determined that the only way Kennedy could win would be to carry the enormous minority districts of Los Angeles County. The Latino neighborhoods of East Los Angeles, and the African-American South-Central area, were the focus of intense mobilizing and voter registration drives.

The campaign set up its headquarters on Wilshire Boulevard in the heart of Los Angeles. Kennedy repeatedly toured the state, and tried to hit each of its three main media markets: Los Angeles, San Diego, and San Francisco. He would sometimes fly from Los Angeles to the Bay Area and back again on the same day, which allowed his appearances to be shown on local newscasts in both Northern and Southern California. His motorcades drew unruly crowds, and his neighborhood tours often ran as the lead story. Jerry Bruno, who had been John Kennedy's advance man, had a well-earned reputation for producing highly successful mob scenes at campaign stops.[9] So enthusiastic were the crowds who swarmed around Kennedy's motorcades in Latino and black neighborhoods, aides feared he would lose white votes if he became overly identified with the aspirations of ethnic minorities.

Kennedy's prospects for winning depended upon grassroots participation and aggressive voter-registration in neighborhoods where poverty and unemployment were the key issues. Yet he did not rely exclusively on the state's lower-income groups and racial minorities. The campaign formed dozens of influential state-level committees of professors, students, law enforcement officials, clergy, and educators. In May 1968, as the campaign unfolded, Kennedy's experienced media managers, led by Frank Mankiewicz and Pierre Salinger, issued daily press releases announcing the formation of committees and new endorsements which gave the impression a bandwagon was rolling along.

Moreover, the campaign almost daily released new proposals on a wide-ranging set of issues, including race relations, poverty, economic policy, pollution, and law enforcement, as well as the war in Vietnam. Neither the Lynch ticket nor the McCarthy campaign could keep up with the sheer volume of Kennedy's press releases, policy statements, and committee announcements. In addition, there were several high-level defectors from the McCarthy campaign, and Mankiewicz and Salinger made the most of these cases.

In California, Latinos comprised the state's largest single minority, and they were central to the campaign's coalition-building efforts, and to the candidate's chances for victory. The leader of the United Farm Workers union (U.F.W.), César Chávez, proved invaluable after he unleashed his small army of organizers, canvassers, and get-out-the-vote activists for Kennedy. He became a Kennedy delegate and state-level campaign official. In an extraordinary move, Chávez temporarily suspended the U.F.W.'s strike and national grape boycott, thereby freeing his unionists to dedicate their time and energy to the campaign.[10]

Under Chávez's leadership, the 13,000-member U.F.W., based in Delano, California, had organized a bitter struggle against California's politically powerful agribusiness interests. The union received help from an idealistic network of young volunteers from the college campuses as well as from progressive Catholic clergy, who played an important role at the local level in aiding migrant workers. In 1968, California's growers remained tenacious in refusing to recognize the union, and the conflict had become a tense stalemate.

Two years earlier, in March 1966, Kennedy had won the support of Chávez and the farm workers when he came to Delano to hold hearings of the Senate Subcommittee on Migrant Labor. He had embraced the U.F.W. cause, and found himself thrust into the center of a volatile political battle: local landowners relentlessly Red-baited Chávez and his union, and even branded priests allied with the U.F.W. "Communist-inspired." They also employed private security guards, who worked hand in glove with local law enforcement officers to harass and disrupt the U.F.W.'s organizing activities.[11] In his final statement before leaving Delano, Kennedy advised the growers' representatives to recognize the U.F.W., because in the end Chávez would be victorious. He also suggested to local sheriffs that they read the U.S. Constitution before engaging in any more preemptive arrests of union organizers. After Kennedy's 1966 visit, the Red-baiting of Chávez and the U.F.W. persisted, but it lost much of its former legitimacy.[12] Kennedy's visit gave badly needed media exposure to the U.F.W.'s struggle, which helped the union gain volunteers and donations. Chávez became a dedicated Kennedy partisan. He was immensely grateful for the Senator's early support for the union, and a close personal friendship had grown up between the two leaders.

The Mexican-American grape and lettuce pickers of Chávez's U.F.W. were among the most destitute workers in the United States. They lived in shanties beside pesticide-laden fields, were paid below the minimum wage, and faced discrimination based on skin color, language, and the ambiguities of citizenship. From 1966 to 1968, Kennedy had called for extending all of the relevant National Labor Relations Act protections to migrant farm workers. He also pushed for reforms at the state and federal level which would allow people who spoke only Spanish to qualify for the vote.[13]

By 1968, Chávez had become far more than a labor organizer; he was a Latino cultural leader who, like Martin Luther King, Jr., promoted the Gandhian principles of nonviolent civil disobedience.[14] Latinos throughout California, Texas, and the Southwest looked to him as their national leader. Chávez's dedication to nonviolence, and his selfless stands against the injustices suffered by the campesinos in the grape, strawberry, and lettuce fields of California's fertile San Joaquin and Salinas Valleys, earned him the admiration of tens of thousands of people nationwide.

In February 1968, after several violent clashes with the police and private security guards, Chávez began a fast in the name of nonviolence to refocus the energies of his supporters on peaceful protest.[15] As Chávez's hunger strike stretched over twenty days and weakened him severely, letters from concerned farm workers flooded Kennedy's office asking the Senator to return to Delano and persuade their leader to end his fast. Some of the U.F.W. letter writers described their fatigue after two-and-a-half years of striking, others were primarily concerned with Chávez's health, while still others wished to share their common ideals with Kennedy. Most of the letters were written in Spanish. "Dear Brother Kennedy," one U.F.W. letter, in English, began:

> I am a farm worker from Delano, California, and I am writing to you to ask for help, because we know you are familiar with our strike and our efforts to organize ourselves into a union and win justice for all farm workers in our country.
>
> Now, we have a problem which is disturbing us greatly, our leader César Chávez has gone on a hunger fast to bring the issue of nonviolence across to people, not only in organizing our union, but nonviolence in general. . . .
>
> We feel that if you come it would cause world-wide attention to the subject of non-violence and therefore persuade César to discontinue his hunger fast.
>
> We would appreciate it from the bottom of our heart.[16]

Several farm workers made direct connections between their struggle for justice in the fields and the aspirations of other aggrieved groups. A member of the U.F.W. Organizing Committee wrote Kennedy that Chávez fasted "to let everyone in this country know that we can accomplish many things without violence, not only in organizing our farm worker union, but elsewhere including [the] Vietnam and Civil Rights Movements."[17]

On March 10, 1968, six days before Kennedy formally announced his presidential candidacy, he returned to Delano to break bread at a Catholic service with Chávez, who was now willing to end his twenty-five day fast. Chávez was so weak he had to be carried to the site on a stretcher, and sat in a lawn chair throughout the ceremony. The event, held outdoors in the Central Valley's sweltering sun, gained national media attention largely because of Kennedy's presence.[18] "I was pleased and proud to go to Delano," Kennedy wrote a constituent after the trip, "to honor a great man, an heroic figure of our time, César Chávez. His non-violent struggle for the rights of the migrant worker is a great achievement which will afford Americans of Mexican descent the full participation in our society which they deserve."[19]

On March 16, when Kennedy declared his candidacy, Chávez and the U.F.W. threw themselves into mobilizing the Latino communities in California for Kennedy. "For every man we had working for John Kennedy" in 1960, Chávez later recalled, "we had fifty men working for Bobby. It was electrifying. The polls will show you. That line is very seldom crossed." It was a product, he added, of "respect, admiration, [and] love."[20] A bilingual Kennedy campaign pamphlet quoted Chávez: "Senator Robert F. Kennedy is a man whose many selfless acts on behalf of struggling farm workers have been expressions of love through practical deeds.[21] Senator Kennedy came at a time when our cause was very hard pressed and we were surrounded by powerful enemies who did not hesitate to viciously attack anyone who was courageous enough to help us. He did not stop to ask whether it would be politically wise for him to come . . . nor did he stop to worry about the color of our skin . . . or what languages we speak. . . . We know from our experience that he cares, he understands, and he acts with compassion and courage."[22]

Other prominent leaders of Latino communities throughout California came forward with offers of help. In addition to Chávez, Bert Corona of the Mexican-American Political Association (M.A.P.A.), who had been a labor organizer since the early C.I.O. days, joined the campaign. Professor Ralph Guzman, the head of the Mexican-American Study Project at the University of California, Los Angeles also signed on. "Please make certain that I and other Chicanos are not left out," Guzman wrote Mankiewicz. "We have a hell of a lot of young Chicano power that identifies with the Senator. . . . We need Senator Robert F. Kennedy and he needs us."[23] Guzman became a Kennedy delegate and state-level campaign official.[24]

Corona's M.A.P.A. organization, which had origins in the Viva Kennedy groups of John Kennedy's 1960 campaign,[25] gave the campaign four of its top organizers, people whom Kennedy's aides considered "real pros" who could "go into an area containing large numbers of Mexican-Americans, and in a very short time have a solid organization."[26] Corona's public endorsement of Kennedy concluded: "We, the Mexican-American and other Spanish-speaking peoples know and have confidence that Bob Kennedy can lead us from the disastrous road, and to the new direction with honest, courageous and effective solutions for our critical problems. He has shown his ability to do so. He has shown his loyalty to our needs and aspirations. We need Bob Kennedy for President."[27]

Corona and M.A.P.A. had the power to press politicians from Latino communities to reconsider their backing of the pro-Humphrey Lynch slate. For example, Corona believed that Congressman Ed Roybal, who was a Lynch delegate, could "be persuaded to back RFK publicly," because Roybal "desperately need[ed] the active support of MAPA to survive politically," and "he would be 'finished' if he sided with Humphrey."[28] Roybal, the incumbent Democrat, ran unopposed in the primary, but the Roybal case illustrates the Kennedy campaign's use of its grassroots political base inside local communities to put the heat on leaders. Corona had large numbers of Mexican-American student volunteers who dedicated their efforts to voter registration drives in behalf of Kennedy.[29] He also proposed to the campaign a number of organizing strategies, including a Spanish-language radio and television blitz, as well as an intensive door-to-door get-out-the-vote effort.[30]

Volunteers set up a group of seventy-five Latino youths in the 21st Congressional District in Los Angeles to galvanize support for Kennedy. They also organized African Americans in the district, an example of black and Latino solidarity for Kennedy.[31] Reports came back to the campaign that there had been "the most astounding outpouring of volunteer help" in many districts, which required the then innovative practice of tracking names on computer punch cards.[32] By the first week of April, the Kennedy headquarters on Wilshire Boulevard, as well as the national headquarters in Washington, D.C., received reports that thousands of Latino farm workers were being added to the voter registration rolls in the San Joaquin Valley. Latino Kennedy volunteers also competed with McCarthy at colleges and universities,[33] and Chávez himself spoke in support of Kennedy on several California campuses.[34]

Kennedy's Catholicism might have been a political liability in some areas of the country, but when it came to wooing support from the Latino communities in California, it was a definite asset. Chávez later said that every

time Kennedy was "put down for being a Catholic this made points with
the Mexicans who are all Catholic." Kennedy was by far the most prominent
national figure to carry the farm workers' cause, and his common faith added
greatly to his appeal among Latinos. He admired Chávez and the union,
and articulated the righteousness of their struggle in language concordant
with the progressive wing of the Catholic Church. Latinos looked on him
"as sort of a minority kind of person himself," Chávez said, and therefore
"with Senator Kennedy it was like he was ours."[35]

With regard to the overall campaign, in early May, California newspapers
reported that Unruh had appointed his own people to key positions in Kennedy's organization, cut off debate on how campaign money should be spent,
and made other vital decisions without consulting delegates. There was even
speculation that Unruh's unilateral moves were directly related to his own
future gubernatorial ambitions.[36] Kennedy's aides were determined to make
certain that Unruh did not become the equivalent in California of what
Edith Green had been in Oregon. The candidate quickly dispatched his
brother-in-law, Steve Smith, Kenneth O'Donnell, and other political professionals to surpass the limitations of Unruh's organizational capabilities,
and to regain operational control.

The Unruh group had focused more attention on courting party stalwarts
than on mobilizing citizens at the grass roots. Soon, complaints began cir-
culating which indicated disaffection with this strategy. The N.A.A.C.P. was
"very unhappy" with the Kennedy office in Los Angeles for not having "a
paid Negro on the staff," and offered the campaign advice on how to rectify
the situation.[37] Unruh's machine had neglected black and Latino voters, the
two groups that campaign strategists well understood would make or break
Kennedy's chances of winning. It was relayed to the Kennedy headquarters
in Washington that the campaign desperately needed someone to head up
the minority groups. "As far as the organization goes in California," one
memo read, "the left hand doesn't know what the right hand is doing."[38]

Unruh reported his sense that a significant segment of the "LBJ vote [was]
peeling off largely to McCarthy." He believed that Kennedy was so far out
in front on "minority group issues," that the "hawks shift[ed] to [the] race
issue," and were "go[ing] with McCarthy."[39] This interpretation explained
Unruh's reluctance to curry favor with blacks and Latinos. Some prowar
Democrats were apparently so fearful of Kennedy's strong identification with
minorities that they backed the peace candidate McCarthy rather than help
Kennedy advance the causes of blacks and browns.

There were conflicting views among Kennedy's allies in California about how to win the McCarthy vote. On April 30, Mankiewicz shared some of his strategy ideas with Steve Smith. The press secretary suggested "play[ing] the Humphrey menace strongly (all the money, Big Labor, Southern governors, Wall Street)," which he believed would "have the effect of driving McCarthy voters to us, particularly if Indiana had show[ed] them that McCarthy is somewhat a lost cause."[40] The "ideal" for the Kennedy campaign, Mankiewicz speculated, would be if Lynch and McCarthy each won 25 percent of the California vote, and Kennedy walked away with the other 50 percent.[41] This was an extraordinarily optimistic scenario.

On May 6, Arthur Schlesinger, after spending a few days in California, informed Kennedy that his standing among the academic community was "not too bad." "While there is predominant faculty and student sentiment for McCarthy on the ground," he wrote, "this appears to be accompanied in most places by entire friendliness toward you." Most McCarthy people Schlesinger encountered "said they expected in due course to support" Kennedy "with enthusiasm." However, he added, this anticipated patronage did "not help in the primaries."[42]

Kennedy volunteers reported to the Washington headquarters that the Youth and Students committee was fighting an uphill battle. In California, as was the case in Oregon, McCarthy had a "very organized" student campaign. The Kennedy youth division was "miserable," they wrote, "everyone [was] in meetings" with little action; it was imperative that the campaign "be able to maximize use of in-state kids," as well as those from out of state who had "come on their own."[43]

Daniel Patrick Moynihan, a former undersecretary of labor who was then the director of the Joint Center for Urban Studies of the Massachusetts Institute of Technology and Harvard University, assessed the situation for the campaign at several California universities. In mid-May, after a quick visit to Santa Barbara, Los Angeles, and Berkeley, Moynihan, who was later elected United States senator from New York, wrote Kennedy: "It was tough, but interesting. I found McCarthy sentiment widespread but not, I thought, very deep. On the other hand, I fear we are in an almost hopeless situation at the universities."[44] In Moynihan's view, the battle shaping up on the campuses was a tough one.

Conceding that McCarthy was stronger among white, middle-class youth, the campaign tapped young people in African-American and Latino communities. "Ghetto youth can be mobilized for voter registration and organization of neighborhood groups," a planning memo stated, and "provide the Senator with opportunities to talk and meet with kids from the central cities to discuss their problems and hopes."[45] The campaign sought to harness the energies of young blacks, many of whom at that time were drifting away from peaceful protest toward a politics of separatism and violence.[46]

The Youth and Student Division came under intense pressure to enlarge its base. It even reached out for support in the heart of the counterculture. Students for Kennedy organized a free Rock Rally in San Francisco's Golden Gate Park billed as "America's first political happening. Admission is free. No speeches. No apple pie." The young activists promised appearances by Sonny and Cher, "a bevy of rock groups," and a number of "surprise guests." "Free oranges, apples and balloons will be served," a Youth for Kennedy spokesperson announced.[47] The Kennedy forces made every possible effort to compete with McCarthy among youth and were having some success.

To compete with McCarthy at colleges and universities, the campaign formed an Academicians for Kennedy committee with Professor Seymour Harris of the University of California at San Diego as the head of its steering committee. Harris claimed a force for Kennedy of "over 450 college and university faculty members from every part of the state," whose ranks were "swelling daily." He was convinced that Kennedy's stands on "the critical issues of the day—the crisis in our cities and the war in Vietnam" could be "translated into effective national action."[48] The committee had coordinators in the San Francisco Bay Area and Los Angeles, and also included scholars from the Rand Corporation.[49]

Enlisting support from labor unions proved difficult for the Kennedy campaign. When a vice president of the United Steel Workers union, Thomas Consiglio, endorsed Kennedy, A.F.L.-C.I.O. President George Meany, who served on the national Humphrey for President Committee, ordered him to rescind his statement, and forbade him to affix his name to the Kennedy delegate slate. Meany blocked by decree Consiglio's endorsement of Kennedy, saying it had not been approved by the official union leadership, and therefore could be falsely construed as coming from the entire steel workers union.[50] This charge illustrated the pressure unionists, even executives, were under from the national leadership. By backing down, Consiglio showed union members the extent of Meany's iron-clad control of political endorsements.[51] The efforts of Meany and other pro-Administration union leaders to enforce discipline led Kennedy's supporters to criticize the Vice President's ties to "big labor."

Kennedy, whose major constituency was working-class whites, could credibly indict the undemocratic practices of labor leaders like Meany, as well as their support for the Vietnam War. There was never a rank-and-file referendum on whether or not the A.F.L.-C.I.O. should promote the war, yet that was what the leadership had done for years. Kennedy's labor support percolated up from the grassroots, not down from the union hierarchy. Despite his problems with the Teamsters Union dating back to the 1950s, when he had doggedly pursued Jimmy Hoffa on corruption charges, Kennedy had the enthusiastic backing of a small but extremely active coterie of labor unionists. Among them were César Chávez, U.A.W. President Walter Reuther, Bert Corona, and Paul Schrade of the 90,000-member United Auto and Aerospace Workers Union, for which he served as western regional director.

Given Humphrey's success in garnering support from the highest echelons of organized labor, Kennedy's allies confronted the Vice President with a direct political and public relations challenge. Unruh had repeatedly offered to introduce legislation in the California Assembly permitting Humphrey to place his name belatedly on the ballot.[52] This reform would allow the Democrats who were already pledged to one of the three delegate slates to switch to Humphrey if they desired, thereby eliminating the need for Lynch to serve as the stand-in candidate. Humphrey concluded that it was not in his political interest to argue the Administration's case for continuing the Vietnam War to the Democratic voters of the nation's most populous state. Instead, he waited out the primaries while helping Lynch and McCarthy behind the scenes to block Kennedy. On April 27, when Humphrey formally announced his candidacy, Unruh responded: "I am particularly pleased he is running because the Johnson Administration needs a spokesman in this campaign, someone to defend and explain the Administration's policies at home and abroad. . . . I regret, however, that the Vice President has decided not to test his vote-getting ability in the California primary, or to accept my offer to introduce legislation which would make it possible for him to place a delegation pledged to him by name on the ballot."[53]

On May 22, Kennedy said in San Francisco that the party must not ignore the "new politics" of mass citizen involvement. He acknowledged that this new politics could not dominate the Democratic National Convention, but warned that "to disregard it would be a great mistake for the Democratic Party." Kennedy described himself and McCarthy as the two chief exponents of participatory democracy, and pointed to their combined victories in New

Hampshire, Wisconsin, Washington, D.C., Indiana, and Nebraska. When coupling Kennedy's and McCarthy's vote totals against Johnson's and Humphrey's, people power had won by a five-to-one margin, he said.[54] Kennedy's analysis was in part an olive branch to the McCarthy campaign, which he credited as being part of this new coalition.

Humphrey, by taking himself out of the primaries at a time of intraparty polarization, had limited his effectiveness in tapping local community action groups, particularly in the cities. The Vice President distanced himself from the post-Kerner Commission debate on race relations, believing that the endorsements from the leadership of the mainstream civil rights organizations would suffice. Civil rights had been one of Humphrey's strengths, but with his reluctance to compete directly with Kennedy for African-American votes in the primaries, he gave the impression that he had conceded, at least for the time being, that Kennedy was more popular among blacks.

McCarthy, on the other hand, seemed uninterested in minority issues, and the black and Latino communities in California understood this. Gerald Hill, who was co-chair of the McCarthy campaign in California, acknowledged Kennedy's gaping lead among minorities, but he dismissed it as a product of "the celebrity factor."[55] These sentiments, along with McCarthy's statement in Oregon that Kennedy's supporters were "less intelligent" than his own, angered African American and Latino community leaders, and strengthened Kennedy's appeal. In Latino neighborhoods, tensions ran high between Kennedy partisans and a tiny group of McCarthy followers. After seeing about twenty Latinos marching with McCarthy placards in East Los Angeles, César Chávez recalled, "There must have been about a thousand people ready to skin them." The McCarthy people did something "stupid," in Chávez's view: "You don't do that in East L.A. or any place where there's blacks and browns"; the U.F.W. considered them "traitors."[56]

In California, the Kennedy campaign gained momentum. It pulled in mainstream Democrats, recruited community activists, formed committees of specific occupational, professional, or social groups, and lined up endorsements from diverse corners of the state's political world. In response, the Humphrey and McCarthy campaigns moved closer to one another, and took on the aura of a "Stop Kennedy" movement. Humphrey wished to avoid a floor fight with Kennedy at the Democratic National Convention, and eliminating him in California would accomplish this goal.

Despite the backing of the D.N.C., the A.F.L.-C.I.O., and nearly a thousand delegates, the Humphrey camp faced the Kennedy threat with trepidation. No matter how many delegates the Vice President brought with him to Chicago, the Humphreyites knew Kennedy could mount a formidable challenge. Few delegations were bound by the unit rule, which restricted the voting freedom of delegates, and there remained the possibility that Kennedy might cut deals and cannibalize existing state delegations, thereby dividing the Humphrey forces. Kennedy's close fellowship with Mayor Daley of Chicago also posed a threat to Humphrey, since Daley controlled not only the Illinois delegation but the voting schedule of the convention. If Kennedy successfully blocked Humphrey on the first ballot (and with Daley's help this was a distinct possibility), then no matter how many delegates Humphrey ostensibly commanded his position would probably erode with each consecutive ballot.

Furthermore, Humphrey and his advisers understood that Kennedy had surrounded himself with talented political professionals who had served President Kennedy, including O'Donnell, O'Brien, Dutton, Smith, Goodwin, Salinger, and Sorensen. Kennedy himself had been his brother's campaign manager, and surprised many more experienced politicians with his ability to maneuver at the 1960 Los Angeles convention. The Humphrey campaign knew that any convention fight with Kennedy would be difficult, and wanted to finish him off in California before he picked up any more steam.

The Johnson Administration helped Humphrey in countless ways. It allowed the Vice President to take vicarious credit for the slightest progress in the Vietnam peace talks that lumbered along in Paris. In the weeks before the California voting, J. Edgar Hoover tried to drive a wedge between Kennedy and his African-American constituency. The FBI leaked documents to the press revealing that Kennedy, when he was attorney general in 1962, had approved a Hoover request to wiretap Martin Luther King, Jr.[57] But aside from prompting some criticism from pro-Johnson journalists (such as Drew Pearson, who had never masked his antipathy for Kennedy), the revelation was politically inconsequential; Kennedy's black support held despite the disclosure, which originated from a source not known for its friendliness toward African Americans. The incident illustrated the underhanded tactics the Administration would tolerate to slow Kennedy's momentum.

After Kennedy lost Oregon he appeared vulnerable, and McCarthy's deep personal dislike for him began to surface. McCarthy already had publicly promised to fight Kennedy all the way to Chicago, and he had hinted that he might throw his delegates to Humphrey. He also seemed unfazed when people left his campaign in protest at what they perceived as McCarthy's backpedaling on the war issue while he dedicated himself to spoiling Kennedy's chances.

Humphrey and McCarthy had what appeared to be a good opportunity in California to knock Kennedy out of the race. Humphrey's behind-the-scenes efforts on behalf of both Lynch and McCarthy pressed Kennedy to seek even stronger ties to grassroots community organizations, and made the campaign all the more dependent on civic groups and local activists. By the end of May, the Kennedy campaign was pitting citizen action against the national party machinery, the prowar labor union bureaucracy, and the McCarthy campaign.

In reply to those who argued that Kennedy was too young, unpredictable, and left wing to be president, the campaign recruited high-profile former Defense and State Department officials. The candidate received dozens of endorsements from past officials of the Kennedy and Johnson Administrations. The former Assistant Secretary of State for Far Eastern Affairs, Roger Hilsman, who had been an architect of some of the failed policies in Vietnam of the early 1960s,[58] now opposed U.S. policy and backed Kennedy. Edwin Reischauer, the Harvard professor and former U.S. ambassador to Japan under Kennedy and Johnson, who was known as an authority on Asia, flew out to California to speak on Kennedy's behalf.[59] Roswell Gilpatrick, a former Deputy Secretary of Defense appointed by President Kennedy, also came to California in support of Kennedy's candidacy.[60]

Kennedy's most controversial endorsement from a national security official came from former Secretary of Defense Robert McNamara, who was then president of the World Bank. Appearing in a taped interview with Theodore Sorensen, McNamara praised Kennedy's skills as a foreign policy crisis manager during the Cuban missile crisis. Kennedy's repeated post-Tet denunciations of U.S. Vietnam policy had established him so clearly as a peace candidate that the campaign gambled he could afford to shore up his right wing with a statement from McNamara. He had remained a close friend of the Defense Secretary's throughout the period of the U.S. military build up in Vietnam. It was a friendship that some of the Senator's advisers found confusing, given his sharp disagreement with the policies that McNamara had consistently defended.[61] Many peace activists and McCarthy supporters, who had fought these policies for years, put forth a convincing critique of Kennedy's willingness to accept McNamara's backing; some of them considered the former defense secretary a "war criminal." The McNamara endorsement aimed to woo moderate voters.

Among representatives of the business community, Kennedy's identification with blacks, Latinos, and low-income whites, along with his belief in
an activist government and his prolabor record, made him, according to
opinion polls, the least favorite candidate. To allay these fears, and show
capital he could be trusted, the campaign assembled a Business for Kennedy
committee that included about forty business owners throughout the state,[62]
with a vice president of the San Francisco-based Golden Grain/Ghirardelli
corporation as its head. However, compared to Humphrey's business and
Wall Street ties, which included two of the most powerful investment bankers in New York, who raised funds for his campaign, Kennedy had a thin
base of support in the private sector.[63]

The calculated promotion of Kennedy's law-and-order credentials to win
the votes of moderates and conservatives generated some division within the
ranks of the campaign. O'Donnell had advised "scrapping" the idea of a Law
Enforcement committee, because he figured Kennedy had "enough of an
image in this area."[64] But in May, Thomas Sheridan, who had been the chief
counsel for the McCone Commission which Governor Brown had appointed
to investigate the causes of the 1965 Watts riot, created the California Law
Enforcement committee for Kennedy. Sheridan backed Kennedy, among
other reasons, because of his local support in the riot-prone black communities
of California.[65] Joining the committee were police chiefs, lawyers (some of
whom had served under Kennedy in the Justice Department), criminology
professors, and local district attorneys from across the state.

Although former California Governor Brown had declared himself a
Humphrey partisan, the Kennedy campaign continued to draw support from
Democrats who had served under him. On May 22, the same day Brown
endorsed Humphrey, the campaign announced that twenty-one key leaders
of Brown's administration now openly backed Kennedy.[66] Five days later,
the campaign released a list of some twenty more people, whom Brown had
appointed to state agencies, who now endorsed Kennedy. One former Brown
appointee, Rafer Johnson, was a 1960 Olympic gold medalist who had served
on Brown's State Recreation Commission, and headed an Athletes for Kennedy committee. Among the events Johnson organized for Kennedy was a
tennis clinic in Oakland featuring the African-American tennis star Arthur
Ashe, along with the San Francisco columnist Herb Caen and the author
George Plimpton.[67] Rafer Johnson often accompanied Kennedy on tours
through black communities, along with the Los Angeles Rams defensive
lineman Roosevelt Grier.

Thomas Braden, who had served for seven years as president of the State Board of Education under Governor Brown, publicly asserted there were more Brown appointees helping Kennedy than Humphrey.[68] Regarding Brown's advocacy of Humphrey, Braden said: "It allies him with the old coalition — Southerners, Big Labor, and back-room politicians," and "it offers further proof that the Vice President is attempting to put together a campaign organization in California without admitting it publicly."[69] The wording of Braden's announcement mirrored a memo that Sorensen had circulated among Kennedy campaign officials. Sorensen argued that Humphrey enlisted support from "the special interest lobbies from Wall Street to oil and the major Republican newspapers," and that "this unholy alliance" played "right into Nixon's hands."[70]

Frank Mankiewicz, who had served as President Kennedy's Peace Corps coordinator for Latin America, organized a Community Action for Kennedy committee, which was primarily composed of former Peace Corps and Vista volunteers, and other "action-oriented" young people. Some of the Peace Corps veterans had worked with Mankiewicz, others had lived in Asia and Africa; the Vista volunteers had assisted antipoverty programs in American cities, on Indian reservations, and in depressed rural regions. "We have worked in the underdeveloped countries of the world, and the underdeveloped parts of America," an organizer announced, and "Senator Kennedy, of all the candidates, is attuned to the needs and the feelings of the people."[71]

The campaign organized a Clergy for Kennedy committee which included Catholic, Protestant, and Jewish clergy and laity who had been active in the civil rights and peace movements. The group brought together clerics as well as professors of theology. Announcing the committee, a Lutheran member said that Kennedy "has demonstrated a capacity for compassion, and for moral leadership which makes demands on complacent consciences. He has earned our support."[72] Clergy for Kennedy illustrated the campaign's ability to reach out to existing networks of progressive people of faith.

The president of the Baptist Ministers' Unions of the San Francisco Bay Area, Reverend G. L. Bedford, endorsed Kennedy. The New York Senator had shown "a concern for the poor peoples of this nation unparalleled by any other government leader."[73] Speaking for a group of some seventy-five clergy and lay people, a professor from the Pacific School of Religion said Kennedy displayed leadership which "harmonizes understanding and compassion, tough minded commitment to administrative realities, and loving appreciation of the ideals we all share."[74]

Michael Harrington, the democratic socialist and author of *The Other America*, flew to California to campaign for Kennedy at several events.[75] John Fell Stevenson, the son of the late presidential candidate Adlai Stevenson, also backed Kennedy.[76] On May 21, the campaign presented its Hollywood for Kennedy committee, which was chaired by the singer Andy Williams. McCarthy had the support of the actors Paul Newman and Dustin Hoffman, but Kennedy had clearly won the Hollywood celebrity count. Included on the Kennedy committee, among many others, were: Lauren Bacall, Milton Berle, Marlene Dietrich, Rita Hayworth, Mahalia Jackson, Janet Leigh, Trini Lopez, Henry Mancini, Elizabeth Montgomery, Kim Novak, Sidney Poitier, Otto Preminger, Connie Stevens, Marlo Thomas, and Shelley Winters.[77]

Kennedy could count on well-known actors and entertainers who shared his views on the war and on race relations. The campaign organized two Kennedy for President galas, one at the Los Angeles Sports Arena on May 24, the other at the San Francisco Civic Auditorium on June 1.[78] These "star-studded," nationally televised events gave Kennedy added exposure inside the "media state." A unique tactical alliance developed between California's exorbitantly wealthy celebrity class and some of the poorest, most dispossessed people of the state. Kennedy's enlistment of the Hollywood elite built on his family ties to the entertainment industry dating back to the 1920s, and helped craft the image that he might restore to the White House some of the glamour of Camelot.[79]

The campaign established a committee to handle the large number of women who wished to work for Kennedy. Dianne Feinstein, who later became Mayor of San Francisco and a United States senator from California, chaired the Northern California Women for Kennedy committee; she organized several fund raisers in the Bay Area.[80] Kennedy's sisters Jean, Patricia, and Eunice, and his mother, Rose Kennedy, attended largely female events throughout the state. Feinstein said that hundreds of women contacted her office in a matter of days offering to volunteer for the campaign. She attributed this "truly amazing" outpouring of support to "their recognition of the contributions made by the women of the Kennedy family."[81]

When San Francisco Mayor Joseph Alioto called Vice President Humphrey "the best qualified candidate to deal with the problems of cities," four Supervisors of the City and County of San Francisco signed a joint statement endorsing Kennedy.[82] Supervisors Roger Boas, John Ertola, Robert Mendelsohn, and Ronald Pelosi stated: Senator Kennedy "wag[ed] his war on urban blight out of conviction and concern. . . . While Robert Kennedy was demanding priority for the cities, Hubert Humphrey was demanding priority for an Asian land war."[83]

On May 30, Kennedy led his presidential campaign on a short whistle-stop railroad tour through the San Joaquin Valley, the state's agricultural heartland. The daylong train ride started in Fresno, and stopped in Madera, Merced, Turlock, Modesto, Stockton, and Lodi on its way to the state capital in Sacramento.[84] Like his tours of rural Indiana, Nebraska, and upstate New York, these were places where such attention from a presidential candidate was a highly unusual event that drew large crowds.

Against the advice of his younger advisers, Kennedy had chosen to ignore McCarthy's repeated challenges to debate, and said he would only debate McCarthy if Humphrey also participated. However, after losing in Oregon it became clear that Kennedy no longer had the luxury of avoiding the Minnesotan, and he agreed to a joint television appearance. Prior to the event, which was scheduled for June 1 in San Francisco, Kennedy campaign staffers circulated a memo saying that "the only real difference between RFK and McCarthy on the issues" was that Kennedy had made "twenty specific proposals on each issue," whereas McCarthy "is always vague [and] never specific."[85] The charge was overstated, but McCarthy had said little about the crisis in America's cities, aside from calling for implementation of the Kerner Commission's recommendations. Kennedy attempted to expose his opponent's apparent lack of interest in the nation's racial tensions, while displaying his own grasp of what needed to be done.

The two candidates generally agreed on the necessity of United States disengagement from Vietnam; their differences were over the specific details of a peace settlement. In March 1967, Kennedy had offered a set of guidelines to end U.S. military involvement, and a detailed outline of the roles of the United Nations and the International Control Commission. He presented the problems involved in maintaining a cease-fire, and offered a prescription for a phased withdrawal of American troops.[86] He had elaborated on these proposals in *To Seek a Newer World*, which was published in November 1967, as well as in lengthy speeches throughout his presidential campaign.

McCarthy had offered proposals for peace in Vietnam that were generally more vague than Kennedy's. He tended to set the Southeast Asian conflict within the broader context of the Cold War, which was popular among his college constituents but avoided many of the thornier requirements of a U.S. withdrawal. In his essays on Vietnam that are collected in his 1967 book

The Limits of Power, it is somewhat frustrating that McCarthy is just as likely to discuss the fiction of Franz Kafka or C. S. Lewis as he is the role of the National Liberation Front and the logistics of removing American troops.[87]

McCarthy had opposed the U.S. escalation of the war, and as a member of the Senate Foreign Relations Committee often asked penetrating questions in hearings with the Administration's national security officials. Although his critique of U.S. Southeast Asia policy, in which he questioned the premises of the Cold War and the role of the C.I.A., seemed more extensive than Kennedy's, he, like Kennedy, stopped short of advocating an abrupt unilateral withdrawal of American military forces.

The long-anticipated Kennedy-McCarthy debate was the focus of intense media attention, but its format limited its effectiveness for delineating the subtle differences between the two candidates. Since McCarthy had made such an issue out of Kennedy's refusal to debate, his followers wanted their candidate to score a knockout blow. Kennedy was the better known of the two, and the prospect of a nationally televised debate with both candidates on an equal playing field appealed to the McCarthy camp.

On June 1, the long-awaited debate was held at Station KGO in San Francisco, with the ABC news broadcaster Frank Reynolds as its moderator; the journalists Bob Clark and Bill Lawrence were the chief questioners. The ground rules had been ironed out between the two campaign staffs.[88] Unlike the more traditional format of the 1960 debates between Richard Nixon and John Kennedy, the Kennedy-McCarthy debate was more akin to a joint press conference. There was no studio audience, there were no opening or closing statements, and "comments on comments" were to be avoided.[89] Instead, the candidates responded in turn to questions from the journalists. Press releases from ABC News referred to the debate as a joint appearance.[90] For such an emotionally charged campaign, with the nation at war and unrest in the cities, it was a neutered set of guidelines. Both campaigns sought to play it safe. Kennedy, McCarthy, and the three journalists were like participants in a political talk show, seated serenely around a coffee table.

On the subject of the Vietnam War, the debate was largely uneventful, and reflected a great deal of agreement between the two candidates. At one point, Reynolds commented: "There don't seem to be too many differences between Senator McCarthy and Senator Kennedy on anything, really."[91] They largely agreed on the need for the U.S. ultimately to get out of Vietnam, with minor differences on the nature of a transitional South Vietnamese government. With peace talks starting up in Paris, and the constantly shifting political and military factions jockeying for power in Saigon, there were simply too many uncontrollable variables for either candidate to be overly rigid. Kennedy did take issue with a McCarthy campaign advertisement, which McCarthy assured him had been pulled, stating that Kennedy had been part of the Johnson Administration at the time of the Dominican Republic invasion, and that he had approved of the military action; neither assertion was true.

During the debate, McCarthy suggested taking the next step against racial segregation by transporting African Americans out of the impoverished inner cities to areas in the suburbs where there were greater employment opportunities. In answering a question about the efficacy of building low-cost housing in the black parts of the larger cities, McCarthy said: "We have got to get to the suburbs, with this kind of housing, because . . . most of the employment now is in the beltline, outside the cities, and I don't think we ought to perpetuate the ghetto, if we can help it, even by putting better houses or low-cost houses there." McCarthy decried "adopting a kind of apartheid in this country," and argued that "some of the housing has got to go out of the ghetto, so there is a distribution of the races throughout the whole structure of our cities and into our rural areas."[92]

Kennedy seized upon McCarthy's idea, and implied that the Minnesota senator advocated moving thousands of blacks into the white suburbs. "Taking 10,000 black people and moving them into Orange County," he said, "would be taking them out where 40 percent of them wouldn't have any jobs at all." If you meant to deal seriously with the problem, "putting them in the suburbs where they couldn't afford the housing, where their children couldn't keep up with the schools, and where there were no vocational schools would be catastrophic." "We have to face the fact," he said, "that a lot of these people are going to live here [in the ghettos] for another several decades. And they can't live under the conditions that they are living under at the present time."[93]

Some in the press accused Kennedy of playing to white fears and "backlash" with his reference to moving 10,000 black people into Orange County, a famous bastion of white conservatism. Kennedy's identification with minorities was so well established that a clumsy attempt to win white votes through provoking racial fears probably would not help him politically. Kennedy's work with the Bedford-Stuyvesant Special Impact program to rebuild an impoverished community had taught him that although the black inner cities were ravaged by poverty and unemployment, which decades of racial discrimination had produced, they were still vibrant communities with a sense of pride, and strong generational and family ties.[94] He believed the success of the Bed-Sty project depended on forging strong ties in the local community, not weakening them. The idea of "moving" blacks in large numbers into the suburbs was simply unrealistic on social, cultural, and political grounds.

Most commentators called the Kennedy-McCarthy debate a draw. It gave Kennedy a boost by putting to rest the McCarthy challenge that had dogged him at campaign stops. He also had held his own against an opponent who, although less well known, was ten years his senior, and had a longer public career.[95] McCarthy showed tens of thousands of people, who knew very little about him, that he was a serious candidate. Media commentators offered their tired observation that both candidates appeared "presidential."

As Kennedy gained momentum in California, Humphrey's supporters used the McCarthy campaign as a vehicle to defeat him. Among the more dubious practices of both the McCarthy and Humphrey campaigns were the transfer of funds, and the running of fraudulent eleventh-hour radio and newspaper advertisements which violated campaign laws.

On May 22, a few days before the Oregon primary, Professor Andrew Robinson, who played a key role for McCarthy in Nebraska, had resigned from his campaign, declaring that "the idealism and the gallantry that Senator McCarthy displayed should not be lost in a pell-mell rush for the Humphrey bandwagon. The torch has now passed to Robert Kennedy."[96] Robinson said the appointment of Thomas Finney, who joined McCarthy as his campaign director in the last weeks of the Oregon campaign, was what had pushed him into the Kennedy camp. Finney, the former C.I.A. official and law partner of Defense Secretary Clark Clifford,[97] maintained close ties to Humphrey. A friend of the Administration was now apparently running McCarthy's campaign, and this was something Robinson could not accept. Finney's emergence on the scene, along with reports that the campaign had received $50,000 from Humphrey partisans, produced a spate of resignations of McCarthy campaign personnel in the final weeks of the California primary.[98]

The Kennedy campaign exploited the divisions within McCarthy's staff that Finney's appointment had stirred.[99] Robinson became the chair of Operation Change-Over, which directed efforts to win over former McCarthyites. Several McCarthy campaign officials abandoned ship, citing the campaign's shift in tactics, its transformation into a Stop Kennedy movement, and its tacit alliance with Humphrey as the key reasons for their departure.[100] Some McCarthy workers may have switched their allegiance to Kennedy simply because they concluded their candidate was going to lose anyway.

Sema Lederman, who had been an important member of McCarthy's national staff, was placed in charge of the Change to Kennedy organization of Northern California.[101] James Bowman, the chairman of the McCarthy campaign in the San Francisco Bay Area, joined the Kennedy cause because, he said, Kennedy related to minority groups and discussed the civil rights issues effectively, while McCarthy did not.[102]

Thomas Page, who had experience as a national public relations director for both Edmund Brown's 1962 gubernatorial campaign and the 1964 Johnson-Humphrey campaign, had been serving as the executive director of the McCarthy for President National Finance Committee. He abandoned the McCarthy campaign and joined Kennedy's staff in San Francisco.[103] The Northern California co-chair of Citizens for McCarthy, Nancy Swadesh, who was the secretary of the national board of directors of the A.D.A., also dumped McCarthy for Kennedy. "It is evident," her announcement read, that Kennedy was "the only candidate who has been able to gain the confidence of the poor and the disadvantaged by coming to grips with their problems and by proposing concrete solutions to them. Kennedy gives us the best chance for peace in the world and at home."[104]

On May 30, five days before Californians went to the polls, the Kennedy campaign charged Humphrey's partisans with deliberately confusing voters.[105] According to transcripts obtained by the campaign, two radio spots, one of sixty seconds, the other of thirty, stated that "only the Tom Lynch delegation includes supporters for all three Democratic presidential candidates—Humphrey, Kennedy, McCarthy."[106] The ads falsely claimed that a vote for the Lynch slate (which represented Humphrey) was actually a vote for Kennedy, because the Lynch delegation was the only official Democratic slate. Stephen Reinhardt, who was the legal counsel for the California Democratic State Central Committee, and Carmen Warschaw, a former chairperson of the Southern California Democratic Committee and a member of the Lynch delegation, both filed formal complaints. The ads also illegally failed to disclose the names of their official sponsors.[107]

Reinhardt sent telegrams to all of the radio stations and newspapers that had run the advertisements notifying them that they were in violation of federal and state election laws, and requested that the ads be pulled immediately.[108] The Kennedy campaign had to rush out its own set of ads to inform the public that "a vote for the Lynch slate was a vote for Humphrey and a vote for the Kennedy slate was a vote for Kennedy."[109]

Radio stations and newspapers continued to run the ads even though the lawyer for the Democratic State Central Committee had already determined they were fraudulent and illegal. On May 30, Warschaw said at a press conference at the Ambassador Hotel in Los Angeles that she was "greatly distressed" that Humphrey's representatives had made no effort to remove the ads. Warschaw and Reinhardt sent telegrams of protest to the United States Attorney General, Ramsey Clark, and to Thomas Lynch, noting that "as Attorney General of California," he had "issued official legal opinions upholding the constitutionality" of the election laws that his supporters now violated.[110]

On June 1, the day of the Kennedy-McCarthy debate in San Francisco, Robinson, of Operation Change Over, stunned the press with the following statement: "The moral basis of McCarthy's candidacy, opposition to the Johnson-Humphrey Vietnam policy, has now been totally destroyed by an increasingly open and cynical coalition of McCarthy and Humphrey forces. . . . Dirty politics in the last days of a campaign are always reprehensible, but it is especially deplorable coming from a candidate whose public posture has been 'holier than thou.' Apparently, we have seen the last of 'Clean Gene.'"[111]

In an embarrassing gaffe, Humphrey's chief fund-raiser, Eugene Wyman, a member of the Democratic National Committee, insisted on television that there was "nothing illegal in the ads," only hours before the Weinberg Milton Advertising Agency of Los Angeles, which produced them, agreed to pull the ads and conceded that they were indeed illegal.

The sponsors of the radio and newspaper blitz were ultimately compelled to capitulate. Although the Weinberg Agency deleted the fraudulent material, the original versions continued to run in the media. The false material was expunged from a full-page ad in the *Los Angeles Times*, but the *San Francisco Chronicle* still ran it in its original form.[112] The Kennedy campaign countered with a ten-second radio spot on June 3, the day before the voting: "There seems to be a little confusion about voting tomorrow. If you want Hubert Humphrey, you vote for the Lynch delegation and if you want Robert F. Kennedy you vote for the Kennedy delegation. It's as simple as that."[113]

On June 3, the day before the election, Kennedy embarked on his most strenuous single day of campaigning. He traveled more than 1,200 miles, and hit each of the state's three media markets. He rode in motorcades through clogged streets in Los Angeles, then flew north to San Francisco for a tour through Chinatown and the neighboring environs, and back down to San Diego for yet another long motorcade into the evening. He had been brought to the brink of physical collapse after eighty-five days of little sleep and nonstop campaigning. Kennedy had conducted a very tactile street campaign. His hands were scabbed and bloodied from the thousands of hand shakes over the past weeks; people often removed his cufflinks and even his shoes; thousands of people felt they had to touch this candidate. On June 4, the day of the election, he rested with Ethel and six of their ten children at the Malibu home of their friend, the movie director John Frankenheimer. Richard Goodwin recalled seeing Kennedy "stretched out across two chairs in the sunlight" out by the Frankenheimers' pool, "his head hanging limply over the chair frame; his unshaven face deeply lined and his lips slightly parted." He was relieved to see that his friend was only in a deep sleep.[114]

Late in the day, as the election results were being tallied, Frankenheimer gave Kennedy a ride to the campaign's election night headquarters at the Ambassador Hotel. That evening, when the vote count in the Los Angeles area trickled in, Kennedy surged ahead of McCarthy in what appeared to be a safe lead. He received large pluralities in Los Angeles County, the state's most populous, and it was apparent he would win despite a likely last-minute swell for McCarthy in the white suburbs. When the final count was made available, Kennedy won with 46.3 percent of the vote to McCarthy's 41.8 percent; the Lynch slate won only 12 percent. It was not an overwhelming victory, but it redeemed the campaign after the Oregon defeat, and the 174 delegate votes greatly strengthened Kennedy's hand as he marched onward to Chicago.

Predictably, the breakdown of the Kennedy districts showed that he won only because large numbers of African Americans, Latinos, and working-class whites voted for him, particularly in the Los Angeles area.[115] The race between McCarthy and Kennedy was close: McCarthy had won 1,267,608 votes to Kennedy's 1,402,911.[116] McCarthy carried twenty more counties than did Kennedy, thirty-eight to eighteen, but Kennedy beat McCarthy handily in Los Angeles County by over 120,000 votes, winning all of the minority precincts by enormous margins.[117] Kennedy's showing in Los Angeles gave him the victory.

When early indicators showed Kennedy would be victorious in California, some members of the campaign turned their attention at once to the post-California strategy. The only chance Kennedy had for winning the nomination was to keep up the pressure on state delegations to be responsive to grassroots citizen action. Kennedy had demonstrated that he could successfully forge a coalition of minorities and working-class whites; he ran best in states where ordinary Democratic voters, as opposed to machine bosses, had a strong voice. One follow-up plan to the California primary called for appointing state coordinators chosen not from "local politicos," but from representatives of the emergent citizens' groups themselves, in an attempt to build on the "growing disenchantment with the political realities of the country."[118]

On election day, David Borden, a Kennedy campaign organizer, wrote to the national office from the Los Angeles headquarters: "The lines have been clearly drawn. Hubert Humphrey has opted for a decision from the top. Senator Kennedy has really no choice but to continue to go to the people. . . . A structure must be provided by which grass-roots organizing can be channeled into delegate confrontation and persuasion."[119] Borden called for a high degree of decentralization, and an expanding network of citizens' groups nationally "to confront and influence local delegates."[120] This strategy sought to sway delegates through direct voter participation, and required a groundswell of support for Kennedy from local peace and civil rights activists. In Chicago, Kennedy would be in a tactical alliance with organizers such as Tom Hayden, who planned massive antiwar demonstrations at the convention.[121] Kennedy strategists hoped to build on the primary election victories by buttressing the campaign's existing ties to civic groups nationwide.

The California victory catapulted Kennedy into a stronger position in the national politics of 1968. The night of the election, he tried to reach Allard Lowenstein several times by phone to enlist his assistance in organizing support in New York's June 18 primary. He also wanted Lowenstein to act as a liaison between the Kennedy and McCarthy campaigns, and bring over McCarthy delegates now that California had proven Kennedy to be the only viable peace candidate. Lowenstein's Dump Johnson movement had created the original impetus for the McCarthy challenge, and now Kennedy sought out the New York activist's help to fortify his own links to the antiwar movement.

On the night of the election, California shaped up to be Kennedy's greatest victory. He waited until it was certain he had won before giving a couple of television interviews from his hotel suite. As the hour arrived at midnight, staffers entreated him to give a statement before it was too late to reach a sizable television audience in the state. The victorious candidate then stepped inside a crowded elevator with a bustling entourage to go down to the Embassy Room to speak. In the clogged ballroom, music, drinking, and merriment reigned. The large chamber was filled with balloons, noisemakers, "Kennedy girls" in Styrofoam boaters, delegates, enthralled campaign workers, and hangers-on of all kinds. A great victory celebration had been underway for hours. Kennedy fought his way through the multitude, and stood at the podium with his wife Ethel, Jesse Unruh, Dolores Huerta of the U.F.W., and members of his campaign staff.

Kennedy's demeanor was calm and contented; he displayed his characteristic humor while calling for the nation to heal its wounds. He was gracious to McCarthy, and praised those who had labored hard in both campaigns. "If there is one clear lesson of this political year," he said, "it is that the people of this country wish to move away from the policies which have led to an endless war abroad and to increasing unrest in our own country. Senator McCarthy demonstrated this in New Hampshire and Wisconsin. He and his supporters deserve the gratitude of the nation for the courageous fight which helped break the political logjam, demonstrated the desire for change, and helped make citizen participation into a new and powerful force of our political life. In the primaries up to now he and I have sought the popular judgment as to which of us should lead the forces of change. That decision has now been made. For it is clear tonight, as it has been for some time, that only the victor in the California primary could hope to win the Democratic nomination."

Kennedy's mood was ebullient, and his ten-minute talk exuded warmth, emotion, and love. His delivery and tone energized the crowd of over a thousand supporters. "Humphrey now appears to be leading in the contest for the nomination," he said. "Yet I do not think he will be successful. In every primary . . . the people have rejected those slates of delegates committed to the Johnson-Humphrey Administration. More than eighty percent of the vote has gone to Senator McCarthy or myself, although we both reject those policies which the Vice President so fervently advocates."

"I cannot believe," Kennedy continued, "that the Democratic Party will nominate a man whose ideas and programs have been so decisively rejected. Yet the Vice President apparently believes he can win the nomination without once submitting his case to the people. I do not believe the Presidential nomination can be a private affair. Yet the Vice President refused to enter his name in primaries, while helping delegates opposed to my candidacy. He has refused to participate in any direct confrontation on the issues." Kennedy called for a face-to-face encounter with Humphrey. "I will go any place any time to meet the Vice President in a televised debate," he said.

"To those who have supported Senator McCarthy, I have only this to say: You have fought well for principles in which you believed. In my judgment, I now remain the only candidate who can be nominated who is also in substantial agreement with those principles. In particular, I am the only candidate committed to a realistic negotiated solution to the Vietnamese war, one embracing all the elements of the South Vietnamese population, and opposed to the use of American military force to carry the major burden of what should be essentially a Vietnamese conflict. In fact, I am the only candidate with policies likely to bring an honorable peace to let the killing stop.

"Yet the forces arrayed against this position are so powerful, I do not believe I can be successful without your help and support. I ask this, not for myself, but for the cause and the ideas which moved you to begin this great popular movement. If we are divided then those who will benefit are those who wish to keep the policies of the past five years. . . . Unlike the Vice President, I do not believe that course is best for the country, nor is it the course the people want to pursue. With you I know we can keep faith with the American need and the American desire for peace and for justice, and for a government dedicated to giving the people mastery over their own affairs and future."[122]

Kennedy then expressed his deep gratitude to his brother-in-law and national campaign manager, Stephen Smith, and went on to thank other members of his family. He injected a light note by including his spaniel Freckles for thanks, whom he had taken with him on the campaign trail.[123] He also thanked his wife Ethel, and the many others who had sacrificed so much for the campaign. He singled out César Chávez and Bert Corona for special appreciation for their work on his behalf in the Latino communities, and Rafer Johnson and Roosevelt Grier for their organizing and registering African-American voters.

"I thank all of you who made this possible this evening," he said. "All the effort that you made, and all of the people whose places I haven't been to, but who made or did all of the work at the precinct level, got out the vote, . . . [and] brought forth all of the efforts required. I was a campaign manager eight years ago, and I know what a difference that kind of effort, and that kind of commitment can make. My thanks to all of you, and on to Chicago."[124] The laughter, music, and cheering blended into an enormous final ovation. Kennedy flashed a quick V for victory gesture with his right hand, brushed back his forelock, stepped from the podium, and started out slowly through the crushing throng toward an exit on his left.

He was led down a cramped, narrow pathway through the hotel kitchen; at the opposite end was a door that opened to a room where a post-victory press conference had been arranged. The kitchen was packed with over seventy campaign workers, celebrants, reporters, and hotel employees. As Kennedy made his way through the pantry, he shook hands with food service workers, and signed a few autographs. There was a sudden burst of commotion to the right of the Senator. Those around him quickly realized someone was discharging a weapon. It was a twenty-two caliber hand gun. Kennedy was shot just behind his right ear. Five others were wounded. The assailant, a disturbed twenty-four year-old Jordanian immigrant, had fired a thirty dollar Iver-Johnson pistol.

With his California victory, Kennedy was on his way to winning the Democratic Party's nomination for president. He had worked harder and longer hours than anyone else on the campaign. He deserved a rewarding, meaningful night of relaxation and celebration. Instead, he found himself collapsed on the greasy concrete floor of the Ambassador Hotel's kitchen pantry.

In the twenty-five hours following the assault, Kennedy was transferred to two hospitals. Neurologists and other specialists were flown in from the east coast. He underwent four hours of emergency brain surgery. In the end, the damage from bullet and bone fragments was too severe. He succumbed to his head wound in the early morning of June 6, 1968. He was forty-two years old.

Eugene McCarthy had suspended his campaign, and paid a visit to Good Samaritan Hospital when Kennedy lay there grasping for life. He read a condolence statement, and linked the shooting to the climate of violence ushered in by the Vietnam War: "It is not enough to say that this is the act of one deranged man," he said. The nation "bears too great a burden of guilt" for "the disposition of violence," which "we have visited upon the rest of the world, or at least part of the world."[125] Lyndon and Lady Bird Johnson sent their respects in telegrams to Ethel Kennedy. Johnson ordered Secret Service protection for all remaining presidential candidates, and offered Air Force One for use by the Kennedy family. He also spoke on national television, where he decried the violence in American society, and he appointed a commission to study its causes.

The shooting sent shock waves all over the world. Condolence letters and telegrams from Poland to South Africa, Vietnam to Argentina, flooded Kennedy's Senate office. Disbelief and sorrow swept the African-American and Latino neighborhoods of California's cities. The director of a black community center in Los Angeles said that an "eerie quietness" had descended over the Watts area in the wake of the shooting. Carl Hampton, the chairman of the Black Congress in Los Angeles, believed that the attack on Kennedy had to be seen in connection with the assassination of Martin Luther King, Jr. "The climate of violence in this country," he said, "is brought on by the unresolved problems relating to black people and the poor, and the fact that unpunished violence long directed against them has now been . . . directed against men of prominent positions."[126]

Another Californian, the executive director of the Latino Community Service Organization said, "Every time anyone speaks out to champion any worthwhile causes for the Spanish-speaking community, he is either knocked down or smeared."[127] A black writer added: "I can't help thinking that all of the unsolved crimes against Negroes have come to an open house of violence."[128] Expressing the sentiments of youth and students, the 21-year-old editor of the *U.C.L.A. Daily Bruin* said he had a "gut feeling, deep inside" that the shooting of Kennedy would "make young people completely unreachable."[129]

* * *

The killing of Robert Kennedy was particularly brutal coming just eight weeks after the assassination of Martin Luther King, Jr., and less than five years after that of President John F. Kennedy. The ideals that the three men shared and their common fate created a lasting association between them in the public mind. But Robert Kennedy's assassination, the last of the three, had the most devastating consequences. The leader of the peace wing of the Democratic Party was removed from national politics with shocking abruptness. His death came at a time when the party was bitterly divided, when there were riots in the cities, when there were over a half million American troops in Southeast Asia. Without him, the prospects for peace abroad and social justice at home were severely diminished. The silencing of Robert Francis Kennedy's voice could not have come at a worse time for the nation.

Conclusion: A Potential Unrealized

Throughout Robert Kennedy's Senate years, an increasingly mobilized citizenry prodded him to take ever bolder stands against the Vietnam War, racism, and social injustice. His dialogue with citizens active in the peace, civil rights, farm worker, and antipoverty movements ultimately came to define his politics. He moved with the times, and also shaped them; he gave legitimacy and strength to the progressive social movements of the period. Kennedy faced some tough political choices along the way, but after some hesitation, he stepped forward to lead the disaffected peace wing of the Democratic Party. He rejected the party leadership which equated support for the war with support for President Lyndon Johnson, and dedicated his energy, political skills, and talents to this final crusade.

Following the Watts riot of August 1965, Kennedy challenged the civil rights movement to focus on alleviating the seemingly intractable problems of poverty and unemployment in the African-American inner cities. He developed an influential set of ventures in his Special Impact Program in Brooklyn. Although he served only three years in the Senate, not nearly long enough to build a legacy, his Bedford-Stuyvesant Renewal and Rehabilitation Corporation has served as a model for other public-private partnerships in impoverished communities. It was an innovative program for community development, a bold response to the devastating urban rebellions in cities across America. Following the Detroit riot of July 1967, the Johnson Administration drifted away from building a Great Society and toward seeking law-and-order solutions. Kennedy, the former attorney general, had moved in the opposite direction.

Although he was a junior senator with no committee assignments relating to foreign affairs, Kennedy became an early critic of intervention in Vietnam. In 1965, he opposed Rolling Thunder, Johnson's "sustained reprisal" bombing of North Vietnam, saying it stymied peace talks, swelled the ranks of the enemy, threatened to bring China into the conflict, and did nothing to shore up the political weakness of the Saigon government. In February 1966, he took an even bolder stand on recognizing the National Liberation Front in South Vietnam, and came under highly publicized attack from Under Secretary of State George Ball, National Security Adviser McGeorge Bundy, and Vice President Hubert Humphrey. Ball, Bundy, and Humphrey went on national television and denounced Kennedy's naiveté for advocating such a course. Ball attacked Kennedy for articulating a view which he privately shared. Kennedy was a far more truthful voice on the entangled issues of the U.S. military mission in Vietnam than any of the spokespersons for the Administration.

In April 1966, Kennedy privately pressed the State Department to take action utilizing third parties, nongovernmental organizations, legal committees, or other nations as intermediaries to secure the release of American prisoners of war in Vietnam. The National Liberation Front held twenty-seven Americans at the time, and had offered a prisoner exchange. The State Department dismissed Kennedy's efforts because such a transfer of prisoners would require a degree of formal recognition of the N.L.F. that the United States was unwilling to give. The Administration hardened its position whenever Kennedy privately or publicly raised virtually any issue regarding Vietnam. This is one of the reasons why he beat a temporary retreat in 1966 in criticizing Johnson about the war.

In March 1967, following a trip to Europe where he gauged the extent of the Western allies' opposition to the U.S. policy in Southeast Asia, Kennedy called for a permanent cessation of the bombing of North Vietnam, a cease-fire, and an expanded role for multilateral institutions such as the International Control Commission. He cited several of the same reasons for stopping the bombing he had presented in 1965. The Administration once again responded with hostility; some in the press speculated Kennedy used his criticism of Johnson's war as a springboard for his own presidential ambitions. Despite his feelings about the war, Kennedy retreated once again, and tried to mend his relationship with the President. Meanwhile, the peace movement's allies inside the Democratic Party stepped up their pressure on Kennedy to break with Johnson.

By the end of 1967, the Administration and the Democratic National Committee became extremely rigid in their demand that Democrats close ranks with Johnson on the war. Johnson loyalists labored to keep the Young Democrats, Americans for Democratic Action, and other groups from bolting in the upcoming 1968 election. Johnson used the FBI to inform him about the actions of the peace wing of the Democratic Party, the National Conference for New Politics, Allard Lowenstein's Dump Johnson movement, and Citizens for Kennedy. He reinforced the divisions inside the party by insisting upon a degree of loyalty to him, and to his Vietnam policy, that tens of thousands of Democrats simply could not give; Kennedy was thrust into the middle of this conflict.

In February 1968, in his first address after the Tet Offensive in South Vietnam, Kennedy's denunciation of the regime of Nguyen Van Thieu broke the logjam of U.S. opinion, and encouraged others, including members of the Senate Foreign Relations Committee and the news anchor Walter Cronkite, to voice similar conclusions contradicting the Administration's claim that Tet was a U.S. victory. When Kennedy spoke out about the war, he spoke to three distinct audiences: mainstream working Americans, people sympathetic to the peace movement, and elite foreign policy planners. As a national political leader, and the brother of the slain President, his views had a profound effect on the Vietnam debate.

At the time of the Tet Offensive, the letters from American G.I.'s in Vietnam who confided in Kennedy reflected their bitterness and their frustration with the war, and with Johnson's leadership. The servicemen knew that the American people were not being told the truth about the war. Although Administration officials portrayed Tet as an unmitigated American military victory, Kennedy disagreed. Many of his key points, such as the deficiencies of the Army of the Republic of Vietnam, the rampant corruption inside General Thieu's government, and the atrocities committed in retaking cities lost during Tet, echoed some of the criticisms going on privately among Johnson's own civilian and military advisers. Publicly, the Administration circled the wagons and sought to refute, point by point, Kennedy's interpretation of Tet. At pivotal moments, Kennedy gambled with his political future to speak the truth about Vietnam.

Lyndon Johnson had been the most successful Democratic president since Franklin Delano Roosevelt, responsible for landmark civil rights, health, education, and consumer safety legislation. He had come to power in 1964 with a healthy mandate. However, by 1968 it was clear that Johnson had wagered his presidency on the success or failure of the Vietnam War; opposing the war became tantamount to opposing the President. The peace movement's ties to the Democratic Party created the political conditions that forced Kennedy to directly challenge Johnson even though he had supported the President's domestic agenda. Kennedy's entrance into the 1968 presidential contest was more a symptom than a cause of the divisions within the party.

In 1968, Kennedy's presidential campaign mobilized civic and church groups, peace and civil rights activists, students, farm workers, progressive labor unionists, blacks, Latinos, working-class whites, students, and New Leftists. At the time of his California victory, he was in the process of forging a new coalition that embraced the social activism of the period. He possessed the unique ability to inspire diverse groups of people from differing income backgrounds to work together for peace and social justice. In the midst of the Indiana primary, after being informed of the assassination of Martin Luther King, Jr., Kennedy's extemporaneous remarks to an African-American audience in Indianapolis stand out as one of the most meaningful short statements on race relations of the 1960s.[1] The African Americans who subsequently wrote Kennedy, some of them from the front lines in Vietnam, poignantly revealed that many blacks looked to Kennedy for leadership after King's killing.

The Kennedy campaign had ambitious plans for the post-California period: a vigorous push for winning New York's 190 delegate votes in mid-June, followed by a brief tour of European capitals — including high-profile meetings with heads of state — and then an attempt to bring the strongest possible alliance of forces to the Democratic National Convention in Chicago that August.[2]

Kennedy's abrupt and cruel removal from the national political scene decapitated the emergent Democratic coalition he had labored so hard to build. In August 1968, the political consequences of that violent act played themselves out at the convention. The nationally televised street battles in downtown Chicago between demonstrators and police, which spilled onto the convention floor in the form of shoving matches between delegates, debilitated the Democratic Party and ultimately enabled Richard Nixon to take the White House. Kennedy's absence from the convention set the scene for a corrosive debate.

Kennedy was the only Democratic politician who could speak the language of the old politics with machine stalwarts such as Mayor Richard Daley, while still engaging in a constructive dialogue with the protesters whom Daley's police had beaten outside the convention hall. The award-winning author Theodore White, whose books on the "Making of the President" transformed campaign journalism, privately shared his impressions of the convention with Ethel Kennedy:

> I write this from Chicago and the Democratic convention—macabre, unbelievable, grotesque parody on the process of American politics. Most macabre is the spectacle of all our old friends split and divided and squabbling and spitting on each other. It is so god-damned sad. There is no comfort for me in the thought, which I always held, that Bob, had he lived, would have marched through this convention as its master—and then on to the Presidency.[3]

Kennedy had drawn upon his direct experiences with municipal politics in Boston, New York, and Chicago, and recognized the potential of a tactical alliance between lower income people of all races and ethnic backgrounds. The rough-and-tumble street politics of the 1968 primaries demanded that Kennedy join with activists and civic groups in small venues and face-to-face meetings. Whether fielding questions in union halls or on college campuses, getting his hands bloodied in ten-hour motorcades, or enduring the berating of militants from a "black caucus" in Oakland, Kennedy made meaningful connections with political activists at the local level, many of whom were far to his left. The energy of the primary campaigns thrust Kennedy into the center of a volatile and dangerous grassroots fervor. César Chávez likened the California campaign to "those heated elections they have south of the border."[4] Kennedy took on the task not only because he needed "people power" to succeed, but because by 1968 he largely agreed with the activists' critiques of American society.

Kennedy appealed to Americans' highest ideals, while telling them the bitter truth about the Vietnam War. Rare among politicians, he showed a faith in the ability of ordinary citizens to recognize and deal with the difficult tasks at hand. He asked the American people to accept the fact that the only truly courageous course for the United States in Vietnam was to get out. In contrast, Nixon (and Hubert Humphrey up until October 1968) offered only vague platitudes about attaining "peace with honor." Before he announced his candidacy, Kennedy had stated publicly that he believed the U.S. must withdraw its troops from Southeast Asia, and that a Nixon presidency would be "unacceptable to the country."[5]

At the time of Kennedy's death, Humphrey already controlled about one thousand delegates of the 1,312 needed to win the nomination. However, Mayor Daley and several key Democratic power brokers in Ohio, Michigan, and other states were awaiting the results of the California and New York primaries before committing to any candidate.[6] The 700 or so delegates who backed Kennedy or were leaning toward him represented a far different Democratic Party than did Humphrey's slate. Kennedy had fought tough primary battles to win his representatives, and had tapped into a community activist sentiment that had defied the Vice President.

Kennedy's presidential campaign sought wherever possible to ally itself with community organizations, which were then drifting away from the party. Even if he had lost his bid for the nomination, his new coalition of mobilized have-nots and have-littles gave promise of providing a counterweight to the politics of racial division which became a mainstay in many campaigns after Nixon launched his "Southern strategy" that same election year.

In August 1968, at the close of the disastrous Chicago convention, the pro-Humphrey leadership flatly rejected a peace plank for the party platform, and repudiated its dove wing. Humphrey, whose defense of the logic and necessity of the Vietnam War did not waver until it was politically fatal, led a dispirited party into the November elections. The political energy that Kennedy and Eugene McCarthy had generated in the primaries had all but evaporated. Nixon won the presidency, and the progressive wing of the Democratic Party, despite its strength in movement politics, lost its influence within the Executive Branch. In the following decades, with the exception of President Jimmy Carter's single term, Nixon's 1968 victory ushered in a quarter-century of Republican domination of the White House, and along with it a prolonged identity crisis for Democrats.

From the time of the administration of Harry S. Truman, the Cold War had nearly unanimous bipartisan support. In the early 1950s, liberal Democrats did not criticize U.S. military action in Korea, nor did they question the global anticommunist crusade generally; in the early 1960s, they led the efforts to undermine Fidel Castro's government in Cuba. But with the Vietnam War, the bipartisan consensus to fight communism everywhere in the world with American blood and treasure began to unravel, and Kennedy became the strongest liberal opponent of the war. There emerged in the 1965–1968 period a moral critique of U.S. policy in Southeast Asia, and along with it a reevaluation of some of the premises of the Cold War that mainstream liberals had never challenged before.

The knee-jerk reaction of Johnson and his powerful Democratic allies to silence their opponents in the peace movement, along with Johnson's willingness to use the FBI and his "Special Office" to thwart what White House memos called the Black Power-Peacenik coalition, pointed to profound contradictions in American liberalism. The Johnson Administration reserved its most bitter attacks for Kennedy. The viciousness of the Johnson Democrats toward Kennedy when he voiced his views of the war showed that liberals were willing to impugn the motives and question the "loyalty" of their critics within the party in order to push them outside the policy debate. Johnson's and Humphrey's bile aimed at Kennedy revealed the problems facing Democrats in their drive to prove constantly their "toughness" against communism and their willingness to use military force in the name of U.S. "national security." Prowar liberals turned on their Democratic detractors with a vindictiveness that surpassed anything directed at the Republicans, who largely supported the Administration's Southeast Asia policy.

The Vietnam War laid bare the contradictions of the Cold War and the limitations of United States power globally. Cold War liberalism broke down in Vietnam, in part, because liberals were forced to make a choice between "guns and butter"; by 1968, Johnson had concluded that guns were more important. The war tore the Democratic Party apart, and liberals who were beholden to seeking a military victory labeled Kennedy a traitor in time of war. The breakdown of the liberal Democratic consensus on foreign policy led to a weakening of the party and ultimately a weakening of the New Deal coalition. In 1968, Kennedy reached out to a mobilized citizenry and attempted to use this grassroots energy to revivify liberalism. He dedicated the final months of his life to furthering progressive social goals, while moving the Democratic Party away from the false Cold War premises exposed in Vietnam.

Robert Kennedy's life was inextricably intertwined with the social activism and élan of the 1960s. During the four-and-a-half years he outlived his brother, he worked to keep President John F. Kennedy's memory alive, while carving out his own political identity in a difficult and divisive time. He said at the close of his final speech: "What I think is quite clear [is] that we can work together in the last analysis, and that what has been going on within the United States over a period of the last three years, the divisions, the violence, the disenchantment with our society—the divisions, whether it's between blacks and whites, between the poor and the more affluent, or between age groups, or on the war in Vietnam—is that we can start to work together. We are a great country, an unselfish country and a compassionate country. I intend to make that the basis for running."[7]

Kennedy's grassroots coalition of working-class whites, African Americans, Latinos, youth and others, whose strength had been demonstrated in the California primary, was an inspiring accomplishment in a decade known for its divisiveness and whose significance has been sharply contested and maligned in the years since. Kennedy's overarching message of seeking common ground among peoples of diverse racial, ethnic, and class backgrounds is as vital today as it was more than three decades ago.

Notes

The following abbreviations are used in these notes:

JFKL	John Fitzgerald Kennedy Library (Boston, Mass)
LBJL	Lyndon Baines Johnson Library (Austin, Texas)
FBI-RFK	FBI File on Robert F. Kennedy
NSFCFVN	LBJ Papers, National Security File, Country File, Vietnam, LBJL
OH-RFK	RFK Oral History Project, JFKL
PCP	RFK Presidential Campaign Papers, 1968, JFKL
PCP, BB	RFK Presidential Campaign Papers, 1968, Black Books
SC-SF	RFK Papers, Senate Correspondence Subject File, JFKL
SC-PF	RFK Papers, Senate Correspondence Personal File, JFKL
TJMN	LBJ Papers, Tom Johnson Meeting Notes, LBJL
WHCF	LBJ Papers, White House Confidential File, LBJL
WHFN	LBJ Papers, White House Famous Names File, LBJL

Prologue

1. Sister Jean and brother Edward followed Robert, born in 1928 and 1932, respectively.
2. James W. Hilty, *Robert Kennedy: Brother Protector* (Philadelphia: Temple University Press, 1997), p. 76.
3. Kennedy wrote a book about his experiences as the chief counsel for the McClellan Committee, *The Enemy Within: The McClellan Committee's Crusade Against Jimmy Hoffa and Corrupt Labor Unions*. Kennedy believed his efforts amounted to a kind of crusade.

4. Quoted in Schaap, *R.F.K.*, p. 85.
5. Dallek, *Flawed Giant*, pp. 6, 63.
6. Ibid., p. 7.
7. The President-elect deflected criticism with humor: "I can't see that it's wrong," he said, "to give Bobby a little legal experience before he goes out to practice law." Quoted in Schaap, *R.F.K.*, p. 87.
8. See Shesol, *Mutual Contempt* and Hilty, *Robert Kennedy: Brother Protector*.
9. Quoted in Weisbrot, *Freedom Bound*, p. 60.
10. Dallek, *Flawed Giant*, p. 135.
11. Margolis, *Last Innocent Year*, p. 159.
12. Dallek, *Flawed Giant*, p. 58. Johnson feared that Kennedy might even receive more write-in votes for vice president than he would for president.
13. Shesol, *Mutual Contempt*, pp. 209–10.
14. Dallek, *Flawed Giant*, pp. 162–63.
15. Shesol, *Mutual Contempt*, pp. 229–30.

Chapter 1

1. Vanden Heuvel and Gwirtzman, *On His Own*, pp. 60–62. Schlesinger, *Robert Kennedy and His Times*, pp. 746–47.
2. Quoted in Schlesinger, *Robert Kennedy and His Times*, p. 737.
3. Vanden Heuvel and Gwirtzman, *On His Own*, p. 217.
4. Dean Rusk's influence had been waning in the final year of the Kennedy Administration. Tom Wicker, *JFK and LBJ*, p. 197; McGeorge Bundy stayed on as Johnson's special assistant for national security affairs until February 1966; Robert McNamara remained a close friend of Robert Kennedy's, and after Johnson eased him out of the Cabinet in late 1967, he campaigned for Kennedy during the 1968 Democratic primaries. McNamara, *In Retrospect*; Rust, *Kennedy in Vietnam*.
5. Frederick G. Dutton to Robert Kennedy, February 8, 1966, RFK Papers, SC-PF, Box 3, File: Dutton, Frederick 1965–1966, JFKL.
6. These statements are taken from Kennedy's speeches and press releases from May 1965 through February 1966 (cited below).
7. Remarks of Senator Robert F. Kennedy on Vietnam and the Dominican Republic, May 6, 1965, *Congressional Record, Proceedings and Debates of the 89th Congress, First Session*, RFK Papers, PCP, Speechwriters' Division, Box 5, File: Vietnam, JFKL. Kennedy reiterated this point in a statement on January 31, 1966.
8. Newsclip, "RFK Asks Social Aid to Viet Nam," January 20, 1966, Adam Walinsky Papers, Box 17, File: Foreign Policy, Vietnam, 2/19/66–2/23/66, JFKL.

This was similar to a statement that President Kennedy had made to Walter Cronkite in September, 1963. Giglio, *The Presidency of John F. Kennedy*, p. 251.

9.   Vanden Heuvel and Gwirtzman, *On His Own*, p. 217.

10. Bowman, *Vietnam War Almanac*, pp. 108–14. Young, *Vietnam Wars*, pp. 142, 160.

11. Isserman, "Michael Harrington and the Vietnam War," p. 390.

12. Wells, *War Within*, pp. 9–62. DeBenedetti, *American Ordeal*, pp. 109–14.

13. See *Reporting Vietnam: American Journalism*, vols. 1 and 2. (New York: Library of America, 1998). The American press corps in Vietnam completely missed the significance of Air Vice Marshall Nguyen Cao Ky's crushing of the Buddhist Struggle Movement in May 1966. See Kahin, *Intervention*, pp. 431–32.

14. Adam Walinsky to Robert Kennedy, May 5, 1965, Adam Walinsky Papers, Box 16, File: Foreign Policy, Vietnam, 4/1965–5/1965, JFKL.

15. Remarks of Senator Robert F. Kennedy on Vietnam and the Dominican Republic, May 6, 1965, *Congressional Record, Proceedings and Debates of the 89th Congress, First Session*, RFK Papers, PCP, Speechwriters' Division, Box 5, File: Vietnam, JFKL.

16. George McT. Kahin, *Intervention*, passim. Kahin shows that the more the United States sought a military solution in South Vietnam, the more it alienated exactly those noncommunist nationalist elements whose support any Saigon government needed to survive.

17. LaFeber, *Inevitable Revolutions*, pp. 156–60.

18. Black, *Good Neighbor*, p. 120.

19. Remarks of Senator Robert F. Kennedy on Vietnam and the Dominican Republic, May 6, 1965, *Congressional Record, Proceedings and Debates of the 89th Congress, First Session*, RFK Papers, PCP, Speechwriters' Division, Box 5, File: Vietnam, JFKL.

20. VanDeMark, *Into The Quagmire*, pp. 206–14.

21. Robert Kennedy to Anthony Lewis, July 19, 1965, RFK Papers, SC-PF, Box 6, File: L: 1965, Lewis-Lo, JFKL.

22. Roger Hilsman to Robert Kennedy, May 11, 1965, RFK Papers, SC-PF, Box 4, File: H: 1965, Harrison-Hodges, JFKL.

23. John Paul Vann to Robert Kennedy, August 14, 1965, Adam Walinsky Papers, Box 16, File: Foreign Policy, Vietnam, 8/1/1965–8/16/1965, JFKL.

24. Ibid. Vann sent Kennedy a draft of a paper he intended to present to the United States ambassador to South Vietnam, Henry Cabot Lodge, Jr., and asked him for "any comments or observations."

25. Johnny Apple (R. W. Apple, Jr.) to Robert Kennedy, October 15, 1965 (from Saigon), RFK Papers, SC-PF, Box 6, File: Kennedy, Edward M., 1965, JFKL. Edward Kennedy was in South Vietnam on a fact-finding mission as the chair-

man of the Judiciary Committee's Subcommittee on Refugees and Escapees. Robert Kennedy wired his brother to "look up" Apple while he was in Saigon. Telegram, Robert Kennedy to Edward Kennedy (Saigon), October 25, 1965, ibid.

26. Johnny Apple (R. W. Apple, Jr.) to Robert Kennedy, October 15, 1965, ibid.

27. Vanden Heuvel and Gwirtzman, *On His Own*, pp. 169–75.

28. George McT. Kahin to Robert Kennedy, August 14, 1965; October 15, 1965, personal papers of George McT. Kahin; Adam Walinsky to Robert Kennedy, n.d., "I don't gather that Saigon is preventing Hanoi from negotiating as he seems to feel on pg 2," Kennedy scribbled to Walinsky on a cover memo to one piece by Kahin entitled "Steps Toward a Settlement." Adam Walinsky Papers, Box 16, File: Foreign Policy, Vietnam, 8/1/1965–8/16/1965, JFKL.

29. Robert Kennedy to George McT. Kahin, November 4, 1965, personal papers of George McT. Kahin.

30. George McT. Kahin, conversation with the author, October 8, 1996.

31. Some Questions Relating to American Policy in Vietnam: Remarks delivered at the Seminar on Southeast Asia of the Council for a Livable World, 5 March 1965, Professor George McT. Kahin, Director, Southeast Asia Program, Cornell University, Ithaca, New York, Adam Walinsky Papers, Box 16, File: Foreign Policy, Vietnam, 1/1965–3/1965, JFKL. Kahin believed the United States' allies in Vietnam had "considerably less of a political base in the South" than at the time of the Geneva agreement of 1954 (which settled the French Indochina War)

32. Ibid.

33. California Governor Edmund Brown appointed the commission, and former Director of Central Intelligence John McCone headed it. Its conclusions were vague and disappointing in their lack of breadth but predicted more Watts-type riots would break out without an infusion of federal aid. Horne, *Fire This Time*, pp. 164–66; 343. Kennedy said it would be a terrible mistake "to limit our efforts to the support of the war in Vietnam," and "postpone action on our pressing domestic needs." Press Release, December 16, 1965, RFK Papers, PCP, Speechwriters' Division, Box 5, File: Vietnam, JFKL.

34. Ibid.

35. "Professor Genovese and Academic Freedom," Richard M. Nixon in Menashe and Radosh, eds., *Teach-Ins*, pp. 233–35.

36. Transcript, Milton Gwirtzman Papers, Box 7, File: Presidential Campaign 1968, K, RF, JFKL.

37. Schlesinger, *Robert Kennedy and His Times*, pp. 789–90.

38. RFK Papers, SC-SF, Box 49, File: Press, 8/1967–2/1968, *Houston Chronicle*, n.d./p. (ca. November 1967), JFKL.

39. Quoted in Carter, *Politics of Rage*, p. 283.

40. Frank Mankiewicz, "Robo" letter, January 2, 1968, RFK Papers, SC-SF, Box 21, File: Foreign Affairs, Vietnam, 1/1/1968–1/8/1968, JFKL.

41. Robert Kennedy to William F. Buckley, Jr., April 4, 1967, RFK Papers, SC-PF, Box 2, File: B: 1967, JFKL. In a follow-up letter, Buckley made an off-color reference to Vidal's homosexuality, William F. Buckley, Jr., to Robert Kennedy, n.d., ibid. (Kennedy and Vidal's mutual contempt for each other was notorious by the mid-1960s.)

42. Senator Ernest Gruening to Robert Kennedy, December 15, 1965, Adam Walinsky Papers, Box 16, File: Foreign Policy, Vietnam, 12/15/1965–12/31/1965, JFKL. Senator Wayne Morse of Oregon was the other senator to vote against the August 1964 Southeast Asia Resolution, which gave Johnson a free hand to deploy the U.S. military to Vietnam.

43. Statement of Senator Robert F. Kennedy, Press Release, December 24, 1965, ibid.

44. Petition sponsored by Mr. and Mrs. E. H. Moscovitch and Mr. and Mrs. B. H. Weston (of Cambridge, Mass., and New Haven, Conn., respectively) to Robert Kennedy, Adam Walinsky Papers, Box 16, File: Foreign Policy, Vietnam, 12/1/1965–12/12/1965, JFKL.

45. Tom Johnson to President Lyndon Johnson, January 11, 1966, WHFN, Box 6, File: Kennedy, Robert F. and Family, 1965–1968, LBJL.

46. *New York Times*, January 30, 1966, n.p.

47. Wells, *War Within*, p. 64.

48. Statement by Senator Robert F. Kennedy, "The President's Decision on the Tragic War in Vietnam," January 31, 1966, *Congressional Record, Proceedings and Debates of the 89th Congress, Second Session*, vol. 112, no. 15, PCP, Speechwriters' Division, Box 5, File: Vietnam, JFKL.

49. Johnson was concerned about provoking the Chinese or the Soviets, leading him to impose strict restrictions on the bombing targets in North Vietnam, which often became a source of bitter criticism among some members of Congress and military officers. Gardner, *Pay Any Price*; Buzzanco, *Masters of War*; Herring, *LBJ and Vietnam*; Steinberg, *Shame and Humiliation*; Berman, *Lyndon Johnson's War*; Bernstein, *Guns Or Butter*.

50. Statement by Senator Robert F. Kennedy, "The President's Decision on the Tragic War in Vietnam," January 31, 1966, *Congressional Record, Proceedings and Debates of the 89th Congress, Second Session*, vol. 112, No. 15, RFK Papers, PCP, Speechwriters' Division, Box 5, File: Vietnam, JFKL.

51. Ibid.

52. George McT. Kahin to Robert Kennedy, February 1, 1966, personal papers of George McT. Kahin.

53. Robert Kennedy to George McT. Kahin, February 3, 1966, personal papers of George McT. Kahin. Kennedy sent Kahin copies of two of his Vietnam

speeches in mid-February. Robert Kennedy to George McT. Kahin, February 15, 1966. Kahin wrote he would be happy to meet with Kennedy, George McT. Kahin to Robert Kennedy, February 17, 1966, ibid.

54. George McT. Kahin to Robert Kennedy, August 14, 1965, Adam Walinsky Papers, Box 16, File: Foreign Policy, Vietnam, 8/1/1965–8/16/1965, JFKL. In notes scribbled on this correspondence Kennedy and Walinsky questioned a couple of Kahin's points relating to negotiations.

55. George McT. Kahin, conversation with the author, October 6, 1996.

56. Frederick G. Dutton to Robert Kennedy, February 8, 1966, RFK Papers, SC-PF, Box 3, File: Dutton, Frederick, 1965–1966, JFKL. Dutton suggested that on the question of Vietnam Kennedy should exert his "leverage more judiciously and over a longer period of time," and "not in one highly publicized trip."

57. Ibid.

58. Ibid.

59. The Administration asked for an additional $12.3 billion for the war in Vietnam, which was linked to other military and foreign appropriation bills. The Congress approved $13.1 billion in supplemental appropriations the following month. Wells, *War Within*, p. 76

60. Newfield, *Robert Kennedy: A Memoir*, pp. 124–25; Schlesinger, *Robert Kennedy and His Times*, p. 793.

61. Statement by Senator Robert F. Kennedy, Vietnam, February 19, 1966, Press Release, Adam Walinsky Papers, Box 17, File: Foreign Policy, Vietnam, 2/19/66–2/23/66, JFKL.

62. Ibid. (Original emphasis.)

63. Memorandum, Conversation Re: U.S. Prisoners in Hands of North Vietnam and Viet Cong, April 14, 1966, 3:30–4:15 P.M., Present: Robert Kennedy, Adam Walinsky, Philip B. Heymann, Administrator, Bureau of Security and Consular Affairs, Department of State, and David Burke, Legislative Assistant to Senator Edward Kennedy. Adam Walinsky Papers, Box 22, File: Foreign Policy, Vietnam, Prisoners of War, JFKL.

64. Fulbright was willing to "recognize" the N.L.F. as an independent entity outside of a Hanoi delegation, but he was unwilling at that time to accept a possible power-sharing agreement.

65. Associated Press, "RFK Sees Confusion in Reaction to Views," February 22, 1966, n.p., Newsclip, Adam Walinsky Papers, Box 17, File: Foreign Policy, Vietnam, 2/19/1966–2/23/1966, JFKL. Guthman and Allen, *RFK: Collected Speeches*, p. 286.

66. Statement by Senator Robert F. Kennedy, Vietnam, February 19, 1966, Press Release, Adam Walinsky Papers, Box 17, File: Foreign Policy, Vietnam, 2/19/66–2/23/66, JFKL. (Original emphasis.)

67. *Long Island Sunday Press*, February 20, 1966, n.p., ibid.

68. United Press International (En Route With Humphrey), "Humphrey Belittles Bob Kennedy's Viet Plan," February 21, 1966, Adam Walinsky Papers, Box 17, File: Foreign Policy, Vietnam, 2/19/1966–2/23/1966, JFKL.

69. United Press International, *New York Journal-American*, "Kennedy Plan Hit," February 21, 1966.

70. Ibid.

71. *New York Herald Tribune*, "Kennedy's Cong Plea—'Absurd,'" February 21, 1966, ibid.

72. McGeorge Bundy, President of the Ford Foundation, to David Ginsburg, March 13, 1967, WHFN, Box 6, File: Kennedy, Robert F. 1968 Campaign, LBJL.

73. *New York Times*, February 23, 1966, p. 12.

74. Bill Moyers to President Lyndon Johnson, February 22, 1966, WHFN, Box 6, File: Kennedy, Robert F. 1968 Campaign, LBJL.

75. Transcript, *Meet the Press*, Sunday, February 20, 1966, RFK Papers, SC-PF, Box 23, File: White House Correspondence, 1966, JFKL.

76. McGeorge Bundy to Robert Kennedy, February 21, 1966, ibid.

77. Ibid.

78. McGeorge Bundy to Robert Kennedy, February 24, 1966, ibid., Bundy included an excerpt of a transcript of a question and answer period he had had when he spoke that Wednesday, February 24, before the National Press Club.

79. Robert Kennedy to McGeorge Bundy, February 24, 1966, ibid.

80. Draft of letter, Robert Kennedy to McGeorge Bundy, February 23, 1966, ibid.

81. DiLeo, *George Ball*; VanDeMark, *Into the Quagmire*, pp. 53, 85–90, 164–66.

82. *New York Herald Tribune*, "Kennedy's Cong Plea—'Absurd,'" February 21, 1966, Adam Walinsky Papers, Box 17, File: Foreign Policy, Vietnam, 2/19/1966–2/23/1966, JFKL.

83. George Ball to Robert Kennedy, February 21, 1966, RFK Papers, SC-PF, Box 1, File: B: 1966, Baggs-Bassett, JFKL. Ball also sent a transcript to Kennedy of his television interview.

84. Robert Kennedy to George Ball, February 24, 1966, ibid.

85. Di Leo, *George Ball*; VanDeMark, *Into The Quagmire*, pp. 53, 85–90, 164–66.

86. *New York Journal American*, "Kennedy Plan Hit," February 21, 1966, Adam Walinsky Papers, Box 17, File: Foreign Policy, Vietnam, 2/19/1966–2/23/1966, JFKL.

87. *New York*, February 22, 1966, ibid.

88. *Rome Sentinel*, New York, "RFK Sees Confusion in Reaction to Views," February 22, 1966, ibid.

89. Frederick Dutton to Robert Kennedy, February 23, 1966, RFK Papers, SC-PF, Box 3, File: Dutton, Frederick, 1965–1966, JFKL.

90. Ibid.

91. *Washington Post*, "Humphrey, R. Kennedy Tangle over Vietcong Role in Settlement," February 28, 1966, Adam Walinsky Papers, Box 17, File: Foreign Policy, Vietnam, 2/19/1966–2/23/1966, JFKL.

92. Ibid.

93. Ibid.

94. Ibid.

95. *Christian Science Monitor*, "Dialogue on Vietnam," March 2, 1966, p. 3.

96. *New York Times*, "Fulbright Backs Kennedy on Role for the Vietcong," February 22, 1966, p. 1, ibid.

97. Newsclip, *Utica Observer-Dispatch*, "Bobby K Has New Fans; The Left Says He's Right," February 21, 1966, ibid.

98. George McT. Kahin to Robert Kennedy, February 21, 1966, personal papers of George Kahin.

99. Frank Church to Robert Kennedy, February 25, 1966, Adam Walinsky Papers, Box 17, File: Foreign Policy, Vietnam, 2/22/1966–2/28/1966, JFKL.

100. "Senator Robert F. Kennedy's Position on Vietnam," Speech of Senator Joseph S. Clark, March 4, 1966, *Congressional Record, Proceedings and Debates of the 89th Congress, Second Session*, RFK Papers, PCP, Speechwriters' Division, Box 5, File: Vietnam, JFKL.

101. Walter Lippmann, *Washington Post*, February 22, 1966, RFK Papers, PCP, Speechwriters' Division, Box 5, File: Vietnam, JFKL.

102. Helen Byrne Lippmann to Robert Kennedy, February 20, 1966, RFK Papers, SC-PF, Box 7, File: L: 1966, Lehman-Lucey, JFKL. Steel, *Walter Lippmann*, pp. 358–61, 365–67.

103. Robert Kennedy to Helen Byrne Lippmann, March 9, 1966, ibid.

104. Theodore Sorensen to Robert Kennedy, February 23, 1966, RFK Papers, SC-PF, Box 10, File: S: 1966: Skakel-Symington, JFKL. Sorensen added: "You put your finger right on the chief bottle-neck in the Administration's development of a rational diplomatic posture and brought them with you most of the way. Congratulations."

105. A. J. Muste to Robert Kennedy, February 18, 1966, Adam Walinsky Papers, Box 17, File: Foreign Policy, Vietnam, 2/1/1966–2/18/1966, JFKL.

106. Robert Vaughn to Robert Kennedy, March 8, 1966, RFK Papers, SC-PF, Box 12, File: V: 1965–1967, JFKL.

107. Anthony Lewis to Robert Kennedy, February 21, 1966, RFK Papers, SC-PF, Box 7, File: L: 1966 Lehman-Lucey, JFKL. Lewis also acknowledged "how hard it must have been for you — and Ethel — in terms of personal feeling toward Taylor and McNamara and so many others. It would be less than human not to look forward with anticipation . . . to its political effects!"

108. Burke Marshall to Robert Kennedy, February 21, 1966, RFK Papers, SC-PF, Box 7, File: M: 1966, Marshall - Martin, JFKL. Marshall added: "Until you

spoke no one suggested in a meaningful way that we would have to give anything up."

109. Press Release, Stanford University News Service, March 15, 1966, Adam Walinsky Papers, Box 22, File: Foreign Policy, Vietnam Poll, JFKL.

110. Ibid.

111. Some knowledgeable observers believed, in a Cold War context, that far from allowing a fox in the chicken coop, direct U.S. negotiations with the N.L.F. might lead to a coalition government in South Vietnam *less* dependent upon Hanoi. Frank C. Child, University of California, Davis, "Disengagement in Vietnam," a 13-pp. report, June 1967. The writer lived in Vietnam in 1959–1961 and returned there in the spring of 1967. Adam Walinsky forwarded this paper to Kennedy who read and initialed it. Adam Walinsky Papers, Box 18, File: Foreign Policy, Vietnam, 6/1967, JFKL.

112. Marine Sergeant Francis J. Ruddy (5th Special Forces Group) to Robert Kennedy, November 24, 1965, RFK Papers, SC-PF, Box 10, File: R: 1966, JFKL.

113. Frederick Dutton to Robert Kennedy, February 23, 1966, RFK Papers, SC-PF, Box 3, File: Dutton, Frederick, 1965–1966, JFKL. Keeping an eye on history, Dutton also noted that Kennedy's Vietnam stand represented a "turning point in any later lifetime biography," that would affect any future assessment of Kennedy's "career and important public contributions."

114. Bickers, "Robert Kennedy and the Press." (Ph.D. dissertation). Bickers shows in this monograph that the press generally became more hostile toward Kennedy the more he spoke out against the Vietnam War.

115. Undersecretary of State George Ball called this the Goldilocks principle: one military option would be too soft, one too hard, one just right, yet all of them increasing the United States role in the war. Young, *Vietnam Wars*, p. 130.

116. Newsclip, "RFK Asks Social Aid to Viet Nam," January 20, 1966, Adam Walinsky Papers, Box 17, File: Foreign Policy, Vietnam, 2/19/66–2/23/66, JFKL.

Chapter 2

1. United States Navy Captain Clarence A. Hill, Jr. to Robert Kennedy, April 7, 1966, Adam Walinsky Papers, Box 22, File: Foreign Policy, Vietnam, Prisoners of War, JFKL. Captain Hill asked Kennedy to help the family of a fellow officer, Commander James Mulligan, a flyer who was shot down over a target in North Vietnam. "I am familiar with your interest in monitoring the efforts of our government in the recovery of prisoners," he wrote. "Although Louise Mulligan is an outstanding Navy wife," Hill added, "there will be a limit to her ability" to raise her "six fine boys."

2. Mrs. Jack Riley, the wife of another prisoner of war, wrote Kennedy about the concerned loved ones of P.O.W.'s: "I'm writing in hopes you may be able to

help us, the families of prisoners of war in Vietnam. Can't the State Department exchange something?" she asked. "Why do we forget our brave young men? Seems there are a lot of people getting rich off our dead bodies of our husbands, sons and sweet hearts. Can't you senators stop this? I ask you to go to the State Department and demand of them to do something. I do hope you will consider running for President," she added. "Mr. Johnson was a big mistake we Americans made," Mrs. Jack Riley to Robert Kennedy, May 5, 1966, ibid. Senator J. William Fulbright, the chairman of the Foreign Relations Committee and a critic of the war, often forwarded letters from family members of American prisoners of war to Kennedy. One letter came from Deborah Brudno, the wife of First Lieutenant Edmund Brudno, who was shot down over North Vietnam on October 18, 1965. She pointed out to Fulbright that "since no declaration of war has been made" there was "very little public knowledge of the whereabouts and actual treatment of the military prisoners." Mrs. Brudno also said that this lack of a formal declaration meant that "the Red Cross cannot inspect the camps." Deborah Brudno, wife of First Lieutenant Edmund Brudno, to Senator J. William Fulbright, May 1, 1966 (forwarded to Robert Kennedy), Adam Walinsky Papers, Box 17, File: Foreign Policy, Vietnam 4/1966, JFKL.

3. Memorandum, Conversation Re: U.S. Prisoners in Hands of North Vietnam and Viet Cong, April 14, 1966, 3:30–4:15 P.M., Present: Robert Kennedy, Adam Walinsky, Philip B. Heymann, Administrator, Bureau of Security and Consular Affairs, Department of State, and David Burke, Legislative Assistant to Senator Edward Kennedy. Adam Walinsky Papers, Box 22, File: Foreign Policy, Vietnam, Prisoners of War, JFKL.

4. Ibid.

5. Ibid.

6. Ibid. Adam Walinsky Papers, Box 22, File: Foreign Policy, Vietnam, Prisoners of War, JFKL

7. Robert Kennedy to Secretary of State Dean Rusk, April 19, 1966, ibid.

8. Secretary of State Dean Rusk to Robert Kennedy, May 13, 1966, ibid.

9. Statement of Senator Robert F. Kennedy, Bombing of North Vietnam, Senate Floor, April 27, 1966, RFK Papers, PCP, Speechwriters' Division, Box 5, File: Vietnam, JFKL.

10. Kahin, *Intervention*, pp. 417–32. Kahin describes in disturbing detail how the government of Nguyen Cao Ky crushed the Buddhist Struggle Movement in the spring of 1966.

11. Ibid.

12. Memorandum for the President (Personal and Confidential), Robert E. Kintner to President Lyndon Johnson, April 28, 1966, WHCF, Box 147, File: Kennedy, Robert F., LBJL.

13. Ibid. Kintner named New York Senator Jacob Javits as a possible choice to counter Kennedy's criticisms. He noted that the *Today* show was "beginning to cover the escalation in a big way."

14. Frederick Dutton prepared a six-page memo on the war for Kennedy prior to his appearance, and forwarded a copy of it to White House Press Secretary Bill Moyers, "Viet Nam Election and De-Escalation Proposal," Frederick Dutton to Robert Kennedy, May 6, 1966, RFK Papers, SC-PF, Box 3, File: Dutton, Frederick, 1965–1968, JFKL.

15. Robert Kennedy to Senator George McGovern, May 23, 1966, RFK Papers, SC-PF, Box 20, File: Kennedy, Robert F. Handwritten Notes and Letters (copies), JFKL.

16. Press Release, Statement of Senator Robert F. Kennedy, On the Bombing of Haiphong, June 29, 1966, RFK Papers, PCP, Speechwriters' Division, Box 5, File: Vietnam, JFKL.

17. Ibid.

18. Statement of Senator Robert F. Kennedy, Senate Floor, Treatment of Prisoners of War, July 15, 1966, ibid.

19. Press Release, Speech by Senator Robert F. Kennedy, New Hampshire Democratic State Convention, September 23, 1966, RFK Papers, PCP, Speechwriters' Division, box 5, File: Vietnam, JFKL.

20. Robert Kennedy to Anthony Lewis, November 25, 1966, RFK Papers, SC-PF, Box 7, File: L: 1966 Lehman - Lucey, JFKL.

21. Robert Kennedy to George McT. Kahin, August 22, 1966, personal papers of George McT. Kahin.

22. Newfield, *Robert Kennedy: A Memoir*, p. 134.

23. Marcus Raskin to Adam Walinsky, August 8, 1966, Adam Walinsky Papers, Box 18, File: Foreign Policy, Vietnam 8/1966–12/1966, JFKL.

24. Adam Walinsky Papers, Boxes 18 through 20, Files: Foreign Policy, Vietnam, JFKL.

25. Ibid. "Alternative Perspectives on Vietnam: Report on an International Conference." Ellsberg later campaigned for Kennedy in California.

26. Daniel Ellsberg notes on the war, November 1967, William Vanden Heuvel Papers, Box 4, File: Vietnam Correspondence, JFKL.

27. Benjamin Spock, M.D. to Robert Kennedy, September 21, 1966, RFK Papers, SC-PF, Box 10, File: S: 1966 Skakel-Symington, JFKL. Spock added: "If such a move is delayed until the last minute it will be called opportunistic rather than statesmanlike."

28. Ibid.

29. Ibid.

30. Richard Goodwin to Angie Novello, October 18, 1966; Robert Kennedy to Benjamin Spock, M.D., October 27, 1966; Benjamin Spock, M.D. to Robert Kennedy, November 9, 1966, ibid.

31. Miller, *Democracy in the Streets*, pp. 260–63.

32. Newfield, *Robert Kennedy: A Memoir*, pp. 134–36.

33. Hayden, *Reunion: A Memoir*, pp. 265.

34. Tom Hayden to Peter Edelman, February 15, 1967, Adam Walinsky Papers, Box 18, File: Foreign Policy, Vietnam 2/1967, JFKL.

35. Ibid.

36. John P. Roche to President Lyndon Johnson, February 9, 1967, Marvin Watson Papers, Box 29, File: Roche, John—Memos, LBJL.

37. Vanden Heuvel and Gwirtzman, *On His Own*, pp. 229–32.

38. Ibid., pp. 235. Kennedy also met with Harvard's professor of international relations, Henry Kissinger, who happened to be in Paris, to discuss possible diplomatic initiatives relating to Southeast Asia.

39. Vanden Heuvel and Gwirtzman, *On His Own*, p. 236.

40. *Newsweek* magazine, February 13, 1967 (Edward Weintal), p. 34.

41. Ho Chi Minh's point number three reads: "The internal affairs of South Vietnam must be settled by the South Vietnamese people themselves in accordance with the program of the National Liberation Front of South Vietnam without any foreign interference." Quoted from "Hanoi's Four Points, April 8, 1965," in Gettleman, et al., *Vietnam and America*, p. 278.

42. Ibid., p. 33.

43. John Gunther Dean, First Secretary to the American Embassy in France, to Joseph Dolan, February 2, 1967, RFK Papers, SC-SF, Box 23, File: Trips, 1/25/1967–2/3/1967 Europe, JFKL.

44. *Newsweek* magazine, February 13, 1967, p. 34.

45. According to Vanden Heuvel and Gwirtzman (*On His Own*, p. 237), the State Department ordered a search of the limited distribution cable files for Europe and Asia, and nothing was found because the Dean cable was classified under general distribution, which was a classification too low to merit inclusion in the department's search.

46. John Gunther Dean, First Secretary to the American Embassy in France, to Joseph Dolan, February 2, 1967, RFK Papers, SC-SF, Box 23, File: Trips, 1/25/1967–2/3/1967 Europe, JFKL. The American Ambassador to France, Charles E. Bohlen, remained outside the fray.

47. Quoted in Vanden Heuvel and Gwirtzman, *On His Own*, p. 237.

48. Ibid., p. 238.

49. Newfield, *Robert Kennedy: A Memoir*, p. 131.

50. At the White House with George Christian, Monday, February 6, 1967, 12:05 E.S.T., LBJ Papers, Daily Diary Backup, Box 54, File: February 6, 1967, LBJL. For a nuanced account about how the peace feeler incident might have affected the secret diplomatic initiatives of the Johnson Administration regarding Vietnam see Gardner's excellent account in *Pay Any Price*, pp. 341–48.

51. White House Daily Diary, February 6, 1967, LBJ Papers, Daily Diary, Box 10, File: Daily Diary, February 1–15, 1967 (log), LBJL.

52. Ibid.

53. Ibid., The meeting lasted from 4:34 to 5:52 P.M.

54. Vanden Heuvel and Gwirtzman, On His Own, pp. 238–40; Schlesinger, Robert Kennedy and His Times, pp. 826–28; Newfield, Robert Kennedy: A Memoir, pp. 128–32.

55. Quoted in Stein and Plimpton, American Journey, pp. 216–17.

56. Ibid.

57. Peter B. Edelman, interview by Larry Hackman, July 15, 1969, interview 1, p. 66, OH-RFK, JFKL.

58. Ibid. 67.

59. Schlesinger, Robert Kennedy and His Times, p. 827.

60. Quoted in Newsweek magazine, February 20, 1967, p. 232.

61. Partial Transcript of Senator Robert Kennedy's Press Conference in West Lobby of White House, February 6, 1967, WHFN, Box 6, File: Kennedy, Robert 1968 Campaign, LBJL.

62. Robert Kennedy to John G. Dean, February 13, 1967, RFK Papers, SC-SF, Box 23, File: Trips, 1/25/1967–2/3/1967, JFKL.

63. Memorandum for the President, Tom Johnson to President Lyndon Johnson, February 6, 1967, 6:40 P.M., LBJ Papers, Daily Diary Backup, Box 54, File: February 7, 1967, LBJL.

64. Walt W. Rostow to President Lyndon Johnson, February 7, 1967, LBJ Papers, Daily Diary Backup, Box 54, File: February 7, 1967, 4:45 P.M., LBJL.

65. Ibid.

66. Press Release, Statement of Senator Robert F. Kennedy, February 13, 1967, RFK Papers, PCP, Speechwriters' Division, Box 5, File: Vietnam, JFKL.

67. R. E. Wick to Cartha DeLoach, February 24, 1967, attachment: article by Robert S. Allen, The Hall Syndicate, FBI File on Robert F. Kennedy, section 6 (microform edition).

68. Ibid.

69. Newsweek magazine, March 20, 1967, pp. 23, 36.

70. Transcript, U.S. State Department, The Today Show, March 7, 1967, 7:00 A.M., Washington, D.C., NSFCFVN, Box 211, File: Vietnam, Senator Robert F. Kennedy, Speech 3/2/1967, and The Today Show Interview, LBJL.

71. U.S. News & World Report, February 6, 1967, p. 13.

72. Adam Walinsky Papers, Box 33, File: Speech Drafts, 3/2/1967, (Vietnam), Correspondence and Memoranda; Box 35, File: Speeches, Drafts, 3/2/1967, (Vietnam), Correspondence and Memoranda, JFKL.

73. Adam Walinsky to Robert Kennedy, Notes on March 2, 1967, speech, n.d., Adam Walinsky Papers, Box 33, Speech Drafts, 3/2/1967, (Vietnam), Correspondence and Memoranda, JFKL.

74. Ibid.

75. Ibid.

76. Adam Walinsky to Robert Kennedy, n.d., Adam Walinsky Papers, Box 35, File: Speeches, Drafts, 3/2/1967, (Vietnam), Correspondence and Memoranda, JFKL.

77. Peter Edelman to Robert Kennedy, February 27, 1967, Adam Walinsky Papers, Box 35, File: Speech Drafts, 3/2/1967, (Vietnam), Correspondence and Memoranda, JFKL.

78. Ibid.

79. Ibid., McGeorge Bundy offered Kennedy the opposite advice from Walinsky and Edelman: "In the long run you would gain by getting independently fixed somewhere between the doves and the hawks." McGeorge Bundy to Robert Kennedy (private and personal), February 18, 1967, RFK Papers, SC-PF, Box 2, File: B: 1967, JFKL.

80. Peter Edelman, interview by Larry Hackett, July 15, 1969, interview 1, p. 44, OH-RFK, JFKL.

81. Arthur Schlesinger to Robert Kennedy, 3-page memo, n.d., ibid.

82. *Newsweek* magazine, March 13, 1967, p. 33.

83. Quoted in Schaap, *R.F.K.*, p. 22.

84. Ibid., p. 24.

85. Quoted in Schaap, *R.F.K.*, p. 27.

86. Ibid., p. 34. Twenty senators showing up to hear a foreign policy speech was an unusually generous turnout.

87. Schaap, *R.F.K.*, pp. 34–36.

88. Text of Remarks by Senator Robert F. Kennedy on Vietnam, Senate Floor, March 2, 1967, RFK Papers, PCP, Speechwriters' Division, Box 5, File: Vietnam, JFKL.

89. Ibid.

90. Ibid.

91. Ibid.

92. Ibid.

93. Wells, *War Within*, p. 123.

94. *Newsweek* magazine, March 13, 1967, p. 34.

95. Memorandum to the President, Fred Panzer to President Lyndon Johnson, March 3, 1967, 5:45 P.M., WHCF, Box 147, File: Kennedy, Robert F., LBJL.

96. *Newsweek* magazine, March 13, 1967, p. 34.

97. Walt W. Rostow to President Lyndon Johnson, March 4, 1967, NSFCFVN, Box 211, File: Vietnam, Senator Robert F. Kennedy Speech 3/2/1967 and The Today Show interview, LBJL.

98. Ibid.

99. Ibid.

100. Secretary of State Dean Rusk statement in response to Robert Kennedy's March 3, 1967 speech, WHCF, Box 72, File: Vietnam, Situation In, LBJL.

101. Secretary of State Dean Rusk to President Lyndon Johnson, March 10, 1967, NSFCFVN, Box 211, File: Vietnam, Senator Robert F. Kennedy Speech 3/2/1967 and The Today Show interview, LBJL.

102. Ibid.

103. Quoted in Schaap, *R.F.K.*, p. 36.

104. Notes of Telephone Request, March 11, 1967, 11:13 A.M., NSFCFVN, Box 212, File: Memos Re: The Pauses 4/1965–5/1967, LBJL.

105. Robert Kennedy to Frank Conniff, Editor, *World Journal Tribune*, April 11, 1967, Adam Walinsky Papers, Box 18, File: Foreign Policy, Vietnam, 4/1967, JFKL.

106. Robert Kennedy to Senator J. William Fulbright, March 6, 1967, RFK Papers, SC-PF, Box 20, File: Kennedy, Robert F., Handwritten Notes and Letters (Copies), JFKL.

107. Tran Van Dinh to Robert Kennedy, March 3, 1967, Adam Walinsky Papers, Box 35, File: Speeches, Drafts, 3/21/1967 (Vietnam) Correspondence and Memoranda, JFKL. The full title of the group was the Overseas Vietnamese Buddhist Association of the United States and Canada.

108. Hugh Sidey to Robert Kennedy, March 4, 1967, RFK Papers, SC-PF, Box 10, File: S: 1967, JFKL. Kennedy answered Sidey with a handwritten thank you note, ibid.

109. Rowland Evans to Robert Kennedy, March 3, 1967, RFK Papers, SC-PF, Box 3, File: E: 1966–1967, JFKL.

110. Transcript, U.S. State Department, The Today Show, March 7, 1967, 7:00 A.M., Washington, D.C., NSFCFVN, Box 211, File: Vietnam, Senator Robert F. Kennedy, Speech 3/2/1967, and The Today Show Interview, LBJL.

111. Ibid.

112. Ibid.

113. Statement of Senator Robert F. Kennedy, March 21, 1967, Adam Walinsky Papers, Box 18, File: Foreign Policy, Vietnam, 3/1967, JFKL.

114. *Newsweek* magazine, March 20, 1967, p. 25.

115. Transcript, U.S. State Department, The Today Show, March 7, 1967, 7:00 A.M., Washington, D.C., NSFCFVN, Box 211, File: Vietnam, Senator Robert F. Kennedy, LBJL.

116. Quotation from Washington Senator Henry Jackson, Senate Floor, February 24, 1967, Adam Walinsky Papers, Box 18, File: Foreign Policy, Vietnam, 2/1967, JFKL. In 1960, Kennedy had favored Jackson over Johnson to be John Kennedy's running mate.

117. Ibid.

118. Bowman, *Vietnam War Almanac*, p. 162.

119. For the fiscal year ending in June 1967 the war cost the United States $21 billion. Ibid., p. 192.
120. It was the lies and deceit of the Johnson Administration regarding the nature of the war which later pushed Senator J. William Fulbright over the edge to full-blown opposition to the war. See Woods, *Fulbright.*

Chapter 3

1. John Bartlow Martin, quotation prepared on a 3 × 5 note card for Robert Kennedy, RFK Papers, SC-PF, Box 20, File: Kennedy, Robert F. Selective Quotations, JFKL.
2. Herman and Brodhead, *Demonstration Elections*, pp. 68–91.
3. Statement of Senator Robert F. Kennedy on Elections in Vietnam—Floor of the Senate, August 11, 1967, RFK Papers, PCP, Speechwriters' Division, Box 5, File: Vietnam, JFKL.
4. Ibid. (Original emphasis.)
5. Although hailed by the Administration's supporters, Johnson's Vietnam speech in San Antonio, Texas, on September 29, 1967 offered the North Vietnamese no concessions other than a temporary bombing halt in exchange for "prompt" and "productive" talks, a position that Hanoi had already rejected. NSFCFVN, Box 103, File: 1954–1968, Documents Pertinent to the War, Its Genesis, LBJL.
6. Howard, *The Sixties*, p. 510.
7. Margolis, *Last Innocent Year.* Margolis shows, among other things, that President Johnson did not hesitate to use the FBI to spy on Robert Kennedy during the 1964 Democratic National Convention (pp. 275–76, 323–24).
8. Frederick Dutton to Robert Kennedy, March 15, 1967. RFK Papers, SC-PF, Box 3, File: Dutton, Frederick, 1965–1968, JFKL. Dutton letters cited below are from this file.
9. Frederick Dutton to Robert Kennedy, November 3, 1967.
10. Frederick Dutton to Robert Kennedy, November 6, 1967. Joseph Dolan to Robert Kennedy, February 14, 1968, Joseph Dolan Papers, Box 1, File: Memoranda 2/14/68–2/29/68, JFKL.
11. Frederick Dutton to Robert Kennedy, November 3, 1967.
12. Frederick Dutton to Robert Kennedy, December 6, 1966.
13. Ibid.
14. Ibid. Kennedy was routinely included in Gallup and Harris polls which attempted to measure President Johnson's relative popularity among Democrats.
15. Frederick Dutton to Robert Kennedy, March 15, 1967.
16. Ibid.
17. Frederick Dutton to Robert Kennedy, April 6, 1966.

18. Joseph Dolan to Robert Kennedy, May 15, 1967, RFK Papers, SC-PF, Box 3, File: Dutton, Frederick, 1967–1968, JFKL.

19. Joseph Dolan to Robert Kennedy, March 22, 1967, Joseph Dolan Papers, Box 1, File: Memoranda, 3/16/1966–3/30/1967, JFKL.

20. Milton Gwirtzman to Robert Kennedy, March 20, 1967, RFK Papers, SC-PF, Box 4, File: G: 1967–1968, JFKL.

21. Ibid.

22. Joseph Alsop to Robert Kennedy, February 1, 1967, RFK Papers, SC-PF, Box 1, File: A: 1967, JFKL.

23. John Kenneth Galbraith to Robert Kennedy, March 18, 1967, RFK Papers, SC-PF, Box 4, File: Galbraith, J. K. 7/20/66–3/25/68, JFKL.

24. Henry Steele Commager to Robert Kennedy, October 4, 1967, RFK Papers, SC-SF, Box 49, File: Press, 3/1968–4/1968, LBJL.

25. Robert Kennedy to Pete Hamill, April 21, 1967, RFK Papers, SC-PF, Box 5, File: H: Halle—Harriman, JFKL.

26. Kennedy had just arrived in New York from England, where he had attended the funeral of Cissy Harlech, and he therefore delivered his "introduction" of the President only after Johnson had already given his speech.

27. *New York Times*, June 4, 1967, p. 1A. Neither Kennedy nor Johnson saw the protesters that evening.

28. Ibid.

29. Remarks of Honorable Robert F. Kennedy, United States Senator from the State of New York, at Democratic State Committee Dinner, at the Americana Hotel, New York City, June 3, 1967, WHFN, Box 6, File: Kennedy, Robert F. and Family, 1965–1968, LBJL.

30. *New York Post*, June 5, 1967; *Newsday*, June 5, 1967, The Records of the Democratic National Committee (D.N.C.), Series I, Box 150, File: Johnson, President Lyndon, Politics, June 3, 1967, Ringing Endorsement of L.B.J. by R.F.K., LBJL.

31. William Vanden Heuvel interview with Doris Kearns, n.d. (ca. August 1968), Milton Gwirtzman Papers, Box 8, File: Testimonials Re: Robert F. Kennedy, JFKL.

32. Newfield, *Robert Kennedy: A Memoir*, p. 184.

33. *Washington Post*, June 5, 1967, The Records of the D.N.C., Series I, Box 150, LBJL.

34. Arthur Schlesinger, Jr., to Robert Kennedy, June 19, 1967, RFK Papers, SC-PF, Box 11, File: Schlesinger, Arthur, 4/1967–8/1967, JFKL. In his 1978 biography of Kennedy, Schlesinger blames the Senator's adulatory words about Johnson that evening on a "hyperbolic paragraph" that Sorensen had inserted shortly before Kennedy's speech. Schlesinger, *Robert Kennedy and His Times*, p. 836.

35. Ibid.

36. Frederick Dutton to Robert Kennedy, December 8, 1966..

37. Allard K. Lowenstein, interview by Larry Hackman, April 23, 1969, p. 40, OH-RFK, JFKL.

38. Matusow, *Unraveling of America*, p. 214. DeBenedetti, *American Ordeal*, p. 161.

39. Lowenstein interview, April 23, 1969, pp. 45–46. OH-RFK, JFKL.

40. Chafe, *Never Stop Running*, p. 284.

41. In April 1967, Kennedy told a student newspaper from the University of Michigan that he had been "paying more attention to students and young people since the protests began." Quoted in Knappman, *Presidential Election 1968*, p. 7.

42. See McAdam, *Freedom Summer*.

43. Teodori, *New Left*, p. 481. See also Wells, *War Within*, chs. 3 and 4, passim. Adam Garfinkle, *Telltale Hearts*, pp. 103–4.

44. Anderson, *The Movement and the Sixties*, p. 178. Norman Mailer, a participant in the Pentagon protest, wrote a novel based on the demonstration, *Armies of the Night*.

45. Chafe, *Never Stop Running*, p. 262.

46. Ibid., p. 269.

47. Ibid.

48. Notes of the President's Meeting with Lyle Denniston, Bob Walters, and Jack Horner of the *Washington Evening Star*, November 15, 1967, TJMN, Box 1, File: Meetings, Correspondence, 7/1967–5/1968, LBJL.

49. John P. Roche to Marvin Watson, August 2, 1967, Marvin Watson Papers, Box 29, File: Roche, John-Memos, LBJL.

50. John P. Roche to President Lyndon Johnson (eyes only), September 25, 1967, Marvin Watson Papers, Box 29, File: Roche, John-Memos, LBJL.

51. John P. Roche to President Lyndon Johnson (eyes only), September 25, 1967, Marvin Watson Papers, Box 29, File: Roche, John-Memos, LBJL. Rauh also helped organize Negotiations Now! in mid-1967 in Washington, D.C., to generate support for the election of delegates to the Democratic National Convention pledged to include a peace plank in the platform. By Rauh's own estimate the plank "would have to be molded to the situation at Convention time in August 1968." Joseph Rauh, "A Proposal to Maximize Political Support for an End to the War in Vietnam," Marvin Watson Papers, Box 32, File: Vietnam, LBJL.

52. John P. Roche to President Lyndon Johnson (eyes only), September 25, 1967, Marvin Watson Papers, Box 29, File: Roche, John-Memos, LBJL. Roche added: "We staked him [Lowenstein] over the ant hill—even Schlesinger and Goodwin helped drive in the stakes—and left him trying to explain to anybody who would listen that he had really won."

53. Ibid. In June 1967, Roche had expressed his joy to President Johnson over what he called "a Rauh-Galbraith schism" brewing inside the A.D.A. Roche to President Johnson, June 9, 1967 (eyes only); in September 1967, Roche urged President Johnson to snub a meeting with John Kenneth Galbraith because it "would be a waste of your time"; Johnson took Roche's advice. Roche to President Johnson, September 23, 1967, ibid.

54. John Roche to President Johnson, September 25, 1967, ibid.

55. John Roche to President Johnson, May 19, 1967. Roche inherited the job of starting the committee from the presidential aide Harry McPherson. Revised Draft Statement of press release announcing the committee, October 4, 1967, ibid.

56. Herring, *LBJ and Vietnam*, p. 144.

57. Revised Draft Statement or press release describing the committee, October 4, 1967, Marvin Watson Papers, Box 29, File: Roche, John-Memos, LBJL.

58. John P. Roche to President Lyndon Johnson, May 19, 1967, ibid.

59. President Lyndon Johnson to Marvin Watson, November 12, 1967, Marvin Watson Papers, box 21, File: DNC/Young Democrats, LBJL.

60. R. Spencer Oliver to Marvin Watson, October 20, 1967, Marvin Watson Papers, Box 21, File: DNC/Young Democrats, LBJL.

61. Paul A. Ecker (County Democratic Chairman, Minnehaha County, South Dakota), to Hon. Billie S. Farnum, Deputy Chairman, D.N.C., October 17, 1967, Marvin Watson Papers, Box 21, File: DNC/Young Democrats, LBJL.

62. Marvin Watson Papers, Box 21, File: DNC/Young Democrats, LBJL.

63. Cartha D. DeLoach was also a key player in the FBI's monitoring of Robert F. Kennedy's activities from the time he was attorney general until his death. *FBI File on Robert F. Kennedy* (microform). The FBI tracked Kennedy beginning in the summer of 1962, chronicling trip itineraries, television show appearances, and speeches.

64. L.N. to Walt Rostow, October 4, 1967, NSFCFVN, Box 103, File: Vietnam, September 29, 1967, San Antonio Speech Commentary, LBJL. For example, following Johnson's September 29, 1967, address in San Antonio, where he announced his San Antonio formula for a negotiated settlement of the war, the President ordered DeLoach to run background checks on citizens who wrote letters and telegrams to the White House criticizing the speech.

65. Memorandum For The Record, July 15, 1967, WHCF, Box 77, File: Political Parties, LBJL.

66. The National Conference for New Politics proved to be an exercise in grassroots democracy that did not succeed in producing a new coalition. See Tomasky, *Left For Dead*, p. 82. DeBenedetti, *American Ordeal*, pp. 191–93.

67. Ibid.

68. Ibid.

69. Garrow, *Bearing the Cross*, p. 577.

70. Chicago, Special Agent in Charge to FBI Director J. Edgar Hoover, November 22, 1967, *FBI File on Robert F. Kennedy* (series 1–4, microform).

71. *FBI File on Robert F. Kennedy*. The FBI informant stated that the communists at the gathering were "functioning through the W.E.B. DuBois Clubs of America and many other organizations in which the communists are active."

72. Special Agent in Charge, Chicago, to FBI Director J. Edgar Hoover, November 22, 1967, *FBI File on Robert F. Kennedy* (microform).

73. Memorandum For the Record, July 15, 1967, WHCF, Box 77, File: Political Parties, LBJL.

74. John P. Roche to President Lyndon Johnson, with attachment (eyes only), April 27, 1967, Marvin Watson Papers, Box 29, File: Roche, John-Memos, LBJL. One of these organizations was the Stern Family Fund, one of whose board members was Johnson's Secretary of Labor, Willard Wirtz. Roche suggested to President Johnson that he tell Secretary Wirtz to "read grant requests a bit more carefully." Ibid.

75. For an overview of the FBI's activities in this period, see Garrow, *FBI and Martin Luther King*; Churchill and Vander Wall, *Agents of Repression*. See also Glick, *War At Home*; Swearingen, *FBI Secrets*.

76. Adam Walinsky to Robert Kennedy, n.d. (ca. late 1967), RFK Papers, SC-PF, Box 20, File: Memoranda: Staff 1967–1968.

77. Ibid.

78. Johnson already had been alerted to rumors that Kennedy planned "to pull a Kefauver in New Hampshire," meaning he would belatedly enter the Democratic primaries in 1968. John P. Roche to President Lyndon Johnson (eyes only), February 20, 1967, Marvin Watson Papers, Box 29, File: Roche, John-Memos, LBJL.

79. Redford and McCulley, *White House Operations*, p. 18. Goodwin became an official member of President Johnson's White House staff in April 1964.

80. Goodwin disseminated his views on the war by writing occasional articles for periodicals. For examples, see Richard Goodwin, "The Lengthening Shadow of War," *Christianity and Crisis*, October 31, 1966; and "What We Can Do About Vietnam," *New Leader*, November 7, 1966.

81. For example, in another memo to Kennedy, Walinsky referred to President Johnson as "Lyndon Pumpkin." Adam Walinsky to Robert Kennedy (ca. November 26, 1967), RFK Papers, SC-PF, Box 20, File: Memoranda: Staff 1967–1968, JFKL.

82. Goodwin also asked: "What can LBJ do anyway[?] He is not smart enough, or tough enough, to cut down [Jesse] Unruh and [Richard] Daley"—as Kennedy had demonstrated his skill at cutting down political rivals in New York State.

Goodwin specifically referred to the Tammany leader Carmine De Sapio, and his protégé Mike Pendergast.

83. Richard N. Goodwin to Robert Kennedy, n.d. (ca. late 1967), RFK Papers, SC-PF, Box 4, File: Goodwin, Richard 1967–1968.

84. Ibid.

85. Ibid.

86. Frederick Dutton to Robert Kennedy, April 6, 1966, RFK Papers, SC-PF, Box 3, File: Dutton, Frederick 1965–1968.

87. Schlesinger, *Robert Kennedy and His Times*, p. 827; Vanden Heuvel and Gwirtzman, *On His Own*, p. 238; see ch. 2.

Chapter 4

1. Citizens for Kennedy mass mailing, June 27, 1967, Marvin Watson Papers, Box 25, File: Kennedy-Fulbright, Citizens for, LBJL.

2. At that time, it was widely rumored that Theodore Sorensen had written most of John Kennedy's *Profiles in Courage.*

3. From the time John Kennedy published his *Profiles In Courage* in 1956, Robert Kennedy understood the power of a book to bolster a politician's public position. It has become standard practice in presidential elections in the ensuing years.

4. Robert F. Kennedy, *To Seek a Newer World.*

5. Both groups asked Robert Kennedy for permission to send out the excerpts, which he quickly granted.

6. *Look* magazine, cover story, "What We Can Do to End the Agony of Vietnam," by Senator Robert F. Kennedy, pp. 35–46, November 28, 1967, vol. 31, no. 24, excerpt from *To Seek a Newer World*. The Washington editor for *Look*, Warren Rogers, became a good friend of Robert Kennedy and his family. See Rogers, *When I Think of Bobby*, p. 144.

7. *Face the Nation*, CBS Television Network and the CBS Radio Network, Sunday, November 26, 1967, Guest: Senator Robert F. Kennedy Democrat of New York. News Correspondents: Martin Agronsky, CBS News; Tom Wicker, *New York Times*; Roger Mudd, CBS News, RFK Papers, PCP, Speechwriters' Division, Box 5, File: Vietnam, JFKL.

8. Ibid.

9. Ibid.

10. Senator George McGovern, interview by Larry Hackman, July 16, 1970, p. 18, OH-RFK, JFKL.

11. Joseph Dolan Robo letter, January 30, 1968, RFK Papers, SC-SF, Box 17, File: Election, Presidential 1/1968, JFKL. Robo letters were "robotic" letters, printed

in large quantities with Kennedy's automated signature, for mass mailings to his supporters.

12.   Averell Harriman to Robert Kennedy, February 1, 1968, RFK Papers, SC-PF, Box 5, File: H: 1968, JFKL.

13.   Peter Edelman interview, July 15, 1969, pp. 49–51, OH-RFK, JFKL.

14.   Joseph Dolan to Robert Kennedy, November 29, 1967, Joseph Dolan Papers, Box 1, File: Memoranda 11/16/1967–11/29/1967, JFKL.

15.   "Eugene McCarthy's 1967 Conscience Quota," Marvin Watson Papers, Box 26, File: McCarthy, Senator Eugene, LBJL. McCarthy disputed all of these discrepancies in his voting record when Kennedy later made them a public issue.

16.   Jack Newfield, "A Look At Kennedy" (ca. May 1968), RFK Papers, PCP, Research Division, Box 45, File: Campaign Literature, General, JFKL.

17.   "Eugene McCarthy's 1967 Conscience Quota," Marvin Watson Papers, Box 26, File: McCarthy, Senator Eugene, LBJL. Kennedy/McCarthy legislative voting comparison (prepared by Robert Kennedy's 1968 campaign staff), April 24, 1968, RFK Papers, PCP, Youth and Student Division, Box 5, File: Issues, JFKL. McCarthy's obfuscation following his vote against the amendment outlawing poll taxes particularly perturbed Kennedy. Peter Edelman interview, July 15, 1969, p. 50 OH-RFK, JFKL.

18.   "Senator McCarthy's Absenteeism," (prepared for Press Secretary George Christian), December 6, 1967. Marvin Watson Papers, Box 26, File: McCarthy, Senator Eugene, LBJL.

19.   Later, when Kennedy and McCarthy were competing in the Democratic primaries, McCarthy claimed that the Kennedy campaign misrepresented his Senate record.

20.   "Eugene McCarthy's 1967 Conscience Quota," ibid. John Roche to President Johnson (eyes only), October 19, 1967, WHCF, Box 77, File: Elections, Campaigns-1967, LBJL. Roche informed President Johnson that McCarthy was "flirting with the Dump Johnson movement . . . playing a real teaser's game. . . . Characteristically, he isn't going to do any work."

21.   Senator George McGovern was willing to make the challenge if Lowenstein could find no one else, but since he was up for reelection in South Dakota in 1968 he would be forced to run two simultaneous campaigns of differing vocabularies and emotional tones. Lowenstein did not think it would be a good idea. See Chafe, *Never Stop Running*, p. 271. (John Kenneth Galbraith would have run but being Canadian precluded it).

22.   Beginning in 1964, Robert Kennedy was routinely included in Gallup and Harris public opinion polls whenever Lyndon Johnson's popularity was gauged. This practice often angered both the Kennedy and Johnson camps.

23.   Robert Kennedy was often invited to dedicate memorials to his slain elder brother. He did so in Europe, Latin America, and Africa.

24. Frederick Dutton to Robert Kennedy, November 3, 1967, RFK Papers, SC-PF, Box 3, File: Dutton, Frederick, 1965–1968, JFKL. Dutton also noted that McCarthy "will create lasting suspicions, if not animosities against his candidacy, by being the first to plunge in."

25. Theodore Sorensen to Robert Kennedy, n.d. (ca. October 1967), RFK Papers, SC-PF, Box 10, File: S: 1967, JFKL.

26. Frederick Dutton to Robert Kennedy, November 6, 1967, RFK Papers, Box 3, File: Dutton, Frederick, 1965–1968, JFKL.

27. When the New Hampshire primary campaign began to heat up Richard Goodwin became the chief source of information on the McCarthy campaign for Robert Kennedy. Peter Edelman interview, July 15, 1969, OH-RFK, JFKL.

28. Colorado State Democratic Chairman William Grant to Robert Kennedy, January 25, 1968, RFK Papers, SC-SF, Box 17, File: Election, Presidential 1/1968, JFKL.

29. Copies of these Robo letters are contained in RFK Papers, SC-SF, Box 17, File: Election, Presidential 1/1968, JFKL.

30. Joseph Dolan to Robert Kennedy, January 9, 1968, Joseph Dolan Papers, Box 1, File: Memoranda, 1/17/1968–1/31/1968, JFKL. Dolan was relaying to Kennedy his own as well as Dutton's concerns.

31. Invitation to the conference, Conference of Concerned Democrats, mass mailing, Harold M. Ickes to W. R. Landrum, New London, Texas, November 18, 1967, Marvin Watson Papers, Box 26, File: McCarthy, Senator Eugene, LBJL.

32. Chafe, *Never Stop Running*, pp. 279–80.

33. Memorandum, Sandy Frucher to Herman Cooper, December 5, 1967, "Re: National Conference of Concerned Democrats in Chicago." William Haddad forwarded a copy of this memo to Kennedy's office. RFK Papers, SC-SF, Box 17, File: Election, Presidential 1/1968, JFKL.

34. Sandy Frucher to Herman Cooper, December 5, 1967.

35. The suspicion of Lowenstein's being a Bobby agent was not unfounded, since Lowenstein admitted repeatedly after Kennedy's death that he never wavered in his loyalty to Kennedy the entire time he worked for McCarthy. Lowenstein was poised to play a pivotal role in unifying the McCarthy and Kennedy delegations after Kennedy's win in the California primary. Kennedy attempted to contact Lowenstein by telephone the night of his California victory to discuss a strategy to bring the two delegations together.

36. Sandy Frucher to Herman Cooper, December 5, 1967.

37. Kaiser, *1968 in America*, p. 57.

38. John Criswell (D.N.C.) to Marvin Watson, November 30, 1967, Marvin Watson Papers, Box 26, File: McCarthy, Senator Eugene, LBJL.

39. Ibid. (The White House also feared that Kennedy money had been behind the National Conference for New Politics).

40. Marty Underwood to James R. Jones, December 4, 1967, ibid.
41. Ibid.
42. Ibid.
43. Fred Panzer to Marvin Watson, December 6, 1967, Marvin Watson Papers, Box 26, File: McCarthy, Senator Eugene, LBJL.
44. Marvin Watson to President Lyndon Johnson, December 7, 1967, ibid. Watson maintained an active file on McCarthy which included relevant press releases, transcripts of speeches, campaign materials, reports from informants within the McCarthy organization, McCarthy campaign financial information, and other relevant items.
45. Marvin Watson to President Lyndon Johnson, December 15, 1967, ibid.
46. John P. Roche to President Lyndon Johnson (eyes only), December 11, 1967, Marvin Watson Papers, Box 29, File: Roche, John P.—Memos, LBJL. Marvin Watson to President Lyndon Johnson, December 5, 1967, Marvin Watson Papers, Box 26, File: Kennedy, Ted. (Roche also referred to what he called McCarthyism in another letter to President Johnson, September 7, 1967, Marvin Watson Papers, Box 29, File: Roche, John—Memos, LBJL.)
47. John P. Roche to President Lyndon Johnson (eyes only), December 11, 1967, Marvin Watson Papers, Box 29, File: Roche, John P.—Memos, LBJL.
48. Ibid.
49. John P. Roche to President Lyndon Johnson (eyes only), December 18, 1967, ibid. (Robert Kennedy's political aide, Joseph Dolan, was indeed making contacts at the time with working-level Democrats across the country, with mixed results.)
50. Ibid.
51. Citizens for Kennedy/Fulbright '68 materials held in Marvin Watson Papers, Box 25, File: Kennedy-Fulbright, Citizens for, LBJL.
52. Background fact sheet, issued October 27, 1967, Citizens For Kennedy/Fulbright '68, ibid.
53. DeBenedetti, *An American Ordeal*, p. 156.
54. RFK Papers, SC-SF, Box 17, File: Election, Presidential 1/1968. This file also contains numerous letters from persons seeking information on Kennedy for President clubs.
55. One such ad appeared in the March 12, 1967 issue of the *New York Times*.
56. Citizens for Kennedy in '68, press release, national office, New York City, October 27, 1967, Marvin Watson Papers, Box 25, File: Kennedy/Fulbright, Citizens for, LBJL.
57. Citizens for Kennedy in '68, Background Fact Sheet, October 27, 1967, ibid. The argument was similar to one that Dolan had privately made to Kennedy. Joseph Dolan to Robert Kennedy, August 22, 1967, Joseph Dolan Papers, Box 1, File: Memoranda 8/11/67–8/29/67, JFKL.

58. Richard A. Raznikov (Citizens for Kennedy/Fulbright '68) to W. R. Landrum, Overton Texas, June 27, 1967, Marvin Watson Papers, Box 25, File: Kennedy/Fulbright, Citizens for, LBJL.

59. John Criswell (D.N.C.) to Marvin Watson, May 16, 1967, ibid.

60. M. A. Jones to Mr. Bishop, August 8, 1967, *FBI File on Robert F. Kennedy* (series 1–4, microform). This document summarizes Kennedy's statements during his appearance August 6, 1967, on the *Meet the Press* television program. Copies of all FBI correspondence regarding Robert Kennedy's activities were forwarded to Cartha DeLoach, President Johnson's liaison with the Bureau.

61. M. A. Jones to Mr. Bishop, August 8, 1967, *FBI File on Robert F. Kennedy* (series 1–4, microform).

62. Robert Kennedy to Emma Guffey Miller, April 18, 1967. Emma Guffey Miller Papers, Women's Studies Manuscript Collection, Series 2: Women in National Politics, Part A: Democrats, Schlesinger Library, Radcliffe College. A power-house in Pennsylvania Democratic politics, the 92-year-old Miller liked to refer to herself as the Old Gray Mare of the Democratic Party.

63. John Seigenthaler to Robert Kennedy, August 29, 1967, RFK Papers, SC-PF, Box 10, File: S: 1967, JFKL.

64. RFK Papers, SC-SF, Box 17, File: Election, 1/1968–2/1968, JFKL. This file is filled with materials from citizens all over the country who implored Kennedy to run for president in 1968.

65. Robert Kennedy to Claude E. Hooton, October 4, 1967, RFK Papers, SC-PF, Box 20, File: Kennedy, Robert F., Handwritten Notes and Letters (Copies), JFKL.

66. John Roche, Marvin Watson, and other presidential assistants at times implied in their internal correspondence that Robert Kennedy was deviously manipulating not only the Citizens for Kennedy groups, but also the peace and civil rights movements, to serve his presidential ambitions.

67. Neither the SC-PF nor the SC-SF of the RFK Papers contain evidence of formal contacts with the Citizens for Kennedy groups other than tracking their activities.

68. Citizens for Kennedy/Fulbright in '68 organizing pamphlet, ca. May 1967, Marvin Watson Papers, Box 25, File: Kennedy/Fulbright, Citizens for, LBJL.

69. Senator Eugene McCarthy agreed to run in the primaries and head Lowenstein's Dump Johnson movement, yet he did not inspire "Citizens for McCarthy" chapters to emerge nationwide as did Kennedy.

70. Bill Phillips ("Intelligence Report") to John Criswell, August 2, 1967, WHCF, Box 147, File: Kennedy, LBJL.

71. Memorandum for Marvin Watson, May 3, 1967, Marvin Watson Papers, Box 25, File: Kennedy/Fulbright, Citizens for, LBJL.

72. Marvin Watson Papers, Box 25, File: Kennedy/Fulbright, Citizens for, LBJL.

73. Robert Spivak routinely gave the Johnson White House advice and suggestions about how best to promote the Administration's views on the Vietnam War, and on ways to attack Johnson's political enemies such as Robert Kennedy and Eugene McCarthy. Notes of Telephone call, March 14, 1968, WHFN, Box 6, File: Kennedy, Robert F. 1968 Campaign; Fred Panzer to Marvin Watson, March 27, 1968, Marvin Watson Papers, Box 31, File: Robert Spivak, LBJL.

74. Ibid.

75. John Criswell to Marvin Watson, September 14, 1967, ibid. The D.N.C. leadership tried to explain to Senator Pell that the mailing "was not against anyone, but an explanation of a situation."

76. John M. Bailey, Chairman of the D.N.C., to J. B. Avery, Democratic Executive Committee of Tennessee, August 31, 1967, ibid.

77. John Criswell to Marvin Watson, October 26, 1967, ibid.

78. Newsclip, Oneonta, New York, September 25, 1967, n.p., RFK Papers, PCP, Press Division, Box 14, File: Politics, 1967, JFKL.

79. Irv Sprague to Marvin Watson, September 20, 1967, Marvin Watson Papers, Box 25, File: Kennedy-Fulbright, Citizens for, LBJL.

80. Robert Kennedy Robo letter, January 2, 1968, RFK Papers, SC-SF, Box 17, File: Election, Presidential 1/1968, JFKL.

81. Martin Shepard, M.D., to Robert Kennedy, January 22, 1968, RFK Papers, SC-SF, Box 17, File: Election, Presidential 1/1968, JFKL. (Original emphasis.)

82. *Face The Nation*, CBS Television Network and the CBS Radio Network, Sunday, November 26, 1967, Guest: Senator Robert F. Kennedy Democrat of New York, News Correspondents: Martin Agronsky, CBS News; Tom Wicker, the *New York Times*; Roger Mudd, CBS News. RFK Papers, PCP, Speechwriters' Division, Box 5, File: Vietnam, JFKL.

83. Frederick Dutton to Robert Kennedy, November 6, 1967, RFK Papers, SC-PF, box 3, File: Dutton, Frederick, 1965–1968, JFKL. (Italics added.)

84. Ibid. Later, when Kennedy entered the race for the Democratic presidential nomination his campaign staff utilized Citizens for Kennedy, either tapping into existing chapters or forming new ones to recruit campaign workers. RFK Papers, PCP, BB, Box 2, File: Alabama-Correspondence, JFKL.

85. Frederick Dutton to Robert Kennedy, November 6, 1967, RFK Papers, SC-PF, Box 3, File: Dutton, Frederick, 1965–1968, JFKL.

86. Newfield, *Robert Kennedy: A Memoir*, p. 198.

87. RFK Papers, SC-SF, Box 49, File: Press, 8/1967–2/1968, *Houston Chronicle*, n.d./p. (ca. November 1967), JFKL.

88. Address by Hon. James A. Farley, Former Chairman of the Democratic National Committee, former Postmaster General, Jefferson-Jackson Day Dinner,

Hartford, Connecticut, February 25, 1967, Marvin Watson Papers, Box 25, File: Kennedy-Fulbright, Citizens for, LBJL.

89. Bert (D.N.C.) to Jim Jones, January 11, 1968, WHCF, Box 147, File: Kennedy, LBJL.

90. Norman Mailer had once written of Farley: "The hell he would consign you to was cold as ice." Norman Mailer, "Superman Comes to the Supermarket," reprinted from *Esquire*, November 1960, in Howard, *The Sixties*, p. 155.

91. Excerpt of James Farley's speech (prepared by Joseph Dolan) taken from the *Salt Lake City Tribune*, "Doves Blistered by Farley; State Democratic Meeting Hears Scorcher," January 14, 1968. Joseph Dolan to Steve Smith, January 15, 1968, Joseph Dolan Papers, Box 1, File: Memoranda, 1/5/1968–1/15/1968, JFKL.

92. D.N.C. Summary of James Farley's remarks in Salt Lake City, January 11, 1968, WHCF, Box 147, File: Kennedy, LBJL.

93. Press Release, Remarks by John M. Bailey, Chairman of the Democratic National Committee, at meeting of the D.N.C., Chicago, Illinois, January 8, 1968, Records of the D.N.C., Box 100, File: Remarks by Chairman Bailey, LBJL.

94. Democratic Party Participating Member Campaign, Democratic National Committee, John M. Bailey, Chairman, letter sent out to working-level Democrats (ca. February 1968); this letter was forwarded to Robert Kennedy's office by an angry constituent, RFK Papers, SC-SF, Box 13, File: Democratic Party, National, JFKL.

95. John M. Bailey, D.N.C. Chairman, form letter to registered Democrats forwarded to Robert Kennedy, February 20, 1968, RFK Papers, SC-SF, ibid.

96. Mrs. Robert Adler (Port Chester, New York) to Robert Kennedy, March 3, 1968, RFK Papers, SC-SF, ibid.

97. David M. Stern (N.Y.C.) to John Bailey (after receiving the donation request), March 13, 1968 (copy forwarded to Robert Kennedy), RFK Papers, SC-SF, ibid.

98. Robert Kennedy to Mrs. Robert Adler, March 7, 1968, RFK Papers, SC-SF, ibid.

99. Joseph Dolan to Robert Kennedy, August 22, 1967, Joseph Dolan Papers, Box 1, File: Memoranda 8/11/67–8/29/67, JFKL.

100. Larry Temple to President Lyndon Johnson, January 18, 1968, Marvin Watson Papers, Box 30, File: Jim Rowe, LBJL.

101. Presidential Special Consultant John P. Roche to President Lyndon Johnson, September 8, 1967 (eyes only/personal), WHCF, Box 77, File: Elections, Campaigns-1967, LBJL.

102. Senators J. William Fulbright of Arkansas, Albert Gore of Tennessee, and Robert Byrd of West Virginia voiced opposition to President Johnson's war policies to varying degrees; even Mississippi Senator John Stennis came to oppose troop

increases in 1968. Notes of Meeting of the President with Senate Committee Chairman, July 25, 1967, TJMN, Box 1, File: July 25, 1967, 6:00 P.M., LBJL.

Chapter 5

1. Remarks by President Lyndon Johnson, December 22, 1967, Video, Episode 7, "Tet: 1968," *Vietnam: A Television History*, WGBH, Boston. Johnson spoke at a stop at the American base at Camranh Bay in South Vietnam. Bowman, *Vietnam War Almanac*, p. 190.

2. The internal debate about the troop request was exposed in a front-page article by Neil Sheehan and Hedrick Smith in the March 10, 1968, *New York Times*.

3. The thesis that the media's inaccurate portrayal of Tet skewed public opinion is most forcefully argued in Braestrup's two-volume work *Big Story*. Oberdorfer's *Tet!* also subscribes to this view. Lyndon Johnson in *Vantage Point*, Maxwell Taylor in *Swords and Plowshares*, and William Westmoreland in *A Soldier Reports* all subscribe to variations of this thesis. For a critique of the Braestrup thesis see Herman and Chomsky, *Manufacturing Consent*, pp. 211–30, and Robert Buzzanco, "The Myth of Tet: American Failure and the Politics of War," in Gilbert and Head, *Tet Offensive*.

4. *New York Times*, February 1, 1968, p. 14.

5. Address by Senator Robert F. Kennedy, Book and Author Luncheon, Chicago, Illinois, February 8, 1968, Adam Walinsky Papers, Box 19, File: Foreign Policy, Vietnam, 2/1/1968–2/18/1968, JFKL.

6. Kaiser, *1968 In America*, p. 64; Oberdorfer, *Tet!*, pp. 30–40; Arnold, *Tet Offensive 1968*, pp. 44–50.

7. Two N.L.F. sappers who participated in the embassy attack were wounded, captured, and tortured by Saigon police. *New York Times*, February 1, 1968, p. 14.

8. Quoted in Anderson, *The Movement and the Sixties*, p. 188. Senator Edward Kennedy, in his first post-Tet address, pointed out that the successful retaking of the embassy—the preeminent symbol of the American presence in Vietnam—"did not mean as much as the fact that for hours it was not in our hands." Address by Senator Edward M. Kennedy before the American Advertising Federation, Washington, D.C., February 5, 1968, Adam Walinsky Papers, Box 19, File: Foreign Policy, Vietnam, 2/1/1968–2/18/1968, JFKL.

9. Oberdorfer, *Tet!*, p. 114.

10. Several of these columnists would later recall this scene in print after Kennedy finally decided to enter the race. Crouse, *Boys on the Bus*, p. 41.

11. Schlesinger, *Robert Kennedy and His Times*, p. 903.

12. Oberdorfer, *Tet!*, p. 114.

13. *New York Times*, February 1, 1968, p. 36.
14. Schlesinger, *Robert Kennedy and His Times*, p. 903; Newfield, *Robert Kennedy: A Memoir*, p. 204.
15. *New York Times*, February 3, 1968, p. 1. There were widespread news accounts of Thieu's forces summarily executing prisoners and looting "liberated" areas; American television showed Thieu's troops rummaging through the pockets of dead bodies.
16. Video, Episode 7, "Tet: 1968," *Vietnam: A Television History*, WGBH, Boston. *New York Times*, February 7, 1968, p. 14. When the battle for Hue ended, evidence was uncovered that the N.L.F. had carried out hundreds of executions. There is a debate among scholars over the true number of victims. See Gareth Porter, "The 'Hue Massacre,'" *Indochina Chronicle*, June 24, 1974, p. 33. See also David Hunt, "Remembering the Tet Offensive," in Gettleman, *Vietnam and America*, pp. 359–77. The Saigon government sent its own assassination teams into Hue when it regained control of the city to root out N.L.F. sympathizers who had exposed themselves during the occupation. See Karnow, *Vietnam: A History*, p. 531.
17. Spector, *After Tet*, p. 319.
18. Ibid., p. 282.
19. Kolko, *Anatomy of a War*, pp. 328–29.
20. Buzzanco, *Masters of War*, p. 335.
21. Spector, *After Tet*, p. 105.
22. Address by Senator Robert F. Kennedy, Book and Author Luncheon, February 8, 1968, Chicago, Illinois. Adam Walinsky Papers, Box 19, File: Foreign Policy, Vietnam, 2/1/1968–2/18/1968, JFKL.
23. An ABC cameraman also filmed the prisoner being handed over to General Loan, but stopped filming at the moment Loan drew his pistol in fear of Loan's retaliation. Kaiser, *1968 in America*, p. 69.
24. Ibid., p. 166, fn.
25. Ibid., p. 170.
26. Assistant Secretary of State for Congressional Relations William B. Macomber, Jr. to Robert Kennedy, May 31, 1968, RFK Papers, SC-SF, Box 24, File: Foreign Affairs, Vietnam 6/1/1968–7/2/1968; Memorandum to Robert Kennedy, February 13, 1968, RFK Papers, PCP, Research Division, Box 53, File: Foreign Policy, Vietnam, 2/1968–6/1968, JFKL.
27. Memorandum, Director of Central Intelligence Richard Helms to White House Press Secretary George Christian, February 9, 1968, Marvin Watson Papers, Box 32, File: Vietnam, LBJL. The White House earlier had been concerned that Loan would use his police power to disrupt the September 3, 1967, elections which were essential for the Administration's portrayal of the Saigon regime as a fledgling democracy.

28. Situation Report in Viet-Nam, August 2, 1967, NSFCFVN, Box 103, File: Vietnam, Situation Room Reports to the President, 6/67–8/31/67, LBJL.

29. Chairman of the Joint Chiefs of Staff General Earle G. Wheeler to Representative Henry S. Reuss (Democrat of Wisconsin), February 3, 1968, NSFCFVN, Box 102, File: Congressional Attitudes and Statements, 12/67–3/68, LBJL.

30. Meeting of the National Security Council, February 7, 1968, TJMN, Box 2, LBJL. No one present at this N.S.C. meeting chose to question Loan's credibility or judgment when Wheeler mentioned his name. It was the only time Wheeler brought up Loan during a meeting with the National Security Council. I reached this conclusion based on examining the files of Tom Johnson's Meeting Notes (TJMN), Boxes 1–4.

31. Telegram, Gaylee Thorness to Robert Kennedy, February 21, 1968, RFK Papers, SC-SF, Box 56, File: To Be Filed, 2/1968, JFKL.

32. *New York Times*, February 7, 1968, p. 15.

33. Address by Senator Robert F. Kennedy, Book and Author Luncheon, Chicago, Illinois, February 8, 1968, Adam Walinsky Papers, Box 19, JFKL.

34. Newfield, *Robert Kennedy: A Memoir*, p. 204.

35. Arthur Schlesinger to Robert Kennedy, February 1, 1968 (with attachment), RFK Papers, SC-PF, Box 11, File: Schlesinger, Arthur 1/1968–5/1968, JFKL.

36. Daniel and Philip Berrigan were already well-known Catholic priest antiwar activists.

37. Thich Nhat Hanh, *Vietnam: Lotus in a Sea of Fire*, p. 108.

38. The V.V.A.W. asked Kennedy for comments and suggestions on a portfolio of advertisements, programs, and documentaries the group was planning. RFK Papers, SC-SF, Box 22, File: Foreign Affairs, Vietnam, 2/20/68, JFKL. Adam Walinsky Papers, Box 19, File: Foreign Policy, Vietnam, JFKL. The Jeanette Rankin Brigade (a sizable group of women peace demonstrators who were barred from protesting on the steps of the Congress) also sent their antiwar materials to Kennedy.

39. My estimate is that Kennedy's mail from Vietnam ran about twenty-to-one against the war. RFK Papers, SC-SF, Boxes 23, 24, Files: Foreign Affairs, Vietnam, JFKL.

40. Army Medical Officer Michael Orr to Robert Kennedy, March 22, RFK Papers, PCP, Speechwriters' Division, Box 1, File: Correspondence, Servicemen Vietnam, JFKL. Enclosed with his letter to Kennedy were his Vietnam Service Medal, National Defense Service Medal, Republic of Vietnam Campaign Medal, Good Conduct Medal, Combat Medical Badge, his Sharpshooter citation, and his Letter of Commendation.

41. Ibid.

42. Richard L. Klingenhogen to Robert Kennedy, March 13, 1968, RFK Papers, SC-SF, Box 4, File: Foreign Affairs, Vietnam, 5/1/1968–5/8/1968, JFKL.

43. Sergeant (S.P. 4) Gabriel C. Mannheim to Robert Kennedy, February 4, 1968, RFK Papers, SC-SF, Box 24, File: Foreign Affairs, Vietnam, 5/1/1968–5/8/1968, JFKL.

44. Warrant Officer Dwight Arthur Dedrick to Douglas Dedrick, January 24, 1968, forwarded to Robert Kennedy, RFK Papers, SC-SF, Box 22, File: Foreign Affairs: Vietnam, 3/5/1968–3/7/1968, JFKL.

45. Robert Kennedy to Captain Samuel R. Bird, February 26, 1968, RFK Papers, SC-PF, Box 2, File: B: 1968, JFKL.

46. "Our brave young men dying in the swamps of Southeast Asia," Kennedy remarked in a subsequent speech. "Which of them might have cured cancer? Which of them might have played in a World Series or given us the gift of laughter from the stage or helped build a bridge or a university? Which of them would have taught a child to read?" Quoted in Dooley, *Robert Kennedy: The Final Years*, p. 108.

47. *New York Times*, February 2, 1968, p. 13.

48. *New York Times*, February 7, 1968, p. 15.

49. Buzzanco, *Masters of War*, 327. Schandler, *Lyndon Johnson and Vietnam*, pp. 210–12.

50. J. William Fulbright, Senate Foreign Relations Committee, to Secretary of Defense Robert McNamara, February 9, 1968, NSFCFVN, Box 102, File: Congressional Attitudes & Statements, 12/67–3/68. LBJL.

51. They would have their chance to grill Secretary of State Dean Rusk in two days of televised hearings in mid-March.

52. Notes of the President's Breakfast with Congressional Leaders (sanitized), January 31, 1968, TJMN, Box 2, LBJL. On January 23, 1968, the North Koreans seized the American intelligence ship U.S.S. *Pueblo*, and held its crew. Negotiations for the crew's release continued throughout 1968.

53. Ibid.

54. Notes of the President's Meeting with Senior Foreign Policy Advisers, February 6, 1968, TJMN, Box 2, LBJL.

55. Notes of the President's Breakfast with Congressional Leaders, January 31, 1968, TJMN, Box 2, LBJL.

56. TJMN, January 23, 24, 1968, Box 2, LBJL.

57. Notes of the President's Meeting with Congressional Leaders and Foreign Policy Advisers, January 31, 1968, TJMN, Box 2, LBJL.

58. Notes of the Tuesday Luncheon, February 6, 1968, TJMN, Box 2, LBJL.

59. Buzzanco, *Masters of War*, pp. 311–40; and Gardner, *Pay Any Price*, pp. 409–30.

60. President Johnson's news conference, February 2, 1968, excerpted in the *New York Times*, February 3, 1968, p. 8.

61. Summary of President's Breakfast with the Boys on the Carrier Constellation, February 18, 1968, TJMN, Box 2, LBJL.

62. Notes of the President's Meeting with the Joint Chiefs of Staff, February 9, 1968, TJMN, Box 2, LBJL.

63. Notes of the President's Meeting with Senior Foreign Policy Advisers, February 11, 1968, TJMN, Box 2, LBJL.

64. Notes of the President's Meeting with Senior Foreign Affairs Advisory Council, February 10, 1968, TJMN, Box 2, LBJL.

65. Robert McNamara's annual report to Congress, February 1, 1968, excerpted in the *New York Times*, February 2, 1968, p. 16.

66. Notes of the President's Meeting with the Joint Chiefs of Staff, February 9, 1968, TJMN, Box 2, LBJL.

67. Notes of the President's Meeting to Discuss General Wheeler's Trip to Vietnam, February 28, 1968, TJMN, Box 2, LBJL. In fact, the desertion rate in 1968 for the South Vietnamese armed forces averaged more than 10,000 a month, reaching a peak of 15,060 in October. Spector, *After Tet*, p. 107.

68. Notes of the President's Meeting to Discuss General Wheeler's Trip to Vietnam, February 28, 1968, TJMN, Box 2, LBJL.

69. Ibid.

70. Notes of the President's Meeting with the Senior Foreign Affairs Advisory Council, in the Mansion, February 10, 1968, TJMN, Box 2, LBJL.

71. Notes of the Democratic Party Leadership Breakfast, February 6, 1968, TJMN, Box 2, LBJL. During this exchange between President Johnson and Senator Byrd, Byrd insisted that he did not agree that the intelligence was good.

72. Lloyd Gardner examines the conflicts between Johnson's military and civilian advisers regarding these changes in bombing policy as well as the troop request in *Pay Any Price*, pp. 409–83.

73. Gardner, *Pay Any Price*, pp. 409–32.

74. Robert Buzzanco argues that one of General Wheeler's principal motivations after Tet was to make bold proposals that would shift the burden of losing the war on to the civilian leadership. *Masters of War*, pp. 316, 325, 330–31.

75. Gardner, *Pay Any Price*, pp. 433–60.

76. Quoted in Bernstein, *Guns or Butter*, p. 478.

77. Braestrup, *Big Story*; Lewy, *America in Vietnam*; Summers, *On Strategy*; Lomperis, *The War Everyone Lost—and Won*; Bergerud, *Dynamics of Defeat*.

Chapter 6

1. Adam Walinsky and Richard N. Goodwin coauthored the speech.

2. Tomasky, *Left for Dead*; Isserman, "Michael Harrington and the Vietnam War."

3. "Bobby Wants You," Progressive Labor Party Pamphlet, September 1967, Hoover Institution Archives, New Left Collection, Box 57, File: New Left Draft Resistance, Stanford University.

4. James C. Scott argues that "many radical attacks originate in critiques within the hegemony [of dominant symbols] . . . To launch an attack in these terms is to, in effect, call upon the elite to take its own rhetoric seriously. Not only is such an attack a legitimate critique by definition, but it always threatens to appeal to sincere members of the elite in a way that an attack from outside their values could not." Scott, *Domination*, pp. 105–6.

5. This notion that Kennedy's disagreement with Johnson in 1967 and 1968 was primarily tactical is still a commonly held misconception. For example, in an issue of the *New York Review of Books* published some thirty years later, Russell Baker, the former columnist for the *New York Times*, writes that Kennedy "made some speeches disagreeing with the Vietnam policy, but his own thinking on Vietnam was still hawkish. The nub of it was that instead of bombing, we should be using counterinsurgency forces." *New York Review of Books*, vol. 44, no. 16 (October 23, 1997), p. 6.

6. Witcover, *85 Days*, p. 39.

7. Palermo, "Johnson Administration Responds," pp. 49–73.

8. Guthman and Allen, *RFK: Collected Speeches*, p. 306.

9. Newfield, *Robert Kennedy: A Memoir*, p. 205.

10. Ibid.

11. Guthman and Allen, *RFK: Collected Speeches*, pp. 306–7.

12. Text of Remarks by Senator Robert F. Kennedy on Vietnam, Senate Floor, March 2, 1967, Adam Walinsky Papers, Box 35, File: Speeches, Draft, 3/2/1967 (Vietnam), #8, JFKL.

13. The Merchandise Mart was an important site for commercial wholesalers and is one of the largest buildings in the United States. *New York Times*, August 30, 1996, p. A21.

14. Giglio, *Presidency of John F. Kennedy*, pp. 18–19. Biles, *Richard J. Daley*.

15. Guthman and Allen, *RFK: Collected Speeches*, p. 307.

16. Vanden Heuvel and Gwirtzman, *On His Own*, p. 296.

17. Quoted in ibid, p. 296.

18. *Washington Post*, February 9, 1968, pp. A1, A2, A10; *Chicago Tribune*, February 9, 1968, pp. 1, 5, 6; February 10, 1968, pp. 3, 7; *New York Times*, February 9, 1968, p. 1, 12, 14.

19. Address by Senator Robert F. Kennedy, Book and Author Luncheon, Ambassador East Hotel, Chicago, Illinois, February 8, 1968, Adam Walinsky Papers, Box 19, File: Foreign Policy, Vietnam, 2/1/1968–2/18/1968, JFKL.

20. Ibid.

21. Ibid.

22. President Kennedy in an interview with Walter Cronkite in early September 1963 said: "We can help them, we can give them equipment, we can send our men . . . as advisers, but they have to win it—the people of Vietnam—against the Communists." Giglio, *Presidency of John F. Kennedy*, p. 251.

23. Address by Senator Robert F. Kennedy, Book and Author Luncheon, February 8, 1968, Chicago, Illinois.

24. Ambassador Ellsworth Bunker to Secretary of State Dean Rusk, January 28, 1968, cables 17179 and 17180, NSFCFVN, Box 102, File: Congressional Attitudes and Statements, LBJL.

25. Address by Robert F. Kennedy, Book and Author Luncheon, February 8, 1968, Chicago, Illinois.

26. In the campaign edition of *To Seek A Newer World*, Kennedy elaborated on his own contribution to the Vietnam tragedy. "I am willing to bear my share of the responsibility," he wrote, "before history and before my fellow citizens," because "past error is no excuse for its own perpetuation." He quoted the *Antigone* of Sophocles: "All men make mistakes, but a good man yields when he knows his course is wrong, and repairs the evil." Kennedy, as late as 1971, had been "the only major official in either Democratic administration who admitted publicly to being wrong about Vietnam." Schlesinger, *Robert Kennedy and His Times*, p. 832.

27. Address by Senator Robert Kennedy, Book and Author Luncheon, Chicago, Illinois, February 8, 1968.

28. Joseph Alsop never wavered from the Administration's line on Vietnam, and he accepted General William Westmoreland's notion that Tet was analogous to the Battle of the Bulge in World War II, a desperation offensive that exhausted the enemy's forces. Joseph Alsop, "Kennedy's Viet Defeatism Contradicts Facts of War," *Washington Post*, March 27, 1968, n.p., RFK Papers, PCP, Research Division, Box 56, File: Kennedy, Robert F., Newsclips 1/1968–3/1968, JFKL.

29. Quoted in Schlesinger, *Robert Kennedy and His Times*, p. 905. Yoder, *Joe Alsop's Cold War*.

30. Quoted by Larry Berman, "The Tet Offensive," excerpt from *Lyndon Johnson's War*, in Rotter, *Light at the End*, p. 152.

31. For an in-depth study of the personal and political rivalry between Kennedy and Johnson (with the accent on the personal), see Shesol, *Mutual Contempt*.

32. Presidential Aide Fred Panzer to President Lyndon Johnson, February 13, 1968, Marvin Watson Papers, Box 32, File: Vietnam, LBJL.

33. Marvin Watson Papers, Box 32, File: Vietnam, LBJL. The article was from the *New York Times*, February 19, 1962.

34. In Lyndon Johnson's memoirs, *The Vantage Point*, he is loath to admit any mistakes in his Vietnam policies. See pages 232–69, 365–424, and 493–531.

35. Associated Press wire service, February 19, 1968, Marvin Watson Papers, Box 32, File: Vietnam, LBJL.
36. Memorandum, Director of Central Intelligence Richard Helms to White House Press Secretary George Christian, February 9, 1968, Marvin Watson Papers, Box 32, File: Vietnam, LBJL.
37. Ibid.
38. *Congressional Record: Proceedings and Debates of the 90th Congress, Second Session,* "Vietnam," February 8, 1968, vol. 114, no. 19. Senator Clark called Kennedy's address "eloquent, cogent, incisive" and of "great moment." Clark had earlier read into the *Record* Kennedy's March 2, 1967, speech as well as excerpts concerning Vietnam from *To Seek A Newer World.*
39. Senator J. William Fulbright to Senator Robert Kennedy, February 10, 1968, RFK Papers, SC-SF, Box 22, File: Foreign Affairs, Vietnam, 2/7/1968–2/12/1968, JFKL.
40. Vietnam Veterans Against the War, Vice-President Executive Committee Carl Rogers to Jeff Greenfield, February 13, 1968, RFK Papers, SC-SF, Box 22, File: Foreign Affairs, Vietnam, 2/17/1968–2/19/1968, JFKL.
41. RFK Papers, SC-SF, SC-PF, Adam Walinsky Papers, JFKL.
42. United States Navy Commander Jack L. Godfrey to Senator Robert Kennedy, February 19, 1968, RFK Papers, SC-SF, Box 22, File: Foreign Affairs, Vietnam, 2/26/1968–2/29/1968, JFKL.
43. Corporal James J. Davies, U.S. Marine Corps, 3rd Battalion, 1st Marines, to Senator Robert Kennedy, February 22, 1968, RFK Papers, SC-SF, Box 22, File: Foreign Affairs, Vietnam, 3/1/1968–3/4/1968, JFKL.
44. Private First Class W. Gafforio to Senator Robert Kennedy, February 16, 1968, ibid., File: Foreign Affairs, Vietnam, 3/8/1968–3/11/1968, JFKL.
45. U.S. Army Specialist 5 John K. Allan to Robert Kennedy, February 23, 1968, Adam Walinsky Papers, Box 19, File: Foreign Policy, Vietnam, 2/21/1968–2/29/1968, JFKL.
46. For example, shortly after Tet, Johnson referred to antiwar protesters in a speech to naval personnel as "hippie and beatnik types . . . zoot suiters and appeasers and isolationists." They were "neurotics," Johnson said, who deserved only pity. Summary of President's Breakfast with the Boys on Carrier Constellation, Sunday, February 18, 1968, TJMN, Box 2, LBJL.
47. Address by Senator Robert Kennedy, Book and Author Luncheon, Chicago, Illinois, February 8, 1968.
48. White, *Making of the President 1968.*
49. Walter Cronkite, C.B.S. News Correspondent, transcript, "Report From Vietnam," Tuesday, February 27, 1968, RFK Papers, SC-SF, Box 23, File: Foreign Affairs: Vietnam, 3/20/1968–3/31/1968, JFKL.
50. According to White House Press Secretary George Christian, Cronkite's report caused "shock waves" to "roll through the Government"; by early March, John-

son's approval rating on his handling of the war had gone from 40 to 26 percent. Bernstein, *Guns or Butter*, pp. 476–77.

51. Ibid.
52. Jack Valenti to Marvin Watson, n.d., ca. February 28, 1968, Marvin Watson Papers, Box 31, File: Jack Valenti, LBJL.
53. United Press International wire service, February 10, 1968, Records of the Democratic National Committee, Series II, Box 121, File: Others on Kennedy Comments, LBJL.
54. "The Torment in the Land," An Address by Senator Frank Church, Member of the Foreign Relations Committee, February 21, 1968, Drew Pearson Papers, Box 6301, File: Vietnam, 1968, LBJL. Said Church: "Year in, year out, the brutal drama penetrates every home until burning villages, screaming children and flowing blood become a routine part of the typical family scene."
55. Appy, *Working-Class War*.

Chapter 7

1. Goodwin, *Remembering America*, pp. 518–522.
2. Dooley, *Robert Kennedy: The Final Years*, p. 113.
3. Joseph Dolan to Robert Kennedy, February 9, 1968, Joseph Dolan Papers, Box 1, File: Memoranda 2/2/1968–2/10/1968, JFKL.
4. Joseph Dolan Papers, Box 1, selected files: Memoranda, 1/1968 to 3/1968, JFKL.
5. Joseph Dolan to Robert Kennedy, March 10, 1s968, Joseph Dolan Papers, Box 1, File: Memoranda 3/1/1968–3/20/1968, JFKL. (Emphasis added.)
6. John P. Roche to President Lyndon Johnson, March 8, 1968 (eyes only), Marvin Watson Papers, Box 32, File: Vietnam, LBJL.
7. President Lyndon Johnson to Marvin Watson, March 8, 1968, 8:30 P.M., ibid.
8. Texas Governor John Connally to President Lyndon Johnson, March 15, 1968, 8:30 P.M., Marvin Watson Papers, Box 25, File: Kennedy, Robert F., LBJL.
9. William Connell to John Criswell (D.N.C.), Jim Rowe, Marvin Watson, March 11, 1968, ibid.
10. Conversation Between Marvin Watson and William White, Friday, March 15, 1968, 5:45 P.M., ibid.
11. Dooley, *Robert Kennedy: The Final Years*, p. 118.
12. United Press International, March 9, 1968, The Records of the Democratic National Committee, Series II, Box 120, File: Kennedy on McCarthy, LBJL.
13. *Time* magazine, vol. 91, no. 12 (March 22, 1968), p. 15.
14. Associated Press, "RFK Denounces Attacks on McCarthy's Loyalty," March 9, 1968, Marvin Watson Papers, Box 25, File: Kennedy, Robert F., LBJL.

15. John Roche to Marvin Watson, March 13, 1968 (eyes only), Marvin Watson Papers, Box 29, File: Roche, John Memos, LBJL. (Original emphasis.)
16. César Chávez interview by Dennis O'Brien, Delano, California, January 28, 1970, OH-RFK, JFKL.
17. *Time* magazine, vol. 91, no. 12 (March 22, 1968), p. 15.
18. Ibid.
19. Marvin Watson Papers, Box 26, File: Labor Bloc, LBJL.
20. Memorandum for the President, New Hampshire Analysis, Fred Panzer to Lyndon Johnson, March 13, 1968, 9:00 P.M., Marvin Watson Papers, Box 28, File: Panzer, Fred, Memos, LBJL.
21. Arthur Schlesinger, Jr. to Robert Kennedy, March 13, 1968, RFK Papers, SC-PF, Box 11, File: Schlesinger, Arthur, 1/1968–5/1968, JFKL.
22. *New York Times*, March 18, 1968, p. 50.
23. John Roche to President Lyndon Johnson, March 14, 1968 (eyes only), Marvin Watson Papers, Box 29, File: Roche, John Memos, LBJL.
24. Ibid.
25. Senator George McGovern, interview by Larry Hackman, July 16, 1970, OH-RFK, JFKL.
26. Witcover, *85 Days*, pp. 73–79.
27. Transcript of Telephone Conversation Between DeVier Pierson at the White House and Ted Sorensen at Senator Robert F. Kennedy's Office, Thursday, March 14, 1968, 6:15 P.M., WHFN, Box 6, File: Kennedy, Robert F., LBJL.
28. Memorandum of Conference with Senator Robert Kennedy and Theodore C. Sorensen, written by Secretary of Defense Clark Clifford, March 14, 1968, ibid.
29. Ibid.
30. Ibid.
31. Ibid.
32. Associated Press, March 19, 1968, ibid.
33. Tom Johnson to President Lyndon Johnson (through Jim Jones), Sunday, March 17, 1968 (confidential), received by the LBJ Ranch CommCenter 2:06 P.M., text of bulletin carried on C.B.S. News, ibid.
34. Tom Johnson to Jim Jones, March 16, 1968, received by the LBJ Ranch CommCenter 6:33 P.M. (secret), ibid.
35. *New York Times*, March 18, 1968, p. 50. Tom Johnson to Jim Jones, March 16, 1968, received by the LBJ Ranch CommCenter 6:33 P.M. (secret), WHFN, Box 6, File: Kennedy, Robert F., LBJL.
36. Notes of the President's Meeting with Senior Foreign Policy Advisers, March 4, 1968, 5:33 P.M., TJMN, Box 2, LBJL.
37. Tom Johnson to Jim Jones, March 16, 1968 (secret), received LBJ Ranch CommCen., 6:00 P.M., Marvin Watson Papers, Box 25, File: Kennedy, Robert F., LBJL.

38. In February 1966, Undersecretary of State George Ball had surprised Kennedy with the contradictory nature of his private and public views of the war; Clifford seems to have done the same thing in March 1968.

39. White House Counsel DeVier Pierson to President Lyndon Johnson, March 14, 1968, 6:35 P.M., WHFN, Box 6, File: Kennedy, Robert F., LBJL.

40. Transcript of Telephone Conversation Between DeVier Pierson at the White House and Ted Sorensen at Senator Robert F. Kennedy's Office, Thursday, March 14, 1968, 6:15 P.M., WHFN, Box 6, File: Kennedy, Robert F., LBJL.

41. Ibid.

42. Theodore Sorensen to Lyndon Johnson, March 16, 1968, ibid.

43. Statement by Senator Robert F. Kennedy, March 17, 1968, William Vanden Heuvel Papers, Box 3, File: Press Releases, 6/7/1967–3/17/1968, JFKL.

44. Ibid.

45. Memorandum of Conference with Senator Robert Kennedy and Theodore C. Sorensen, written by Secretary of Defense Clark Clifford, March 14, 1968, WHFN, Box 6, File: Kennedy, Robert F., LBJL.

46. Ibid.

47. Statement by Senator Robert F. Kennedy, March 17, 1968, William Vanden Heuvel Papers, JFKL.

48. John Stewart to Robert Kennedy, March 9, 1968, RFK Papers, SC-PF, Box 10, File: S: 1967, JFKL.

49. Robert Kennedy to John Stewart, March 13, 1968, ibid.

50. Dick Schaap to Robert Kennedy, March 14, 1968, William Vanden Heuvel Papers, Box 1, File: Campaign, 1968 General; Telegram, James Whittaker to Robert Kennedy, March 13, 1968, RFK Papers, PCP, BB, Box 12, File: North Dakota Correspondence, JFKL.

51. Joseph Dolan to Robert Kennedy, March 8, 1968, Joseph Dolan Papers, Box 1, File: Memoranda 2/14/1968–2/29/1968, JFKL.

52. Robert Kennedy to Anthony Lewis, March 13, 1968, RFK Papers, SC-PF, Box 6, File: L: 1965, Lewis-Lo, JFKL.

53. Telegram, Robert Kennedy to Speaker of the House of Representatives John McCormack, March 15, 1968, John McCormack Papers, Box 130, File: 7, Boston University Archives.

54. Goodwin insisted on finsihing what he had begun in the Wisconsin primary for McCarthy. A McCarthy victory in Wisconsin would help Kennedy politically in any case. He assisted both campaigns until the April 13 election, and then worked soley for Kennedy. (Kennedy's name was not on the ballot in Wisconsin.) Goodwin, *Remembering America*, pp. 518–522.

55. Conversation with Richard Goodwin on April 28, 1968, Re: Edward Kennedy's trip to Green Bay, Wisconsin, on March 15, 1968, William Vanden Heuvel Papers, Box 1, File: Campaign, 1968 General, JFKL.

56. Teletype from Lloyd Hackler to Jim Jones at Ranch, March 16, 1968, re: Press Conference of Senator Eugene McCarthy, WHCF, Box 77, File: Election Campaign 1968, LBJL.

57. Conversation between W. Marvin Watson and Governor Harold Hughes, Friday, March 15, 1968, 10:49 A.M.

58. Notes of telephone conversation, March 14, 1968, 3:00 P.M., WHFN, Box 6, File: Kennedy, Robert F., 1968 Campaign, LBJL.

59. Fred Panzer to Lyndon Johnson, March 15, 1968, 4:00 P.M., WHCF, Box 77, Election Campaign 1968, LBJL. The hawks favored Johnson over Kennedy, 50 percent to 36 percent (prowar voters were estimated to comprise 61 percent of the adult population). Among doves (estimated at only 23 percent of the adult population), Kennedy won handily, 57 percent to Johnson's 27 percent.

60. Kearns, *Lyndon Johnson and the American Dream*, p. 343.

61. Statement by Senator Robert Kennedy announcing candidacy, March 16, 1968, 10:00 A.M., and transcript of subsequent press conference, WHCF, Box 77, File: Election Campaign 1968, LBJL.

62. Ibid.

63. Ibid.

64. Ibid.

65. Ibid.

66. Senator Eugene McCarthy, transcript of press conference, March 16, 1968, ibid.

67. Notes, Vice President Hubert Humphrey, Democratic Meeting, French Lick, Indiana, March 16, 1968, Marvin Watson Papers, Box 31, File: Vice President, LBJL.

68. Ibid.

69. For the President, through Barefoot Sanders, Charles D. Roche, March 19, 1968, Harold Barefoot Sanders Papers, Box 27, File: Political Canvass, March 1968, LBJL.

70. Memorandum for Barefoot Sanders, Sherwin Markman, March 18, 1968, ibid.

71. Ibid.

72. Memo, Night Reading, Fraser Barron to Robert Kennedy, April 11, 1968, RFK Papers, PCP, Youth/Student Division, Box 5, File: Grassroots Activities, JFKL.

73. Memorandum to Barefoot Sanders, Bill Blackburn, March 18, 1968, Harold Barefoot Sanders Papers, Box 27, File: Political Canvass, March 1968, LBJL.

74. Cloward and Piven, *Politics of Turmoil*, pp. 272–77.

75. Congressional Contacts, Barefoot Sanders, March 28, 1968, Barefoot Sanders Papers, Box 27, File: Political Canvass, March 1968, LBJL.

76. Ibid.

77. Ibid.

78. Congressional Contacts, Barefoot Sanders, March 19, 1968, ibid.
79. Memorandum for the President, John Gonella, March 20, 1968, ibid.
80. Ibid. The Democratic commentator was from South Carolina.
81. For the President, Barefoot Sanders, March 22, 1968, ibid.
82. For the President, Barefoot Sanders, March 20, 1968, Barefoot Sanders Papers, Box 17, File: Campaign 1968, LBJL.
83. "The Goal," Barefoot Sanders to Lyndon Johnson, March 25, 1968, Barefoot Sanders Papers, Box 17, File: Campaign 1968, LBJL.
84. Ibid.
85. Ibid.
86. Ibid.
87. For the President, Charles D. Roche, March 20, 1968, ibid.
88. Ibid.
89. Congressional Contacts, Barefoot Sanders, March 19, 1968, ibid.
90. Ibid.
91. Memorandum for Barefoot Sanders, Sherwin Markman, March 19, 1968, ibid.
92. For the President, Charles D. Roche, re: Conversations with Members, March 18, 1968, ibid.
93. Ibid.
94. Memorandum to Barefoot Sanders, Sherwin Markman, March 19, 1968, ibid.
95. Congressional Contacts, Barefoot Sanders, March 19, 1968, ibid.
96. Ibid.
97. For the President, Charles D. Roche, March 21, 1968, ibid.
98. For the President, Barefoot Sanders, March 22, 1968, ibid.
99. Ibid.
100. Ibid.
101. Press Release, Jesse Unruh, March 26, 1968, RFK Papers, PCP, Press Division, Box 15, File: California, JFKL.
102. *Washington Post*, March 22, 1968.
103. RFK Papers, PCP, BB, JFKL.
104. Notes of Meeting, EMK Office, Morning, March 16, 1968, Milton Gwirtzman Papers, Box 5, File: Memoranda, undated, JFKL.
105. Witcover, *85 Days*, p. 83.
106. *Pentagon Papers*, p. 591.
107. Schandler, *Lyndon Johnson and Vietnam*, p. 259.
108. McNamara, *In Retrospect*; Shapley, *Promise and Power*.
109. Kolko, *Anatomy of a War*, pp. 283–311; Bernstein, *Guns or Butter*, pp. 367–78; Gardner, *Pay Any Price*, pp. 410–14.
110. Schandler, *Lyndon Johnson and Vietnam*, p. 227.
111. Berman, *Lyndon Johnson's War*, p. 198.

112. President Lyndon Johnson meeting with the Joint Chiefs of Staff, March 26, 1968, TJMN, Box 3, LBJL.

113. *Washington Post*, March 31, 1968, RFK Papers, PCP, Press Division, Box 14, File: Polls, 1968, JFKL.

114. Governor John Connally to Lyndon Johnson (through George Christian), March 31, 1968, 4:35 P.M., LBJ Papers, Daily Diary Backup, Box 94, File: March 31, 1968, LBJL.

115. Text of the Remarks of the President to the Nation from the President's Oval Office, 9:00 P.M., EST, March 31, 1968, ibid.

116. Quoted in Schandler, *Lyndon Johnson and Vietnam*, p. 287.

117. Comments of Cabinet Members, Larry Temple, March 31, 1968, LBJ Papers, Daily Diary Backup, Box 94, File: March 31, 1968, LBJL.

118. Anderson, *The Movement and the Sixties*, pp. 190–91.

119. Press Conference Number 122 of the President of the United States, March 31, 1968, 11:00 P.M., ibid.

120. Schlesinger, *Robert Kennedy and His Times*, p. 932.

121. LBJ Papers, Daily Diary Backup, Box 94, File: March 31, 1968, LBJL

122. Telegram, Robert Kennedy to Lyndon Johnson, March 31, 1968, 11:43 P.M., RFK Papers, SC-PF, Box 23, File: White House Correspondence, JFKL.

123. *Evening Star*, Washington, D.C., April 1, 1968, RFK Papers, PCP, Research Division, Box 56, File: Newsclips, 4/1968, JFKL.

124. Quoted in Shesol, *Mutual Contempt*, p. 441.

125. Ibid., p. 442.

126. Memorandum of Conversation: The President, Senator Robert F. Kennedy, Theodore Sorensen, Charles Murphy, and W. W. Rostow, 10:00 A.M., April 3, 1968, WHFN, Box 6, File: Kennedy, Robert F. 1968 Campaign, LBJL.

127. Ibid.

128. Ibid.

129. Ibid.

130. Ibid.

131. Ibid.

132. Ibid.

133. Memorandum of Conversation, Wednesday, April 3, 1968, W. W. Rostow, Participants: The President; the Vice President; Charles Murphy; W. W. Rostow, WHFN, Box 6, File: Kennedy, Robert F. 1968 Campaign, LBJL.

134. Ibid.

135. Shesol, *Mutual Contempt*, p. 444.

136. Kenneth O'Donnell, interview by Paige Mulhorn, July 23, 1969, OH-RFK, JFKL.

137. Carter, *From George Wallace to Newt Gingrich*, p. 24.

138. Doris Kearns notes of interview by William Vanden Heuvel, n.d. (ca. late 1968), Milton Gwirtzman Papers, Box 8, File: Testimonials Re; Robert F. Kennedy, JFKL.

Chapter 8

1. *Report of the National Advisory Commission on Civil Disorders*, pp. 1–2.
2. Gardner, *Pay Any Price*, p. 439.
3. Robert Kennedy, "Announcement of Candidacy for President," in Guthman and Allen, *RFK: Collected Speeches*, p. 320.
4. "Conversation with Martin Luther King," March 25, 1968, Rabbinical Assembly, in Washington, *Testament of Hope*, appendix, p. 677.
5. Address by Senator Robert F. Kennedy, State Convention of Independent Order of Odd Fellows, Spring Valley, New York, August 18, 1965, *Congressional Record-Senate: Proceedings and Debates of the 89th Congress, First Session*, vol. 111, part 16, pp. 21492–93.
6. King, "A Christmas Sermon on Peace," December 24, 1967, *Testament of Hope*, p. 257.
7. Andrew Young to William Vanden Heuvel, May 14, 1969, William Vanden Heuvel Papers, Box 3, File: Tributes, JFKL.
8. Guthman, *RFK: Collected Speeches*, p. 200.
9. Charles Evers, *Have No Fear*, pp. 229–30. "Ever since Medgar had been killed," Charles later wrote, "Bobby had been my best friend in the world."
10. Telegram, Charles Evers to Robert Kennedy, May 8, 1968, RFK Papers, PCP, BB, Box 9, File: Mississippi Correspondence, JFKL.
11. Clarence Mitchell, Director, N.A.A.C.P. Washington Bureau, to Robert Kennedy, June 14, 1965, RFK Papers, SC-PF, Box 7, File: M: Meany-Moorhead, JFKL.
12. Jerry Bruno Papers, Box 8, Files: Senate Files, Trips, 3/18/66–3/19/66, Alabama, Mississippi; Senate Papers, 1966 Correspondence, JFKL.
13. RFK Papers, PCP, Research Division, Box 47, File: Civil Rights 1/1968–3/1968, JFKL.
14. Robert F. Kennedy, "Suppose God Is Black," *Look* magazine, vol. 30, no. 17 (August 23, 1966), pp. 45–48.
15. Ibid.
16. Guthman and Allen, *RFK: Collected Speeches*, p. 200.
17. Hampton and Fayer, *Voices of Freedom*, pp. 452–53.
18. Bloom, *Class, Race, and the Civil Rights Movement*, p. 201; Horne, *Fire This Time*; *Los Angeles Times*, August 13–18, 1965.
19. *Los Angeles Times*, August 18, 1965, p. 17.

20. Andrew Young, *An Easy Burden*, p. 380.

21. *Los Angeles Times*, August 20, 1965, pp. 1, 3. Yorty even opposed Governor Edmund G. Brown's appointment of a commission to study the underlying social causes of the riot.

22. *Los Angeles Times*, August 21, 1965, p. 4.

23. *Los Angeles Times*, August 15, 1968, p. 24.

24. Address By Senator Robert F. Kennedy, State Convention of Independent Order of Odd Fellows, Spring Valley, New York, August 18, 1965, *Congressional Record-Senate, 89th Congress, First Session*, vol. 111, part 16, pp. 21491–92. "The rate of Negro unemployment is twice the white rate," Kennedy said.

25. Ibid.

26. The Kerner Commission also confirmed Kennedy's assessment of Watts and the other uprisings.

27. *Congressional Record: Proceedings and Debates of the 89th Congress, first session, Index*, vol. 111, part 22, p. 592; second session, *Index*, p. 513; 90th Congress, first session, *Index*, p. 751.

28. Guthman and Allen, *RFK: Collected Speeches*, p. 177.

29. *Congressional Record-Senate, 89th Congress, Second Session*, October 3, 1966, vol. 112, part 18, pp. 24794–96. Kennedy cited Labor Department statistics which estimated that 75 percent of black teenagers were unemployed in some areas, and reports that out of 950,000 new jobs created for teenagers the previous year, only about 3 percent went to blacks.

30. *Congressional Record, 89th Congress, second session, Index*, p. 513; *90th Congress, first session. Index*, p. 751.

31. Guthman and Allen, *RFK: Collected Speeches*, pp. 185–86.

32. Text of Remarks of Senator Robert F. Kennedy, Saturday, December 10, 1966, Bedford Stuyvesant, *Congressional Record-Senate, 90th Congress, First Session*, January 23, 1967, vol. 113, part 1, pp. 1209–11.

33. Over the next two years, a community hall was rebuilt, some 300 homes were renovated, and I.B.M. was in the process of creating 300 jobs. Eighty banks and insurance companies agreed to offer conventional-rate mortgages guaranteed by the Federal Housing Administration. *Newsweek* described the project as "the most sweeping and comprehensive rehabilitation effort ever brought to bear on a single American community." *Newsweek* magazine, May 7, 1968, quoted in Dooley, *Robert Kennedy: The Final Years*, p. 32.

34. McAdam, *Political Process*, p. 222.

35. Bloom, *Class, Race, and the Civil Rights Movement*, p. 200.

36. McAdam, *Political Process*, p. 222.

37. President Johnson's news conference, February 2, 1968, excerpted in the *New York Times*, February 3, 1968, p. 8.

38. Notes of the President's Meeting with the Senior Foreign Affairs Advisory Council, February 10, 1968, 3:17 P.M., TJMN, Box 2, LBJL.

39. "RFK Urges War Freeze, Billions to Erase Slums," August 7, 1967, newsclip, *FBI File on Robert F. Kennedy* (microform).

40. Robert F. Kennedy, *To Seek a Newer World*, p. 46 fn. Kennedy's proposals in these two bills of 1967 were remarkably similar to the ideas of subsequent researchers. See Wilson, *Truly Disadvantaged*. Kennedy wished to "develop a system based on need, and not on artificial barriers of any kind."

41. Dooley, *Robert Kennedy: The Final Years*, p. 31.

42. Memo, May 15, 1968, RFK Papers, PCP, BB, Box 12, File: Oregon Background and Intelligence, 3/19/1968–5/19/1968, JFKL.

43. Edsall with Mary D. Edsall, *Chain Reaction*; Radosh, *Divided They Fall*; Aistrup, *Southern Strategy Revisited*; Brennan, *Turning Right in the Sixties*; Goldberg, *Barry Goldwater*; Berman, *America's Right Turn*; Phillips, *Emerging Republican Majority*; Dent, *Prodigal South*; Murphy and Gulliver, *Southern Strategy*; Kalk, "Wormley's Hotel Revisited."

44. Kalk, "Wormley's Hotel Revisited," pp. 88–90; Murphy and Gulliver, *The Southern Strategy*, pp. 5–20.

45. Robert F. Kennedy to Hodding Carter III, April 25, 1968. Kennedy referred to Seigenthaler as the Southern point man and wrote: "It is most encouraging to know that the Carters are on our side." RFK Papers, PCP, Box 9, File: Mississippi Correspondence, JFKL.

46. Carson, *In Struggle*, pp.215–28.

47. Evers, *Have No Fear*, p. 233.

48. Frederick C. Berger to Joseph Dolan, March 28, 1968, RFK Papers, PCP, BB, Box 9, File: Mississippi Correspondence, JFKL.

49. The classic study of the changing social and economic trends in the South is Key, *Southern Politics in State and Nation*; see also Dollard, *Caste and Class in a Southern Town*; Bloom, *Class, Race, and the Civil Rights Movement*; Scher, *Politics in the New South*; Applebome, *Dixie Rising*.

50. Memo, Ted McLaughlin, May 28, 1968, RFK Papers, PCP, BB, Box 16, File: Summary, 6/3/1968 Kentucky-Mississippi, JFKL.

51. Memo, April 27, 1968, RFK Papers, PCP, Box 9, File: Mississippi Background and Intelligence, JFKL. Carson, *In Struggle*, pp. 98–99, 123, 128, 139, 232.

52. Frederick C. Berger to Joseph Dolan, March 28, 1968, RFK Papers, PCP, BB, Box 9, File: Mississippi Correspondence, JFKL.

53. Bill Silver to William Vanden Heuvel, May 2, 1968, RFK Papers, PCP, BB, Box 2, File: Alabama Correspondence, JFKL. The memo went on: "The coalition of NAACP, FDP, students and labor which the Kennedys helped to create provid[ed] the Senator with his best chance of carrying Mississippi at the convention."

54. David Vann to Joseph Dolan, March 16, 1968, RFK Papers, PCP, BB, Box 2, File: Alabama Background and Intelligence, JFKL.

55. Governor Lurleen Wallace, the spousal caretaker of the governor's mansion who was battling cancer at the time, welcomed Kennedy to Alabama. "It is always a pleasure to have a distinguished United States Senator and Presidential candidate visit us here in the 'heart of Dixie,'" she wired Kennedy. Telegram, Governor Lurleen Wallace to Robert Kennedy, March 21, 1968, RFK Papers, PCP, BB, Box 2, File: Alabama Correspondence, JFKL.

56. Guthman and Allen, *RFK: Collected Speeches*, p. 334.

57. Telegram, William D. Smith, Alabama delegate from the 6th Congressional District, to Robert Kennedy, March 28, 1968, RFK Papers, PCP, BB, Box 2, Alabama Correspondence, JFKL.

58. King, *Where Do We Go From Here?*, pp. 152–53.

59. Ibid, p. 147.

60. Memorandum, Bill Geoghegan to Edward Kennedy, March 22, 1968, re: conversation with Conyer, RFK Papers, PCP, BB, Box 9, File: Michigan, Background and Intelligence, 3/18/1968–4/15/1968, JFKL.

61. Andrew Young to William Vanden Heuvel, May 14, 1969.

62. Memorandum, Bill Geoghegan to Edward Kennedy, re: conversation with Conyers.

63. Dooley, *Final Years*, p. 121.

64. Garrow, *Bearing The Cross*, pp. 576, 618.

65. Andrew Young to William Vanden Heuvel, May 14, 1969, William Vanden Heuvel Papers, Box 3, File: Tributes, JFKL. This quote closes with Young lamenting the two leaders' "common tragic destiny."

66. *Congressional Record-Senate, 89th Congress, Second Session*, October 3, 1966, vol. 112, part 18, pp. 24794–96.

67. King, *Where Do We Go From Here?*, p. 7.

68. Noer, "Martin Luther King, Jr. and the Cold War," p. 126.

69. Garrow, *The FBI and Martin Luther King, Jr*; O'Reilly, "*Racial Matters*"; O'Reilly, *Black Americans: The FBI Files*; Friedly and Gallen, *Martin Luther King, Jr.: The FBI File*; Churchill and Vander Wall, *Agents of Repression*; Pepper, *Orders To Kill*.

70. *FBI File on Robert F. Kennedy* (series 1–4, microform).

71. King, "Showdown for Nonviolence," *Testamnent of Hope*, p. 64.

72. King, *Where Do We Go From Here?*, p. 17.

73. Ibid., p. 132.

74. "Conversation with Martin Luther King," *Testament of Hope*, appendix, p. 678.

75. Ibid.

76. King, "The Drum Major Instinct," *Testament of Hope*, p. 264. The "poor white" had been put into a position, he wrote, "where through blindness and preju-

dice, he is forced to support his oppressors, and the only thing he has going for him is the false feeling that he is superior because his skin is white. And [he] can't hardly eat and make his ends meet week in and week out."

77. J. W. Coover, Special Assistant Office of Senator Robert F. Kennedy, June 10, 1968, RFK Papers, SC-SF, Box 6, File: Civil Rights 6/1968, JFKL.

78. Michael Harrington, *The Other America*.

79. Garrow, *Bearing The Cross*, pp. 601, 608.

80. Newfield, *Robert Kennedy: A Memoir*, pp. 259, 274; Schlesinger, *Robert Kennedy and His Times*, p. 966; Witcover, *85 Days*, p. 231. Another link between the Kennedy campaign and King's Poor People's March was George Wiley, the executive director of the National Welfare Rights Organization, who supported both efforts. Garrow, *Bearing The Cross*, p. 595; Schlesinger, *Robert Kennedy and His Times*, p. 966.

81. Harrington, *Toward a Democratic Left*, p. 96.

82. J. Edwin Stanfield, "In Memphis: Tragedy Unaverted," April 3, 1968, Supplement to Special Report of March 22, 1968, Southern Regional Council, RFK Papers, PCP, Research Division, Box 46, File: Cities: Civil Disorders, 1968, JFKL.

83. Garrow, *Bearing The Cross*, p. 611.

84. *Wall Street Journal*, April 3, 1968, quoted in Dooley, *Robert Kennedy: The Final Years*, p. 122.

85. King, "Remaining Awake Through a Great Revolution," *Testament of Hope*, p. 274.

86. Garrow, *Bearing The Cross*, pp. 595–96.

87. King, "I See the Promised Land," *Testament of Hope*, p. 285.

88. Ibid., p. 286

89. Senator Robert Kennedy's Schedule for Thursday, April 4, 1968, Jerry Bruno Papers, Box 12, File: 1968 Campaign Scheduling, 4/2/1968–4/15/1968, JFKL. Walter Sheridan and John Lewis helped arrange the rally.

90. T. E. Bishop to Cartha DeLoach, April 3, 1968, re: "John Treanor, Member of Senator Robert F. Kennedy's Campaign Staff," *FBI File on Robert F. Kennedy* (series 1–4, microform).

91. Robert F. Kennedy's remarks on the death of Martin Luther King, Jr., April 4, 1968, Indianapolis, Indiana, in Guthman and Allen, *RFK: Collected Speeches*, pp. 355–58; Audio Tape, *Selected Speeches*, Edwin Guthman and Richard Allen, eds., Tape Two (New York: Penguin-Highbridge Audio, 1993).

92. David Blyth to Dun Gifford, April 8, 1968, RFK Papers, PCP, BB, Box 13, File: Pennsylvania Correspondence, JFKL.

93. Coretta Scott King, *My Life with Martin Luther King, Jr.*, pp. 322, 338–39.

94. Teletype, Atlanta FBI Headquarters to J. Edgar Hoover, April 9, 1968, *FBI File on Robert F. Kennedy*. The names of the informants are censored in FBI doc-

uments. The FBI had previously tracked the activities of Kennedy's advance man in Indianapolis, John Treanor, who was arranging the Senator's appearances in some of the black communities. T. E. Bishop to Cartha DeLoach, April 3, 1968, re: "John Treanor, Member of Senator Robert F. Kennedy's Campaign Staff," ibid.

95. Copy of wire service article, February 6, 1967, ibid.

96. FBI Director J. Edgar Hoover to James Neagle, April 29, 1968, ibid.

97. Memorandum for the Record, July 15, 1967, WHCF, Box 77, File: Political Parties, LBJL.

98. The connection between the assassination of King and President Kennedy weighed on Kennedy's mind. He turned to his young aides after a long silence and said: "You know, that Harvey Lee Oswald, whatever his name is, set something loose in this country." Quoted in Guthman and Allen, *RFK: Collected Speeches*, p. 359.

99. Guthman and Allen, *RFK: Collected Speeches*, pp. 360–61.

100. Sargeant Curtis Gilleglen et al. to Robert Kennedy, April 6, 1968, RFK Papers, SC-SF, Box 24, File: Foreign Affairs, Vietnam, 5/9/1968, JFKL.

101. Telegram, the National Association of Colored Women's Clubs to Robert Kennedy, April 6, 1968, RFK Papers, SC-SF, Box 6, File: Civil Rights 5/1/1968–5/15/1968, JFKL.

102. Telegram, The Black Women's Boycott, New Haven, Connecticut to Robert Kennedy, April 12, 1968, RFK Papers, SC-SF, Box 6, File: Civil Rights, 6/1968, JFKL. Kennedy's office forwarded a copy of the telegram to the Justice Department with a request for action.

103. Quoted in Guthman and Allen, *RFK: Collected Speeches*, p. 362.

104. Branch, *Parting the Waters*, pp. 40–43.

105. LBJ Papers, Daily Diary, Box 15, File: April 1–15, 1968, LBJL.

106. Kaiser, *1968 In America*, pp. 146–47.

107. Ibid., pp. 147–48.

108. Robert F. Kennedy, *To Seek a Newer World*, pp. 39–43.

109. Robert Kennedy to Mrs. Lillian Horton, New Rochelle, New York, May 30, 1968, RFK Papers, PCP, Research Division, Box 46, File: Correspondence 5/28/1968–6/12/1968, JFKL.

Chapter 9

1. George Gallup, Gallup Report, "Kennedy, LBJ Show Equal Pull With Democrats," *Hartford Courant*, Hartford, Connecticut, RFK Papers, PCP, Press Division, Box 14, File: Polls, 1968, JFKL. The President, the poll estimated, received support from 45 percent of the nation's Democrats to Kennedy's 44 percent

2. Laurence Kraus to Adam Walinsky, March 20, 1968, RFK Papers, PCP, BB, Box 2, File: California Correspondence, 3/16/1968–4/15/1968, JFKL.

3. Memorandum for Edward Kennedy, Steven Smith, Theodore Sorensen, et al., March 25, 1968, RFK Papers, PCP, Youth and Student Division, Box 5, File: Memoranda to Campaign Headquarters, JFKL.

4. Witcover, *85 Days*, p. 110.

5. Ibid., pp. 122, 147, 203.

6. The unit rule, which Hubert Humphrey's supporters tried to impose in several states including Pennsylvania and Texas, required the state delegations, once committed to a candidate, to vote as a unit or not at all, thereby preventing alternative candidates from peeling off delegates at the convention. Blocking the unit rule wherever possible was one issue upon which Kennedy and McCarthy agreed fully.

7. Unger and Unger, *Turning Point: 1968*, p. 338.

8. Quoted in Kopkind, "The Liberal's Progress," *Thirty Years' War*, p. 97.

9. Powers, *Vietnam: The War at Home*, p. 285.

10. Richard Reeves, "The Making of a Candidate, 1968: The Kennedy Machine is Moving," *New York Times Magazine*, March 31, 1968.

11. Reeves's *New York Times Magazine* piece, and the Indianapolis *Star* and *News* (both owned by the conservative Pullium family publishing empire), offered similar descriptions of the Kennedy campaign, which were less than accurate. It was the opposite of the political game of "poor-mouthing," where candidates attempt to cultivate the underdog image to keep their supporters mobilized. The *New York Times* seldom gave Kennedy good press, which he found frustrating given the paper's reputation as a liberal mouthpiece.

12. Notes of Meeting-Edward Kennedy Office-Morning March 16, 1968, Milton Gwirtzman Papers, Box 5, File: Memoranda, Undated; Suggested Division of Responsibility, Milton Gwirtzman Papers, Box 7, File: Presidential Campaign 1968, JFKL. For example, Edward Kennedy was given the responsibility for contacting key Democratic officials in nonprimary states.

13. Arthur Schlesinger to RFK Campaign Headquarters, March 23, 1968, RFK Papers, SC-PF, Box 11, File: Arthur Schlesinger, 1/1968–5/1968, JFKL.

14. Statement by Senator Robert F. Kennedy, Alfred M. Landon Lecture Series, Kansas State University, Ahern Fieldhouse, Manhattan, Kansas, March 18, 1968, 10:00 A.M., RFK Papers, PCP, Speech Writers' Division, Box 5, File: Vietnam, JFKL.

15. Ibid.

16. Witcover, *85 Days*, pp. 117–18. Richard Goodwin was credited with the "darker impulses" line, and the negative press response led Kennedy to tone down the emotional appeals in subsequent speeches.

17. Mass mailing, Citizens for Kennedy, Philip Lilienthal, Peace Corps volunteer,

Ethiopia, 1967 (ca. April 1968), RFK Papers, PCP, Press Division, Box 16, File: Campaign Literature, Kennedy, Robert F., JFKL.

18. Paul Tsongas to Jeff Greenfield, April 3, 1968, RFK Papers, PCP, Speech Writers' Division, Box 3, File: Presidential Campaign: Resume and Job Inquiries, JFKL. Tsongas wrote this letter offering to volunteer for the campaign from St. Thomas, the Virgin Islands Peace Corps Training Center. He was inspired to help the campaign after attending a seminar conducted by Harris Wofford, a Kennedy friend and adviser who also later became a United States senator.

19. Memo, Kennedy Youth Action: History, Present and Future (ca. April 1968), RFK Papers, PCP, Youth and Student Division, Box 6, File: Purpose and Goals of Youth Student Division, JFKL. (Allard Lowenstein had been an organizer of Vietnam Summer, which itself was modeled on the Freedom Summer civil rights actions of 1964 in Mississippi, and involved thousands of student volunteers.)

20. Ibid. The memo also states: "It is also possible that a Kennedy volunteer, with experience, can work with the group in terms of solving its own needs." This is exactly what the campaign did with César Chávez's United Farm Workers in California.

21. Robert Scheer, "A Political Portrait of Robert Kennedy," *Ramparts*, February, 1967, pp. 11–16, and "Scheer Analyzes 'Presidential Mess'—Criticizes Everyone," *Communiqué for New Politics: Left-Out News* Berkeley, Calif., vol. 2, no. 11 (April 25, 1968); Hoover Institution Archives, New Left Collection, Box 57, File: New Left, Stanford University. Similar materials can be found in the Lawrence Kramer New Left Collection, Cornell University: Papers 1966–1972. Scheer's *Ramparts* piece appeared, coincidentally, the same month Kennedy met with Tom Hayden and Staughton Lynd.

22. Scheer, "A Political Portrait of Robert Kennedy," pp. 11–16.

23. "Bobby Wants You," Progressive Labor Party pamphlet, text of a forum held in San Francisco, September 22, 1967, entitled: "Kennedyism—The Liberal Offensive Against the Anti-War Movement," Allen Solganick and John Roemer. Hoover Institution Archives, New Left Collection, Box 57, File: New Left, Draft Resistance, Stanford University.

24. Quoted in Hayden, *Reunion*, p. 263.

25. Kopkind, "Waiting for Lefty," June 1, 1967, *Thirty Years' War*, p. 70.

26. Kopkind, "All Fool's Eve," April 5, 1968, *Thirty Years' War*, p. 112. Kopkind's pro-Kennedy sentiments later led Gore Vidal to pronounce Kopkind "Bobby-enthralled as of 1967." Gore Vidal review of *The Thirty Years' War* in *The Nation*, vol. 260, no. 23 (June 12, 1995). See the subsequent exchange between the author and Gore Vidal about this in *The Nation*, vol. 261, no. 3 (July 17/24, 1995), p. 74.

27. Kopkind, "The Cord Snaps," *Thirty Years' War*, p. 118.

28. Ibid., p. 71.

29. Hayden, *Reunion*, pp. 266–67.

30. Dowd, *Blues for America*, p. 148. These political strains included pacifists, middle-class reformers, "yippie" libertarians, anarchists, Socialists, Communists, antinuclear activists, and others. Dowd, a Cornell Economics professor who served on the Mobe's steering committee from the beginning, recalled how a "small but aggressive element" of Trotskyists from the Socialist Workers Party (S.W.P.), had maneuvered themselves on to the committee, and employed obstructionist tactics to try to move the Mobe in their ideological direction.

31. The vast majority of writers who were strongly sympathetic to the antiwar movement and the New Left of the 1960s, including Charles DeBenedetti, Todd Gitlin, Terry Anderson, Doug Dowd, Gerald Hill, Thomas Powers, Tom Wells, and others, concede that the movement never functioned as a hierarchical, ideologically rigid institution and displayed little overall agreement and unity among its constituent groups, except for their belief that the Vietnam War had to be stopped.

32. Francine du Plessix Gray, *Divine Disobedience*; Mitchell Kent Hall, "Clergy and Laymen Concerned About Vietnam: A Study of Opposition to the Vietnam War," Ph.D. diss., University of Kentucky, 1987.

33. Quoted in Powers, *Vietnam: The War at Home*, p. 293; also quoted by Hayden in *Reunion*, p. 264. The speech was on March 10, 1968.

34. The journal *Studies on the Left*, which came out of the University of Wisconsin in the late 1950s, was very influential in promoting a radical critique of American foreign policy and racism, and had a significant impact on the founders of the S.D.S. The work of William Appleman Williams and C. Wright Mills was also path-breaking and important. See Jacobs and Landau, *New Radicals*; Jacobs and Landau with Pell, *To Serve The Devil*.

35. The question here is whether a "left" can politically subsist outside of a base of support among progressive labor unions. The movement in the United States had nothing close to the student-worker alliance which emerged in Paris in 1968. It was precisely the New Left's lack of a viable political base with the working class that led it to fragment, and degenerate into sectarianism. This fragmentation, over the next two years, led a tiny collection of "action factions" to embrace violent revolutionary tactics, and ultimately delegitimize secular left politics. See Powers, *Diana: The Making of a Terrorist*. By the mid-1970s, again reflecting the lack of a sustainable working-class base, the left became synonymous with middle-class "identity politics," while the far right of the Republican Party succeeded in defining the national political agenda (even for the Democrats). See Tomasky, *Left For Dead*; Gitlin, *Twilight of Common Dreams*; and Berman, *Tale of Two Utopias*.

36. Campaign Leaflet, RFK Papers, PCP, Research Division, Box 45, File: Campaign Literature, Indiana. (The quote was taken from a Kennedy speech in Miami, Florida, May 18, 1965).
37. Lichtenstein, *Most Dangerous Man in Detroit*, pp. 356, 425.
38. Cormier and Eaton, *Reuther*, pp. 386, 391; Gould and Hickok, *Walter Reuther*, p. 373.
39. John Roche to President Lyndon Johnson, March 18, 1968 (eyes only), Marvin Watson Papers, Box 26, File: Labor Bloc, LBJL.
40. White House Aide Robert Hardesty to Harold Barefoot Sanders at the White House, March 26, 1968, 7:45 P.M., Harold Barefoot Sanders Papers, Box 27, File: Political Canvass March 1968, LBJL.
41. Message to the President from Jim Rowe, March 19, 1968, ibid.
42. Press Release, June 2, 1968, RFK Papers, PCP, BB, Box 9, File: Michigan, JFKL.
43. Press Release, April 26, 1968, Kennedy for President, Indianapolis, Indiana, RFK Papers, PCP, Press Division, Box 15, File: Indiana, 4/22/1968–4/29/1968, JFKL.
44. Report of Meeting, May 17, 1968, RFK Papers, PCP, BB, Box 14, File: South Dakota, Background and Intelligence, 5/1968 & undated, JFKL.
45. Newfield, *Robert Kennedy: A Memoir*, p. 269. Kennedy had problems with the state's Teamsters Union, which was still resentful of his prosecution as a Senate lawyer of Jimmy Hoffa in the 1950s.
46. Press Release, Cecil Tibbit, May 24, 1968, RFK Papers, PCP, Press Division, Box 15, File: Oregon, 5/19/1968–5/27/1968.
47. RFK Papers, PCP, Press Division, Box 14, File: Polls, 1968, JFKL.
48. Appy, *Working-Class War*.
49. Conversation Between Senator Hart and Marvin Watson, March 23, 1968, Marvin Watson Papers, Box 32, File: Marvin Watson Conversations, LBJL.
50. John Douglas to Edward Kennedy, Re: White and Blue Collar Vote, March 28, 1968, Milton Gwirtzman Papers, Box 5, File: Memoranda 8/1964–3/1968, JFKL.
51. *AFL-CIO American Federationist*, vol. 74, no. 3 (March 1967); vol. 74, no. 10 (October 1967); vol. 74, no. 11 (November 1967); vol. 75, no. 1 (January 1968); vol. 75, no. 3 (March 1968); vol. 75, no. 4 (April 1968).
52. Knappmann, *Presidential Election 1968*, p. 19.
53. Wayne E. Glenn, Vice-President, International Brotherhood of Pulp, Sulphite and Paper Mill Workers, to Robert Kennedy, April 30, 1968, RFK Papers, PCP, BB, Box 2, File: Arkansas Correspondence, JFKL. Glenn was also a veteran of both World War II and the Korean War.
54. Appy, *Working-Class War*, pp. 6–7.

55. Ibid., p. 22. Appy shows that at the same time the American combat forces in Vietnam were becoming more integrated by race, they became more stratified by class. The college deferments functioned in a classist manner; middle-class whites, blacks, and Latinos could shield themselves from the draft by going to college.

56. *UAW Solidarity*, vol. 11, no. 6 (June 1968), p. 15.

57. Witcover, *85 Days*, p. 124.

58. Chester, et al., *American Melodrama*, p. 161. The president was Michael Riley.

59. Memorandum from Robert Kennedy to Youth and Students, RFK Papers, PCP, Youth and Student Division, Box 5, File: Memoranda, Edward and Robert Kennedy to Students, JFKL.

60. Arthur Schlesinger, Jr. to Robert Kennedy, April 9, 1968, RFK Papers, SC-PF, Box 11, File: Schlesinger, Arthur, 1/1968–5/1968, JFKL.

61. Witcover, *85 Days*, p. 136.

62. Ibid., p. 167.

63. News Clip, RFK Papers, PCP, BB, Box 6, File: Indiana Newsclips 4/17/1968–4/22/1968, JFKL.

64. Jim Flug to Edward Kennedy, Gerald Dougherty, J. Douglas, R. Goodwin, R. Pritchard, April 28, 1968, RFK Papers, PCP, Youth and Student Division, Box 5, File: Memoranda to Campaign Headquarters, JFKL.

65. Chester, et al., *American Melodrama*, pp. 175–76.

66. Jim Flug to Edward Kennedy, Gerald Dougherty, J. Douglas, R. Goodwin, R. Pritchard, April 28, 1968, RFK Papers, PCP, Youth and Student Division, Box 5, File: Memoranda to Campaign Headquarters, JFKL.

67. "The Route of the Wabash Cannon Ball, Whistle Stop Tour of Senator Robert F. Kennedy," Jerry Bruno Papers, Box 12, File: 1968 Campaign Scheduling, 4/23/1968–4/27/1968, JFKL. The Wabash Cannon Ball had been immortalized in 1904 with a song by William Kindt that Dizzy Dean used to sing during lulls in games, when he was a broadcaster for the St. Louis Cardinal baseball team. The Wabash Cannon Ball originally referred to the St. Louis-Omaha train route that began in the 1880s; Indiana was added to the route in 1950.

68. Allan Gardner to Don Wilson, April 30, 1968, Foreign Language Radio and Newspapers, RFK Papers, PCP, BB, Box 6, File: Indiana Background and Intelligence, 4/1–4/30/1968, JFKL. The total cost for the radio spots was only $1,384.

69. Newfield, *Robert Kennedy: A Memoir*, p. 260.

70. Chester, et al., *American Melodrama*, p. 162.

71. Vanden Heuvel and Gwirtzman, *On His Own*, p. 343.

72. Larry O'Brien to Edward Kennedy, April 27, 1968, Get Out the Vote Program for Indiana Primary Day, RFK Papers, PCP, BB, Box 6, File: Indiana Background and Intelligence 4/1–4/30/1968, JFKL.

73. Copy of "Complaint for Injunction," filed in Marion County Circuit Court, May 6, 1968, The American Legion, Department of Indiana (plaintiff) vs. Robert F. Kennedy, "Robert F. Kennedy President Ballot Committee," Kennedy for President Committee, AVCO Broadcasting Corporation, Time-Life Broadcasting, Inc., and Papert, Koenig and Lois, Inc. (defendants), RFK Papers, PCP, Youth/Student Division, Box 6, File: Legal Problems, American Legion Law Suit, JFKL.

74. Press Release, Kennedy for President, Monday, May 6, 1968, ibid.

75. Chester, et al., *An American Melodrama*, p. 176.

76. Witcover, *85 Days*, p. 180.

77. Newfield, *Robert Kennedy: A Memoir*, pp. 262–63.

78. Witcover, *85 Days*, p. 178.

79. Knappmann, *Presidential Election 1968*, p. 85.

80. Dooley, *Robert Kennedy: The Final Years*, p. 127.

81. Newfield, *Robert Kennedy: A Memoir*, pp. 263–65.

82. Schlesinger, *Robert Kennedy and His Times*, p. 949.

83. Anthony Lewis to Robert Kennedy, May 8, 1968, RFK Papers, SC-PF, Box 6, File, L: 1967–1968, JFKL.

84. Newfield, *Robert Kennedy: A Memoir*, p. 261.

85. Press Release, Nebraska Vote Summary (for background only), RFK Papers, PCP, Press Division, Box 15, File: Nebraska, 4/1968–5/1968, JFKL.

86. Joseph Dolan to Robert Kennedy, March 9, 1968, Joseph Dolan Papers, Box 1, File: Memoranda, 3/1/1968–3/20/1968, JFKL.

87. Chester, et al., *American Melodrama*, p. 178. The total Democratic vote was 162,611.

88. Quoted by Witcover, *85 Days*, p. 185.

89. McCarthy, *Year of the People*, pp. 120–34.

90. Quoted by Witcover, *85 Days*, p. 185.

91. McCarthy, *Year of the People*, p. 143.

92. Dooley, *Robert Kennedy: The Final Years*, pp. 127–28; Witcover, *85 Days*, pp. 196–97.

93. *Chicago Daily News*, May 15, 1968, RFK Papers, PCP, RD, 45, F: Campaign Literature.

94. Press Release, Nebraska Vote Summary (For Background Only), ibid.

95. *Washington Post*, April 16, 1968.

96. Night Reading, May 3, 1968, RFK Papers, PCP, BB, Box 14, File: South Dakota, Background and Intelligence, 5/1968 & undated, JFKL.

97. Summary, May 1, 1968, ibid.

98. Report on Meeting, May 17, 1968, ibid.

99. Notes from Meeting, May 1, 1968, ibid.; Press Release, Robert Kennedy, February 1968, "The American Indian—An American Tragedy."

100. RFK Papers, PCP, BB, Box 14, File: South Dakota, Background & Intelligence, 5/1968 & Undated, JFKL. Bill Byler was the executive director.

101. Report on Meeting, May 17, 1968, ibid.

102. Ibid. Edward Kennedy would be in California on the night of the June 4 election.

103. Dooley, *Robert Kennedy: The Final Years*, p. 134.

104. Phil Sherburne to Jim Flug, March 21, 1968, RFK Papers, PCP, BB, Box 12, File: Oregon Background and Intelligence, 3/19/1968–5/19/1968, JFKL.

105. Youth/Student Field Report, Peter Countryman, April 1, 1968, ibid.

106. Field Report, April 19, 1968, ibid. At that time the campaign expected to fare better in Portland and Salem.

107. Field Report, April 29, 1968, ibid.

108. *Eugene Register-Guard*, April 14, 1968, ibid., File: Oregon Newsclips, 4/1968.

109. William Vanden Heuvel, Oregon Papers, n.d., William Vanden Heuvel Papers, Box 2, File: Campaign Memoranda Undated, JFKL.

110. Field Report, n.d.; *Oregonian*, n.d., ibid., File: Newsclips 5/1968 & Undated. A campaign staffer scribbled "What?" next to the paragraph of the article that contained the Leiken quotation.

111. *Washington Post*, April 20, 1968, ibid.

112. Ibid.

113. *Washington Post*, April 18, 1968, ibid., File: Oregon Newsclips, 4/1968.

114. William Vanden Heuvel, Oregon Papers, n.d., William Vanden Heuvel Papers, Box 2, File: Campaign Memoranda Undated, JFKL.

115. RFK Papers, PCP, BB, Box 12, Files: Oregon Newsclips, 4/1968; 5/1968 & Undated.

116. RFK Papers, PCP, BB, Box 12, File: Oregon Newsclips, 5/1968 & Undated.

117. Quoted in Witcover, *85 Days*, p. 204.

118. *Eugene Register-Guard*, n.d., RFK Papers, PCP, BB, Box 12, File: Oregon Newsclips, 5/1968 & Undated.

119. Ross Pritchard to "Ted" (Ted Kennedy or Ted Sorensen), n.d., RFK Papers, PCP, Youth/Student Division, Box 5, File: Memoranda: To Campaign Headquarters.

120. Schlesinger, *Robert Kennedy and His Times*, p. 972.

121. *New York Times*, May 22, 1968, RFK Papers, PCP, BB, Box 12, File: Oregon Newsclips, 5/1968 & Undated, JFKL.

122. Witcover, *85 Days*, p. 209.

123. *San Antonio Express*, March 19, 1968, RFK Papers, PCP, BB, Box 14, File: Texas Newsclips, 3/18/1968–4/15/1968, JFKL.

124. Ibid.

125. Witcover, *85 Days*, pp. 213–14; Newfield, *Robert Kennedy: A Memoir*, pp. 270–71; Chester, et al., *American Melodrama*, pp. 304–05.

126. Robert Kennedy to Eugene McCarthy, May 25, 1968, RFK Papers, PCP, Press Division, Box 15, File: Oregon, 5/19/1968–5/27/1968.

127. Quoted in Chester, et al., *American Melodrama*, p. 304.

128. Quoted in Witcover, *85 Days*, p. 209.

129. Telegram, William Vanden Heuvel to Thomas Finney, McCarthy Campaign Director, May 27, 1968, RFK Papers, PCP, Press Division, Box 15, File: Oregon 5/19/1968–5/27/1968, JFKL.

130. Statement by Pierre Salinger, Benson Hotel, May 27, 1968, 10:30 A.M., ibid.

131. Ibid.

132. Press Release, May 22, 1968, RFK Papers, PCP, Press Division, Box 15, File: California, Los Angeles, 5/14/1968–5/24/1968, JFKL. Professor Andrew Robinson resigned from the McCarthy campaign and announced his support for Kennedy.

133. Chester, et al., *American Melodrama*, p. 300.

134. Morse was also an outspoken critic of the war and in 1964 he had been, along with Senator Ernest Gruening of Alaska, one of the only two members of Congress to vote against the Gulf of Tonkin Resolution.

135. William Vanden Heuvel, Oregon Papers, n.d., William Vanden Heuvel Papers, Box 2, File: Campaign Memoranda Undated, JFKL.

136. William Vanden Heuvel, Oregon Papers, n.d., William Vanden Heuvel Papers, Box 2, File: Campaign Memoranda Undated, JFKL.

137. Quoted in Witcover, *85 Days*, p. 221.

138. Chester, et al., *American Melodrama*, p. 306.

139. Quoted in ibid., pp. 306–7.

140. Ibid., p. 224.

141. Chester, et al., *American Melodrama*, pp. 302–3. In a major speech given both in Oregon and at the Cow Palace in San Francisco, McCarthy attacked the late President Kennedy (and Robert Kennedy) for their roles in deepening United States involvement in Vietnam.

142. Paid Advertisement inserted by Republicans for McCarthy, RFK Papers, PCP, BB, Box 14, File: South Dakota Newspaper Clippings, JFKL.

143. McCarthy, *Year of the People*, p. 144.

144. In his memoir, McCarthy boasts that he was the only Democratic candidate in 1968 who could win Republican votes. *Year of the People*, p. 152.

145. *Dallas Morning News*, March 25, 1968.

146. Garcia, *Memories of Chicano History*, pp. 234–37. Corona, who had been a labor leader for decades and a strong political ally of Humphrey's, tells a story of riding in the Vice President's limousine in San Francisco in late 1967 on the way to a speaking engagement, when crowds of his own supporters among the local labor and Latino communities yelled "scab" at him for being seen with Humphrey; Corona and other leaders refused to appear on the podium with Humphrey out of fear of losing local support.

147. Remarks of Vice President Hubert H. Humphrey, Announcement, April 27,1968, Washington, D.C., RFK Papers, PCP, Research Division, Box 56, File: Humphrey, Hubert, Press Releases and Remarks, JFKL.

148. Nixon reaped "maximum advantage from the troubles of the year" 1968, Garry Wills writes, "using a coolly orchestrated politics of discontent." Wills, *Nixon Agonistes*, p. 76.

Chapter 10

1. Janet Lee Auchincloss to Robert Kennedy, May 31, 1968, RFK Papers, SC-PF, Box 1, File: A: 1968, JFKL.

2. In the spring of 1968, there were over four million registered Democrats, and about three million registered Republicans in California.

3. Press Release, May 22, 1968, RFK Papers, PCP, Press Division, Box 15, File: California, LA 5/14/1968–5/24/1968, JFKL.

4. *Los Angeles Times*, April 2, 1968, RFK Papers, PCP, BB, Box 3, File: Ca. Newsclips.

5. *Los Angeles Times*, April 1, 1968, RFK Papers, PCP, BB, Box 3, File: California Newsclips, 4/1/1968–4/30/1968, JFKL.

6. Press Release, April 23, 1968, RFK Papers, PCP, Press Division, Box 15, File: California Index 3/26/1968–5/13/1968, JFKL.

7. *Los Angeles Times*, April 4, 1968, RFK Papers, PCP, BB, Box 3, File: California Newsclips, 4/1/1968–4/30/1968, JFKL.

8. Notes From Meeting, April 5, 1968, RFK Papers, PCP, BB, Box 2, File: California, Background and Intelligence, JFKL.

9. Bruno was known for his "break-away" barricades where the goal was to create the largest looking crowd possible by allowing people to stampede feebly assembled barriers.

10. César Chávez interview, January 28, 1970, p. 23, OH-RFK,

11. South Central Farmers Committee, "The Delano Story" (ca. April 1968), Hoover Institution, New Left Collection, Stanford University, Box 39, File: Delano Grape Strike.

12. Ibid., 7. From 1966 to 1968, growers' organizations continued to label Chávez a communist.

13. Memorandum, April 6, 1968, Peter Fishbein to Joseph Dolan, RFK Papers, PCP, Research Division, Box 46, File: Memoranda, JFKL. California's constitution required that persons be able to read English before they could vote. Kennedy had fought for a similar lifting of the language barrier for New York City's large Puerto Rican population.

14. Ferris and Sandoval, *Fight in the Fields*; Griswold del Castillo and Garcia, *César Chávez: A Triumph of Spirit*; Levy, *César Chávez: Autobiography of La Causa*.

15. A militant Latino youth group, the Brown Berets, that had been loosely allied with the U.F.W. had rejected Chávez's calls to remain non-violent, just as elements of the Student Non-Violent Coordinating Committee (S.N.C.C.) had rejected Martin Luther King, Jr.'s similar pleas.

16. Miss Helen Serda to Robert Kennedy, March 3, 1968, RFK Papers, SC-SF, Box 30, File: Labor, Migrant 3/1968–6/1968, JFKL.

17. Mr. Catalino Tacliban to Robert Kennedy, March 3, 1968, ibid.

18. When Kennedy left Delano this time, Chávez, Dolores Huerta, and other U.F.W. leaders, along with the labor organizer Bert Corona of M.A.P.A., were convinced that Kennedy was on the verge of announcing his candidacy. César Chávez interview by Dennis O'Brien, January 28, 1970, pp. 13 and 21, OH-RFK, JFKL. Garcia, *Memories of Chicano History*, pp. 236–44.

19. Robert Kennedy to Mr. and Mrs. Edmund Wianecki, March 19, 1968, RFK Papers, SC-SF, Box 30, File: Labor, Migrant 3/1968–6/1968, JFKL.

20. César Chávez interview, January 28, 1970, p. 17, OH-RFK, JFKL.

21. César Chávez quotation on Kennedy campaign pamphlet, ca. May 1968, RFK Papers, PCP, Box 45, File: Campaign Literature, General, JFKL.

22. Ibid.

23. Ralph Guzman to Frank Mankiewicz, March 19, 1968, RFK Papers, PCP, Press Division, Box 1, File: Correspondence, E,F,G, JFKL.

24. Frank Mankiewicz to Ralph Guzman, April 9, 1968, RFK Papers, PCP, Box 1, File: Correspondence, E,F,G, JFKL.

25. Garcia, *Memories of Chicano History*, p. 208.

26. Fraser Barron to Dave Hackett, April 6, 1968, RFK Papers, PCP, BB, Box 6, File: Indiana, Background and Intelligence, 4/1/1968–4/30/1968, JFKL.

27. Press Release, n.d., Statement of Bert N. Corona on Behalf of Senator Robert F. Kennedy for President, RFK Papers, PCP, Press Division, Box 15, File: California, Los Angeles, 5/25/1968–6/3/1968, JFKL.

28. Fraser Barron to Dave Hackett, April 6, 1968, RFK Papers, BB, Box 2, File: California, Background and Intelligence, JFKL.

29. Memorandum, n.d., re: David Hackett conversation with Richard Boone, RFK Papers, PCP, BB, Box 2, File: California, Background and Intelligence, JFKL.

30. Bert Corona, Memorandum to the National RFK Headquarters, May 1, 1968, RFK Papers, PCP, Press Division, Box 19, File: Memoranda 3/1968–6/1968, JFKL.

31. Ronald Sugarman to Jim Flug, March 31, 1968, RFK Papers, PCP, Speech Writers' Division, Box 2, File: Presidential Campaign, General, JFKL.

32. Clayton Rost to Jesse Unruh, March 28, 1968, RFK Papers, PCP, BB, Box 2, California Correspondence, 3/16/1968–4/15/1968, JFKL.

33. Vincent Lavery, Chairman of Citizens for Kennedy '68 in Merced County, to Dun Gifford, April 8, 1968, RFK Papers, PCP, BB, 2, ibid.

34. César Chávez interview, January 28, 1970, pp. 22–23, OH-RFK, JFKL.

35. Ibid, pp. 16 and 17.

36. *Los Angeles Times*, May 1, 1968, RFK Papers, PCP, BB, Box 3, File: California Newsclips, 5/1/1968–5/31/1968, and Undated, JFKL.

37. Night Reading, April 17, 1968, report of phone call from Mattie Williams of the N.A.A.C.P., RFK Papers, PCP, BB, Box 2, File: California, Background and Intelligence, JFKL. Williams suggested getting Steve Smith to do something about the situation.

38. Memorandum, April 15, 1968, RFK Papers, PCP, BB, Box 2, File: Ca. Background and Intelligence, JFKL.

39. Typed notes of a phone conversation with Jesse Unruh, April 23, 1968, RFK Papers, PCP, BB, Box 2, File: California, Background and Intelligence, JFKL. Unruh also believed at that time that Hubert Humphrey, who had not yet formerly announced his candidacy, was distancing himself from the Lynch slate.

40. Frank Mankiewicz to Stephen Smith, April 30, 1968, RFK Papers, PCP, Press Division, Box 19, File: Memoranda 3/1968–6/1968, JFKL.

41. Ibid.

42. Arthur Schlesinger to Robert Kennedy, May 6, 1968, RFK Papers, SC-PF, Box 11, File: Schlesinger, Arthur 1/1968–5/1968, JFKL.

43. Notes of Meeting, Youth and Students for Kennedy, May 10, 1968, RFK Papers, PCP, Youth and Student Division, Box 6, File: Regional Activities of Youth/ Student Division, JFKL.

44. Daniel Patrick Moynihan to Robert Kennedy, May 21, 1968, RFK Papers, PCP, Press Division, Box 1, File: Correspondence: M, JFKL.

45. Undated 7-page Memorandum, David Rosenbloom outlining the goals of the Youth and Student Division of the Kennedy campaign, RFK Papers, PCP, Youth and Student Division, Box 6, File: Purpose and Goals of the Youth/ Student Division, JFKL. The memo goes on to state that the youthful minorities could also create "hoopla" around Kennedy campaign appearances and do so relatively cheaply.

46. Ibid. By the time Kennedy decided to run for president the Black Power movement was already two years old.

47. Press Release, Student Press, Students for Kennedy, n.d. (ca. May 25, 1968), RFK Papers, PCP, Press Division, Box 15, File: California, San Francisco, 5/15/1968– 6/3/1968, JFKL.

48. Press Release, May 27, 1968 (No. 88A), ibid.

49. Press Release, May 27, 1968 (No. 88B), ibid.

50. Thomas G. Consiglio, Coordinator, District 38 Legislative Education, United Steel Workers of America, to Jesse Unruh, April 2, 1968, RFK Papers, PCP, Press Division, Box 2, File: Correspondence, T-Z, JFKL.

51. Chester, et al., *American Melodrama*, p. 317.

52. Press Release, April 25 & 26, 1968, RFK Papers, PCP, Press Division, Box 15, File: California Index, 3/26/1968–5/13/1968, JFKL.

53. Press Release, April 27, 1968, Jesse Unruh's statement on Hubert Humphrey's entry into the race, ibid.

54. *Washington Post*, May 22, 1968 (William Chapman), n.p., RFK Papers, PCP, BB, Box 3, File: California Newsclips 5/1/1968–5/31/1968, JFKL.

55. *San Francisco Chronicle*, April 17, 1968, RFK Papers, PCP, BB, Box 3, California Newsclips, 4/1–30/1968, JFKL.

56. César Chávez interview, January 28, 1970, p. 20, OH-RFK, JFKL.

57. C. D. DeLoach to C. Tolson, May 17, 1968, *FBI File on Robert F. Kennedy* (microform).

58. Press Release, May 21, 1968, RFK Papers, PCP, Press Division, Box 15, File: California, San Francisco, 5/15/1968–6/3/1968, JFKL.

59. Press Release, May 24, 1968, ibid.

60. Press Release, May 26, 1968, ibid.

61. Goodwin, *Remembering America*, p. 462.

62. Press Release, May 27, 1968, RFK Papers, PCP, Press Division, Box 15, File: California, San Francisco, 5/15/1968–6/3/1968, JFKL. Paul DeDominico headed "Business for Kennedy."

63. Gwirtzman and Vanden Heuvel, *On His Own*, p. 354. The bankers were Sidney Weinberg and John Loeb.

64. Kenneth O'Donnell to William Vanden Heuvel, April 8, 1968, Milton Gwirtzman Papers, Box 5, File: Memoranda 4/1968–8/1969, JFKL. O'Donnell believed that "people in this group could be more effective if they worked through quiet contact rather than an open group."

65. Press Release, May 9, 1968, RFK Papers, PCP, Press Division, Box 15, File: California, Los Angeles Index 3/26/1968–5/13/1968, JFKL.

66. Press Release, May 22, 1968, RFK Papers, PCP, Press Division, Box 15, File: California, San Francisco, 5/15/1968–6/3/1968, JFKL. Kennedy's political aide, Frederick Dutton, had served on the Board of Regents of the University of California, and had been an executive secretary to Governor Brown.

67. Press Release, May 27, 1968, RFK Papers, PCP, Press Division, Box 15, File: California, San Francisco, 5/15/1968–6/3/1968, JFKL. Given Johnson's status as a celebrity athlete and sports announcer for NBC, he also served on the Hollywood for Kennedy Committee.

68. Press Release, May 22, 1968, RFK Papers, PCP, Press Division, Box 15, File: California, Los Angeles, 5/14/1968–5/24/1968, JFKL.

69. Press Release, May 21, 1968, ibid.

70. Theodore Sorensen, April 26, 1968, RFK Papers, PCP, BB, Box 2, File: California Background and Intelligence, JFKL.

71. Press Release, May 15, 1968, RFK Papers, PCP, Press Division, Box 15, File: California, San Francisco 5/1/1968–5/15/1968, JFKL.

72. Press Release, May 25, 1968, RFK Papers, PCP, Press Division, Box 15, File: California, San Francisco, 5/15/1968–6/3/1968, JFKL.

73. Press Release, May 27, 1968, ibid.

74. Press Release, n.d., ibid.

75. Press Release, May 27, 1968, ibid.

76. Press Release, May 28, 1968, ibid.

77. Press Release, May 21, 1968, ibid. Serving also as committee coordinators were Jackie Cooper, Steven Gelders, Roy Huggins, Ben Irwin, Norman Jewison, Peter Lawford (Kennedy's brother-in-law), Irving Lazar, Henry Mancini, and Elizabeth Montgomery.

78. Press Release, May 14, 1968, RFK Papers, PCP, Press Division, Box 15, File: California, Los Angeles Index 3/26/1968–5/13/1968, JFKL.

79. *San Francisco Chronicle*, April 17, 1968, RFK Papers, PCP, BB, Box 3, California Newsclips, 4/1–30/1968, JFKL.

80. Press Release, n.d., RFK Papers, PCP, Press Division, Box 15, File: California, San Francisco, 5/1/1968–5/15/1968, JFKL.

81. Press Release, May 8, 1968, May 29, 1968, RFK Papers, PCP, Press Division, Box 15, File: California, Los Angeles, 5/25/1968–6/3/1968, JFKL. Yvonne Braithwaite, March Fong, and Mrs. Henry Grady were honorary chairpersons. Many spouses of prominent figures also participated, such as Renée Carpenter, the wife of the astronaut Scott Carpenter.

82. Press Release, May 14, 1968, RFK Papers, PCP, Press Division, Box 15, File: California, San Francisco, 5/1/1968–5/15/1968, JFKL.

83. Ibid.

84. Press Release, May 29, 1968, RFK Papers, PCP, Press Division, Box 15, File: California, Los Angeles, 5/25/1968–6/3/1968, JFKL.

85. Bill Smith to Theodore Sorensen, n.d. (ca. May 30, 1968), Milton Gwirtzman Papers, Box 5, File: Memoranda Undated, JFKL.

86. Text of Remarks by Senator Robert F. Kennedy on Vietnam, Senate Floor, March 2, 1967, RFK Papers, PCP, Speech Writers' Division, Box 5, File: Vietnam, JFKL.

87. McCarthy, *Limits of Power*, pp. 99–101, 192, 194.

88. Pierre Salinger to John Siegenthaler, May 30, 1968, RFK Papers, PCP, Press Division, Box 22, File: Telex Messages, 4/22/1968–6/4/1968, JFKL.

89. Press Release summary, Peggy Whedon (producer), June 1, 1968, RFK Papers, PCP, Youth and Student Division, Box 5, File: Issues and Answers, June 1, 1968, JFKL.

90. Ibid.

91. Witcover, *85 Days*, p. 241.

92. Quoted in ibid., p. 244.

93. Quoted in ibid., pp. 244–45.

94. Most blacks did not want to leave their communities but wanted the govern-
    ment to protect them against discrimination, develop the schools and infrastruc-
    ture, and prod the private sector to create employment. In the late 1960s, prior
    to the massive "black flight" from the inner cities that occurred in the 1970s,
    these African-American urban communities, although poor with high unem-
    ployment, still possessed a cross-section of occupations, as well as a class of
    small shop owners. There was the hope that through government action in
    partnership with private enterprise these communities could improve their con-
    ditions. See Wilson, *Truly Disadvantaged*.

95. Witcover, *85 Days*, pp. 245–46; Newfield, *Robert Kennedy: A Memoir*, p. 282;
    Schlesinger, *Robert Kennedy and His Times*, p. 979; Gwirtzman and Vanden
    Heuvel, *On His Own*, p. 378.

96. Press Release, May 22, 1968, RFK Papers, PCP, Press Division, Box 15, File:
    California, San Francisco, 5/16/1968–5/23/1968, JFKL.

97. Ibid.

98. Dooley, *Robert Kennedy: The Final Years*, p. 131; Herzog, *McCarthy for Presi-
    dent*, p. 149.

99. Statement by Pierre Salinger, Benson Hotel, May 27, 1968, 10:30 A.M., RFK
    Papers, PCP, Press Division, Box 15, File: Oregon 5/19/1968–5/27/1968, JFKL.

100. Ibid.

101. Press Release, May 27, 1968, Sema Lederman (21-year-old graduate of the
    University of Michigan appointed by Professor Andrew Robinson to head
    Northern California Change to Kennedy committee), RFK Papers, PCP,
    Press Division, Box 15, File: California, San Francisco, 5/15/1968–6/3/1968,
    JFKL.

102. Press Release, May 28, 1968, James Boman, a manufacturing engineer for
    Fibreboard Corporation and vice president of the Walnut Creek Democratic
    Club, RFK Papers, PCP, Press Division, Box 15, File: California, San Fran-
    cisco, 5/15/1968–6/3/1968, JFKL. Bowman's base of operations was in Walnut
    Creek, northeast of San Francisco.

103. Art Seltzer, who was chairman of the Kennedy campaign in California, was
    delighted to have the help of this experienced publicist in the media state. Press
    Release, n.d., RFK Papers, PCP, Press Division, Box 15, File: California, San
    Francisco, 5/1/1968–5/15/1968, JFKL.

104. Press Release, May 28, 1968, RFK Papers, PCP, Press Division, Box 15, File:
    California, San Francisco, 5/15/1968–6/3/1968, JFKL. Swadesh was also an
    active member of the Lowenstein-affiliated California Democratic Council.

105. Press Release, May 30, 1968, RFK Papers, PCP, BB, Box 3, File: California
    Newsclips 5/1/1968–5/31/1968, JFKL.

106. Transcripts of Lynch Delegation Radio Spots, May 30, 1968, RFK Papers, PCP, Press Division, Box 15, File: California, Los Angeles 5/25/1968–6/3/1968, and undated, JFKL.

107. Press Release, May 30, 1968 (Dick Kline), RFK Papers, PCP, Press Division, Box 22, File: Telex Messages, 4/22/1968–6/4/1968, JFKL.

108. Telegram sent to radio stations carrying the Lynch spots by Attorney Stephen Reinhardt; telegram sent to newspapers carrying Lynch spots by Attorney Stephen Reinhardt, May 30, 1968, RFK Papers, PCP, Press Division, Box 15, File: California, Los Angeles 5/25/1968–6/3/1968, and undated; Press Division, Box 2, File: Correspondence, T-Z, JFKL. Reinhardt pointed out that the ads violated California Elections Code Sections 11702, 11703, and 11706; and Federal Election Disclosure laws Title 18, United States Code, Section 612.

109. Ibid.

110. Ibid.

111. Press Release, June 1, 1968, RFK Papers, PCP, Press Division, Box 15, File: California, Los Angeles 5/25/1968–6/3/1968, and undated, JFKL.

112. Press Release, May 31, 1968 (#89), ibid.

113. 10-Second Spot Announcement, June 2, 1968, ibid.

114. Goodwin, *Remembering America*, p. 535

115. Knappman, *Presidential Election 1968*, p. 99.

116. *Los Angeles Times*, June 6, 1968, p. 19; Fresno County was not included in this tally.

117. Ibid.

118. David Borden (Kennedy Campaign Los Angeles Headquarters) to James Flug (Kennedy Washington Headquarters), June 4, 1968, RFK Papers, PCP, Press Division Box 22, File: Telex Messages, 4/22/1968–6/4/1968, JFKL.

119. Ibid.

120. Ibid.

121. Ibid.

122. Statement by Senator Robert F. Kennedy, Ambassador Hotel, Los Angeles, California, June 4, 1968, RFK Papers, PCP, Press Division, Box 22, File: Transcripts, 4/14/1968–6/11/1968 (television and radio), JFKL.

123. Kennedy said that Freckles "has been maligned, and as F.D.R. said, 'I don't mind what you say about me, but leave my dog alone.'" McCarthy had criticized Kennedy's public appearances with his dog.

124. Quoted in Witcover, *85 Days*, p. 264.

125. *Los Angeles Times*, June 6, 1968, p. 3B.

126. Ibid., Part II, p. 1.

127. Ibid., Part II, p. 8.

128. Ibid.

129. Ibid., Part II, p. 1.

Conclusion

1. Kennedy's remarks in Indianapolis after King's assassination appear in chapter 8 above.
2. Jerry Bruno Papers, Box 12, File: 1968 Campaign Scheduling, 6/7/1968–6/17/1968; RFK Papers, PCP, Press Division, Box 19, File: Memoranda 3/1968–6/1968, JFKL.
3. Theodore White to Ethel Kennedy, August 23, 1968, Theodore White Papers, Box 49, Folder 11, Series 1, Harvard University Archives.
4. César Chávez interview January 28, 1970, p. 20, OH-RFK, JFKL.
5. Newfield, *Robert Kennedy: A Memoir*, p. 295.
6. Gwirtzman and Vanden Heuvel, *On His Own*, p. 363.
7. Quoted in Jules Witcover, *85 Days*, p. 263.

Bibliography

Collections

John Fitzgerald Kennedy Library, Boston, Massachusetts (JFKL)

Gerald J. Bruno Papers
McGeorge Bundy Papers
Joseph Dolan Papers
Peter Edelman Papers
Milton Gwirtzman Papers
Thomas M. Johnston Papers
Robert Francis Kennedy Papers
        Senate Papers 1964–1968
        Personal File (SC-PF)
        Subject File (SC-SF)
        Presidential Campaign Papers, 1968 (PCP)
Arthur M. Schlesinger, Jr. Papers
Theodore C. Sorensen Papers
William J. vanden Heuvel Papers
Adam Walinsky Papers

Lyndon Baines Johnson Library, Austin, Texas (LBJL)

Democratic National Committee Papers
National Security File, Country File, Vietnam (NSFCFVN)
Tom Johnson Meeting Notes
Drew Pearson Papers
Harold "Barefoot" Sanders Papers

Marvin Watson Papers
White House Central Files
Appointment Files: Daily Diary and Diary Backup
White House Confidential File (WHCF)
White House Famous Names File (WHFN)

Other Collections

FBI File on Robert F. Kennedy, Scholarly Resources
Personal Papers of George McT. Kahin
Hoover Institution Archives, New Left Collection, Stanford University
Lawrence Kramer New Left Collection, Cornell University
John McCormack Papers, Boston University
Emma Guffey Miller Papers, Schlesinger Library, Radcliffe College
Dick Schaap Papers, Cornell University
Theodore H. White Papers, Harvard University

Oral Histories

John Fitzgerald Kennedy Library (OH-RFK)

César Chávez
Peter Edelman
Allard Lowenstein
George McGovern
Kenneth O'Donnell

Lyndon Baines Johnson Library

Frederick G. Dutton
Hubert H. Humphrey
Nicholas deB. Katzenbach
John W. McCormack
George McGovern
Harry McPherson
Lawrence O'Brien
Kenny O'Donnell
Harold "Barefoot" Sanders
Larry Temple
Jack Valenti

Government Records

Congressional Record, Proceedings and Debates of the 89th Congress, First Session.
Congressional Record, Proceedings and Debates of the 89th Congress, Second Session.
Congressional Record, Proceedings and Debates of the 90th Congress, First Session.
Congressional Record, Proceedings and Debates of the 90th Congress, Second Session.

Journal Articles

Altschuler, Bruce E. "Kennedy Decides to Run: 1968." *Presidential Studies Quarterly* (Summer 1980): 348–52.

Best, James J. "Who Talked to the President When?" *Political Science Quarterly* (Fall 1988): 531–45.

Dallek, Robert. "Lyndon Johnson and Vietnam: The Making of a Tragedy." *Diplomatic History* (Spring 1996): 147–62.

Isserman, Maurice. "Michael Harrington and the Vietnam War: The Failure of Anti-Stalinism in the 1960s." *Peace & Change*, vol. 21, no. 4 (October 1996): 383–408.

Kalk, Bruce H. "Wormley's Hotel Revisited: Richard Nixon's Southern Strategy and the End of the Second Reconstruction," *North Carolina Historical Review*, vol. 71, no. 1 (January 1994): 85–104.

Noer, Thomas J. "Martin Luther King, Jr. and the Cold War," *Peace and Change*, vol. 22, no. 2 (April 1997): 126.

Oates, Stephen B. "Tribune of the Underclass," *Reviews in American History* (June 1979): 286–92.

Palermo, Joseph. "The Johnson Administration Responds to Sen. Edward M. Kennedy's Trip to South Vietnam, January 1968." *Peace & Change*, vol. 23, no. 1 (January 1998): 49–73.

Palermo, Joseph. "Black Power on Campus: The Beginnings." *San Jose Studies* (Spring 1988): 31–48.

Newspapers

Birmingham Post Herald
Chicago Daily News
Chicago Tribune
Eugene Register-Guard
Dallas Morning News
Houston Chronicle
Knickerbocker News
Long Island Sunday Press
New York Journal-American

New York Herald-Tribune
Rome Sentinel
St. Louis Post-Dispatch
Salt Lake City Tribune
San Antonio Express
The Christian Science Monitor
The Montgomery Advertiser
The Oregonian
The New York Post
The New York Times
The Los Angeles Times
The San Francisco Chronicle
The Wall Street Journal
The Washington Post

Magazines

AFL-CIO American Federationist
Christianity and Crisis
Esquire
Look
Life
New Leader
Newsweek
Ramparts
The Nation
The New Republic
The New York Times Magazine
Time Magazine
U.A.W. Solidarity
U.S. News and World Report

Unpublished Dissertations and Theses

Bickers, Patrick M. "Robert Kennedy and the Press." Ph.D. dissertation. Ball State
    University, 1984.
Hall, Mitchell Kent. "Clergy and Laymen Concerned About Vietnam: A Study of
    Opposition to the Vietnam War," Ph.D. dissertation, University of Kentucky,
    1987.

Lee, Ronald Emery. "The Rhetoric of the 'New Politics': A Case Study of Robert F. Kennedy's 1968 Presidential Campaign." Ph.D. dissertation. University of Iowa, 1981.

Palermo, Joseph. "The Racial Discrimination Crisis at San Jose State College, September 1967." Masters Thesis. San Jose State University, 1986.

Sanders, Frederick Clarke, Jr. "The Rhetorical Strategies of Senator Robert Kennedy and Senator Eugene McCarthy in the 1968 Presidential Primaries." Ph.D. dissertation. University of Oregon, 1973.

Books

Aistrup, Joseph A. *The Southern Strategy Revisited: Republican Top-Down Advancement in the South.* Lexington: University Press of Kentucky , 1996.

Anderson, Terry H. *The Movement and the Sixties.* New York: Oxford University Press, 1995.

Applebome, Peter. *Dixie Rising: How the South Is Shaping American Values, Politics, and Culture.* New York: Random House, 1996.

Appy, Christian G. *Working-Class War: American Combat Soldiers and Vietnam.* Chapel Hill: University of North Carolina Press, 1993.

Arnold, James R. *Tet Offensive 1968: Turning Point in Vietnam*, Campaign Series Four. London: Osprey Publishing, 1990.

Beran, Michael Knox. *The Last Patrician: Bobby Kennedy and the End of American Aristocracy.* New York: St. Martin's, 1998.

Bergerud, Eric M. *The Dynamics of Defeat: The Vietnam War in Hau Nghia Province.* Boulder, Colo.: Westview, 1991.

Berman, Larry. *Lyndon Johnson's War: The Road to Stalemate in Vietnam.* New York: Norton, 1989.

Berman, Paul. *A Tale of Two Utopias: The Political Journey of the Generation of 1968.* New York: Norton, 1996.

Berman, William C. *America's Right Turn: From Nixon to Bush.* Baltimore, Md.: Johns Hopkins University Press, 1994.

Bernstein, Irving. *Guns or Butter: The Presidency of Lyndon Johnson.* New York: Oxford University Press, 1996.

Beschloss, Michael B. *Taking Charge: The Johnson White House Tapes, 1963–1964.* New York: Simon & Schuster, 1997.

Biles, Roger. *Richard J. Daley: Politics, Race, and the Governing of Chicago.* De Kalb: Northern Illinois University Press, 1995.

Black, George. *The Good Neighbor: How the United States Wrote the History of Central America and the Caribbean.* New York: Pantheon, 1988.

Bloom, Jack. *Class, Race, and the Civil Rights Movement.* Bloomington: Indiana University Press, 1988.

Bowman, John S. *The Vietnam War: An Almanac*. New York: World Almanac Publications, 1985.

Braestrup, Peter. *Big Story: How the American Press and Television Reported and Interpreted the Crisis of Tet 1968 in Vietnam and Washington*. Boulder, Colo.: Westview, 1977.

Branch, Taylor. *Parting the Waters: America in the King Years, 1953–1963*. New York: Simon & Schuster, 1988.

Branch, Taylor. *Pillar of Fire: America in the King Years, 1963–1965*. New York: Simon & Schuster, 1998.

Brennan, Mary C. *Turning Right in the Sixties: The Conservative Capture of the G.O.P.* Chapel Hill: University of North Carolina Press, 1995.

Brown, Lt. Col. Richard L. *Palace Gate: Under Siege in Hue City Tet January 1968*. Atglen, Pa.: Schiffer Military Aviation History, 1995.

Burner, David. *Making Peace with the 60s*. Princeton, N. J.: Princeton University Press, 1996.

Buzzanco, Robert. *Masters of War: Military Dissent and Politics in the Vietnam Era*. New York: Oxford University Press, 1996.

Carson, Clayborne. *In Struggle: SNCC and the Black Awakening of the 1960s*. Cambridge: Harvard University Press, 1981.

Carter, Dan T. *From George Wallace to Newt Gingrich: Race in the Conservative Counterrevolution, 1963–1994*. Baton Rouge: Louisiana State University Press, 1996.

Carter, Dan T. *The Politics of Rage: George Wallace, the Origins of the New Conservatism, and the Transformation of American Politics*. New York: Simon & Schuster, 1995.

Chafe, William. *Never Stop Running*. New York: HarperCollins, 1993.

Chester, Lewis, et al. *An American Melodrama: The Presidential Campaign of 1968*. New York: Viking. 1969.

Churchill, Ward and Jim Vander Wall. *Agents of Repression: The FBI's Secret Wars Against the Black Panther Party and the American Indian Movement*. Boston: South End Press, 1988.

Cloward, Richard A. and France Fox Piven. *The Politics of Turmoil: Poverty, Race, and the Urban Crisis*. New York: Vintage, 1975.

Conkin, Paul K. *Big Daddy from the Pedernales: Lyndon Baines Johnson*. Boston: Twayne, 1986.

Cormier, Frank and William J. Eaton. *Reuther*. Englewood Cliffs, N. J.: Prentice-Hall, 1970.

Crouse, Timothy. *The Boys on the Bus: Riding with the Campaign Press Corps*. New York: Ballantine, 1972.

Dallek, Robert. *Hail to the Chief: The Making and Unmaking of American Presidents*. New York: Hyperion, 1996.

Dallek, Robert. *Flawed Giant: Lyndon Johnson and His Times 1961–1973*. New York: Oxford University Press, 1998.

DeBenedetti, Charles, with Charles Chatfield. *An American Ordeal: The Antiwar Movement of the Vietnam Era*. Syracuse, N. Y.: Syracuse University Press, 1990.

Dent, Harry S. *The Prodigal South Returns to Power*. New York: Wiley, 1978.

DiLeo, David L. *George Ball, Vietnam, and the Rethinking of Containment*. Chapel Hill: University of North Carolina Press, 1991.

Dollard, John. *Caste and Class in a Southern Town*. Garden City, N.Y.: Doubleday, 1957.

Dooley, Brian. *Robert Kennedy: The Final Years*. Staffordshire, England: Keele University Press, 1995.

Dowd, Doug. *Blues for America: A Critique, a Lament, and Some Memories*. New York: Monthly Review Press, 1997.

Edsall, Thomas Byrne with Mary D. Edsall. *Chain Reaction: The Impact of Race, Rights, and Taxes on American Politics*. New York: Norton, 1991.

Ellsberg, Daniel. *Papers on the War*. New York: Simon & Schuster, 1972.

Evers, Charles. *Have No Fear: The Charles Evers Story*. New York: Wiley, 1997.

Ferris, Susan and Ricardo Sandoval. *The Fight in the Fields: César Chávez and the Farmworkers Movement*. New York: Harcourt Brace, 1997.

Foner, Eric. *The Story of American Freedom*. New York: Norton, 1998.

Friedly, Michael and David Gallen. *Martin Luther King, Jr.: The FBI File*. New York: Carroll and Graf, 1993.

Garcia, Mario T. *Memories of Chicano History: The Life and Narrative of Bert Corona*. Berkeley: University of California Press, 1994.

Gardner, Lloyd C. *Pay Any Price: Lyndon Johnson and the Wars for Vietnam*. Chicago: Ivan R. Dee, 1995.

Gardner, Gerald. *Robert Kennedy in New York: The Campaign for the Senate*. New York: Random House, 1965.

Garfinkle, Adam. *Telltale Hearts: The Origins and Impact of the Vietnam Antiwar Movement*. New York: St. Martin's. 1995.

Garrow, David J. *Bearing the Cross: Martin Luther King, Jr. and the Southern Christian Leadership Conference*. New York: Vintage, 1986.

Garrow, David J. *The FBI and Martin Luther King, Jr*. New York: Penguin, 1981.

Gettleman, Marvin E. et al., eds. *Vietnam and America: The Most Comprehensive Documented History of the Vietnam War*. New York: Grove, 1995.

Giglio, James N. *The Presidency of John F. Kennedy*. University Press of Kansas, 1991.

Gilbert, Marc Jason and William Head, eds. *The Tet Offensive*. Westport, Conn.: Praeger, 1996.

Gillon, Steven M. *The Democrats' Dilemma: Walter F. Mondale and the Liberal Legacy*. New York: Columbia University Press, 1992.

Gitlin, Todd. *The Twilight of Common Dreams: Why America Is Wracked by Culture Wars*. New York: Holt, 1995.

Gitlin, Todd. *The Sixties: Years of Hope, Days of Rage*. New York: Bantam, 1987.

Glick, Brian. *War at Home: Covert Action Against U.S. Activists and What We Can Do About It*. Boston, Mass.: South End Press, 1989.

Goldberg, Robert Alan. *Barry Goldwater*. New Haven: Yale University Press, 1995.

Goodwin, Richard N. *Remembering America: A Voice from the Sixties*. New York: Harper & Row, 1988.

Gould, Jean and Lorena Hickok. *Walter Reuther: Labor's Rugged Individualist*. New York: Dodd, Mead, 1972.

Gray, Francine du Plessix. *Divine Disobedience: Profiles in Catholic Radicalism*. New York: Vintage, 1971.

Griswold del Castillo, Richard and Richard A. Garcia. *César Chávez: A Triumph of Spirit*. Norman, Okla.: University of Oklahoma Press, 1995.

Guide To U.S. Elections, 3rd ed. Washington, D.C., Congressional Quarterly, 1994,

Guthman Edwin O. and Richard C. Allen, eds. *RFK: Collected Speeches*. New York: Viking, 1993.

Guthman, Edwin O. *We Band of Brothers*. New York: Harper & Row, 1971.

Guthman, Edwin O. and Jeffrey Shulman, eds. *Robert Kennedy: In His Own Words*. New York: Bantam, 1988.

Halberstam, David. *The Unfinished Odyssey of Robert Kennedy*. New York: Random House, 1968.

Halberstam, David. *The Best and the Brightest*. New York: Random House, 1969.

Hampton, Henry and Steve Fayer with Sarah Flynn. *Voices of Freedom: An Oral History of the Civil Rights Movement from the 1950s Through the 1980s*. New York: Bantam, 1990.

Harrington, Michael. *The Other America: Poverty in the United States*. Baltimore, Md: Penguin, 1962.

Harrington, Michael. *Toward a Democratic Left: A Radical Program for a New Majority*. Baltimore, Md.: Penguin, 1969.

Hayden, Tom. *Reunion: A Memior*. New York: Random House, 1988.

Henggeler, Paul R. *The Kennedy Persuasion: The Politics of Style since JFK*, Chicago: Ivan R. Dee, 1995.

Herring, George C. *LBJ and Vietnam: A Different Kind of War*. Austin: University of Texas Press, 1994.

Herman, Edward S. and Frank Brodhead. *Demonstration Elections: U.S.-Staged Elections in the Dominican Republic, Vietnam, and El Salvador*. Boston, Mass.: South End Press, 1984.

Herman, Edward and Noam Chomsky. *Manufacturing Consent: The Political Economy of the Mass Media*. New York: Pantheon, 1988.

Herzog, Arthur. *McCarthy for President*. New York: Viking, 1969.

Horne, Gerald. *Fire This Time: The Watts Uprising and the 1960s*. Charlottesville, Va.: University of Virginia Press, 1995.

Howard, Gerald, ed. *The Sixties: The Art, Attitudes, Politics, and Media of Our Most Explosive Decade*. New York: Marlowe, 1991.

Humphrey, Hubert H. *The Education of a Public Man: My Life and Politics*. Norman Sherman, ed. Garden City, N.Y.: Doubleday, 1976.

Jacobs, Paul and Saul Landau. *The New Radicals: A Report with Documents*. New York: Vintage, 1966.

Jacobs, Paul and Saul Landau with Eve Pell. *To Serve the Devil: A Documentary Analysis of America's Racial History and Why It Has Been Kept Hidden*. New York: Vintage, 1971.

Johnson, Lyndon. *The Vantage Point: Perspectives of the Presidency, 1963–1969*. New York: Popular Library, 1971.

Kahin, George McT. *Intervention: How America Became Involved in Vietnam*. Garden City, N.Y.: Anchor, 1987.

Kaiser, Charles. *1968 in America: Music, Politics, Chaos, Counterculture, and the Shaping of a Generation*. New York: Weidenfeld & Nicolson, 1988.

Karnow, Stanley. *Vietnam: A History*. New York: Penguin, 1983.

Kearns, Doris. *Lyndon Johnson and the American Dream*. New York: Harper & Row, 1976.

Kennedy, Maxwell Taylor, ed. *Make Gentle the Life of This World: The Vision of Robert F. Kennedy*. New York: Harcourt Brace, 1998.

Kennedy, Robert F. *The Pursuit of Justice*. Theodore J. Lowi, ed. New York: Harper & Row, 1964.

Kennedy, Robert F. *To Seek A Newer World*. April 1968 ed. New York: Bantam, 1968.

Kennedy, Robert F. *The Enemy Within: The McClellan Committee's Crusade Against Jimmy Hoffa and Corrupt Labor Unions*. New York: Da Capo Press, 1960.

Kennedy, Robert F. *Thirteen Days: A Memoir of the Cuban Missile Crisis*. New York: Norton, 1969.

Key, Jr., V. O. *Southern Politics in State and Nation*. Knoxville: University of Tennessee Press, 1949.

King, Coretta Scott. *My Life with Martin Luther King, Jr*. New York: Holt, Rinehart and Winston, 1969.

King, Jr., Martin Luther. *Where Do We Go From Here?: Chaos or Community?* Boston: Beacon, 1967.

Knappmann, Edmund W., ed. *Presidential Election 1968*. New York: Facts on File, 1970.

Kolko, Gabriel. *Anatomy of a War: Vietnam, the United States, and the Modern Historical Experience*. New York: Random House, 1985.

Kopkind, Andrew, edited by JoAnn Wypijewski, *The Thirty Years' War: Dispatches and Diversions of a Radical Journalist*. New York: Verso, 1995.

LaFeber, Walter. *Inevitable Revolutions: The United States in Central America*. New York: Norton, 1984.

Landau, Saul. *The Dangerous Doctrine: National Security and U.S. Foreign Policy*. Boulder, Colo.: Westview, 1988.

Larner, Jeremy. *Nobody Knows: Reflections on the McCarthy Campaign of 1968*. New York: Macmillan, 1970.

Leuchtenburg, William E. *Under the Shadow of FDR: From Harry Truman to Ronald Reagan*. Ithaca, N.Y.: Cornell University Press, 1983.

Levy, Jacques E. *César Chávez: Autobiography of La Causa*. New York: Norton, 1975.

Lichtenstein, Nelson. *The Most Dangerous Man in Detroit: Walter Reuther and the Fate of American Labor*. New York: Basic Books, 1995.

Lomperis, Timothy J. *The War Everyone Lost—and Won*. Baton Rouge: Lousiana State University Press, 1984.

Mailer, Norman. *Armies of the Night: History as a Novel, the Novel as History*. New York: Signet, 1968.

Mann, Robert. *The Walls of Jericho: Lyndon Johnson, Hubert Humphrey, Richard Russell and the Struggle for Civil Rights*. New York: Harcourt Brace, 1996.

Margolis, Jon. *The Last Innocent Year: America in 1964: The Beginning of the "Sixties."* New York: Morrow, 1999.

Matusow, Arthur. *The Unraveling of America: The History of Liberalism in the 1960s*. New York: Harper & Row, 1984.

McAdam, Doug. *Political Process and the Development of Black Insurgency, 1930–1970*. University of Chicago Press, 1982.

McAdam, Doug. *Freedom Summer*. New York: Oxford University Press, 1988.

McCarthy, Eugene. *The Limits of Power: America's Role in the World*. New York: Holt, Rinehart and Winston, 1967.

McCarthy, Eugene. *The Year of the People*. New York: Doubleday, 1969.

McCarthy, Eugene. *Up 'Til Now: A Memoir*. San Diego: Harcourt Brace Jovanovich, 1987.

McCoy, Alfred. *The Politics of Heroin in Southeast Asia*. New York: Harper & Row, 1972.

McNamara, Robert S. *In Retrospect: The Tragedy and Lessons of Vietnam*. New York: Times Books, 1995.

McPherson, Harry C. *A Political Education*. Boston: Little, Brown, 1972.

Menashe, Louis and Ronald Radosh, eds. *Teach-Ins: U.S.A., Reports, Opinions, Documents*. New York: Praeger, 1967.

Miller, James. *Democracy in the Streets: From Port Huron to the Siege of Chicago*. Cambridge: Harvard University Press, 1987.

Morgenthau, Hans J. *Truth and Power: Essays of a Decade, 1960–1970*. New York: Praeger, 1970.

Moynihan, Daniel P. *Maximum Feasible Misunderstanding*. New York: Free Press, 1969.

Murphy, Reg and Hal Gulliver. *The Southern Strategy*. New York: Scribner, 1971.

Newfield, Jack. *Robert Kennedy: A Memoir*. New York: Penguin, 1969.

Nhat Hanh, Thich. *Peace Is Every Step*. New York: Bantam, 1991.

Nhat Hanh, Thich.*Vietnam: Lotus in a Sea of Fire*. New York: Hill & Wang, 1967.

Nolan, Keith William. *Battle for Hue: Tet 1968*. Novato, Calif.: Presidio, 1983.

Oberdorfer, Don. *Tet!: The Turning Point in the Vietnam War*. New York: Doubleday, 1971.

O'Brien, Lawrence F. *No Final Victories: A Life in Politics—from John F. Kennedy to Watergate*. Garden City, N.Y.: Doubleday, 1974.

O'Reilly, Kenneth. *Nixon's Piano: Presidents and Racial Politics from Washington to Clinton*. New York: Free Press, 1995.

O'Reilly, Kenneth, ed. *Black Americans: The FBI Files*. New York: Carroll & Graf, 1994.

O'Reilly, Kenneth. *"Racial Matters": The FBI's Secret File on Black America, 1960–1972*. New York: Free Press, 1989.

Parenti, Michael. *Dirty Truths: Reflections on Politics, Media, Ideology, Conspiracy, Ethnic Life and Class Power*. San Francisco, Calif.: City Lights, 1996.

Parmet, Herbert S. *JFK: The Presidency of John Kennedy*. New York: Dial, 1983.

Pentagon Papers. Senator Gravel ed., vol. 4. Boston: Beacon, 1970.

Pepper, William F. *Orders to Kill: The Truth Behind the Murder of Martin Luther King*. New York: Carroll and Graf, 1995.

Phillips, Kevin. *The Emerging Republican Majority*. New Rochelle, N.Y.: Arlington House, 1969.

Polenberg, Richard. *One Nation Divisible: Class, Race, and Ethnicity in the United States since 1938*. New York: Penguin, 1980.

Powers, Thomas. *Vietnam: The War at Home*. Boston: G. K. Hall, 1973.

Powers, Thomas. *Diana: The Making of a Terrorist*. New York: Bantam, 1971.

Radosh, Ronald. *Divided They Fall: The Demise of the Democratic Party, 1964–1996*. New York: Free Press, 1996.

Redford, Emmette S. and Richard T. McCulley. *White House Operations: The Johnson Presidency*. Austin: University of Texas Press, 1986.

Report of the National Advisory Commission on Civil Disorders. New York: Bantam, 1968.

Reuther, Victor G. *The Brothers Reuther and the Story of the UAW*. Boston: Houghton Mifflin, 1976.

Rogers, Warren. *When I Think of Bobby: A Personal Memoir of the Kennedy Years.* New York: HarperPerennial, 1993.

Rotter, Andrew J. *The Light at the End of the Tunnel.* Wilmington, Del.: Scholarly Resources, 1999.

Rust, William J. *Kennedy in Vietnam: American Vietnam Policy 1960–1963.* New York: Da Capo Press, 1985.

Schaap, Dick. *R.F.K.* New York: Signet, 1967.

Schandler, Herbert Y. *Lyndon Johnson and Vietnam: The Unmaking of a President.* Princeton, N. J.: Princeton University Press, 1977.

Scher, Richard K. *Politics in the New South: Republicanism, Race and Leadership in the Twentieth Century.* New York: Paragon, 1992.

Schlesinger, Jr., Arthur M. *Robert Kennedy and His Times.* New York: Ballantine, 1978.

Scott, James C. *Domination and the Arts of Resistance: Hidden Transcripts.* New Haven, Conn.: Yale University Press, 1990.

Shannon, William V. *The Heir Apparent: Robert Kennedy and the Struggle for Power.* New York: Macmillan, 1967.

Shapley, Deborah. *Promise and Power: The Life and Times of Robert McNamara.* Boston: Little Brown, 1993.

Sheehan, Neil. *A Bright Shining Lie: John Paul Vann and America in Vietnam.* New York: Vintage, 1988.

Shesol, Jeff. *Mutual Contempt: Lyndon Johnson, Robert Kennedy, and the Feud that Defined a Decade.* New York: Norton, 1997.

Sidey, Hugh. *A Very Personal Presidency: Lyndon Johnson in the White House.* New York: Atheneum, 1968.

Sorensen, Theodore C. *Kennedy.* New York: Harper & Row, 1965.

Sorensen, Theodore C. *The Kennedy Legacy.* New York: Macmillan, 1969.

Spector, Ronald. *After Tet: The Bloodiest Year of the War.* New York: Free Press, 1985.

Steel, Ronald. *Walter Lippmann and the American Century.* New York: Vintage, 1981.

Steigerwald, David. *The Sixties and the End of Modern America.* New York: St. Martin's, 1995.

Stein, Jean and George Plimpton, eds. *American Journey: The Times of Robert Kennedy.* New York: Harcourt Brace Jovanovich, 1970.

Steinberg, Blema S. *Shame and Humiliation: Presidential Decision Making on Vietnam.* University Press of Pittsburgh, 1996.

Stone, Gregory and Douglas Lowenstein, eds. *Lowenstein: Acts of Courage and Belief.* New York: Harcourt Brace Jovanovich, 1983.

Summers, Jr., Harry G. *On Strategy: The Vietnam War in Context.* Carlisle Barracks, Pa.: Strategic Studies Institute, U.S. Army War College, 1981.

Swearingen, M. Wesley. *FBI Secrets: An Agent's Expose*. Boston: South End Press, 1995.

Taylor, Maxwell. *Swords and Plowshares*. New York: Norton, 1972.

Teodori, Massimo, ed. *The New Left: A Documentary History*. New York: Bobbs-Merrill, 1969.

Toledano, Ralph de. *R.F.K.: The Man Who Would Be President*. New York: Putnam, 1967.

Tomasky, Michael. *Left For Dead: The Life, Death, and Possible Resurrection of Progressive Politics in America*. New York: Free Press, 1996.

Unger, Irwin and Debi Unger. *Turning Point: 1968*. New York: Scribner, 1988.

Vanden Heuvel, William and William Gwirtzman. *On His Own: Robert F. Kennedy 1964–1968*. New York: Doubleday, 1970.

VanDeMark, Brian. *Into the Quagmire: Lyndon Johnson and the Escalation of the Vietnam War*. New York: Oxford University Press, 1995.

Warner, Roger. *Back Fire: The CIA's Secret War in Laos and Its Link to the Vietnam War*. New York: Simon & Schuster, 1995.

Washington, James M., ed. *A Testament of Hope: The Essential Writings and Speeches of Martin Luther King, Jr.* New York: HarperCollins, 1986.

Weisbrot, Robert. *Freedom Bound: A History of America's Civil Rights Movement*. New York: Plume, 1990.

Wells, Tom. *The War Within: America's Battle over Vietnam*. New York: Holt, 1994.

Westmoreland, William. *A Soldier Reports*. New York: Doubleday, 1980.

White, Theodore H. *The Making of the President 1964*. New York: New American Library, 1965.

White, Theodore H. *The Making of the President 1968*. New York: Atheneum, 1969.

Wicker, Tom. *JFK and LBJ: The Influence of Personality upon Politics*. Baltimore, Md.: Penguin, 1968.

Wilkins, Roger W. *A Man's Life: An Autobiography*. New York: Simon & Schuster, 1982.

Wills, Garry. *Nixon Agonistes: The Crisis of the Self-Made Man*. New York: Houghton Mifflin, 1969.

Wilson, William Julius. *The Truly Disadvantaged: The Inner City, the Underclass, and Public Policy*. University of Chicago Press, 1987.

Witcover, Jules. *85 Days: The Last Campaign of Robert F. Kennedy*. New York: Morrow, 1969.

Witcover, Jules. *The Year the Dream Died: Revisiting 1968 in America*. New York: Warner, 1997.

Wofford, Harris. *Of Kennedys and Kings: Making Sense of the Sixties*. New York: Farrar, Straus & Giroux, 1980.

Woods, Randall Bennett. *Fulbright: A Biography*. New York: Cambridge University Press, 1995.

Wright, Lawrence. *In the New World: Growing Up with America 1960–1984*. New York: Knopf, 1988.

Yoder, Edwin M. *Joe Alsop's Cold War: A Study of Journalistic Influence and Intrigue*. Chapel Hill: University of North Carolina Press, 1995.

Young, Marilyn B. *The Vietnam Wars, 1945–1990*. New York: HarperPerennial, 1991.

Young, Andrew. *An Easy Burden: The Civil Rights Movement and the Transformation of America*. New York: HarperCollins, 1996.

Index